The Descent of the Imagination

THE DESCENT
OF THE IMAGINATION

Postromantic Culture in
the Later Novels of Thomas Hardy

Kevin Z. Moore

New York University Press
NEW YORK AND LONDON

Library of Congress Cataloging-in-Publication Data
Moore, Kevin Z.
The descent of the imagination : postromantic culture in the later
novels of Thomas Hardy / Kevin Z. Moore.
p. cm.
Includes bibliographical references (p.)
ISBN 0-8147-5451-1 (alk. paper)
1. Hardy, Thomas, 1840–1928—Criticism and interpretation.
2. Romanticism—England. I. Title.
PR4757.R64M66 1990
823'.8—dc20   89-28685
CIP

Book design by Ken Venezio

For William E. Buckler and Alan Singer,
valued teachers, colleagues, and friends
past and present.

Remarks: (1) The intertext is not necessarily a field of influences; rather it is a music of figures, metaphors, thought-words; it is the signifier as *siren*.

Roland Barthes, Roland Barthes

Contents

Acknowledgments

I would like, first of all, to thank my colleagues and friends at Temple University for the support and encouragement they have shown me during the three years I spent completing my study. In particular I have profited from conversations with Professors Susan Stewart, Timothy Corrigan, and Susan Wells. I would also like to thank Frazer Cocks, curator of the Hardy Collection at Colby College, for the rewarding summer I spent there when I first began to compose my study. I owe a further debt of gratitude to the Department of English at the University of Pennsylvania for providing me the opportunity to air my views regarding English romanticism during the fall semester of 1988 when I was bringing this study to its completion. And I owe a debt of gratitude to the anonymous reader at Duke University Press whose criticism and commentary on an early draft helped me to shape my presentation. In this regard, I would like to thank Ms. Despina Papazoglou Gimbel at New York University Press for the professional care she and her staff have given my manuscript and Nadia Kravchenko at Temple University whose help in the preparation of the manuscript was invaluable.

Institutional acknowledgments to one side, I would like to thank Professor Marjorie Levinson for her astute reading of my introductory chapter and Professor Alan Singer for his enthusiastic reading of a then overly long theoretical introduction to Hardy's representations of late-romantic culture. Finally, it gives me great pleasure to thank Professor John Maynard for reading the manuscript and for his continued interest in and support of my work since that time.

The Descent of the Imagination

Disenchanting Wessex:
Hardy's Trading in Romantic Signs

*If you look closely enough, every character in a
novel is a monster, and all art consists in preventing
the reader from looking too closely.*
Simone de Beauvoir, *The Mandarins*

*Am more and more confirmed in an idea I have
long held, as a matter of common sense, long before
I thought of any old aphorism bearing on the subject:* Ars est celare artem.
Hardy, *Life and Work*

IN J. HILLIS MILLER's extended study of "the linguistic moment," he
pauses in his chapter on Shelley to comment that "as is well-known
. . . Hardy's work is so inhabited by echoes of Shelley's work that it
almost might be defined as, from beginning to end, a large-scale interpretation of Shelley, one of the best and strongest that we have" (*Linguistic
Moment*, 115). In the present book, I have taken this critical commonplace as the starting point for a theoretically interested investigation of
Hardy's relationship to British romanticism.[1] The well-known relationship between Hardy's and Shelley's writing is exemplary of the relatively unknown relationship between his narratives and the writings of
Wordsworth, Keats, and Carlyle as well as Arnold's and Pater's critiques
of romantic writing. As Miller's comment implies, Hardy's intertextual
dialogue with romanticism just might be "one of the best and strongest"
readings of nineteenth-century culture that we have.

Read at full length, Wessex is preoccupied with the themes, forms,
notions, and concerns of English romanticism. From *Desperate Remedies*
to *The Dynasts,* it is always romanticism that is covertly and overtly at
issue. Covertly, typically romantic contentions infiltrate the early nov-

I

els, such as the contention between science and poetry which structures *Desperate Remedies*, while overtly such contentions become the "philosophic" material of his later fictions, those from *The Mayor of Casterbridge* to *Jude*. *The Dynasts*, Hardy's last novel-length work, is a dramatized epic of the failure of romanticism which must be read in conjunction with those works written during the fictionalized time of the epic drama, roughly 1800 to 1815.

Putting to one side Hardy's early novels where he was working his way toward a method, I have concentrated my efforts on his final or latter-day Wessex, those works published between 1886 and 1896. During that time, Hardy systematically interrogates some typically romantic views on subjectivity, the imagination, and history—on man, on nature, and on human experience—by contextualizing in the novels representative figures and incidents drawn from the romantic canon. For example, Henchard's fate is predicated upon Carlyle's dialogue between dynamism and mechanism, Marty South is a revisionary form of Wordsworth's Margaret of "The Ruined Cottage," and Jude's life is Hardy's reading of Shelley's *Alastor*.

Just as "Wordsworth reproaches Pope for having abandoned the imaginative use of figural diction in favor of a merely decorative allegorization" (de Man, *Rhetoric of Romanticism*, 1), Hardy in his turn reproaches Wordsworth for *his* imaginative abuse of metaphor. Hardy will then return the intent of romantic metaphor to the realm of the "merely decorative," rhetorical, and allegorical. In this scheme of reversals, Wordsworth redresses the lack he finds in Pope's poetry, while Hardy takes issue with Wordsworth's philosophical poetry by interrogating its claims in his novels. Failing to give his consent to the claims of the romantic imagination in ways that Coleridge did, Hardy was compelled to reiterate the "adventure of [the failure of romantic intent] in an infinite variety of forms and versions" (*Rhetoric of Romanticism*, 7) as his version of the quest myth. It is this version of the quest myth which constitutes the most significant thematic, formal, and stylistic considerations in the later Wessex novels. Wessex is a literary anthology or fragmented ensemble of specific themes, forms, and figures drawn from the British romantic tradition. Hardy renders this tradition—such as he understood it—the figural substance of Wessex. The recent past of romantic writing returns under interrogation in his mature novels which define their themes in reference to and in refutation of those cultural claims and pronouncements testamental to the "faith" of the early century.

Forged from the figural debris of the explosive dispersal of romantic writing in the nineteenth century, Wessex writing derives its characteristics from that canon of interrelated texts "which may be defined as extending from the childhood of Blake and Wordsworth to the present moment" (Bloom, *Ringers in the Tower,* 14), which for Hardy was the literary culture of the eighties and nineties. As this study will presently demonstrate, all major characters in the latter-day Wessex find their immediate heritage in those "Characters of the great Apocalypse" of an earlier age. Because he was so unsure of himself as a writer, because novel writing was a professional concern to him and not a spiritual practice, and because he knew that a culturally responsible fiction had to be dense with allusion, Hardy constructed his narratives from the established dramas of a recent romantic culture. It is not "life" which motivates his fictions but "text." Wessex is a Frankensteinian body of literature wherein the recognizable parts of other bodies of work are stitched together into the semblance of a whole. This semblance never lives as organically cohesive texts do, or are purported to, though it does simulate that life.

As simulated models of romantic life, characters in Wessex are critical allegories of the romantic self. Thus in Hardy's fiction the typical characteristics of the romantic self return as a classical typology of selfhood. The subject of romantic culture becomes the "subject of subjectivity" in Wessex where "life is a psychological phenomenon" *(Tess)* dominated by Spencer's "Principle of Uncertainty." The events enacted by Hardy's romantic types constitute romantic emblems turned round upon themselves and become critical of their own constituent features and desires. Wessex writing then is always allegorical (and not symbolic), following Coleridge's distinction between the two modes of representation, and always a double writing, a writing about writing which futilely quests after a pure silence where the voice of authenticity might once again begin to speak its timely utterances.

If the portrayal of character is a sign of a novelist's acquisition of knowledge about society and culture, then Hardy's characters signal his awareness that inauthenticity dominates a remnant romanticism which has fallen into a dogmatic phase and is itself in need of "romanticization" or redemption. Characters in Wessex are characteristic of those romantic figures who once bore within themselves the grounds of their own authority. In Wessex, character appears as a textual formality and not a personality, that "whole man" or coherent individuality which romanticism understood as an autonomous subjectivity enjoying some degree of creative self-expression. It is the "myth" of this myth that is put on display in Wessex.

Such a display demonstrates a loss or absence of the romantic impetus within a parody of presence. In *Tess,* Hardy will call this loss the "ache of modernism." What he means by this phrase is the triumph of time or history over all forms of "life" as correspondence and transcendence.[2] Hardy's phrase echoes and plays off of Wordsworth's sense of aching joys in "Tintern Abbey." In "Tintern Abbey," Wordsworth remarks upon the passing of his primitive or naive form of romanticism with these words: "That time is past, and all its *aching* joys are now no more,/ And all its dizzy raptures" (83–85). It is Wordsworth's "no more" which defines the aching lack in modern Wessex. Despite the loss of his primitive romanticism, Wordsworth could still claim that it is "not for this/ Faint I, nor morne nor murmur; other gifts/ Have followed; for such a loss, I would believe,/ Abundant recompense (85–88). The abundant recompense which Wordsworth found in sentimental forms of romanticism does not materialize in Wessex where secondary, sentimental, or idealistic forms of romanticism either fail outright or fail to appear. The ache of the modern is then the effect of a double failure or loss whose cause Hardy attributed to the "burden of history" or, in Shelley's fine phrase, to "The Triumph of Life." The overall effect of such a double loss is the complete absence of redemption, which is why Wessex is so tragic a domain.

One thematic result of such a triumph is that latter-day Wessex romantics dramatize the gaps, discontinuities, ambiguities, and problems which poets before them had successfully overcome or evaded, and by so doing legitimized their creative vision by embodying that vision within a poetry of presence. In Wessex, the repressed skeptical and cynical content of such a poetry is liberated, and with calculatedly tragic results. Read as a response to the aspirations of romantic poetics, Hardy's mature narratives "decompose" the coherent results composed by romantic rhetoric. The upshot of such decompositions is that the impossibilist position held by the various members of the visionary company becomes more apparently just that. It is an "unedited" or incoherent romanticism which returns in Hardy's writing in order to elaborate the real horror from which the romantic imagination recoiled. That horror was succinctly stated by Shelley when he wrote that the "deep truth is imageless" in order to justify the necessity of imaginative evasions of vacancy. Hardy in his turn understood Shelley's words to mean that all images are therefore without truth, and it is from this standpoint that he created Wessex as a challenging reply to Shelley's unsettling question: "And what were thou, and earth, and stars, and sea,/ If to the human mind's imaginings/ Silence and solitude were vacancy?" ("Mont Blanc," 141–44).

What indeed but a chaos of anecdotal principles embodied in images metonymically related to some "reality" they intend to describe? And what could such a metonymical form of writing signify but the failure of the intentional structure of the romantic metaphor? It is, then, the end of romantic writing which constitutes the beginning of Wessex writing in its modern or mature phase.

We can see this conclusion for instance in *The Woodlanders* where it is the silence and solitude of Shelley's unimaginably vacant Mont Blanc which rises up before John South's eyes and kills him. It can kill him because his life depends upon a reverie on an elm tree. Though we need not go into particulars here, the tree plays a central role in romantic writing where it stands as a symbol for tradition and custom (Wordsworth had characterized Burke as an oak in *The Prelude* 7:520–30.) and as a model for the corresponding relations between man and nature, society and culture. South's "romantic Igdrasil" is cut down by the "scientist" and aesthete Dr. Fitzpiers who quotes Shelley by heart. It is Fitzpiers who decides that South's imaginative relationship with his genealogical tree of power should be severed. In Hardy's woodland allegory, the aesthetic doctor armed with art and science—or "upstart theory" in Wordsworth's estimate *(Prelude,* 7:529)—cuts John off from his tree of power. Such a disempowerment refigures the playful contention in Wordsworth's "Expostulation and Reply" and "The Tables Turned," and with tragic results. Moreover, the drama between South and Fitzpiers recasts the contention between Wordsworth and Shelley, the one a traditionalist, the other a figure of rational Enlightenment or "upstart theory."

In the Hintock woodlands, the Wordsworthian imagination is portrayed as a neurotic fancy which renders the subject-creator dependent upon nature rather than an individual of resolute independence supported by nature. Thus the imagination fallen to the condition of neurosis and reason become unsympathetic to imaginative relationships are tragically at odds in Hardy's woodlands. In effect, Hardy has recast the two great empowering agents of the romantic revolution as corrupt, fallen, and frivolous.

The story develops tragically because John South's fanciful relationship with his tree is clearly neurotic and not redemptive. In Hardy's allegory, there is a genealogical relationship of descent between John (of the) South and his "tree of power" and William of the North and his invocations to a redemptive nature. This "descent of the imagination" typifies the reactionary posture Hardy took toward that tradition or faith which initially shaped his desire to write. As this brief example of the fall of nature as "mother and nurse" demonstrates, Wessex underscores the fictional character of the romantic figure in order to interrogate the expectations which those figures typically bring or "apply" to life in accordance with Wordsworth's and then Arnold's recommendation for a culturally responsible literature.

The deliberate figuration of such a literature of interrogation is admittedly a complicated process, one which Hardy invented when "feeling his way to a method" (Preface, *Desperate Remedies,* Orel, 3) of becoming "a good-hand at the serial [novel]" (*Life and Work,* 102). His emphasis on method and manipulation should not go unnoticed for it is by mechanical means that his narratives are constructed in a calculated response to his understanding of the one thing necessary for great fiction at the close of the nineteenth century, a complete engagement with high or scriptural culture. By understanding literally Arnold's dictum that fiction should appropriate "the best that was known and thought in the world," Hardy produced novels dense in unassimilated cultural critique and literary history on loan from the journals, gazettes, and books of his day.

After much formal experimentation between 1877 and 1885 which saw only one remarkable novel produced, *The Return of the Native* (1878), Hardy increased the density of cultural allusion in his novels by borrowing directly from his "literary" notebooks-cum-sourcebooks. Replete with undisclosed textual borrowings, Hardy's latter-day Wessex is implicitly intertextual and not just occasionally or theoretically so.[3] By allusion, homology, and disguised grafting, Hardy incorporated as critical commentary previously published texts. He undoubtedly understood these texts as a kind of public domain or material *zeitgeist*. Given this method of construction, the romantic "work" of many hands such as the *Lyrical Ballads* returns as a work of many texts. For instance, when we read Hardy's own account of how he combed the pages of the *Dorset County Chronicle* for an actual incident upon which to build the novel that would eventually appear as *The Mayor of Casterbridge,* it is not a unique instance that he reveals but a usual practice. This "practice" will find its greatest work in *The Dynasts,* nearly all of which is comprised of borrowed material.[4] Then, too, if we reflect upon his "borrowing" of Leopardi's phrase "the world is only a cerebral phenomenon" (*Literary Notebooks,* 2:473) and placing it nearly verbatim into *Tess,* we establish a model of Hardy's literary method. Hardy usually finds his narrative positions "elsewhere" in contemporary cultural publications, while his characters and events are derived from those key romantic poems and poetic biographies (in effect the same thing) upon which the cultural publications "philosophized."

By redefining truth as an impression and an impression as the effect of any credible philosophy, Hardy justified his incorporation of all manner of textual positions into a fiction that was not intended to criticize any particular view as false in order to assert another as true. Such determinations had become difficult by the 1880s because the enabling principles of romanticism had become either anecdotal or suspect. In Hardy's "narrative ensembles," idealism is demoted to fancy, in Coleridge's senses of the less than imaginative, while realism becomes an allegory of history, a less than fanciful discourse which is doubly delusive because coerced by reason to appear coherent, directed, comprehensible, and purposeful. Inscribed between fancy and history, Wessex narratives "irrealize" the symbol. Wessex vision represents the distance, and not the identity, between man's understanding of the real and the real itself. Hardy's irrealized symbolism (his realized metonymic constructions) are inversely romantic, signs of loss which point to a gain in another direction. Paradoxically, what is gained in Wessex is an awareness of loss. There, man the mythmaker is cast as historical man anguished by nostalgic fancies of satisfaction or redemption which never materialize.

Through the perfect recommencement of the empty ceremony of significance futilely aspiring to ritual, romanticism returns in Wessex as gesture and not as act. As both waning sentimental and waxing aesthetic romantics in Wessex demonstrate, Hardy rejects the possibility of an ontologically credible fiction and refuses to comply with the then current reformulations of a responsible cultural past in the irresponsible belletrist eighties and nineties. Because Wessex narratives are distanced from both idealism and aestheticism, we might understand Hardy's brand of impressionism as the realistic effect of an insistent refusal of all ideologies as insubstantial forms of knowledge. Directed against the very notion of ideology, Wessex narratives offer us a way of "seeing" romanticism as Hardy did, as a specular discourse on the imagination which had lost its credibility.

As the source of its drama Wessex writing reproduces the romantic origins of its own nostalgia within a nihilistic context that points up the illusory, speculative character of its own fondest desires. In this sense, Wessex thrives on self-frustration generated by narrators who interrogate the sources of their nostalgia. The combination of reproduction within denial results in specular investigations of the very status of the spectacle (figural investigations of the status of the figure). That is, Wessex narratives convey their own insecurity regarding their ability to narrate knowledge authentically and originally. Ironically, it is by the very narration of anxiety and insecurity that they gain a secure place in the canon of late nineteenth-century romantic writing.

Born of the sign, Wessex writing does not pretend to figure its way out of the problematic of language and significance. The romantic scenario for the "growth and development of the mind" as it "dialogues with itself," so as to integrate perceptual/experiential fragments into a self-mastering authenticity, is a lost mode of overcoming in Wessex. There, characters attempt to narrate themselves into coherence and fail because the narrative constituents of their egos are not prone to cohere given the failure of those principles which could guide them to wholeness. Moreover, the terms by which they seek a unified point of view are themselves involved in too many cultural debates to be able to supply the desired rhetorical effect of organic growth and development. Each "romantic" ego in Wessex is the product of cultural contingency. Subjectivity itself is a replication in the mind of complex contextual priorities "happed" upon by the questing self as it desperately seeks remedies for such complexities, otherwise called romantic redemption.

The failure of redemption within character is reflexively motivated by the author's failure to do more than mechanically or logically organize his tale. Hence Hardy's reliance upon rationalized structures to insure a readability guaranteed by the teleological expectations of genre. For Hardy, the novel was an unredeemed genre, an organized chaos produced by an "author" who was himself a "chaos of principles." The complex, intertextual mosaic of his self-presentation in his autobiographical *Life and Work* is like that of any major character's in a novel. Such "con-fabular" characters, in turn, are emblematic of the narrative itself. Generically speaking, all Hardy's textual productions, including himself (his authorial self), are of a piece, or of pieces methodically organized to appear organic when it is just this romantic imperative that they place in jeopardy.

From this angle, we might see Hardy as a practitioner of what Jameson has called "pure point of view." Such purity "ushers in a kind of total relativism, in which we are obligated to accept any narrator on his own terms, and which results in the destruction of all absolute values and standards of judgment, and consequently, of the very source of literary effects as well" (*Marxism and Form,* 356). Hardy's narratives (and we must now include his autobiography in this set) cancel all literary effects as their own special literary effect. Wessex is thus best defined as a literature of cancellation. Cancellation is the sort of "purity" Hardy had in mind in *Tess of the d'Urbervilles* wherein Tess, the woman, seeks the purity of pure point of view which can only be found in the unwritten margins of her densely inscribed culture. She seeks to escape from the effects of culture and thereby become Tess, the woman, and not Tess, the subject of a romantic novel. Thus while *Tess,* the novel, remains cunningly "solutionless," it points to the solution which lies in the silencing of those romantic texts which inform Tess, the character. It is by interdiction, and not by "diction" or speaking further, that redemption can arise as a refinding of the silence of the uninscribed body of desire.

By the time Hardy completes *Jude,* he will have accepted the wisdom of his own narrative understanding and write no more novels. Accordingly, the "philosophic" poetry that the twentieth-century Hardy will write will be a poetry of interdiction wherein romantic "signseekers" are relentlessly disappointed and time always triumphs over romantic hopes.

In sum, it is through an exhaustive refiguration of romanticism's tropes that Hardy depletes romantic desire. No new "circus animals," in Yeats's sense of the performing romantic figure, appear in the Wessex forests of the night where the old animals wander, become exhausted, and die. By recalling only to discredit the many forms of romanticism, Wessex narratives provide a continuous commentary through stylistic example upon the historic fate of romantic writing. Overall, that fate was to exchange intimations of plentitude for those of the abyss. Wessex, then, is the *paysage démoralisé* of romantic writing. It is a folkloric domain of the ballad deprived of its lyrical moment of self-shattering. The gloom which was background in the romantic topography becomes the shadow in the foreground of Wessex.

Everything that had been construed as *private* in romantic writing is construed as *public* in Hardy's writing. This means that the boundary between inner and outer is nearly dissolved in Hardy's fictions. This weakening is symptomatic of the autodidact's crisis of authority, but it is also symptomatic of a cultural moment dominated by the literal as its most capable form of profundity. That is to say, in Wessex all "timely utterances," Wordsworth's summary phrase for lyrical release, have become time-bound or historic categories of selfhood which articulate the character of self-expression as repetition without alteration, which is to say without redemption.

Curiously, this self-consuming artifact of Wessex read at full length and in relation to romantic poetics suggests that Hardy eventually understood that romantic writing was very much like his and not more authentic or more original than his own, as he initially imagined. All along he had been unwittingly romantic in exploring the doubtful demands and figurative desires of romanticism. The novels are then the epistemological laboratory out of which the poet is born. It is too the wisdom of the novelist that produces the romantic satire of *The Dynasts,* a Carlylean anti-epic of the latter days of the French Revolution featuring romanticism's representational devices and modalities *as* a conflict of interests. In and through novel writing, Hardy came to recognize that a culturally responsible writing would highlight the problems within romantic forms of subjectivity and idealism and not repress them. The growth of Hardy's "mind" from a longing for a coherent point of view, such as that advocated in *The Prelude,* to the acceptance of an undesirable but acknowledged chaos of fragments as the only form of completeness available to culture, reverses the romantic rhythm of redemption. And it is this reversal of direction that informs all narrative critiques in the latter-day Wessex.

In his "Apology" to *Late Lyrics and Earlier* of 1922, Hardy wrote that "[He] must trust for right note-catching to those finely-touched spirits who can divine without half a whisper, whose intuitiveness is proof against all the accidents of inconsequence" in order that the different poetic voices and positions in his poetry be heard (Orel, "Apology," 55). How closely we are to listen and catch notes so as to hear the embedded sources and allusions is a determination that criticism has not yet established to its own best interest. This determination is especially pressing when we consider that the very paragraph in which we are invoked to note-catch evinces traces from the finale to Eliot's *Middlemarch*, the need for "note-catching" being exemplified in the very injunction to do so.

Uncaught notes from romantic writing resound throughout Hardy's writing. For instance, in the preface to *The Dynasts*, Hardy sums up his theme by quoting Schiller without bothering to mention that his "thing signified" refers to the German romantic's "thing signified" in his *On Naive and Sentimental Poetry*.[5] If we caught this note, we could have returned to Schiller and learnt that the "thing signified" of *The Dynasts* is an awareness that all romantic signs succeed by intention only, that the imagination is distinct from actuality and does not correspond to it, and that metaphor does not "disappear completely in the thing signified [but is] forever heterogeneous and alien to the thing signified" (Schiller, 98). Schiller's inherently rhetorical view of metaphor partly explains the specular and speculative character of *The Dynasts,* a book which Hardy said was "Wessex writ large" (Orel, "1912 Preface to Novels," 48).

To this particular, unacknowledged quotation, we can add quite a list of others which legislate theme and form in *The Dynasts*. The title page presents an unacknowledged quotation from Tennyson's "A Dream of Fair Women," while the introduction incorporates textual fragments from Shelley, Wordsworth, Coleridge, and Schlegel. In this connection it is of interest to note that in the 1903 preface Hardy had promised to supply a footnote annotating the history texts from which he directly borrowed speeches. He never supplied the annotation and later deleted the promise. Though he admits that "paraphrase" accounts for much of the dialogue in the *The Dynasts,* he means this glancing acknowledgment to cover, via the practices of the historical novelist, his usual need to borrow and to paraphrase. To this observation we might add that Hardy never admits that he has "paraphrased" from poets and novelists in composing *The Dynasts,* which he has. Moreover, he vehemently denied that he had even read Tolstoy's *War and Peace* when he was composing his epic-drama. In fact, not only had he read Tolstoy's book when he was composing, he had annotated specific passages which he later incorporated into the text.[6] Although he admits his "indebtedness for detail to the abundant pages of the historian, the biographer, and the journalist, English and Foreign" which he states was continuous throughout the course of composition (Preface, *The Dynasts*), he chooses to remain silent on his debt to the poets and novelists.

Hardy could admit borrowing from historians because his expertise was not theirs and because it was common practice for the historical novelist to do so. Yet even in the face of such a common practice, Hardy withdraws his initial pledge to cite sources. Meanwhile, his debt to romantic and Victorian poets, novelists, and essayists had to remain obscure because their profession was his. To the instance of *The Dynasts,* we might add that of his "Apology" to *Late Lyrics and Earlier* which is thick with unacknowledged loanwords and phrases from Wordsworth, Coleridge, Arnold, Browning, Bacon, Newman, and Carlyle in addition to Eliot, whose phrase on note-catching we have already mentioning. In this regard, we might recall that in the past critics have suspected Hardy of forgery only to excuse him of it or to work around the problem. How to handle his debt to the literary past was a methodological problem for Hardy as well, which he too had to either work around, excuse, and in every event, suppress. Nor is it unusual for critics to spot a large debt to a particular writer in a single novel, in effect seeing a symbiotic relationship between host and parasite. Much of Hardy's thinking about art as a formalist and therefore implicitly expressionist practice should be viewed as one of the ways he came to theorize authenticity and claim it for himself despite the derivative character of his practice of writing novels. In the serialized version of his novels, moreover, he would cite an author in one run and then delete the citing in the next, thereby displaying his anxiety of attribution. Given this anxiety, it should come as no surprise that "towards the end of his life, [he] destroyed most of his personal notebooks and diaries" (Björk,

Literary Notebooks, 1: xxxi) and that there is no authentic holograph of any single novel. Hardy's literary bonfires at Max Gate during the early years of the twentieth century and concluding with one final effort in 1928 shortly before he died now appear to have been set alight for more than personal motives regarding privacy, for there was a literary identity to protect as well, that of "The Man of Letters."

I have cited these instances as a prelude to my intertextual investigation of Hardy's narratives which I understand to be consciously forged from the published word. We are not speaking here of an anxiety of influence, in Bloom's sense, but of an anxiety of professional competence. Given Hardy's anxiety of competence, we must listen closely to the intertextual weave of his narrative voices in order to hear their heteroglossic richness. As chiefly second-degree writing in Barthes's sense, Wessex is uniformly parodic and replete with surreptitious quotations.[7] Working within the constraints of a culture greatly invested in the aesthetic rubric of an inspired and organic creativity, Hardy saw himself as somewhat uninspired and therefore second rate. Thus, his speaking of his career as a novelest in less than laudable terms, as he did later in life, should not be attributed to a self-effacing modesty, but to rare moments of candor about the character of English fiction he practiced professionally.

Hardy's candor suggests that we need to take his requisite full look at the worst rather than indict him for criminal negligence or, what is worse, conspire along with him to hide or excuse his forgeries. That worst is that character and event in Hardy's novels are constructed from consciously borrowed, thinly disguised revisions of figures and philosphies lifted either wholly or in part from romantic texts. If, as Hardy suggested, "the way to a better" can be found by taking a full look at the worst, then the better we seek in exposing Hardy's sources is a more accurate assessment of the character and quality of his achievement.

No Wessex romantic experiences a healthy imagination empowered to transform the world into a redeeming image of its beloved, though tragic parodies of redemption abound. In effect, Wessex is populated by those figures of selfhood which romantics tried to overcome with varying degrees of success: figures reminiscent of Blake's Specter of Urthona (*The Mayor of Casterbridge*); of a flightless Shelleyanism *(Tess* and *Jude); of Wordsworthian gloom and perplexity from which the imagination flees, its very flight transforming the sublime of terror into the classically beautiful *(The Woodlanders);* and of Coleridge in dejection musing upon a "hope that refuses to be fed" (Tess at Stonehenge).

In concluding, we might consider Hardy's last published novel, *The Well-Beloved,* as a type of all we have been discussing. *The Well-Beloved* is an allegory depicting the plight of one form of romantic idealism as it encounters history. The tempting and elusive Shelleyan "form all light" and "one shape of many names" of the allegory is successively named Avice, I, II, and III. More explicitly, she represents "a vice" which inhabits three generations of desire—romantic, Victorian-romantic, and late-Victorian[8]—each more tragically than the last. By its blatantly allegorical structure, its "close reading" of Shelley, its reformulation of the natural immortality of the Keatsean nightingale, and its depiction of the "triumph of time" in Marcia's unveiled face at the conclusion, *The Well-Beloved* is the "legend" text to that wider literary topography of Wessex which I seek to map in this study.

It is one of the aims of this intertextual study to apply the appropriate aesthetic frame to Hardy's mature novels by upgrading the scholarly labor of annotation to the critical art of interpretation. My study goes about accomplishing its task by providing a systematic exegesis of romantic sources and analogues of character and incident in Wessex. Theoretically, such an exegesis should define the thematically stable context by which Hardy measured his differences from his predecessors, differences which amount to his reading of the instabilities within British romantic culture.

Those textual sources I have been able to locate are presumed with good cause to have been purposefully interwoven into narratives which are implicitly and explicitly metacritical forms: implicitly, by their revisionist figures and dramas; explicitly by their structure. In order to approach the unapparent "thing signified" in Hardy's texts, we must understand annotation rhetorically and classically as a drawing forth of figures from the image-reservoir of approved cultural material. Although there must be a degree of unconscious textual echoing in Wessex, it is to the consciously garnered referent that I have directed my attention and which I seek to establish as the trace of a deliberate textual practice.

Once we acknowledge Hardy's concern with inauthenticity, Wessex forgeries can be seen to harbor an anxiety of authority which Hardy could neither ignore nor overcome. In terms of an Oedipal struggle enacted within cultural history as "a family" of texts, Hardy's inability to identify with his romantic precursors means that he could not replace them. Thus each narrative mimics the coherence of idealism's strong textual moments without being able to genuinely recall or replicate them. The authority of romanticism's "vision" or perspective is not evoked by Hardy's narratives, while the very inability to speak/write authoritatively becomes thematically central to all of his later or mature novels. It is then the art of "unconvincing" that informs Hardy's texts with their most "convincing" themes.

Informed by the unconvincing, Hardy's mature novels are ensembles of fragments dreaming nostalgically of their lost totality. The act of witnessing or directing our attention toward these ensembles highlights what romanticism would evade, hide, repress, or transform, while the systematic exegesis of these "acts of witnessing" requires that we *not* suspend our disbelief. Instead we must activate our disbelief in order to understand the ways in which Hardy suspended all beliefs promoted by romantic rhetoric. It is Hardy's skepticism of those beliefs which informs his fiction and renders it a parodic, metonymic form, while it is specifically its parodic character which requires that we apply postmodern methods of literary analysis as those most appropriate to investigating the form of fiction he wrote.

In order to organize this systematic exegesis, I have constructed a master narrative of the latter-day Wessex, a heuristic fiction wherein each novel published between 1886 and 1896 is imagined as one chapter in a literary history constituted of an interlocking domain of texts. Based on the formal, generic, and historical evidence that remains for us after Hardy's bonfires and those of Sir Sydney Cockerell, his literary executor, I will argue that each of Hardy's novels features one particular poet as the target of a critique which enfolds other poets and other texts as well. Thus in *The Mayor of Casterbridge,* Hardy refigures Carlyle's romantic critique of the thirties in order to demonstrate that romanticism's last strong prophetic voice had not been listened to, though it certainly had been heard. It is this denial and repression of romanticism which informs the remaining Wessex novels. Next comes *The Woodlanders* which is primarily directed against Wordsworth, the fathering "romantic woodlander" par excellence. *Tess* follows. In that novel, Hardy is primarily concerned with Keats's romantic reformulation of Milton's "Dream of Adam" and with Keats's literary revolt against literary culture. *Jude* is the omega of the set. In this novel, Hardy presents the historic fate of Shelleyan forms of romanticism. Essentially, and by essence I mean the structural center, *Jude the Obscure* is a retelling of Shelley's *Alastor,* a mini-epic concerned with the punishing spirit of idealistic solitude which is itself a response to Wordsworthian forms of idealism. Each novel or chapter represents a discrete reflex to a particular set of poetic texts which voice a specific position within the romantic cultural problematic, thus collectively the ensemble of novels (the ensemble of ensembles) circumscribes Hardy's ongoing debate with English romanticism. And it is that debate which informs Wessex. Paradoxically, it is the reactionary and reproductive character of these novels which constitutes their claim to originality.

In his "General Preface to the Novels and Poetry (1912)," Hardy defined the art of narrative as an "objectless consistency" (Orel, 49). He meant that his Wessex narratives are highly formal constructions without an object (or end or something to be proven) and without objects, since all "things" therein contained were subjects and all subjects were textual. "Objectlessness" here signifies the aimless linguistic, an aesthetic realm of the ungrounded figure, while "consistency" is the effect of a rationalized method of plot development understood as the structural equivalent of an organic growth to coherence. The latter-day Wessex I seek to define is then an outline of this form of forms, itself no more than a formally organized illusion about the illusion of organic form. My intent in proceeding in this way is explained by Hardy's novels themselves. That is, if his Wessex is an allegory about allegories in search of the lyric, then my study is yet one allegory (or reading) more in that network of texts.

Because mimetic of romanticism's positions, these narratives reflect as well as reflect upon the inability of narrative itself (and of the author) to say anything further. The recognition of this impotence of metaphoricity and, further, its thematization as the subject of Wessex is Hardy's one defense against falling into silence during a time when he could not afford to do so (and we note that as soon as he could afford to do so, professionally and financially, he did indeed quit novelizing). That is to say that his strategy of revision prevented him from engaging in untenable repetitions as the repetition of the untenable, of an unbelievable form of knowledge invoked by the easy authority of the spoken word. In addition, it is our understanding that Hardy used his novel-writing practice as a means of developing a poetic which he would then employ as a poet in the twentieth century. In effect, the latter-day Wessex is Hardy's "Prelude." Collectively, the novels are a literary autobiography wherein the growth of the poet's mind toward his acceptance of cultural chaos within an indeterminate and indeterminable history is centrally at issue.

The latter-day Wessex opens with *The Mayor of Casterbridge* (1886) and closes with *Jude the Obscure* (1896). Henchard is a radical realist dominated by materialistic ambitions; Jude a radical idealist prone to every form of enchantment. Henchard depends upon material props and market methods to support his character, Jude upon mentalistic props and idealism's procedures to support his. Each novel interrogates one form of nineteenth-century character: Henchard is the "man of character"; Jude, "the whole man" of romantic redemption. The former is a realist without enthusiasms; the latter, a fantasist with little other than his cultural enthusiasms to motivate him. In Hardy's revisionist reading, both forms are inadequate; thus both novels are satires upon their respective type.

Henchard's Casterbridge is the inverse of Jude's Christminster, as the alliteration between city names implies. Jude flees "Casterbridge" realities in order to find Christminster dreams; Henchard divorces himself from "Christminster" dreams in order to become a master of Casterbridge realities. Between the two characteristic domains of discourse, there is no dialectical exchange. Were there, Hardy would have only reconstituted Wessex as an idealized form of romantic culture ruled by the integrative imaginative reason. And it is the absence of this dialectical agency at every level of writing, from plot to character to language, which is the source of tragedy in Wessex as well as the source of Hardy's particularly "wooden," primitive, or pretentious style, as it has been variously characterized. More philosophically, Hardy's portrayal of a world without access to the imagination creates a literature which imagines the imagination dead as a way of "taking a full look at the worst." Such a literature is preeminently postmodern and needs to be dealt with as such.

We begin our brief overview of the master narrative by noting that *The Mayor of Casterbridge* opens "one evening of late summer, before the nineteenth century had reached one-third its span (69)." Specifically, the novel opens at the very moment when Carlyle began his assessment of the "spiritual" slippage within romantic culture. As the narrator's oblique cue suggests, Casterbridge's thematic (that is textual) center is found in Carlyle's writings of the thirties. It is Carlyle's debate between culture and society, between the dynamical and the mechanical, and between the past organic universe of wonder and the present "Steam-Engine universe" of mechanism and skeptical "pulling-down" which is articulated in Hardy's "story of a man of character."

Henchard finds his way to Casterbridge by an act of romantic betrayal. He sells his wife and child who are constituted in the text as his little cosmos of traditional order; they represent, overall, the virtues of romantic eros such as Wordsworth's Margaret had found and then lost. As it is cast in the narrative, Henchard's bargain is Faustian, but it is to Carlyle's Faust that we must turn if we are to accurately designate the Faust type the narrator has in mind when naming the mayor "a vehement gloomy being" (186). Specifically, Henchard is a revised figure derived from Faust as he appears in Carlyle's "Goethe's *Helena,*" while it is Carlyle's translation and extended commentary of this fragment of German romanticism which bears directly upon the themes and forms of Hardy's *Kunstmärchen.*

When we first see him on the road to Weydon, Henchard bears in train the waning constellation of his romantic cosmos which he will soon manufacture into a great chaos. We can summarily present this position and all that it implies by recalling M. H. Abrams's account of the marriage emblem in Wordsworth's prospectus to *The Recluse.* Abrams's claim is that marriage is a sign for the agency of the imagination and for all those correspondences it fosters between man, nature, and society. For Abrams, marriage is a "prominent period-metaphor which served a number of major writers, English and German, as the central figure in a similar complex of ideas concerning the history and destiny of man and the role of the visionary poet as both herald and inaugurator of a new and supremely better world" (*Natural Supernaturalism,* 27). In opening *The Mayor of Casterbridge* with a scene of divorce, Hardy presents us with as radically divergent an emblem from that which is "central [to] the Romantic enterprise" as he could imagine. As the antithetical emblem to marriage, the Weydon divorce initiates a narrative concerned with disintegration, disfiguration, decay, and death.

In sum, it is a narrative concerned with the disappearance of all that an early romanticism had married together or tried to and which Carlyle had tried to redeem.

The Weydon divorce is then a negative emblem contradicting all sympathetic acts and agencies of romanticism's natural supernaturalism. Dominated by the death wish, Henchard's life proceeds by a degeneration of the self in order to fulfill the ultimate aim of his desire which is to have his life "unbe." Henchard is a Carlylean "demon of the Void" who rules over the capital of Wessex, a city where man is divorced from his fellow man (or held together by the bondage of the cash nexus), where man is divorced from woman, man from nature and from his "better nature" or best self of romantic culture, where father is divorced from daughter, brother from brother (figuratively, Farfrae, who resembles Henchard's dead brother), where leadership is divorced from the qualities of good government, and where authorship is divorced from the power to authorize solutions on a cosmic, traditional, or individually redemptive register.

Henchard's story is set against the totality of romantic possibilities for enlightenment discussed in Carlyle's "Characteristics" and "Signs of the Times." In this way, his "character" is a "sign of the times," an introductory representation of Hardy's understanding of romantic collapse in the 1880s. Henchard's history depicts all kinds of divorce, right down to the divorce of sign from significance, the romantic metaphor from its intent, and of romance (idealism) from history (materialism). As he appears in the narrative, Henchard is a wooden man, his character not more than a social construction "enlivened" by a will toward romantic denial as presumably its best method of getting on in the world. More radically, Henchard is a figure of time itself or history understood as an unidealized "vacancy," in Shelley's phrase ("Mont Blanc") or as "a soulless image on the eye" in Wordsworth's (*Prelude*, 6:527).

As "Father Time," he is Little Father Time writ large as well as a smaller, more provincial rendition of Father Chronos of *The Dynasts*. More complexly characterized, he is a man who turns away from a narcissistically inclined romanticism and toward the social world of ambition. By divorcing his wife and casting off his child, he fathers himself into historical being as a character without internal, imaginative resources. Divorced from a lyrical interiority which resides in the past, he is born into the present as a figure of "pure" or brute history.

19

Introduction

Another way we might imagine his characterization is to invoke Jacques Lacan's semantics of selfhood. Post-Weydon Henchard represents the fate of the "je" or ego ideal radically detached from the "moi" or ideal ego. The result of this detachment is that he forfeits the power to idealize or "self-shatter" his ego ideals. Thus, he becomes an externally directed personality without access to the internal sources and resources of romantic individuality forged in the metaphorics of the lyric. Bereft of this lyrical capability, he is a "man of character," as Hardy names him, whose destiny is thoroughly mediated by the materialistic forces of economic production and its concomitant social affects. In this reading, he is exactly *un*like the whole man of romantic culture by which he defines his difference.

Intertextually, Michael Henchard is a mirror image of Wordsworth's Michael, the Good Shepherd. Those domestic and spiritual virtues practiced faithfully by Michael of the North are rejected out of hand by Michael of the South. By reading Henchard's character against Wordsworth's Michael, we enrich our understanding of the complex, antiromantic character of the mayor. Nor is such a reading entirely speculative, for Hardy alludes to "Tintern Abbey" in his prologue (chapter 1) to a novel which is the "Prelude" to the latter-day Wessex.

Farfrae's romantic character also partakes of the north-south or past-present dialogue of romantic representation. He is a Scot who descends from the North, a "Borderer" from Edinburgh whose lineage suggests the successful invasion of England by Walter Scott's sentimental romanticism, while his talent for balladry recalls the cultural premises of Wordsworth's and Coleridge's lyrical ballads. Intertextually, Farfrae's split sensibility is deliberately constructed from Hardy's reading of Carlyle's response in "Characteristics" (1831) to Thomas Hope's utilitarian *Essay on the Origins and Prospects of Man* (1830) and Friedrich von Schlegel's *Philosophical Lectures* (1831). As it is depicted in the narrative, Farfrae's character is a combination of both "philosophic" possibilities. He is a "comparmentalized" character, half romantic and half utilitarian, who will degenerate toward his pragmatic aspect after Henchard inadvertently murders his romantic life with Lucetta.

The Mayor of Casterbridge concludes with the narrator's outlining Elizabeth-Jane's "secret of making limited opportunities endurable . . . in the cunning enlargement, by a species of microscopic treatment, of those minute forms of satisfaction" (410) which haphazardly become available to her. Her minimal happiness replaces the grand revolutionary enthusiasms and cosmic joys of an earlier, more imaginatively daring epoch. Such expansive and sublime movements are not to be expected in latter-day Wessex where one must *mechanically* enlarge "minute forms" of satisfaction. Though minimal forms of recuperation are available, they are by no means an equivalent form to the romantic redemption imagined by Carlyle, nor do they bring with them an equivalent measure of satisfaction.

The satire enfolded within the narrator's concluding statement can only be fully measured by comparing it to the prevalent line of metaphor in Carlyle's early writings. There, the mechanical is set over against the dynamical, while it is hoped that the dynamical will dominate culture. In Hardy's revision, a low-voltage form of the dynamical can be achieved by mechanical or "microscopic" means. In effect, it is a cash nexus society that comes to dominate imaginative culture, precisely as Carlyle hoped it would not. Through this collapsing of Carlyle's distinctions between an organic culture and mechanistic society, Hardy achieves his satire on romantic aspirations. Society and culture (mechanism and dynamism) do collude within Elizabeth-Jane, yet without the therapeutic effect of a widening of vision which Carlyle had hoped for. In this way, the narrator implies that the present will not see a return of the glorious past despite Carlyle's titanic efforts to have it so "before the nineteenth-century had run one third its span."

In *The Woodlanders* (1887), Hardy continues his critique of British romanticism by combining a fable written against Wordsworth with a tale of Shelleyan romanticism degenerated into a self-serving aestheticism of erotic delight. This description accords well with what we know about the construction of the narrative. Hardy had sketched the "Giles Winterborne" story ten years earlier as a tragic elaboration of Gabriel Oak's comedy of romantic obsession. To this woodland story, he added "Fitzpiers at Hintock" (Hardy's title in draft), the story of an adulterous aesthetic doctor. Giles's woodland tale is a critique of Wordsworthian pastoralism, while Fitzpiers's story critiques the "decadent" permutation of Shelley's romanticism in the belletristic eighties.

We can schematically present the narrative results of this splicing if we recall that in "The Tables Turned" Wordsworth says that we have had "Enough of Science and of Art," thus we should "Close up those barren leaves;/ Come forth, and bring with you a heart/ That watches and receives" its nourishment from nature (29–32). The price of not so doing is to "grow double" (2). In *The Woodlanders* we witness an aesthetic doctor (science/art) who has grown double, meaning he has become cultured and "cultivated." Fitzpiers comes from old woodland stock, and he returns to the woods as the last scion of a family that once felt at home in rural England. For him, the woodlands are a region of "barren leaves," while it is the "natural man," Giles the woodlander, whom he outromances because he is well-read, cultured, and artful. Fitzpiers wins Grace's hand (the quest) because he has grown double, as has she at finishing school. It is the very "doubling" of her consciousness, half of which is Wordsworthian, and half Paterian, which constitutes the conflict in her existence as a returned native. Moreover, Giles's Wordsworthian "wise passiveness" and singleness of vision is not a help to him; rather it is this very passiveness which is the source of his defeat and destruction. At the conclusion of the struggle, we witness a romantic "grace" tragically married to art and science and the Wordsworthian naturalist dead.

During the course of the narrative, Fitzpiers's infidelities aptly depict the character of a frivolous and adulterous romanticism out to please itself as an "art for art's sake." His demonstrated inability to correspond with anything except himself marks him as romantic man fallen into a narcissistic phase of self-gratification, one which accepts the Paterian "thick wall of self" as the limit of sympathy. In this way, Fitzpiers is a portrait of an unsuccessful romantic in Bloom's scenario, one who fails to overcome self-enthrallments and engage in the "still sad music" of history *(Ringers in the Tower)*. The scientific aesthetician's "rainbow casting" which projects his aura of desire onto a temporary well-beloved mocks the very premise of an early romanticism which desired to see into the life of things and in which the individual redeemed himself from isolation through creative sympathy.

For Blake and for Wordsworth, the rainbow was a symbol of hope, a "visionary" bridge as real as it was imaginary which linked heaven to earth (*A Vision of the Last Judgment;* "My Heart Leaps Up When I Behold"). In the Hintocks, the romantic rainbow returns as a fanciful harbinger of despair. The degenerate form of the rainbow finds its closest analogue in Shelley's poetry in general and in particular in his *Prometheus Unbound* where flowers "hide with thin and rainbow wings/ The shape of Death (2.4.62–63). It is the "shape of Death" or nature as the abyss and history as pure process that is highlighted in Fitzpiers's rainbow casting. Tilottama Rajan's gloss on Shelley's floral rainbow, that it "points to the self-deconstructing duplicity in which a whole category of acts, including hope, dream, and fiction find themselves trapped" (*Dark Interpreter*, 54) applies with equal force to Fitzpiers's rainbow-casting in Hardy's *Woodlanders*. By emphasizing the romantic problematic of ephemerality, the novel offers us a reading of a wide range of existential problems such as those concerned with the epistemological status of an imagination once asserted to be a powerful substantiating agent for various perceptions of truth, beauty, and reality.

Spliced together, Fitzpiers's and Giles's tales constitute an emblematic refutation of the available forms of romanticism, the naive and the sentimental. In the Hintocks, traditional forms of romanticism die to be replaced by aesthetic forms which are insufficient to the task of organizing a coherent and self-regulating society. We can begin to uncover this subtextual critique by noting that Fitzpiers's adulterous affair with Felice Charmond is partly predicated upon Hardy's reading of Pater's *The Renaissance* whose themes of cultural renovation are interdicted in a narrative about decay, collapse, corruption, mutilation, and death in the woodlands. Although the theme of romantic decay exceeds its figural predicates as, perhaps, does the interpersonal drama of the fable, it is nonetheless the figural predicates which design and inform the cultural allegory of the narrative. In particular, Hardy draws his romantic figures from Pater's essay on "Leonardo." Fitzpiers is a reworking of Pater's "wizard-artist" Leonardo to whom he is compared in the narrative. Concomitantly, Mrs. Charmond, the "flesh of the world," is a reworking of Pater's famous portrait of La Gioconda, while Grace Melbury's evanescent character is derived from Pater's fading "face of grace," the Christ portrait of Leonardo's *Ultima Cena*.

Grace is initially a Wordsworthian romantic who is then "educated" to become the aesthetic mate of Fitzpiers. Her story features trace events from Wordsworth's epic "Grace Darling" (1843) whose intent Hardy inverts to write an anti-epic concerned with "the mis-education of Grace." She is mis-educated because taught to give priority to "city" fashions over "woodland" sentiments of being. In allegory, her fable demonstrates the erosion of the primitivism that sustained Wordsworth even when he was away from the woods. Because her youthful primitivism is weakened by her "finishing" school education, Grace eventually leaves the woods. With her gone and Giles dead, the woodlands are devoid of the potential to be the scene of romantic regeneration.

Giles Winterborne is a portrait of an early romantic sensibility superannuated into postromantic times. Like the stream he is named after, Winterborne is unfortunately born into Arnold's mid-century "Iron Time" which is hostile to his form of consciousness. His death by drowning and by fever conflate the two ways which, according to Hardy, romantic poets typically die. Hardy is of course thinking of the deaths of Shelley and Keats, and his understanding is satirical (Millgate, *Hardy*, 505). Yet it is this sort of deadly satire which informs a novel which concludes by demonstrating how Giles's name is "written on water" in ways which Keats's was not.

Intertextually, Giles's character is predicated upon Balder's from Arnold's *Balder Dead*. The narrator compares the Hintocks to Arnold's Jarnvid Wood while the iron character of the woods alludes to the "Iron Time" into which Arnold said romantic culture had fallen in his eulogy to Wordsworth entitled "Memorial Verses." In this reading, *The Woodlanders* eulogizes a past and passing romanticism. As Hardy depicts them, the woods are indeed iron; they are a manufactory of punishing labor where the sylvan spirit of freedom and joy is rarely felt.

In Hardy's southern woods, the romantic self is lost and not (re)found. The core metaphor Hardy uses to modulate his woodland motifs is derived from Shelley's trope of the decayed Rousseau, who is figured in *The Triumph of Life* as an old, distorted root. The rotten breath of the decomposing romantic inspiration mouthed by Shelley's wooden marionette of romantic origins suffuses the Hintock woods. Thus it is with Shelley's inconclusive (and unconcluded) critique of Wordsworth's "gentle breezes" and "voiced valleys" of salvation that Hardy concludes *The Woodlanders*.

Marty South is a complexly revised figure of Wordsworthian despair and Paterian impotence. Primarily, her character bears strong traces from Wordsworth's Margaret of *The Recluse*, while her fable reiterates the terms of loss in Wordsworth's mini-epic. Marty dwells in a "ruined cottage" as does Margaret; the copse of elm trees surrounding Margaret's cottage is reduced to the single elm which figures so prominently in Hardy's novel. Marty's staunch faithfulness to Giles replicates Margaret's to Robert, yet the marital commitment of Wordsworth's romantic couple returns as Marty's unrequited, fantasy attachment to Giles. Marty's full name is, after all, Margaret; the shortened, masculine form of her name speaks of her severance from her precursor's feminine strengths. Marty is also an incarnation of Pater's "Beauty in the Abstract" which we learn in the preface to *The Renaissance* is useless because unable to inspire culture to appreciate life as beauty. Indeed, the weak and pathetic character of Marty's masochistic romanticism serves as a prelude to Tess's fable of rape insofar as *Tess* tells of a "concrete beauty" sufficiently potent to inspire culture's new poets to revolutionary gestures appropriate to their time. That Tess does not become the new muse or Urania of romantic inspiration completes Hardy's critique of both concrete (embodied) and abstract (disembodied) forms of beauty.

Marty's final prayer at Giles's grave is based upon Hardy's reading of Arnold's "Memorial Verses." There, the poet-critic of cultural restraint inveighs us to "to keep fresh the grass" upon Wordsworth's grave until another such spirit comes along to revive culture. Marty's nostalgia which verges on necrophilia and our awareness of the impossibility of Giles's renascence further situates Hardy's response to a lost and soon-to-be-forgotten form of romanticism. In her instance, memory does not inaugurate a ritual of redemption; rather it motivates a compulsive repetition of erotic frustration and futility in reply to Arnold's recommendation regarding the romantic past in "Memorial Verses."

Like Marty, Tess bears the foreshortened name of an earlier and more potent romanticism. Read with its repressed content restored, Tess, whose full name is Theresa, is a latter-day Saint Theresa of Avila. Specifically, it is George Eliot's St. Theresa whom Hardy had in mind when writing *Tess of the d'Urbervilles.* Moreover, his sense of tragedy in *Tess* owes much to Eliot's in *Middlemarch*. Eliot's novel, we will recall, concluded with the suggestion that "our daily words . . . are preparing the lives of many Dorotheas, some of which may present a far sadder sacrifice than that of the Dorothea whose story we know" (Finale, 896). This "far sadder" Dorothea is Tess, while it is the failure of romantic culture (of words) which "prepares" the way for her tragedy.[9]

If Eliot's intention in *Middlemarch* is to describe culture in the "middle" of an itinerary first mapped by Kant in his *Cosmopolitan History,* Hardy's intention in *Tess* is to describe the "end-march" or last phase of that crusade. That "other side of silence" where Eliot's narrator locates the cacophony of cultural discord (*Middlemarch,* chapter 23) is the narrative space or figural terrain of Hardy's *Tess*. As a more severely punished

Introduction

Dorothea Brooke, Tess wanders through a culture thickly inscribed with romances and inhabited by poseurs who seduce her into becoming their romance. Tess's transformations by first Alec's and then Angel's romantic fancies best define the sense of "rape" in the novel. Yet once the intertextual relationship is established, this should come as no surprise for this form of intercourse is the tragic agency in *Middlemarch* too where Hardy found it. In her summing up of the novel, Eliot's narrator tells us that "there is no creature whose inward being is so strong that it is not greatly determined by what lies outside it (Finale, 896). It is by "what lies outside her" that Tess is raped. Cultural impositions mediated inward by language and act are the source of Tess's sorrow and destruction. Significantly, it is by murder that she tries to set herself (her-self) free from those enchantments which others have cast upon her. To find the purity of the uninscribed, she must get beyond the laws (or letters) of culture where the body can begin to determine the fate of its own desire. This marginal space of freedom where the body in question can determine—or in Tess's case redetermine—the direction of its own desire constitutes the fantasy of redemption through ecstasy which is implemented in the narrative at Bramshurst Court.

At the hands of her two Shelleys, Tess falls prey to a form of culture-philistinism. Like Flaubert's Madame Bovary, she is compelled to define herself in and through romantic forms which provide only "sustenance for the inauthenticity of those who consciously shape [their] experience by it" (Trilling, *Sincerity and Authenticity,* 104–5). As a deft reworking of a ballad of a fallen maiden, *Tess* critiques various romantic positions in ways similar to Flaubert's novel where the story of a romantic heroine critiques the very expectancies of that form of literature and its relations to life. Paradoxically, romantic culture imposes on Tess "the peculiar inauthenticity which comes from basing a life on the very best cultural objects" (Trilling, 104), while it is by such impositions (rapes) that Tess's body becomes the locus of various allegories of character (ballads of self) which long for a moment of self-defining "purity" (lyrical self-expression).[10]

Yet unlike Emma Bovary whom we may see as choosing her forms of literary poison, Tess is forced to swallow romances which paradoxically destroy her potential for genuinely romantic experiences. These pseudo-romances are delivered by messengers like Angel and conquerors like Alec who seduce and rape Tess by misreading her. Though she never fully comprehends what she wants, Tess seeks self-transgression in order to free herself from a culture which has trespassed upon her. She seeks, that is, to break free of those allegories which bind her desire and prevent her from becoming either a romantic Prometheus in her own right or a muse who could inspire a poetical character like Angel to become one. The ballad of her failure implicitly reflects upon "the expectations imposed on life by literary romances" as well as "the expectations which those same romances raise concerning literature itself" (Bersani, *A Future for Astyanax*, 99).

If the terms of incarceration are Eliot's, the terms of liberation are Keats's. In order to find an acceptable form of lyrical liberation from literary culture, Hardy read deeply in the Buxton Foreman edition of Keats's *Works* which included Keats's letters on aesthetic concerns.[11] Hardy's reading results in a narrative meditation upon Keats's "Beauty is Truth, Truth Beauty." "Big Beauty" was one of Tess's names in manuscript, and it is the story of Hardy's Big Beauty which tells the sad truth about the inability of art to encourage productive transgressions of art as its particular form of truth. Hardy inverted the marriage metaphor in Keats's "Ode to Psyche" to construct the novel's central metaphor of rape. In this way, Keats's emblem of erotic intercourse between beauty and truth degenerates into Hardy's emblem of deadly impositions wherein life is divorced from art by the conjunction of fancy and the seductive lie. Rape then is Hardy's metaphor for a divorce between life and art. And it is this form of divorce that structures a text obsessed with the decline and fall of the romantic imagination's capacity to encourage "marriages," characterized as sympathetic acts of intercourse between man, society, and nature. In *Tess*, life is art but art is not life.

In order to impute an epic (or anti-epic) dimension to this reading, Hardy usurped Keats's emblem for the vital imagination, "The Dream of Adam," which Keats, in turn, had borrowed from Milton's *Paradise Lost*, Book Eight. Keats's "Dream of Adam" is, of course, his allegory for the potent creative imagination which can make its desires real. Hardy recasts Keats's "Dream of Adam" as Tess's nightmare of rape, for it is she who becomes the form of another's desire. This other never "sees into the life" of Tess's desire and thus misrepresnts her as someone who represents his wishes for her. She then becomes "like" his idea of romantic beauty which fails to express the truth of her being. She becomes, that is, a metonym of desire in search of an apt metaphorical definition, one which would leave her idea of self intact as it expresses the idea.

Hardy reiterates Keats's Miltonic "Dream of Adam" *nine* times in the narrative; each time the dreams returns it structures a moment when Tess is negatively transformed (or raped) by the poetic-creative word into a romance of herself, or in Hardy's sense, into a fancy of some Adam or other. In all nine instances, rape is best understood as a cultural affair. Starting out in Marlott as a nearly white gown, or *tabula rasa,* Tess winds up in Wintoncester an overinscribed black flag, a palimpsest written to illegibility by the numerous fancies men have imposed upon her. Their inscriptions cast her (or "write" her) life as "Sorrow," the name of her illegitimate child, rather than "joy," the legitimate heir of romantic culture.

Read as a parable about cultural intercourse as mistaken identity, *Tess* is also concerned with the status of writing as representation and with authorship as a therapeutic procedure. For instance, we might draw our attention to the itinerant "red paint pot preacher" who writes *upon* nature in a parody of the penetrative imagination's capacity to read *into* nature and write. Then, too, Prince, the d'Urberville horse whom Tess replaces "in harness," is penetrated by a "mail-man" hurrying along in the dark before dawn to deliver his letters. In his official capacity as a "male mailman," he is a double signifier of the dominant cultural or "lettered" ideologies. His inadvertently penetrating Prince with the running shaft of his vehicle is proleptic of those scenes of metaphoric rape in which male carriers of the cultural letter penetrate Tess, the d'Urberville princess, with their "vehicles" and thus change the "tenor" of her life.

In order to construct his two "Adams" or "mailmen," Hardy incorporates a reading of two then recent views of Shelley. Alec and Angel are fabricated from Hardy's response to Dowden's biography of Shelley (1886) and to Arnold's critical manipulation of Dowden's *Shelley* in his 1888 essay entitled "Shelley." Hardy had read both pieces in the nineties in preparation for writing *Tess* (*Literary Notebooks,* 2:510). Arnold represents Dowden's Shelley as both a libertine and a liberal, a womanizer and an idealist. Alec and Angel are derived from Hardy's reading of Arnold's Shelley. Hardy's two characters replicate Arnold's strategy of splitting Shelley's ego, yet with a different effect. Whereas Arnold recommends that culture repress the sexual Shelley and embrace the idealist Shelley, Hardy's narrative tacitly recommends that we embrace both as a way of reconfiguring the whole man of a powerfully transgressive romanticism who can effectively rebel against and reform society's ethically bourgeois sense of romance and relationship.

As Hardy's narrative demonstrates, without a strong desire to transgress, the Arnoldian Angel is indeed "ineffectual." In contradistinction to Arnold's negative estimation of an erotomaniacally "sick" Shelley, Hardy discreetly applauds Alec's sexuality, though not its lascivious enactments. Had Angel possessed Alec's sexual drive he would have consummated his marriage with Tess specifically because narrative imperatives regarding purity would not have stood in the way of his desire to possess her physically. In possessing her, he would have broken the stranglehold that cultural narratives had upon her and upon him. His "legal" act of transgression (he is married to her) would have revolutionized—or romanticized—both their lives. Instead, he remains enthralled to Arnoldian notions of a rational restraint and propriety as his form of cultural philistinism. Ironically, in acting according to the highest and best that is thought by culture, Angel fails to become the modern prometheus.

When it came time to pattern a brief vignette of saving grace in *Tess,* Hardy turned to Keats's "Ode to Psyche" for guidance. In effect, he inverts his own initial inversion (negates his negation) to arrive at a Keatsean moment of genuine romance. At Bramshurst Court, a "court of love" where eros can speak its mind, Hardy portrays Tess as Keats's Psyche and Angel as her Cupid, the winged god. Both are weakened forms of Psyche and Cupid however, just as the narrator is a weakened form of Keats's poet-observer who will not be empowered to create a new poetry after gazing upon a liberated body's marriage with the soul of its desire.

As a Psyche figure, Tess momentarily becomes the inspiration for a new manner of worship, which, following Keats's intent in the Ode, would instigate a new or "romantic" form of poetry. In this sense, Hardy seeks in *Tess* what Keats sought in the "Ode," a new language of self-expression spoken by an authentically creative self who would not be at a loss for words, as Tess always is. Because Tess has reached Bramshurst Court by transgressing or shattering all romances, the lost triumvirate of Muse/Psyche, Eros/Cupid, and Poet/Priest returns briefly in an unrented mansion "dispossessed" of language. There the body is at liberty to speak its desire. It is thus as outlaws living in a vacant space marginal to society that Tess and Angel enact a genuine romantic epithalamium.

That form of culture which victimized Tess becomes Jude's chosen form of self-victimization. In fable, he is a self-persecuting and ineffectual Angel Clare who becomes Alec-like when he forces Sue to commit herself bodily to becoming his counterpart. Jude is an embodiment of the star-soul of romantic idealism in eclipse as he is named in the epigram to part second, "Christminster." There we learn that "save his own soul he hath no guide." This characterization of his subjectivity casts him as a figure of an imagination which rises in Wordsworth's *Prelude* and sets in Swinburne's *Songs Before Sunrise,* a title whose temporal moment must be read in conjunction with the blissful dawn of the romantic enterprise. In Hardy's skeptical reading of romantic culture, the glad day seemed about to dawn, yet the dawn never broke. And it is the failure of this expectation which is narrated in Jude Fawley's quest for redemption in the twilight culture of the romantic gods, a culture which has been poised "before sunrise" for nearly a century.

Contrary to popular critical belief and in accordance with the numerous overt and covert references to romantic writing in the narrative, romantic culture is, collectively, the "letter" which "killeth" Jude's vitality. In one sense, Jude stands where all romantics stand, *before* Wordsworth's dawn of bliss expecting a genuinely enlightened culture to soon arise. The mirage of Christminster, we note, always floats on the horizon; it never touches the ground of history. In another sense, Jude stands at the dead end of the romantic tradition because a century of such "songs before sunrise" had passed and the dawn still had not come. Jude is thus an alpha and omega figure who represents the origins and conclusion of romantic forms of idealism in England. That is, in *Jude* Hardy paradoxically (and perhaps inadvertently) becomes a romantic writer by critically demonstrating the impossibility of becoming a romantic writer.

Briefly, Jude is Hardy's Don Quixote. He is a man possessed by a fabulous form of consciousness which cannot dispossess itself of its enchantments. The fable of his life is a "mental picaresque." Like Blake's "Mental Traveller," Jude is enthralled within cycles of illusion which evade, repress, or deny a history of concrete commitments to the ordinary, and it is these commitments which return with a vengeance through the defiles of Jude's self-entrapping fanciful evasions. "Christminster" is Jude's word for his labyrinth of denial. It is the home of the "lost causes" of his joy in solitude, which is why Hardy borrows Arnold's Oxford, the home of lost causes, as the model for Jude's hypothetical capital of the pleasure principle.

Jude's enthrallment to Christminster's "glowing dome" is a sign of his fixation upon a narcissistic inwardness to the exclusion or suppression of outward perception. If, as Barbara Schapiro argues, "the finest Romantic poetry . . . reveals the efforts of [the narcissistic self] to overcome its angry, self-destructive attachment to the mother and itself" (*Romantic Mother,* 130), then Hardy's novel portrays a less-than-fine romantic who cannot overcome his attachment to the mother-imago. In this reading, *Jude* is a fable about romantic culture's failure to engage history. Jude rejects low Christminster culture as vulgar and he is rejected by high Christminster culture because he is vulgar. Thus he lives an isolated, quixotic existence in which he both evades history and relentlessly pursues his own destruction on a quest for a self-constructed and highly limited idea of perfection.

The thematics of isolation point to the textual sources of *Jude* which are to be found in Shelley's reading of Wordsworth. More specifically, *Jude* is predicated upon Shelley's *Alastor* and Wordsworth's "Arabian Dream" in Book Five of *The Prelude*. There, Wordsworth relates his "bookish" visionary romance of an Arab-Quixote, a "semi-Quixote" whose fantastic quest the poet admires but has the good sense not to pursue. It is this good sense, combined with the strength to "overcome" the "maniac's fond anxiety" and desist from partaking of the idealist's self-consuming quest (*Prelude* 5:160–63), that marks Wordsworth as a successful romantic. His ability to overcome enchantments is precisely what Jude does not possess, which is why Wordsworth's dream sequence constitutes the "solution" to Jude's form of idealism.

Jude's failure to overcome his enthrallments point to his character as a "reading" of Shelley. And it is to Shelley's life as well as his *Alastor* that Hardy turned in order to construct his fable of the "Arab phantom." Just as Wordsworth and then Shelley gave this phantom substance by fancying "him a living man/ A gentle dweller in the desert, crazed/ By

love and feeling, and internal thought/ Protracted among endless solitudes. . . . wandering on his quest" (*Prelude* 5:142–47), so too does
Hardy in his turn and by their example.

Unlike Wordsworth but very much like Shelley, Jude cannot overcome his "entrancement" to Christminster. Because he cannot, his life
is tragic. The agency of this tragedy is "culture," in Wordsworth's sense
—the poet is entranced by Shakespeare, Milton, and the *Tales of the
Arabian Nights*—and in Shelley's whose Alastor-poet "reads runes" when
seeking the secrets of life. Jude will ruin his life by reading too. Phillotson
is Jude's teacher-hero who inspires him to become a cultural philistine.
Jude's desire for Culture with a capital "C" is his tragic flaw or, in
Shelley's phrase, his "generous error." Hardly uses Shelley's *Alastor* to
write a tale about the fall of the House of Romanticism which is brought
down by the failure of things as they are (or history) to merge with
things as they ought to be (or idealism) (the formulation is Hardy's from
his "New Year's thought" for 1879, *Life and Work*, 127).

To flesh out his tale, Hardy followed Dowden's biography of Shelley
and Arnold's critique of it, as he did in *Tess*. It is more than the close
proximity in time of composition that marks these two novels as alike,
it is the identity of their shared Shelleyan source texts. Like the Shelley
of Dowden's biography, Jude "gives the impression of encountering no
enchantment he does not embrace" (Bloom, *Ringers in the Tower*, 27).
His autodidactic cultural character is built from introjected and then
projected fragments of books he reads, ones significantly antique and
out of date. In this way, he inverts romanticism's dialogue between a
living past and a dead present. Jude studies dead languages in order to
produce a "studied" character of perfection. In him, the dead past informs the living present, killing its ability to be either fully present or
fully alive. In this sense, his cultural ambition is comparable to Henchard's
social ambition. Both forms of aspiration lead to the ruthless solitude of
death-in-life, Henchard's because abysmally materialistic and external,
Jude's because radically ethereal and internal.

Hardy's allegory closely follows Shelley's *Alastor*. His choice of the
stone-cutting profession for Jude is derived from Dowden's view that
"*Sculpture* . . . presenting beauty or passion in an immortal abstraction
from all that is temporary and accidental—appealed in a peculiar degree
to Shelley's imagination" (Hardy's *Literary Notebooks*, 2:69, emphasis

Hardy's). As a type of sculptor, Jude's consciousness is an "immortal abstraction" removed from history, the realm of the temporary and accidental. His status as a copyist of past forms suggests that his very character is a copy of past forms which he trys to restore to life in the present. Like the gothic forms he trades in, Jude is a statuesque (or rigid) copy of a once-sublime form. Otherwise put, he represents the dead letter of romantic culture.

Like his predecessor the Alastor-poet, Jude leaves Marygreen, the possible site of Wordsworthian forms of naive romanticism, to seek the "solemn vision, and bright silver dream" of Christminster. In allegory, we see a boy who rejects Nature in its high romantic formulation in order to embrace culture in its bookish formations. Jude likes "school" as the Wordsworthian "Boy" does not. Jude's cultural father is Phillotson, Wordsworth's is mother nature. Jude's form of romanticism heads him toward the city, that specular St. Bartholomew Fair from which Wordsworth fled in horror back to the reality of "Mary-Green" or mother nature. In terms of literary history, Jude's ambitions represent those of second-generation romantics who sought a Hellenic reformulation of the Hebraic ideals of the first generation. Jude relives both generations' ideals: he begins as a Hebraic sentimentalist and winds up a Hellenic idealist, thanks to Sue's tutelage. Significantly, he is never a naive romantic, never a "naked" savage running joyfully through the woods uncaring of his isolation because "in love" with natural forms.

Like the Alastor-poet, Jude first becomes distracted from his high calling by an encounter with Arabella, his "Arab Maiden." They reenact the Arab Maiden's carnal temptation in *Alastor* when she offers the scholar gypsy "meat" from her father's tent. Significantly, Arabella hurls a pig's pizzle at Jude to offer him the role of the father-husband. In accepting her offer, he breaks off his bookish enchantments and bears himself into history, momentarily waking as it were from a dream. (We will recall that in *The Prelude,* Book Five, it is those who "take in charge/ Their wives, their children, and their virgin loves" [154] who are *not* on the quixotic quest.) The pizzle is the incarnated castrating word of the father which symbolically denies Jude access to his oceanic fantasy of the breast (Christminster) and invites him to become a father in his own right by engaging in biological and social reproduction. Appropriately, the child of their union appears first as a fancy or fable (the terms are synonymous in Blake and Coleridge) fostering a weak correspondence—Arabella feigns pregnancy in order to compel Jude to marry her—and second as Little Father Time, a minimal version of history in Wordsworth's sense of a "spot of time." Little Time is the agent of revenge who "punishes" Jude for not breaking with his enchantments and attempting to live continually in a "space like a heaven filled up with northern lights, /here, nowhere, there, and everywhere at once" (*Prelude*, 5:530–33).

In the wake of his divorce from Arabella, Jude pursues his second veiled maiden, Sue Bridehead. Sue's name recalls Shelley's veiled maiden from *Alastor,* and she will sing Jude a hymn to intellectual beauty and enthrall him to her form of romance. She is like Jude insofar as she too must deny history in its biological form to enact her enchantment. By the self-defining poetry she has Jude quote and by her pet name of "little bird," Sue is a refiguring of Shelley's Skylark, the blithe spirit of Jude's narcissistic delight. Her "intellectual" nature becomes his "mother nature." Together, Jude and Sue reenact Shelley's "Hymn to Pan" and its companion piece, the "Hymn to Apollo." As an enactment of Shelley's "one shape of many names" (*Laon and Cythna,* 1, 27:3), Sue will be one more form of the name of Christminster. In this Shelleyan reading, Sue's second name "Mary" refers to Mary Shelley, of whom she is weak successor, while Florence, Sue's third name, is derived from Florence Henniker, Hardy's Shelleyan "companion" and "epipsychidion." Mrs. Henniker burst Hardy's fantasy of adultery in order to keep faith with her husband. Her faithlessness to Hardy's Shelleyan ideal of transgression enacted by "spirits" sharing elective affinities is "punished" in the narrative when he depicts Sue Florence's "cowardly" betrayal and abandonment of Jude. Her betrayal is a crime against Jude's "generous error" of idealizing her which imbues her with an heroic character she does not possess.

As a figure of history, Little Father Time is Jude's repressed antiself. He is the perverse Wordsworthian child who fathers Jude into the permanent vacancy of a world not colored by his rainbow projections of culture. Derived from Shelley's "Chariot of the Hours," Little Time inverts the redemptive moment in *Prometheus Unbound* when "life" triumphs over time. In Hardy's revision, time triumphs over life. Furthermore, Little Time presents us with a cameo appearance of Henchard's form of character. As such, Henchard and Little Time are the alpha and omega characters of a Wessex where "time conquers all his romances" as the narrator tells us outright in *Tess*.

Time has not been Jude's "fair seed field" as Wordsworth and Carlyle had promised it might be if culture could marry with society. Thus Jude dies asking us to forget that he ever lived by reciting lines from *Job*. The scriptural character of his last will and testament is reflective of his having "grown double" by reading books like the figure of cultural absorption in Wordsworth's "The Tables Turned." Born of "the letter," he ultimately seeks the appropriate letter which will erase his scriptural character. Significantly, he finds it in the Book of Job wherein a good man is punished for his "generous error" of belief. By reiterating Job's curse, Jude asks us to forget his life; indirectly, we are asked to abandon quests after obscure and misleading forms of culture which displace us from history. His dying in the "real" Christminster (and not his dream vision of it) signifies that he has finally learned the lesson of Wordsworthian overcoming; like Don Quixote before him, Jude dies condemning those "tales of the Arabian Nights" which have led him on a "maniac's errand."

In death, Jude is portrayed as a statue, a beautiful monument to a passing form of romanticism. As an ostensibly beautiful figure—his beauty is twice commented upon by the Widow Edlin—he invokes Burke's category of the Beautiful in order to revoke romanticism's category of the gothic or Miltonic Sublime. Pale because consumptive and white because speckled with marble dust, Jude finally appears in the narrative as a figure of "Grecian art, and purest poesy" (*Prelude*, 5:459) representing all that he had tried to evade by his enchantments and, concomitantly, all that those enchantments needed to recognize in order to be vital. Jude's quixotic life has been folly as his surname of Fawley implies. His life in letters is an extended critique of the narcissistic imbalances within early romanticism; his "epic" in prose illuminates the self-threatening knowledge repressed in and by earlier epic representations of sublime possibilities.

In *Jude the Obscure*, Hardy's theme is that "far greater uneasiness about the limits of poetic idealism than might appear from the theoretical statements of [romantic] poets themselves" (Rajan, 29). Subject to such a powerfully disturbing discontent, Wessex is indeed one of the finest readings of romanticism that we have, one for which Hardy's adopted classical rubric that "art conceals art" is aptly suited, for it covertly reveals his desire to artfully explore the textual sources and resources of romanticism's obscure aesthetic effects.

The critical arguments and revisionist interpretations I have sought should be understood as a search for a more accurate understanding of Hardy's uneasiness with all forms of romantic ideology. He named the source of this discomfort "Non-Rationality" (*Life and Work*, 332), a neologism which defines the rhetoric and intent of Wessex writing. A Marxist might define nonrationality as that form of "negativity" which bears an intuition of concrete history apperceived in the gap between contending ideologies as each dissolves the other's purchase on perception. A Lacanian might understand nonrationality as the place of the real in the constitution of the subject, that "real" being nothing more substantial than the effect of absence within the interplay of imaginary and symbolic agencies of representation.

However we might construe it, and here we are speaking only of finding a suitable allegory of reference, Hardy's nonrationality is best understood as a nonsynthetic contradiction of terms. The discursive result of such a "principle" is that every truth claim within narrative returns as fiction. Constructed from fictions revised to highlight their own inherent fictionality, Wessex mimes earlier forms of writing that claimed to be both beautiful and true. In order to interrogate Hardy's mimesis of fiction we should follow Roland Barthes's advice and explore narratives by "deliberately pretend[ing] to remain within this consciousness [presented in narrative]" so as "to dismantle it, to weaken it, to break it down on the spot, as we would do a lump of sugar by steeping it in water. Hence *decomposition* is here contrary to *destruction*" (*Barthes on Barthes*, 63). By decomposing Wessex narratives we deploy as an analytical insight the same nonrational principle which informs the construction of Wessex and permits Hardy himself to remain interior to a romanticism he is out to interrogate. In effect, we figure out Wessex in accordance with the one principle by which Hardy had "figured it in."

In the preceding reading of Wessex, I have sought to describe the overall effects of nonrationality in narratives arising between *The Mayor of Casterbridge* and *Jude the Obscure*; Jude who lives in the imaginary, Henchard who dwells in the symbolic; Jude who lives in the empty plenitude of culture as a function of its lost desire, Henchard who dwells in an empty or loveless society as a social functionary, a mayor of Casterbridge. No one novel represents solutions to or absolutions from the problems it sets out to define, though all narratives are "solutions" which suspend the terms of the problematic. This nonrational structure of suspensions which informs Wessex will repeat itself one more time in *The Dynasts*. There, where all of Wessex is writ large, Hardy takes nonrationality as his most central issue. In *The Dynasts*, the much-debated "It" is a self-referential signifier without significance which rules a history (the underworld) and a metaphysic (the overworld) which can only be formally present as a function of language and debate.

As a writer in search of significance, Hardy's position in literary history is akin to that of a late Augustan or preromantic poet's with, of course, a difference in time. Like his much-admired Gray (whose poetry and poetics play a significant role in *Desperate Remedies*), Hardy pondered the exhaustion of the poetical character and of a tradition of forms and formulations which had run their course and could only return as artifice and decoration, as a sentimental repetition of the poetry of sentiment. Yet Hardy arrives on the scene of poetic invention one century after Gray and in the wake of Wordsworth who had defined the new poetical character and its function. Thus Gray's difficulty in discovering the authentic poetical character translates, with historical difference, into the difficulty Hardy experiences in losing that poetic character, or, what amounts to the same thing, not being able to (re)find it. In effect, Hardy's anxiety of authority mirrors (inverts and reflects) Gray's.

This anxiety and insecurity within the authorial temper has been aptly described by Weiskel in his analysis of the preromantic poet (*The Romantic Sublime*, 107–36). Because an anxiety of authority informs Wessex, Hardy's narratives return an already constituted cultural episteme back to its originary moment constituted of conflicting groups of writers in the historical world. By this I mean that within any late Hardy novel, apparently authoritative statements are returned to the historical moment when they themselves were insecure assertions struggling for hegemony over the cultural episteme. In this reading, Hardy's fictions are understood as chronicles, as he liked to think of them, which reengage the historical struggle for authority between various ideological positions in the late eighteenth and early nineteenth centuries. Because his intertextual constructions reengage this past, Hardy's writing is implicitly "historic." In representing the similitude between the moment of initiation/composition and the moment of decay/decomposition, Wessex parodies the romantic desire for an identity between past and present and in so doing demonstrates that from the point of view of history (and not literary history) there never was any ideal, systemically organized "romantic" faith which might return at the present's beckoning.

Hardy's mature awareness of the always unfulfilled desires of romantic writing is evidenced by the following two epistolary statements on art which he inserted into his *Life and Work* in the year 1901. The date of the entry helps us to define his sense of the pathology of "the century's corpse outleant" (cf. Hardy's poem "The Darkling Thrush") which he will anatomize in *The Dynasts*. Though it is incidental to our purpose, it is worthwhile noting that the date of insertion could be symbolic. The letter was never sent and, in the absence of corroborating evidence, we cannot say for certain when it was written, chronology being but one feature more at issue in his autobiography-miscellany.

My own interest lies largely in non-rationalistic subjects, since non-rationality seems, so far as one can perceive, to be the principle of the Universe. By which I do not mean foolishness but rather a principle for which there is no exact name, lying at the indifference-point between rationality and irrationality. (332)

Following this statement, Hardy inserts this entry on the "unimaginative" function of literature at the present time.

I do not think that there will be any permanent revival of the old transcendental ideals; but I think there may gradually be developed an Idealism of Fancy; that is, an idealism in which fancy is no longer tricked out and made to masquerade as belief, but is frankly and honestly accepted as an imaginative solace in the lack of any substantial solace to be found in life. (333)

Both statements bear witness to Hardy's interest in nonrational subjects; both pit the poetics of the year 1800 against those of 1900. Standing as he does at the still point between reason and irrationalist intuition, the nonrational writer draws upon fictions created by both discredited representational modes, relocating the figures and claims of these fictions within narratives that negate the desired effect of a beautiful truth. Written from the standpoint of Carlyle's "Center of Indifference" slouching toward the "Eternal Nay," Wessex texts are neither beautiful nor true, although they do have much to say about the ways in which romanticism legitimizes beauty and truth.

In this vein, we might note also that although Hardy's sense of impressionism closely approximates Pater's, himself a romantic revisionist of the eighties, the nondialectical character of nonrationality produces no gemlike flames of art capable of generating a cultural renaissance. His resistance to Pater's aestheticism gives us cause to suggest that while Hardy's fictions dismantle recent, local manifestations of romanticism, they also provide sufficient material for reflections upon romanticism and the romantic temper extending back from Pater to his Petrarchan sources in the West.

The immediate results (or the immediate narrative causes) of Hardy's reformulation of imaginative reason in 1901 appear early in his career with the publication of *Desperate Remedies* (1871). As a case in point, *Desperate Remedies* combines a rational calendrics of time and date with a gothic fable of intuition. The rational narrative traces the progress of a detective architect, Edward Springrove; the irrational narrative follows the plight of his intuitively acute fiancée Cytheria who solves the murder mystery almost as quickly as does her detective lover. The double structure of the narrative combines the rational with the irrational without allowing the two categories to dialectically merge. Structurally, *Desperate Remedies* does not represent the sort of marriage Wordsworth had in mind in his prospectus to *The Recluse* or that Blake had imagined when wedding Heaven to Hell.

We might further enhance out understanding of Hardy's principle of nonrationality by defining his neologism as a perilous extension of Mill's corrosive argument against religion in "Nature and Utility of Religion" written between 1858 and 1860 when Hardy was a student of Mill's (*Life and Work*, 355–56). Mill's argument has been summarized in the following manner: religious belief "is neither rational nor irrational. It is simply non-rational, but to base morality on non-rational foundations is to weaken it, perhaps even to sow the seeds of its destruction. Hence the prosecuting attorney lurks in Mill behind the earnest and fair logician" (Nakhnikian, *Nature and Utility of Religion*, xxiv). Hardy extends Mill's overt logic and covert rhetoric to "sow the seeds of destruction" in all forms of poetic faith, thereby corrupting all forms of narrative legitimation. Hence we might say with equal force that the prosecuting attorney lurks in Hardy behind the earnest and fair chronicler of events.

In a remarkable turning about of Blake's imaginative assertion that "All Religions are One" to the poetic genius, Hardy ironically claims that indeed all faiths, including poetic faiths, are identical insofar as all are fanciful rhetorics which shape perception in accordance with temperament and ideology. This claim, which runs counter to the spirit of the high romantic age, is the basis for Hardy's suggesting that in postromantic times *"every man* [should] *make a philosophy for himself out of his own experience"* (*Life and Work,* 333, emphasis Hardy's). In the construction of such a philosophy Hardy notes that "[Nobody] will . . . be able to escape using terms and phraseology from earlier philosophies" (333). Here, stated in Hardy's own words and from motives that now should be clear, is the rationale underlying his methodology of narrative construction. In principle, Hardy states that everybody should do in life as he has done in narrative—forge and combine, borrow and incorporate "terms and phraseology" gleaned from earlier philosophies in order to "construct" a philosophy suitable to his experience.

Though a novelist "could not escape" borrowing "terms and phraseology from earlier" writers, the special duty of an author is "to avoid adopting their theories if he values his own mental life" (*Life and Work,* 333). So construed, a valued mental life is reactive and not productive; it generates new fictional ensembles by reproducing and reorganizing philosophies while remaining ironically distanced from their claims. Authenticity, the "duty" of the author, is achieved through a calculated distancing of mind from all manner of mediated representations or ideologies as itself a way of mediating the thoroughly representational character of consciousness. Fiction is thus constituted by a calculated avoidance of and engagement with culture. In effect, a supplementary authenticity is gained through irony and the labor of cultural reproduction. Written with this form of authenticity in mind, Hardy's novels are properly understood as tragedies of significance whose deliberate regress from the Coleridgean symbol to allegory recuperates meaning by indicating the collapse of the very form and intent in the rhetoric it reproduces in order to communicate collapse.

To these reflections upon method, we should add that toward the close of the nineteenth century, Hardy felt compelled to reformulate "the confusion of thought" he "observed" in "Wordsworth's teachings on the imagination in his essay in the Appendix to 'Lyrical Ballads' " (*Life and Work,* 329). Hardy locates the source of Wordsworth's confusion as "chiefly" arising "out of his use of the word 'imagination' " (*Life and Work,* 329). Amazingly, he "corrects" the confusion by deleting the imagination from Wordsworth's conception of poetic language. Under

Hardy's revising hand, Wordsworth's "imagination" is deleted from the category of "imagination and sentiment" and replaced by "passion," thereby substituting the key transcendental signifier of romantic writing with one derived from the psychology of the emotions. Such a substitution returns the authority within romantic writing to its origin in late-eighteenth-century psychology as a way of adjusting its claims to late-nineteenth-century perceptions about romantic obscurity. As though his "way of putting it better" were not damning enough, Hardy goes on to equate Wordsworth's category of the imagination with fancy, thereby collapsing the two concepts into one. Far from restoring credibility to poetry, such a revision completely demolishes the supreme fiction and main enabling agency of British romantic poetry.

To comprehend just how devastating this demolition is, we must refer to Coleridge's writing, as Hardy did toward the conclusion of his *Life and Work.* Then, he cautions himself to "remember the fate of Coleridge." The fate Hardy wishes to keep in mind is that of the systematizer who seeks to produce a coherent explanation of the faculties of perception within a principled frame. For Hardy, Coleridge stood as a warning to all would-be romantics seeking coherent philosophical narratives which would transcend historical contradictions and establish their view as more than an ideological response validated by temperament and taste. If we recall that Wordsworth's discussion of the imagination and fancy in his 1815 preface instigated Coleridge's theoretical elaboration in *Biographia Literaria* in 1817, then it is not difficult to see that in revising Wordsworth, Hardy effectively takes Coleridge to task as well.

Before considering Hardy's views on Coleridge, it is worth our while to pause and note that the above reformulations and connections were written around 1900 during which time "[Hardy] was preparing for the press a number of lyrics and other verses" which would further define the role of fancy within history (*Life and Work,* 332). These lyrics and verses would appear in *Poems of the Past and the Present* (1901), a title which relates Hardy's poetry to Wordsworth's and Coleridge's. My point here is that Hardy is deliberately situating the inaugural moment of his own poetic career in opposition to Wordsworth's and Coleridge's nearly one hundred years after their poetic revolution. Hardy's canon of poetry constitutes a counterrevolution to theirs and is intended as such. The reference to "Past and Present" in the title demonstrates his awareness of the counterrevolutionary posture he has taken. The title further implies that Hardy worked against the romantic grain from the beginning since one of the references to the "past" of Hardy's title is his own past poetic compositions. We can confirm this by recalling that *Poems of the Past and the Present* includes such items as "The Lacking Sense" and "The Sleep Worker," both of which are critical of the romantic faith although Christianity is their ostensible target. As Hardy all but states in these lyrics and in poems such as "The Impercipient," the poet who lacks the imaginative sense can only be a "sleep worker," a skillful manipulator of dreams or fancies, and a "sign seeker" whose awareness of the abyss between sign and reference is his sole purchase on significance.

As allegorical productions of Blake's "Daughters of Memory" forged without access to the transcendental imagination, Hardy's nonrational narratives can be theoretically elaborated through the defiles of Coleridge's notions on the romantic subject. In brief, Hardy removes the imagination from its position of priority in Coleridge's hierarchy so as to produce a fiction dominated by fancy reigning over history. In Hardy's revision, Coleridge's model of the poetical character remains intact, yet with an empty slot or cipher at the site where the imagination once stood. Nostalgia keeps this space open for possibilities which reason and temperament understand are unlikely to arise. Hardy's reformulated Coleridgean model materializes as the structure of *The Dynasts*. It is as though the course of his narrative investigations in Wessex finally enabled him to represent the obscure absence that had been tragically at issue all along. As a linguistic counter holding the place where the imagination once stood as the guarantor of cultural meaningfulness, the It of *The Dynasts* represents the absence of a creative authority in a Wessex now writ large to represent nineteenth-century culture.

The It of *The Dynasts* is an equivalent term for Hardy's neologism of nonrationality, one neologism of incertitude standing in for another as it were, the net gain of significance between the two being zero. In form and in function, both metaphors stand for the absence of any stance as the key determinative position in Wessex writing. Decentered as it is, Wessex is devoid of Coleridge's "primary imagination," defined as "the repetition in the finite mind of the eternal act of creation in the infinite I AM" which joins temporal (history) to transcendental (mind) dimensions and thus locates a center or truth. In the absence of the primary

42

imagination, Hardy's method of composition depends partly upon Coleridge's mechanical "secondary imagination" which "dissolves, diffuses, and dissipates in order to create" (*Biographia Literaria,* chapter 13) and partly upon Coleridge's specular realm of history.

Without the primary imagination as a guarantor of principled creativity, what is to Coleridge a difference in degree becomes to Hardy a difference in kind. The result of this difference is the failure of the secondary imagination to "idealize and unify." Specifically, Hardy's characters dwell in a culture of ungrounded secondary imaginings which are insidious because deprived of the benefit of the primary imagination's ordering principles. Severed from correspondences of any kind, characters ultimately describe their form of consciousness as "chaotic" *(The Mayor of Casterbridge)* and unprincipled *(Jude).* The "fable" of how this occurs is intended to "dissolve, diffuse, and dissipate"—in short, to decompose—the claims of the romantic imagination operating within an organic subjectivity.

"Fancy," Coleridge tells us, "has no other counters to play with but fixities and definites." Coleridge's linguistic "counters" become "signs" in Hardy's narratives, those key signifiers that invade Tess, inhabit Jude, and determine the self as an allegory of character. The fixedness of these counters shape but do not "unify" the subject, giving the self an allegorical form of character. Any self so informed is deprived of dialectical flexibility, as we have noted of Farfrae as a case in point. Character as a "fixity" can exchange fancies or "counters," but it cannot integrate or unify them. Nor can it "grow" into personality, romantically conceived. Instead it collects views which accumulate into a chaotic and unprincipled miscellany, the ultimate destiny of the self in Wessex, of which Hardy's "autobiography"—no more than an assemblage of idealized cultural positions disguised as self-representation—is our best example.

Constituted by the Coleridgean fancy, character can only gesture its desire to act otherwise. The tragic outcome of such implicitly frustrating gestures is the desire to "unbe" in order to disburden the self of its "fixities" and so "be" for the first time.[12] Otherwise stated, the apex of awareness in Wessex occurs when a character understands that "seeming to be" is "seeming as being" after which they desire to "unbe." In their genuine desire to "unbe," Wessex romantics ironically achieve a moment of authentic specular presence. That is, they imagine that the fanciful character of their own consciousnesses is the authentic end (in the sense of aim and conclusion) of the romantic discourse on the subject. Having achieved such a "theoretical" position, they desire to die (unbe) as a sign of their authentic understanding of their cultural predicament. In this way, authenticity in Wessex is an effect of nihilism and death.

Though characters such as Tess and Jude might seem to represent "symbols of living power," they are actually remnants of such figures motivated by a "lifeless mechanism" of the sign, in Coleridge's distinction between the vital metaphorics of the symbol and the deadening metonymics of allegory. Yet all is not lost in them nor is their insignificance insignificant. Devoid of "free and vital originality," they assume an originality all their own by representing themselves (their selves) collectively as a "servile imitation" of their genuine precursors, in Coleridge's condemnatory assessment of the subjected position of the allegorical figure (*Shakespearean Criticism,* 1:197). Engaging in a mimesis of romantic subjectivity achieved by a "blind copying of effects instead of a true imitation of essential principles," Hardy's characters depict a false mimesis as well as a mimesis of falsity. In presentation, Wessex characters are purely formal, mechanical men and women. As Coleridge defines it, "the form is mechanic when on any given material we impress a predetermined form not necessarily arising out of the properties of the material as when to a mass of wet clay we give whatever shape we wish it to retain when hardened" (*Shakespearean Criticism,* 1:198). This mode of "impressing" defines Tess's rape by cultural myths, while the agency of rape reflects the destructive form of culture which Hardy's nonrational impressionism is intended to communicate to the reader. In conjunction with this characterization, we might profitably recall that in composing a poem, Hardy would first construct a metered scaffolding without words, like a crossword puzzle, then fill in the blanks later on when a suitable word came to his attention. Upon the materiality of language, Hardy would impress a "predetermined form not necessarily arising out of the properties of the material" (Coleridge, *Shakespearean Criticism,* 1:198) in order to produce the perfect simulacrum of an organically conceived poem. In Coleridge's determination, Hardy's method produces a poetry that ceases to be poetry because it has sunk "into a mechanical art" (*Biographia Literaria,* chapter 18; henceforth cited as *BL*). Because the product of morphosis and not the creation of poiesis, Hardy's

44

poetry is "a deceptive counterfeit" of genuinely imaginative poetry (*BL,* 18).

Likewise, Hardy's well-balanced plots are substitute structures for organic narratives understood as literary forms developing in accordance with internal principles. The pride Hardy took in pointing out just how well made they were is the pomp of the artificer and the architect whose skill copies and recombines types and orders from the past into a serviceable and allusive structure. The exteriority of Hardy's well-made plot is subversive to the interiority of organic plot structures characterized as "the growth of the poet's mind" in accordance with the laws and principles of his or her being. This subversion occurs at the level of character too, which imparts to Hardy's narratives a doubly mechanical and thoroughly exterior character. For instance, Tess and Jude's bodies are impressed like wet clay with forms of romantic consciousness derived from the materiality of the *zeitgeist;* thus their subjectivities are exterior, received and not innate, reflective of temporal forms of consciousness yet significantly without that "genial understanding directing self-consciously a power and an implicit wisdom deeper than consciousness" in Coleridge's assessment of the one thing necessary for romantic genius (*Shakespearean Criticism,* I:198). Written as a double exteriority then, Wessex has no interior. There is no "heart" of Hardy country which is all surface with no depth, and yet paradoxically this superficial condition constitutes its most profound heart of darkness.

Although this critique of the romantic idiom might be extended to the realm of textual allusions in general as a shaper and misshaper of experience, that wider encompassment has not been attempted in my study. As de Man convincingly argues in another context, there is an infinite regress involved in studying the intertextuality of narratives for which there can be no precise method of analysis *(Rhetoric of Romanticism).* Any method deployed would only construct an allegory of the interpreter's desire out of the materials at hand. Yet if we understand Hardy's relationship to romanticism as dialogic, insofar as Wessex relates to a specific set of utterances circumscribed by those romantic allusions and copytexts found in his notebooks, letters, autobiography, and novels, then de Man's infinite regress is halted where, presumably, Hardy began to construct his fictions. In curtailing an infinite regress where, hypothetically, Hardy began to react to and reform his materials (and so beginning my analysis where Hardy began his), we do no more than

45

accept Hardy's myth of Eden in order to understand a Wessex born of its fall into history.

Framed within this limitation, this book follows the path of John Livingston Lowe's *Road to Xanadu,* yet with a critical difference. Whereas Lowe ultimately subscribes to the Coleridgean imagination in order to explain its literary productions and thereby conspires with the very myth he sets out to interrogate, I have sought to locate the richly allusive character of Hardy's fictions in the materiality of the inherited word which Hardy consciously sculpted into narratives. Such narratives are the products of a calculated professional risk dealing in recent—and not remote—cultural matters. Hardy's forgeries are not attributable to Lowe's "Imagination Creatrix," but to a cunning placed at the service of a will to succeed by an author who saw himself primarily as a producer of cultural commodities. Although there may well indeed be an anxious, latent response to romantic influence in his narratives, a Lacanian *refoulement* of secondary repression, my primary aim has been to cite and elaborate instances of Hardy's professional practice of decomposing romantic texts within his own compositions in order to maintain the distance required by his one guiding principle of nonrationality.

Exceeding simplistic formulations of aesthetic disinterestedness, Hardy's nonrational narratives are Rabelaisian, in Bakhtin's sense of a writing on the frontiers of cultural collapse which constructs from the debris an "image of *man growing* in *national-historic time*" (*Speech Genres,* "The *Bildungsroman,*" 25). Wessex is a baroque or carnivalesque narrative space where the novels represent the desire for poetic faith and the demand for the suspension of all such faiths as forms of "bad faith." It is my understanding that Hardy's nostalgia (as a form of reverence) and skepticism impart to his writing its unique character. By locating romantic irruptions in this baroque narrative space, by listening for certain key words or clusters of words reiterative of romantic poetry, and by tracing displaced figures from, say, Coleridge's *Statesman's Manual* where an orchard reflected in a lake returns as Giles Winterborne's disappearing "plot" of arcadian romanticism, we initiate the project of unearthing (by counterediting) the hidden life of Hardy's art.

Failing to succeed where Yeats and Stevens would succeed by half, Hardy produced a literature against the romantic gain, unique for its time and valuable because rudely unaccommodating to romanticism's deepest desires and most profound intentions. Wessex is a literature of

Introduction

fancy, invention, and history and not of imagination, originality, and the sublime. So defined, fictional Wessex is uncannily more real than imaginary because constituted of a writing where the imaginary conditions of the real are depicted as imaginary. Confined within a cultural space of collapse, a black hole of skeptical writing which envelops idealistic texts to feed its own bizarrely inverting energies, Hardy began to fancy the imagination dead as his particular form of empowering self-deception. It is to the negating, consumptive, and demystifying strategies of his form of truth that I have given my full critical attention, imagining in my turn a literature uninspired by the romantic imagination, a purely specular literature without future returns, a historic literature without ringers in the tower, a Wessex without towers.

PART ONE

HEBRAIC SATIRES

[1]

Dissembling Henchard:
The Mayor of Casterbridge

*If thou beest he—but O how fallen! How changed
From him who, in the happy realms of light
Clothed with transcendent brightness, didst outshine
Myriads, though bright!*

Paradise Lost

*In Hardy, almost for the first time, we have an author
who is counter to the central tendencies of his age.*

Frederick Karl, *"The Mayor of Casterbridge:*
A New Fiction Defined"

THOUGH IT MIGHT seem excessive to compare Michael Henchard to Milton's fallen Satan, the distant comparison locates the proximate source of Henchard's character in Carlyle's romantic formulation of Goethe's Mephistopheles. As we shall see, Hardy's "man of character" is Carlyle's Demon of the Void, "a child of Darkness, an emissary of the primeval Nothing" and the "best and only Devil of these latter times" ("Goethe's *Helena*," *Essays*, 1:158). The impending spiritual void of Carlyle's "latter times" paradoxically constitutes a rich source of themes and figures in Hardy's mature fiction, of which Henchard's story is the prologue. Henchard is an ambitious materialist who commits his ungenerous error by revolting against romantic eros in order to dominate the capital of Wessex; thus, he is "satanic" because his character is contrary to the central themes and tendencies of imaginative literature from Blake to Carlyle.

As Carlyle's Mephisto, Henchard represents a return to "the void" or abyss which the romantic imagination had attempted to obliterate by fostering correspondences between man and nature, man and man, and man and society. By divorce, Henchard cuts himself off from potential correspondences of any sort. At Weydon, he severs himself from the totality of communal and transcendental possibilities promoted by romantic love. In so doing, he damns himself to a hell of despair and, ultimately, to work without hope of gaining either sympathy or love. Though not as forceful a presentation as "the Sole positive of Night" in Coleridge's "Ne Plus Ultra," Henchard nonetheless is a portrait of "The Substance that still casts the shadow Death!" the "unrevealable,/ And hidden one" and "sole despair/ Of both th'eternities in Heaven" (1–15).

Rather than a typically romantic allegory of regeneration, *The Mayor of Casterbridge* presents us with a postromantic epic of degeneration. In order to construct this negative emblem (or positive negation, in Coleridge's sense), Hardy read deeply in Carlyle's admonitory cultural writings of the 1830s. In those tracts for the times, Carlyle assumed the mantle of a latter-day Coleridge recalling a backsliding Albion to the romantic faith. Hardy's intimate knowledge of Carlyle was instrumental in the production of *The Mayor of Casterbridge,* which presents us with a "reading" of the message and impact of Carlyle's writing.[1] In Hardy's reading, the Scot's plea had fallen upon deaf ears; thus since the thirties England had become a Casterbridge, a place of getting and spending which laid to waste its ever-weakening imaginative powers as it moved further away from the aspirations and tenets of Carlyle's gospel of "The Everlasting Yea" *(Sartor Resartus).*

At Weydon Priors, Henchard commits his "original" sin for which he will be exiled from the garden of romantic possibilities defined by the "Hebraic" line of English romantics—those strongly influenced by German romanticism—from Wordsworth to Carlyle. Henchard's divorce completes his turning away from a romantic past in order that he might acquire a modern present. In essence, he interdicts Wordsworth's and Carlyle's desire that the past inspire the present in traditional and imaginative ways. By selling his wife and child, Henchard initiates the tragedy of a deracinated selfhood which Hardy entitles "the story of a man of character." Ambition is Henchard's crime; possession of the world in its historical, factual, and mechanical forms both his reward and his punishment. In betraying his romantic self, Henchard becomes public man, a social being whose consciousness Wordsworth characterized as a "pensioner/ On outward forms," "rich one moment to be poor for ever" *(Prelude,* 6:736–38). In short, he is Carlyle's mechanical man, the willful dynamo of the "Steam-Engine Universe" and the antithetical self to the dynamic personality.

Dissembling Henchard: The Mayor of Casterbridge

Divorce then is the midwife or agent which bears Henchard into history as fallen, public man cut off from his interiority. Bizarrely, Henchard is nonsubjective man, a fantastically objective character whose subjectivity is completely superficial and therefore deeply problematic. One way of comprehending this form of character is to read it literally. Henchard's character is like a character in the alphabet. He is quite literally presented as a social being whose essence is a social construction, whose actions are public performances, and whose life is valued in quantities and not qualities. In this reading, his character bears comparison to Blake's Urizen as he appears in *The Book of Urizen*. Henchard is Urizen-like after Weydon where he falls from the romantic eternity of desire, an interior condition which redeems the external world from its very externality. Divided from his redemptive powers, Henchard becomes a self-enclosed, all-repelling, and gloomy worshiper of his own limited self-creation called the mayor of Casterbridge. Both Hardy's and Blake's epics or prophecies of history depict the fate of a willful subjectivity which divides, separates, limits, and diminishes its own existence in order to rule a mechanical universe of satanic wheels within wheels cut off from the imagination's resourceful eternity. Born of divorce, Henchard is a self-divisive character, and Casterbridge is his walled city of self-destructive limitations.

Though Hardy did not have Blake in mind when he drafted *The Mayor of Casterbridge,* he did have Carlyle's formulation of the Urizenic "mechanical" character which by the eighties had become a critical commonplace in romantic culture's debate with history. The terms of that debate opposed culture to society, the lyric to the narrative, romance to realism, and the imagination to fancy, and it is these terms which return to inform the drama of Henchard's narrative. *The Mayor of Casterbridge* continues this debate by portraying a character who favors social narratives over cultural lyrics, realism and history over idealism and romance, spectacles of the "Phantom Opera" (Wordsworth's emblem of London) to the realities of the imagination, and the proprieties of expression over the vitalities of self-expression. The story of this form of character is one of spiritual loss achieved through material gain, and in this way it constitutes a continuation of Carlyle's tragedy of romanticism, his worst-case scenario for historical man.

Read at its simplest, Henchard's fable depicts the triumph of death over life, of thanatos over eros. The totality of the defeat is indicated in many ways: by the allegorical (and not symbolic) character of the narrative, by the absence of poetry and dreams in Henchard's life, by the vacant and unenlightened character of nature surrounding Casterbridge, by the relentless incursion of the mechanical into the town's daily life—from Farfrae's "mechanical miracle" which cures Henchard's "grow'd wheat" to the seed-drill which replaces the sower in the fields, by Hardy's casting Weydon Priors as Wordsworth's St. Bartholomew Fair from Book Seven of *The Prelude,* and by the description of the Casterbridge Roman Ring as a Wordsworthian "spot of time" whose terror cannot be imaginatively transformed into a moral lesson for world-historical man. Moreover, Henchard is portrayed as a character who disintegrates rather than as a personality who integrates as his mode of being. His character is depicted as a collection of "fixed counters" in Coleridge's phrase for the elements of allegory, and his three attempts to idealize a relationship—once with Farfrae and again with Lucetta and finally with the second Elizabeth-Jane—result in strife.

When we first see him on the road to Weydon during the "preludium" to his history, Henchard walks beside his family, willfully setting himself apart from them, treating them as though they were an albatross hung round his neck which prevents his ambitious ascent in the world. Wandering in search of a more prosperous form of labor, the narrator initially portrays him as an unregenerate mariner "that on a lonesome road/ Doth walk in fear and dread,/ And having once turned round walks on, /And turns no more his head;/ Because he knows, a frightful fiend/ Doth close behind him tread" (*Rime of the Ancient Mariner* 6:445–51).

The demon which dogs his heels is the spirit of a perverted Promethean ambition with whom Henchard strikes a bargain at Weydon. There, he enters the modern capital of Wessex—Henchard's provincial version of Wordsworth's "vast mill" of London (*Prelude,* 7:719)—with the assistance of the furmity woman, his "modern Merlin." Intoxicated by her adulterated potion, Henchard divorces his wife. In so doing, he puts "the whole creative powers of man asleep," in Wordsworth's estimation of the dangers which lay in store for those who crave the seductive spectacles of the city. Years later, Henchard appears as mayor, the chief showman in the Phantom Opera of Casterbridge.

Henchard is "discreative" man. Understood in terms of the Carlylean cultural debate, *The Mayor of Casterbridge* depicts antiromantic man subject to time, chance, and change. Subject to time and a subject of time, history will be his nemesis. Because he uproots himself from "timeless" community rituals and traditional structures of relationship, he places himself in the jeopardy of history. The furmity woman exemplifies history as nemesis, for among other things she is an agent of history. It is she who holds the secret to his past, that spot of time which, when recalled, causes Henchard to forfeit his good name, that professional name invested with mayoral power for which he sold his wife, child, and rural past.

As devastating as this loss is, it would not be so disastrous were Henchard permitted to regain his forfeited romantic capacity and thereby achieve the redeemed state of "organized innocence" after his fall from grace. But he is not given this opportunity for regeneration, even after he begins to desire such. This is one reason why Hardy's novel is so unremittingly gloomy and dark, while it exemplifies Hardy's shift away from the reiteration of romantic tales of redemption as the expected form of public, literary therapy. As a type for all of Hardy's late novels, *The Mayor of Casterbridge* is written on the cusp between a desire for romantic redemption and the recognition that history does not afford opportunities for recuperation. Time destroys all romances—even Henchard's paradoxical romance not to be romantic or idealistic. Thus, the recognition of loss in the later Wessex does not lead to gain or restitution. It leads rather to a literal or purely historical awareness that time is difference and that difference means a disappearance of all that was vital in the past without any hope whatsoever that it will reappear once its value is recognized.

Divorce, the agent of Henchard's primal loss, becomes particularly significant in light of the weight which M. H. Abrams gives to epithalamic metaphors in romantic writing. According to Abrams, marriage is "the prominent period-metaphor which served a number of major writers, English and German, as the central figure in a similar complex of ideas concerning the history and destiny of man and the role of the visionary poet as both herald and inaugurator of a new and supremely better world" (*Natural Supernaturalism*, 27). Henchard inaugurates his fate (his character) through divorce, an act at odds with marriage, the central figure for the romantic complex of ideas in England and in Germany. If marriage is but another word for "correspondence," which undoubtedly it is, and if the doctrine of correspondence in its various formulations describes summarily the utopian agency of the supremely better world envisioned by romantic idealism, then Henchard's divorce and the story of its results should be read as Hardy's supremely negative fiction representing the fate of historical consciousness cut off from all idealistic principles and from the very desire for idealism itself.

Initiated by divorce, Henchard's life goes against everything implied by the romantic metaphor of marriage, which is quite a lot. By juxtaposing epithalamium to divorce, we define by contrast Hardy's position regarding the prominent themes and forms of the "Germanic" or mystic strain of English romanticism from Wordsworth and Coleridge to Carlyle. Divorce, and not marriage, is Hardy's great theme in his mature fictions. And we shall see that Hardy overtly and covertly deploys the emblem of divorce to define his sense of tragedy without redemption. Otherwise put, it is history divorced from the imagination that is on display in Wessex. Such a display can only be specular, "a picture-language which is itself nothing but an abstraction from objects of the sense" and a "phantom proxy [of] empty echoes" in Coleridge's definition of allegory ("Symbol and Allegory," from *The Statesman's Manual*, 437). Given that Wessex is such a place of divorcement, we might say along with Coleridge, "Alas, for the flocks that are to be led forth to such pastures!" ("Symbol and Allegory").

The antipastoral character of such a history appears first on the road to Weydon. There Henchard willfully refuses to acknowledge the presence of his wife or child, nor does he hear the nightingale singing in the bush. In emblem, we see a man willfully recoiling away from romantic eros, from family, tradition, generation, nature, and from that gothic "sense of a past" which romantics like Carlyle hoped would return and dominate the present. In sum, we see a man overcome by a "savage torpor," feeling a "peasant disgust" toward those realms of pastoral delight to which romantics had once fled from the horrors of the city (quotation from Wordsworth's *Preface, Second Edition of the Lyrical Ballads* [1800], 449).

Instead of holding a sustaining intercourse with nature and family, Henchard stares steadily at the dusty ground. He never lifts his eyes into the distance as Jude does to see the glowing dome of Christminster, nor does he reflect upon the beauty of his companion as does Angel. Beauty and imaginative truth do not exist for him. Nature, too, is a dead thing in his eyes as it was not for the solitary, wandering characters in

Dissembling Henchard: The Mayor of Casterbridge

Wordsworth's fiction. As a premise to the whole, we see a Henchard whose heart is "dry as dust," in Coleridge's and then Carlyle's pejorative description of a "loveless," uncharitable, murdering man, in, respectively, *The Rime of the Ancient Mariner* and *Sartor Resartus*. We see too a man who "attempt[s] to exist without human sympathy," a "selfish, blind, and torpid" man who will experience "the lasting misery and loneliness of the world," in Shelley's description of unromantic, Hobbesian man. Because he is one of those "who love not their fellow beings," Henchard will live "a fruitless life" in preparation for "a miserable grave," his "heart dry as summer's dust" (the very dust we see him tread on his way to Weydon), "burning to the socket" (quoted and paraphrased from Shelley's Preface, *Alastor*, 70). Lastly, we see Coleridge's Ancient Mariner in the act of shooting the albatross. Indeed, Coleridge's mariner returns in Hardy's novel as Newson, the regenerate mariner who accepts the cast-off woman and child and presides over the second Elizabeth-Jane's wedding in place of Henchard, the uninvited wedding guest.

Although these crimes against the heart are clear enough as analogues to Henchard's fate, the character and destiny they describe are extremely difficult to comprehend. As unromantic man, Henchard represents Hardyan "unbeing," a condition which we might understand as motivated by the compulsion to disintegrate. Driven by the Freudian death drive whose aims are antipathetic to those of the libido and whose mechanisms are to date poorly understood,[2] Henchard is radically "unerotic" man. Subject to (or a subject of) the death-drive, he cannot properly be described in Freudian psychoanalytic terms which belong to the realm of eros and the libido. Thus, Henchard's story can only be told, not analyzed. In this way, he is a portrait of Burke's "sublime" of terror, yet his character is genuinely mysterious and not just mystically so. The fable of such a mysterious will to unbe depicts what we might call the "historical sublime" wherein terror arises as an effect of history in conjunction with a perverse desire for nothingness enacted through the acquisition of property and power. Part of the terror arises because we do not know the "law" or "essence" of his being, all we see are its effects in time.

In this connection, we might note that all seemingly romantic or libidinous moments in Henchard's life are mechanical and deadly attachments bound by the letter of convention and not by any sense of an elective affinity which exceeds that letter. That is, the narrator depicts each and every one of his "marriages" as a business "contract" and not a love affair. At Casterbridge, he contracts to remarry a "ghostly" and dispirited Susan whom he does not love; he strikes a bargain with Farfrae to keep him in town because the Scot reminds him of his dead brother, and he demands that Lucetta marry him as though she were breaking a contract by not doing so. His stepdaughter, Elizabeth-Jane, can live with him provided that she follows the letter of his laws on propriety, while he returns Lucetta's love letters with an air of giving her back a contract which she did not honor. Even in death Henchard prohibits the resurgence of eros. His last will and testament demands that all forget him; in effect, he prohibits the therapy of recollection and recital which constitutes the terms of the Ancient Mariner's redemption. It is explicitly by "not forgetting" or by recollecting the horror of his isolation and his drive toward unbeing that some small recompense could arise and, if cultivated, adjust the future; yet it is precisely this therapy that his last will and testament prohibits.

If we imagine him as Hardy did, as a gloomy Wordsworthian "spot of time," we see that it is by constructively overcoming the memory of Henchard that beauty and joy can arise. If we agree further that romantic representations of joy arise as the imagination recoils from history and that correspondences occur when we repress the awareness of strife and difference, then it would seem apparent that those who manage to either flee or overcome the memory of Henchard would be able to recuperate some small portion of romantic contentment. Thus by ignoring Henchard's last will and testament and recalling the lesson of his life, the second Elizabeth-Jane partially romanticizes her life. By denying the anti-romantic character she has called father and acknowledging Newson's natural paternity, she becomes a somewhat romantic character in her own right.

This calculus is borne out by the narrative. Freed of Henchard by her small inheritance, Lucetta falls in love with Farfrae, while Elizabeth-Jane is capable ultimately of finding "microscopic" joys in small acts of social welfare after Henchard's death. In this respect, Henchard's interaction with Abel Whittle is a negative parable of remarkable proportions, especially when Abel accompanies his "brother," Cain-Henchard, into the wilderness. Then, the mayor's "desire not to desire" finally achieves its perverse goal and the archetypal murderer of brotherly, familiar, and sacred love is murdered in turn by his own hand as an act of kindness toward himself and others. Ironically, it is through the doubly negative effect of his will to die (of his desire to kill his desire not to desire) that Henchard achieves the equivalent of redemption, which is oblivion. That is to say that by escaping from himself he becomes worthy of an equivalent form of that grace which others have merited and received by escaping from him.

What is truly remarkable about Henchard is that he exists as pure quantity without quality. Henchard is repeatedly referred to as a quantum whose stock of "goods" is eroded by time and chance. He has no purchase on anything eternal and immutable; he is thoroughly temporal man. The narrator describes Henchard's temporality by charting his "fall" as though a stock were falling in value on the stock exchange. We will recall that Mr. Fall is instrumental in his "fall," that Fall's nickname is Wide-O, which names Henchard's sin (he widowed himself) as well as the zero that he is, and that Henchard's fall is precipitated by his distrust in the prophet of nature's prophecy, which turns out to be true. Devoid of natural qualities, Henchard is perhaps the first narrative portrait of modernism's "man without qualities," a radically pathological extension of the typically Victorian villain of materialism who appears in fiction from Dickens to Galsworthy.

Given the pure exteriority of his character, Henchard can only acquire culture in its purely specular forms. He is a man for whom beauty and learning are but the thespian acquisitions of "the quality," a word whose social ironies are thematically central to Hardy's satirical intent in the novel. It is this specular sense of culture that interests Henchard in his concern for his good name and for Elizabeth-Jane's education. We will recall that he prohibits his stepdaughter from helping Nance Mockridge with her chores and that he demands that she not speak the "familiar" dialect of Wessex. His demands require that she abandon romantic culture (cast as mercy, love, pity, peace, tradition, community, and "the real language of men") and embrace the "mannered" culture of the quality. To remain his daughter and live "under his roof," she must divorce herself from romantic culture as he did many years ago when he began his ascent to the mayoral mansion.

It is only after he is "honeycombed clean out of his good character" that Henchard begins to desire home and marriage and all that those redemptive metaphors represent. He will live with Elizabeth-Jane in a little cottage from which he sells seeds in an attempt to reconstitute the "Dear tranquil time, when the sweet sense of Home/ Is sweetest! moments for their own sake hailed/ And more desired" (Coleridge, "To Wordsworth," 93–95). Henchard will be denied this form of redemption when he symbolically "murders" his stepdaughter or "a daughter" for the second time in his life. He repeats his original crime by telling Newson that "his" daughter is dead. By so doing, he kills any love that he had won back for himself by behaving "romantically" in Wordsworth's and Coleridge's domestic sense of romance. Ultimately, Henchard is denied access to hearth and home at Elizabeth-Jane's wedding. Though he can approach the wedding under the sign of the nightingale (the caged goldfinch he carries), he must remain apart from the communal and connubial rites of spring with its choric dancing and song. Hardy's point in this denial is clear: having sold his "marriage rites" at Weydon, Henchard cannot buy them back. Otherwise put, when Henchard finally desires redemption, he fails in his attempt to remarry or reintegrate his "lettered" self with his divorced erotic potential. In terms of the Faustian underpinning of Hardy's fable, Faust-Henchard is denied an eleventh-hour reprieve from the demonic deal he had struck with history at Weydon.

This denial is important, for its consequences will reverberate throughout the narratives of the latter-day Wessex where romanticism's quests are reengaged without recalling their triumphs. Whereas redemption seemed probable to Blake, possible to Wordsworth, necessary to Coleridge, and demandable to Carlyle, it was not expected by Hardy whose last comic novel of significance had been *Far From the Madding Crowd*. Equally as important, Henchard's damnation helps explain Hardy's penchant to favor the skepticism of second-generation romantics such as Shelley and Keats over the "faith" of first-generation romantics such as Wordsworth and Coleridge. That is to say, the more skeptical the romantic, the more closely his vision approximates Hardy's. And it is in this sense that Hardy is a last "last romantic" whose vision is more skeptical than that of skeptical romanticism's last romantics.

Henchard's radical disenchantment with all forms of idealization mark him as the most unnarcissistic character in Wessex and the antithetical counterpart to Jude, the most narcissistic. Henchard's character is dominated by Freud's ego-ideal (of social demands and representations), while

Jude's is dominated by the Freudian ideal ego (of unrestrained narcissistic desires). On the one hand, we have Henchard who is outwardly turned and who has forfeited all access to the mother as nature, as woman, and as correspondence. On the other, we have Jude who is inwardly turned and who moves always toward the lost mother, always seeking to bind himself to the woman. It takes no remarkable feat of calculation to see that Jude marries about as many times as Henchard divorces, taking into account Henchard's many figurative divorces. After his primary (and I would say "primal" divorce) at Weydon, Henchard's life is constrained by law only. His life is "bound" by chronology and contract; there is no timeless or mythic dimension to him and he never dreams until he loses all of his possessions, summarily named his "character." Jude's life, conversely, evinces the anomic character of the dream which follows its own logic, the logic of desire. Jude has little sense of real time and real society, which is his romantic flaw, while his cultural fancies are collectively the "letter" that kills him.

We can elaborate this binary opposition by understanding that Henchard is flawed or wounded because he has abandoned his Jude-like aspect while Jude receives his wound by abandoning his Henchard-like character. It is Henchard's radical severance from *jouissance,* the felt effect of an imaginary union between the infant and the (m)other, that describes the severity of his alienation.[3] If we understand *jouissance* to be the source of romantic joy in its most radical or "oceanic" formulations as Barbara Schapiro does in *The Romantic Mother,* then we are compelled to see Henchard as a man divorced from the capacity for a lyrical exuberance understood to have its source in pre-egoistic (prelinguistic) apperceptions of the mother–child relationship. Indeed, the one time Henchard attempts song in the Three Mariners inn, he transforms a sacred hymn into a secular curse and by so doing prevents a "timeless" community ritual from recurring.

By closing himself off from that dawn of innocence when it was a joy to be alive, Henchard arrives on the stage of history and never once looks back to the past he has left behind. He never integrates past with present to arrive at an organic sense of self; rather, he willfully represses the past when he dwelt with mother nature as a Wessex native and "heathen" or son of the heath. His act of repression or disjunction is figured at Weydon when he sells Susan and Elizabeth-Jane (the imago of mother and child) in order to purchase a pure, dis-illusioned form of experience.

Turned away from the fantasy of the breast (which perhaps is why the road to Weydon is so terribly dry) and toward the fantasy of empiricism and Hobbesian realism, Henchard presents us with an imaginary portrait of the Lacanian "je" (or ego) cut off from its "moi-fixations" on the mother. Disconnected in this way, he is a figure in the narrative representing narrative forms of representation, an ego that is only an ego, a ballad of self divorced from its lyrical component. Stated otherwise, he is a figure enclosed within the prison house of language and denied the reprieve of lyrical originality. In this reading, we might see Henchard as a radically empirical man whose story is a "Descriptive Sketch" of "Guilt and Sorrow" (the sorrow of not being able to overcome himself, of not being able to shatter his mayoral ego ideal, the guilt of his entry into history) like those written by Wordsworth before the dawn of his strong imaginative power for self-shattering, the source of his authority, authenticity, and originality.

Once displaced from his position of authority as mayor, Henchard drifts aimlessly upon the heath, a nobody endlessly circling the scene of his lost character. He will seek to recuperate his lost identity as a desiring and desirable individual by clutching onto fragments of Elizabeth-Jane's clothing. His doing so tells us that he is partially recovered for he has learned to love fragments. His fetishism reveals furthermore his inability to see "wholes" because he is a collection of disjointed parts himself. We will recall that poised on the threshold of eros at Elizabeth-Jane's wedding Henchard "could see only fractional parts of the dancers . . . chiefly in the shape of the skirts of dresses and streaming curls of hair" (400). As a fetishist, he can only see part of the dance, never the entire figure. When mayor, he had possessed objects and not people. All along, he had lived in a world of parts unrelated to any communal whole while governing a thespian society of "parts." Wandering the heath clutching the eroticized fragments of Elizabeth-Jane's clothing, his "story" comes full circle, ending just where it began when he wandered the heath with a family falling to pieces. And it is during this moment of finale that the narrative offers up its most profound understanding of romantic representation and desire.

Succinctly, that understanding is this. Positioned between the loss of

Dissembling Henchard: The Mayor of Casterbridge

his character and his being refused love, Henchard represents the pure signifier. Without a secure allegiance to either a "romantic" (idealist) or a "realist" (historical) context of representation, he ceaselessly orbits the lost realms of desire and demand. Because he never settles into either field of representation, he becomes a figure of pure equivocality laden with the burden of a nostalgia for a "home" or position within a certifiable system of significance, a "field of representation" and its commitments. Henchard's story, the "story of a man of character," ultimately represents the fate of the signifier (of the letter or character) within late-romantic British writing. And it is this fatality of the romantic metaphor that determines the character of Henchard's fate in accordance with the novel's tragic ratio that "character is fate" (185).

Read at full length, *The Mayor of Casterbridge* is a fable about the fate of writing in an episteme characterized by the disengagement of sign from significance. The total effect of the narrative of Henchard's life is a suspension of the traditional character of narrative as a symbolization of desire (the romantic epic) or as an allegory of social comportment (the Victorian novel). Ideally, romantic narrative poems such as Wordsworth's "Michael" offer a way of mediating both realms. Significantly, Hardy's Michael negates that mediation.

Henchard begins his life where he ends it, on the road between: between culture and society, between narcissism and egoism, between inwardness and outwardness, between interiority and exteriority, between idealism and mercantilism, between communal correspondence and the bonds of the cash nexus, and between time and intimations of immortality. Between everything, he is a wandering signifier in search of significance, a character in search of an author. All Hardy's upcoming novels will be written from this position on "the road between" where we first and last witness Henchard disconsolately walking. Failing to identify with either culture or society and highly satirical (that is to say critical) of both, Wessex writing remains disengaged and "in between." And it is this disengagement which constitutes its most original contribution to "modern" literature.

In *The Mayor of Casterbridge* then, we witness a writing about disengagement and reproduction within a narrative which details the reproduction of disengagement, which is to say disintegration. The story of Henchard's gradually winding down to zero encompasses the motives,

63

agencies, and trajectory of Hardy's mature Wessex writing. Aware that he too disconsolately wanders a wilderness of cultural possibilities, imaginative or otherwise, Hardy stands "in between" all fields of discourse, claiming this road to be his own, wishing all along that it could be otherwise but understanding why it cannot.

In Hardy's mature novels, we witness the unwitting inauguration of a literature set against itself, one positioned in the margin between literature as philosophy and philosophy as literature. From the "road between" where we first and last see Henchard, all subsequent Wessex novels level a radically disruptive reading of the romantic character and the character of romanticism. Paradoxically, the deep effect of such a highly subjected literary domain that is anxiously aware of its own subjection is the covert production of a literature endowed or infected with a profoundly problematic originality. In short, the suspension of romantic being is the chief characteristic of Wessex, while it is a portrayal of "the life and death" of the romantic self which opens the pageant of literary history in *The Mayor of Casterbridge*.

Because the subtitle to *The Mayor of Casterbridge* is "the story of a man of character," it is crucial that we locate as best we can the immediate sources and relevant definitions of "character" which Hardy had in mind. The narrator provides a clue to one source when he proclaims that "Henchard's character . . . might just be described as Faust has been described—as a vehement gloomy being who had quitted the ways of vulgar men, without light to guide him on a better way (chapter 17, 185–86). By indirection we are directed to Goethe's Faust. The narrator's description is immediately followed by this pronouncement: "Character is Fate, said Novalis" (185). Now, we are led to implicate Novalis and German romanticism in general.

In fact, neither are directly implicated in Hardy's construction of character. Though there has been much ado about the source of these quotations, both are derived from Carlyle whose translations and characterizations of German romanticism in general and its authors in particular in the late twenties and early thirties account for the Germanic themes of Hardy's novel. Henchard's story opens "One evening of late summer, before the nineteenth century had reached one-third of its span" (chapter 1, 69), precisely when Carlyle had begun to publish his translations of Germanic literature regarding the character and fate of romantic man as Goethe and the Jena group of the *Atheneum* had defined him.

By withholding his source in the first instance and supplying a red herring in the second, Hardy suppresses the immediate source of character which is to be found in Carlyle's writing of the late twenties and early thirties. Hardy knew Carlyle's writing extremely well, while he knew little German at all. In order to hide the English source of his intertextual citations and thereby impress upon his writing the cosmopolitan character essential to the professional man of letters, Hardy borrowed liberally from Carlyle and then deleted all references except those suggesting the international tone of the well-read author. Were Carlyle's name cited as often as it might be, Hardy's novel would seem secondary and second-rate—a reading—when compared to its very proximate English source.

Although we are quickly pointed to Faust by the narrator, his precise reference is to Carlyle's version of Goethe's Faust. Specifically, Henchard's Faustian character is derived from Carlyle's translation and commentary upon "Goethe's *Helena*" published in 1828 when the century had run "nearly" one-third its course. In addition to this, Hardy relies heavily on two of Carlyle's seminal essays, his "Characteristics" of 1831 and his "Signs of the Times" of 1830, to inform his cultural critique of a backsliding England unwilling to "summon back from lonesome banishment" early romantic writers in order to once more "make them dwellers in the hearts of men/ Now living or to live in future years" (Wordsworth, *Prelude*, 1:164–67).

As Carlyle describes it in his extended prefatory analysis, Goethe's *Helena* tells of a man who successfully bargains for love incarnate or Helen of Troy. Goethe's tale recounts the fate of an "erring" wife who returns to "salute her paternal and nuptial mansion" (*"Helena,"* 168) and then precedes to once again leave Agamemnon to engage in an "unexampled courtship" with Faust. Their phantasmagoric courtship depicts the triumph of romantic art in the union or "marriage" of desire and form, classical beauty and sublime possibilities. Hardy will invert Carlyle's fable to portray a man who divorces himself from Helen of Troy or love incarnate and thereby deforms romantic art and its existential intent. Hardy's fable will depict the triumph of adultery over marriage, of history over myth, or of brute reality over the beautifying imagination.

Both Hardy's and Carlyle's Fausts are "mayors"; Carlyle's rules a tower's keep, Hardy's, roman Casterbridge. Carlyle describes Goethe's *Helena* as a "gay gorgeous masque" of "Romantic Pomp." Hardy will invert the character of this description to produce a gloomy masque of capitalist pomp and specular culture. The masquelike character of the novel is most apparent during the visit of the royal personage and its companion spectacle, the skimmington ride. If Goethe's *Helena* shows us a "light scene, divided by chasms and unknown distances from that other country of gloom" called history, as Carlyle noted it did, then *The Mayor of Casterbridge* shows us "that other country of gloom" *("Helena,"* 164) or "history."

In Goethe's *Helena,* Faust's desire marries with Helen's beauty to produce Euphorion, their romantic child and joy (euphoria) incarnate. Hardy's *Mayor of Casterbridge* inverts marriage as the central agent of the allegory to produce a fable about divorce, the joyless implications of which we have already discussed. The demonic agent in the *Helena* is called Phorcyas, a "hard-tempered and dreadfully ugly old lady" whom Carlyle names a "wise old Stewardess" for the role she plays as Faust's pimp. She will reappear in Hardy's novel as Mrs. Goodenough, a "haggish creature" (73) who twice mediates Henchard's damnation, once as the instigator of his crime against love (it is her potion that liberates his will toward divorce) and then again as an agent of history when she sets the record straight in the courts and brings the law to bear upon Henchard's good character.

As "a man who has quitted the ways of vulgar men, without light to guide him on a better way" (185), Henchard is Carlyle's unredeemed Faust. Unredeemed because he had "quitted the ways of vulgar men," ways which Wordsworth had struggled to institute as a form of cultural wisdom. Possessed by the "demon of the void," Hardy's Faust is "no longer restricted by the sympathies, the common interests and common persuasions by which the mass of mortals, each individually ignorant . . . as to the proper aim of life, are yet held together" *("Helena,"* 159–60). Cut off from common sympathies and interests, he has only uncommon interests and antipathies to guide him. He is thus portrayed as "the slave of impulses, which are stronger, not truer or better [than sympathy], and the more unsafe that they are solitary" ("*Helena,*" 160). Carlyle's wayward and impulsive Faust becomes Hardy's erring and impulsive Henchard, and his impulses are not depicted as stronger or truer than the common human sympathy from which they cut him off. Rather, they compel him to isolate himself, first from his family and then from the community as a mayor distanced from those he governs.

Once a Wessex laborer and presumably a part of the rural community, Henchard comes to disdain the vulgarity of common man and seeks always to set himself apart from the community. "Himself he feels to be peculiar [and] not as other men, he is '*with* them, not *of* them' " as Carlyle wrote of Faust ("*Helena,*" 160, emphasis Carlyle's). When we first see Henchard he is "set apart" from his wife and child. When next we see him, he is "framed" in a window which sets him apart from the crowds below, and when we last see him he is wandering alone with Abel Whittle, a shadow figure of his lost ability to be common, sympathetic, appetitive man.

Devoid of "the sentiment of companionship," Henchard's character is "the beginning of madness itself," in Carlyle's estimate of Faust's problem in the *Helena.* The madness Carlyle has in mind is not sacred but profane; it inspires one toward disintegration rather than integration within communal rituals. Henchard's Faustian madness opens onto those "unspeakable abysses of despair" which in time Faust reaches ("*Helena,*" 160). Then, too, like Carlyle's Faust, Henchard "is divided from his fellows," a type of the "one man" who stands over against romanticism's whole man capable of elective affinities; "Pride and self-love" are "the mainsprings of [Faust's] conduct" as they will be for Henchard, and "knowledge is precious with him because it is power" ("*Helena,*" 167).

Carlyle warns his readers that "To invest a man of this character" with power "is but enabling him to repeat his error on a larger scale, to play the same false game with a deeper and more ruinous stake" ("*Helena,*" 161). Carlyle's warning outlines the fate of Hardy's mayor whose story is structured by a relentless repetition of his first error, the divorce, which was not "generous" in Shelley's sense of an idealistic transgression. We first see Henchard err ungenerously with his family and then we see him "play the same false game" in Casterbridge with deeper and more ruinous results.

The Mayor of Casterbridge inversely traces the curve of ascent mapped by Goethe's *Helena,* a complete translation of which appeared in Carlyle's article describing its aesthetic merits. That is, the reconstruction of a failing romantic ideal represented in Goethe's allegory is mirrored by the deconstruction of that same ideal in Hardy's. During his rise to power, we can imagine that Casterbridge is Henchard's "gay island of existence"; yet from the time that Susan returns, it becomes "the ancient realm of Night" (quotations from Carlyle's *"Helena"*). On the road to Weydon, we witness a Henchard "goaded by despair," as was his Faustian namesake. To relieve the pressure of despair, Faust "unites himself with the Fiend." The "fiend" that both Carlyle and then Hardy have in mind is a "denier both of heart and head, a child of Darkness, an emissary of the primeval Nothing" (*"Helena,"* 158). Once freed of love and family, Henchard's Faustian ambition creates him an "emissary of the primeval nothing," motivated by the denial of head and heart (as Farfrae will partially redeem both when he first arrives), and a character who exists solely as the difference from and a deferral of those erotic, redemptive characteristics typical of romantic man.

Modeled upon Carlyle's Faust-Mephisto combination, Henchard is a portrait of "the best and only genuine Devil of these latter times" (*"Helena,"* 158). The latter times of the reference span the years 1827 and 1828 when Carlyle was engaged in reintroducing German romanticism into an England that had seemingly forgotten the import of Wordsworth's and Coleridge's cultural formulations in the wake of rapid industrial expansion. The virulent optimism expressed by Carlyle during this time reverts to a qualified pessimism in Wessex. In effect, Hardy declares that Carlyle's efforts had failed to turn back the course of history onto more idealistic paths.

Appropriately, it is "the pessimist" who first names the character of Weydon. When Henchard asks him if there is "any trade doing here," the pessimist informs the solitary wanderer that "pulling down" is more the "nater" of the place (71) and not building-up or construction. "Pulling down" is Carlyle's colloquialism for skeptical consciousness in *Sartor Resartus,* while Henchard's inquiring after "trade" brings to mind the Faustian character of his bargain. Ironically, it is Carlyle's optimism that is pulled down on the road to Weydon. After Henchard trades eros for thanatos, he is seen to disintegrate or "pull down" his organic, dynamic, and communal character in a narrative which displays the unbuilding of a romantic selfhood.

Dissembling Henchard: The Mayor of Casterbridge

In "Goethe's *Helena*," Carlyle had declared that the romantic problem set forth in *Faust* was neither complete nor "capable of completion" (*"Helena,"* 161). This was because Faust's story was the emblem of the perennial romantic problematic and therefore always worthy of rewriting and revising so as to characterize the coloration that problematic took at a particular point in time. Carlyle's challenge set Hardy to writing his version or "phantasmagoria" on romanticism in order to characterize the impact history had upon the hopes and desires of Carlyle's form of romanticism.[4]

As a portrait of Carlyle's unredeemed Faust, Henchard is "a monster" with a "vehement, keen, and stormful nature." When his monstrous nature is "stung into fury, as he thinks of all he has endured and lost; he broods in gloomy meditation" (*"Helena,"* 160). Twice we will see Henchard brood in gloomy meditation among the romantic ruins of Casterbridge's priory. The Franciscan priory (and here we think of Arnold's St. Francis, the patron saint of romantic joy) had been a mill before it had fallen into disuse. As a monastery and as a grain mill, the priory has positive connotations in Carlyle's calculous of work and prayer. Yet when Henchard arrives at this double scene of faith (in God and in communal man), it lays in ruins, a violated figure of traditional "ghostly forms" like the Grand Chartreuse in Book Six of *The Prelude* or like the scattered and fragmented remains of Abbot Joycelyn's monastery in Carlyle's *Past and Present*. Unlike a Wordsworth meditating above the ruins of Tintern Abbey (and in a scene to which it bears comparison), Henchard will not reestablish the severed connection between past and present by meditating upon the ancient ruin above the Casterbridge Schwarzwasser. Thus contrary to Carlyle's sense of organic history wherein the present incorporates the past into a continuum, Henchard's mechanical life begins in the gap or rift of disruption between past and present, while it is the opening of the rift between past and present (between romantic programs and aspirations and postromantic satires of such) which constitutes the theme of the narrative.

Goethe's *Helena* concludes with the marriage of Faust (a figure of gothic desire) and Helen (a figure of classical form or beauty) which then "magically" produces Euphorion, the "offspring of Modern Poesy" (191). It is just this offspring which does not arise in Casterbridge. There, beauty and power (or culture and society) do not dialectically merge to produce "modern poesy." Unlike Goethe's *Helena* which progresses by contraries, Hardy's *The Mayor of Casterbridge* maintains the distance between inherited contradictions until both beauty and power are worn down to "microscopic joys." In Casterbridge, the romantic revolution does not "save [itself] from the straits and fetters of Worldly Life in the loftier regions of Art, or in that temper of mind by which those regions can be reached, and permanently dwelt in" as it does in Goethe's *Helena* (161). Henchard does not attain that region of life-bearing grace because he has fallen permanently under "the influence of Doubt, Denial, and Obstruction, or Mephistopheles, who is the symbol and spokesman of these" (161).

The incapacity of the redemptive grace of modern poetry is given its most Carlylean cast when Casterbridge celebrates the triumph of the "Steam-Engine Universe of dead fact" when honoring the royal personage who visits there. Historically, Hardy models the event upon Prince Albert's 1849 visit to Dorchester by train to inaugurate the Portland breakwater project. Albert was well known for his enthusiasm for engineering and rational planning, and he stopped in Dorset on his way to celebrate the progress of both. Hardy has his "prince" come to Casterbridge by carriage to suppress the historical referent which could only serve to recall the great age of English railroad expansion in the 1840s as well as Carlyle's jeremiads against the mechanical universe in all of its forms. We will recall in this respect that Henchard dominates the spectacle with a spectacle of his own and that his mayoral costume and character have become as "rusty" as a worn steam engine by this time.

The "Steam-Engine Universe" continues to expand and refine its dominion under Farfrae whose "virtue" is that he is more organized than Henchard and hence his historic son and heir. Farfrae's split personality, half-romantic and half-utilitarian, recalls somewhat the character of Euphorion in Goethe's *Helena,* and for a while he is cast as a poetical character. More to the point though, Farfrae's two aspects are derived from Carlyle's "Characteristics" (1831). We will recall that "Characteristics" first appeared in the *Edinburgh Review* and that Farfrae comes from Edinburgh, that he is on his way to America when he passes through Casterbridge, and that Carlyle often recommended emigration to America as a solution to the overcrowded condition of England. Furthermore, in "Characteristics" Carlyle reviews two recently published books, one discussing romantic philosophy, the other, utilitarianism. In Carlyle's review, he notes that Thomas Hope's *An Essay on the*

Dissembling Henchard: The Mayor of Casterbridge

Origin and Prospects of Man (1830) discusses the origin and prospects of "organized" man, while Friedrich von Schlegel's *Philosophical Lectures* (1831) outlines the origins and prospects for "organic" man. Carlyle refers to these two books toward the conclusion of his essay in which he does not synthesize their prospects but sets them at odds, only to declare that a redeemed future belongs to Schlegel's organic man and not Hope's organized man, or so he hoped.

Farfrae is at once a sentimentalist and a utilitarian. Read in light of Carlyle's essay, his character conforms to the two programs and possibilities therein outlined. When he first appears in the narrative, Farfrae is a balanced character with a romantic and a practical side. Both sides or aspects are held apart—as they are in Carlyle's essay. Yet he gradually loses his balance and slides toward Henchard's form of damnation. Significantly, Farfrae backslides after he loses Lucetta and her unborn child because he has discovered that she had once been involved with Henchard, whose name is always death. Acting the Mephisto in this instance, Henchard is the haggish agent who effects Farfrae's divorce from his romantic aspect. And it is that divorce which decides against Carlyle's hope that the future belonged to Schlegel's Jena romanticism and not to Hope's English utilitarianism.

In "Characteristics," Carlyle predicted that despite the prevalence of disease in all branches of knowledge, "Man is still Man" and so "the genius of Mechanism, as was once before predicted, will not always sit like a choking incubus on our soul; but at length, when by a new magic Word the old spell is broken, [mechanism and mechanistic knowledge] will become our slave, and as a familiar spirit do all our bidding" (42–43). As we have been at pains to explain, *The Mayor of Casterbridge* denies a future to that prediction because the verdict of history had already been reached when Hardy sat down to write. In Henchard's Casterbridge, the incubus of materialism holds the office of mayor. The descent of this incubus from, roughly, 1830 when the Weydon deal was struck to 1848 when Farfrae comes to town is clearly traceable in the novel's three successive "mayors." Henchard is fully in love with death; he is followed by a "Mr. Chaulkfield," as Carlylean and "dry-as-dust" a name as Hardy could find, who is in turn followed by Farfrae, a man half in love with death who will gradually slide toward Henchard's full commitment to the universe of death.

In Carlyle's terminology, Henchard is but "a Body" without a soul, a purely "material" being who solves "the problem of philosophical dualism" by becoming totally "mechanical" (the quoted distinctions are Carlyle's from "Characteristics"). Thus, his character "lies open to us" like a denotative language deprived of its connotative register. Henchard is not the romantic "body of desire" characterized by Wordsworth's naked savage, but a body of earth, of dust—a pure corpus of materialistic history and an unimaginably empirical being who embodies the abyss itself. Devoid of a "dynamical . . . vitality" and without access to meditation's "quiet mysterious depths," Henchard is a "manufactured unity," a composite of pure exteriority and an historical "body" which "thinks" without "thought" in Carlyle's distinction between rational/empirical and sympathetic/idealizing mental processes.

By way of concluding my comparison, I would note that the structure of *The Mayor of Casterbridge* reflects the triadic structure of Goethe's *Helena* which encompasses a prologue, dramatic phantasmagoria, and an epilogue. Chapters 1 and 2 of the novel serve as the prologue (69–85). During this time, we see Henchard cross over the threshold from eros to thanatos, from romance to history. The prologue is followed by a silent period of eighteen years, a gap in the narrative which exceeds the speaking time of the narrative proper. The silence of Henchard's ascent to power is remarkable because it implies that he bears with him a barren and unpoetical time about which there is nothing to say. When represented as the abyss of pure processes, nature, man, and society have no voice.

It had been the task of the romantic imagination to give a voice to the abyss. Thus, it is only when love and its imaginative possibilities return to Casterbridge in the persons of Susan and Elizabeth-Jane that the narrative once again begins to speak. Significantly, Susan is the name Hardy usually connects with desire: it is one of Tess's manuscript names; it appears in *The Woodlanders* as Suke Damson, and it is the name of Jude's Sue. Elizabeth-Jane's name also bears strong romantic connotations; both of her names are taken from two of Hardy's early fiancées, Eliza Nicholls and, unremarkable for Hardy, her sister Jane. When we consider that the Elizabeth-Jane who comes to Casterbridge is not Henchard's daughter but Newson's, the romantic signature of her name doubles and then triples because Richard Newson is intended to be the redeemed ancient mariner of the novel. Thus Elizabeth-Jane is the true daughter of "the wedding guest" (Newson is the honored guest at her wedding), who believes that "he prayeth well who loveth well/ Both man and bird and beast" ("The Rime of the Ancient Mariner," 612–13) as Henchard does not, although he arrives at the wedding with a bird in order to appear as though he does or might if given the chance. That he is not given a third chance—he had been given a second chance when he lived with Elizabeth-Jane in a small cottage—is, of course, thematic in a novel representing the status of romanticism after Carlyle, who tried to give England a second chance.

Between chapters 3 and 43 (86–382), the character of Henchard's fate unwinds. During this time, we witness the death drive in action as Henchard "undoes" himself and proceeds to "unbe." When he is depleted of his wealth and its effects, he proclaims that he has been "honeycombed clean out of all the character and standing that's been building up these eighteen years" (178). The irony of his self-reflection should not be missed: quality is quantity, self is a storehouse of characteristics worthy because commanding obedience, and standing is a function of one's position in society. In sum, Henchard's subjectivity is objective, social, exterior, literal, and completely disconnected from all sources and reserves of imaginative power.

The narrative of his disintegration concludes with chapter 43 at which point Henchard leaves Casterbridge. The two-chapter epilogue which follows (chapters 44 and 45) provides a balanced reflection to the prologue (chapters 1 and 2). During the prologue, we witness Henchard abandon work and family, the two grand Carlylean signifiers of social and cultural health which relate his form of romanticism to Wordsworth's and to Goethe's. Returned to the heath in the epilogue, Henchard seeks to revive the natural man he had killed to become the mayor of Casterbridge. Costumed exactly as he was prior to Weydon, he enacts a parody of his former self by miming a selfhood capable of unconscious "natural" activity. Like Wordsworth in "Nutting," Henchard tricks himself out "in proud disguise of cast-off weeds/ Which for that service had been husbanded" (9–10). Dressed as a "figure quaint" of his former vulgar self, he mimes his lost desire in the hope that the desire will return during the course of his ritual of repentance. That is, by investing himself in the costume of romantic salvation, he expects to be saved. Moreover, by dressing as he had in the past, he expects his natural past to shape his artificial present in ways Carlyle suggested it might. Henchard's use of the past is, of course, parodic, and his parody presents us with an insubstantial, mechanical, and specular version of Carlyle's program for self and cultural rejuvenation.

Dressed as he is, Henchard is self-consciously archaic and rustic. His "poetical character" is metonymic and not metaphoric. His quest is enacted by a metonymic character in search of his lost metaphoric identity. In this reading, he is a weak sentimentalist who longs for a naive romanticism as well as a figure of loss enacting an identity "as" in the hope of awakening an identification "with." Otherwise put, his self-representation is a simulacrum. As a romantic simulator, Henchard's mimesis of desire produces an "artificial resurrection of romanticism as a system of signs which is sheltered from the imaginary, and from any distinction between the real and the imaginary . . . the produced and the authentic" (Baudrillard, *Simulations,* 5–7). And it is with this "artificial resurrection of romanticism" that the story of his character closes.

From *The Mayor of Casterbridge* forward, we shall witness only "the orbital recurrence of models and the simulated generation of difference" (Baudrillard, 4) as the most prevalent form of Wessex romanticism. Characters such as Fitzpiers, Angel, and Jude are like Henchard on the heath, costumed as a rustic. All parody their romantic desires in the futile hope that they can put themselves in touch with a successful form of romantic idealism. It is then Henchard who begins to help us define the difference in similitude exemplified by romantic analogues and complexes in Wessex. His final orbiting of Elizabeth-Jane circumscribes the field of Hardyan nostalgia for a lost idealism, while his costume drama characterizes the forms of romanticism which will appear in all forthcoming novels. It is solely the desire for desire that Hardy sees as the modern impetus toward enacting as gesture a romanticism which then represents a double loss by copying that which it cannot reinstate, reproducing that which it can no longer produce.

Structurally, I have made the intent of the novel clear: Henchard exchanges eros and a principled cosmos for thanatos and a history tending toward chaos. At Weydon, he trades in his ability to correspond to transcendent and communal orders of significance in order to acquire the liberty to ply all mechanistic modes of possession. The imaginative nexus is traded for the cash nexus, thus his Casterbridge character is not the romantic self, his history one of disintegration rather than integration.

This history begins in the prologue where we witness the foreclosing of romantic idealism. On the journey to Weydon, Hardy portrays Henchard as a fading sentimentalist seeking release from his sentimental commitments. Hardy achieves this portrayal by presenting Henchard's journey as a perverse rendition of the Holy Family's journey to Egypt. As the narrator describes them, the Henchards are surrounded by a "nimbus" of "stale familiarity" as "they mov[e] down the road" toward a Casterbridge that he will later compare to Egypt during the time of the Old Testament plagues.

As they walk toward Weydon, the Henchards are portrayed as a deceptively loose group of once erotically bound individuals. They are a group portrait of the Freudian family romance in decay as well as an emblem of preindustrial England as it approaches the Industrial Revolution, the great Weydon Fair of communal disconnections. At this pivotal point in personal and public history, Henchard is a hay-trusser drifting away from his trade in search of more ambitious engagements. He carries a knife and wimble, the tools of his trade and heraldic signs of his communal identity. The knife is for cutting, the wimble for binding. In the time-honored fashion of his trade, cutting is followed by binding. Significantly, it is the binding phase which lends his trade its name and which locates him in the community's hierarchy.

Yet the knife and the wimble also identify Henchard as a man living on the threshold between cutting and binding. His tools figure forth the edge or boundary line on which he walks, while they forecast the reversals he will enact a Weydon. Post-Weydon, binding is followed by loosening until Henchard has nothing left to lose, at which point he appears in the narrative as "disappearance," as nothing, and as absence. Born under the sign of the knife, the mayor of Casterbridge will have to purchase everything that had once been freely given to him for love, a liberality to which his wife bears apt witness in her tolerating his unnatural silence as "a natural thing" (70).

Although they appear a coherent family, at this time the Henchards are the simulacrum of this basic social group. They are *like* a family, but not identical to romanticism's best definitions of family and home. In the prologue, the narrator tells us that "they walked side by side in such a way as to suggest *afar off* the low, easy, confidential chat of people full of reciprocity; but on *closer* view it could be discerned that the man was reading, or pretending to read, a ballad sheet which he kept before his eyes" (69, emphasis added). Romantic congeniality and reciprocity are only apparent here, not real. Thus, our first view of the Henchards is deceptive, and the narrator is quick to point out the illusion. His disenchanting us is a model of the narrative agency which informs the entire novel and constitutes its most significant theme. Moreover, his manner establishes the precedent for all subsequent Wessex narrators who will continue to disenchant us of our romantic illusions. From "afar off," Wessex characters will seem genuinely romantic, while "on closer view" they will reveal themselves to be simulacra which highlight idealistic expectations as they disabuse us of them.

The narrator's act of revelation or "close reading" is repeated once more when he describes Susan's face, "the chief attraction" of which is "its mobility" (70). Her face is flexible and "alive" when she looks at her baby daughter, while it becomes rigid and "dead" when she thinks (70). "The first phase was the work of Nature, the second probably of civilization" (70), the narrator tells us. For the critical edge in his description the narrator depends upon Carlyle's critique of conscious thinking or "self-consciousness" as opposed to romantic unselfconsciousness. Susan's face is "lyrical" when turned in the narcissistic direction (when she looks at her child) and "historical" when she looks toward the father. The failure of her two aspects or faces, or the two directions of her gaze, to integrate suggests the cause of decay in her family romance, while it tells us that Henchard's Casterbridge will be dominated by "the name of the father," by laws, chronologies, duties, and society's instruments and instrumentalities.

In order to escape "an intercourse that would have been irksome to him" (70), Henchard reads a ballad sheet, or seems to. The silence between "the man" and "the women" (the narrator portrays them generically in the prologue), seems "a natural thing" to them. Their artificial sense of "the natural" has replaced the "naturalness" of the romantic pair whose intercourse is crucial to redemption in the poetry of Wordsworth and Coleridge. There is no "conversation poem" going on between them, no lyrical ballad which could redeem a wintry present by relating it to other, spring-like pasts.

Whether or not the play of allusion between Weydon Priors and

Tintern Abbey above the Wye is intended or incidental, the relationship between the two scenes of balladry are worthy of comparison for the reasons we have just mentioned. Wordsworth's "Lines Composed a Few Miles Above Tintern Abbey on Revisiting the Wye" were first published in the *Lyrical Ballads* and the Wye flows in the south, in Wales. In contradistinction to Wordsworth's reconnecting past to present after five long winters of discontent in the city, Hardy depicts a man who disconnects his past from his present after an undefined period of discontent in the country. Contrary to Wordsworth's intent and direction, Henchard heads for the city where he fancies he will find contentment. What I am suggesting here is that the terms of Hardy's inversion are exact. Wordsworth rediscovers love and joy above Tintern Abbey at the Wye, Henchard discovers lovelessness and loneliness at Weydon where he permanently alienates himself from wife, child, and woodland trade, from all to which Wordsworth had reconnected himself on his journey to Tintern Abbey.

As though allusion were not enough, Hardy freights his introductory scene with negative figures which invert Wordsworth's positive meanings. Henchard's "springless step" and "dogged and cynical indifference personal to himself" (69) suggests that he is moving into "a winter of discontent" and not out of one. If the lyrical ballads encouraged readers to contemplate nature and to establish affectionate ties of reciprocity with a "Dear Friend," then Henchard's ballad reading encourages precisely the opposite. Reading a ballad prevents him from intercourse with either nature or his "dear friend" Susan. Neither now nor later does the "green pastoral landscape" become "dear" to him, nor can the presence of his wife and child help him "catch/ the language of [his] former heart, and read/ [His] former pleasures" there ("Tintern Abbey," 115–20). Unlike Wordsworth's persona in "Tintern Abbey," Henchard permits and even encourages his "genial spirits to decay." Eventually, he will dwell "In darkness and amid the many shapes/ Of joyless daylight" in Casterbridge where "the fretful stir/ Unprofitable, and the fever of the world" possess him totally.

The point at issue in this comparison is that typically inspiring Wordsworthian strategies for redemption are not inspiring to Henchard. For the sentimental soul of early romanticism such isolated scenes tended to "impress/ Thoughts of a more deep seclusion" upon the mind and compel the individual to "connect/ The landscape with the quiet sky"

The Descent of the Imagination

("Tintern Abbey," 6–9) as a prelude to greater and more far-reaching connections. In Hardy's revisionist fable, scenes of silence and solitude become more and not less isolating and lonely because the capacity for correspondences of any sort, be it the Wordsworthian imagination, the sympathetic fallacy, or even elementary human sympathy, is either weak or not existent. Those "beauteous forms" which preserve the natural-supernaturalist from an insistent sense of radical alienation are "As a landscape to a blind man's eye" ("Tintern Abbey," 24) to Henchard. Henchard is Wordsworth's "blind man" when we first see him disconsolately journeying toward the "lonely rooms . . . of towns and cities" to accept as his form of salvation, "greetings where no kindness is" and "all/ The dreary intercourse of daily life" ("Tintern Abbey," 128–31).

In his denial of a personal past, Hardy's Michael is antithetical to Wordsworth's. Thematically, *The Mayor of Casterbridge* is related by inversion to "Michael," which appeared in the second edition of the *Lyrical Ballads* (1800). Giles was Henchard's name in manuscript. As he appears in *The Woodlanders* Giles is a revised form of Gabriel Oak who is like Wordsworth's shepherd Michael. In this regard, we might note that Oak's romantic adventures begin with a retelling of Wordsworth's "The Last of the Flock" and that Gabriel's first name pairs up with Michael's, both being archangels. In Hardy's handling of these names, Gabriel and Giles are romantic angels, while Henchard is the fallen angel of romantic discord, Carlyle's "demon of the void."

Though this connection must remain speculative, the relationship by contrast between Wordsworth's Michael and Hardy's gains an added credibility when we examine the intent and import of each character. In a letter of 11 October 1800 to Thomas Poole, Wordsworth explains that his Michael is "agitated by two of the most powerful affections of the human heart; the parental affection and the love of property, landed property, including the feelings of inheritance, home, and personal and family dependence." Hardy's hay-trusser is "agitated" by an inversion (or perversion) of Wordsworth's "two most powerful affections." Henchard does not desire to remain a parent and he does not love "property" in Wordsworth's sense of a familiar region of affectionate attachments. "Feelings of inheritance, home, and personal family dependence" are alien to Henchard's mentality, though he seems to have experienced

78

them in the past. But this is precisely the romantic past from which he severs himself at Weydon.

Wordsworth's Michael struggles to keep his family together and to build a stone cottage for their permanent residence, a rock of all ages that will survive the onslaughts of history. Tropologically, Wordsworth's Michael is an Abel, the shepherd figure whose stone altar—the sheep pen—is pleasing to the romantic gods. Henchard, though, is a Cain *figura* and named as such in the narrative. The biblical Cain was a farmer and Henchard is a hay-trusser; both renounce their Edenic inheritances in violent ways and both are marked as outcasts. Henchard will even be seen "beating" or harassing "Abel Whittle," a whittled-down figure of his great namesake. Figuratively then, the conclusion of Wordsworth's "Michael" inaugurates the beginning of Henchard's story. Hardy's Michael is an ex-rustic like "Luke" who "in the dissolute city gave himself to evil courses." As Hardy recasts it, Luke's London is Casterbridge, while the fate of Michael's son in London informs the lesson of Henchard's fable in Casterbridge. In effect, Wordsworth's text "fathers" Hardy's.

The heartstrong stability of Wordsworth's Michael converts into the headstrong tenacity of Hardy's Henchard. Set upon by adversity, Michael of the North claims that "There is a comfort in the strength of love;/ Twill make a thing endurable, *which else/* Would overset the brain, or break the heart" ("Michael," 448–80, emphasis added). Michael of the South (or "southron" Michael as the narrator designates him) can make no such claim, though eventually he will wish that he could. In fact, we might see Wordsworth's "which else" as naming the very motive for Henchard's suicide. Deprived of the strength of love, Henchard is "overset" by despair despite his boast that his fate is not more than he can bear. Clearly, it is more than he cares to endure. In this reading, Henchard's costume tragedy on the heath is understood as his attempt at recuperating the "comfort in the strength of love" enjoyed by his lost counterpart, Michael, the Good Shepherd.

As Hardy's Michael journeys toward the part he will play in "the real history of a town called Casterbridge" (67) and not any lyrical ballad of such, the only sound to be heard is "the voice of a weak bird singing a trite old evening song" which is neither unique nor valuable and which could have been "heard . . . at any sunset of that season for centuries untold" (71). The weak Wessex songster is a direct descendant of Keats's once-powerful nightingale, itself a revision of Wordsworth's nightingale whose "voice was buried among trees,/Yet to be come at by the breeze" ("O Nightingale! Thou Surely Art," 13–14). Once a sign of the poet's lyrical capability and joy (witness Coleridge's "Nightingale"), the Wessex nightingale now warbles a "trite old song" of no interest to anyone, and especially not to Henchard. Buried among the trees, the Wessex bird is precisely positioned where Wordsworth had initially found it and where Keats rediscovered it.

If we recall the expansive role both Coleridge and Keats wrote for Wordsworth's nightingale and then compare it to the minimal role which Hardy's narrator gives it in the scheme of things, then we will be alert to the purely literal realm of description we are about to enter in *The Mayor of Casterbridge*. The narrator's mentioning that the bird had sung its song for "centuries untold" is surely a glancing allusion to Keats's "Ode to a Nightingale" wherein repetition of the type suggests a form of natural immortality as well as a sameness in difference. Born into time, Keats's bird escapes from time on the wings of genealogy. Hardy's bird, conversely, becomes time-bound by the same genealogical process of transformation and descent. The once-lyrical figure of the romantic muse has become (once again) a figure of natural history, an uninteresting bird in a bush whose transcendental possibilities are "unheard." In effect, the sign of the bird has been returned to the discursive realm of late-Augustan poetry. Returned to its origins in decorative allegory, the bird becomes a figure of loss proleptic of the loss Henchard will acquire at Weydon.

In *The Mayor of Casterbridge*, romanticism is conspicuous by its absence. Wessex longs for a draught of the vintage Provençal lyric to forget "[t]he weariness, the fever, and the fret," of a place like Casterbridge. And no one will long for this draught more than Henchard eventually will. Though "still" the bird "would sing," and indeed the narrator draws our intention to its continuance, Henchard has "To [its] high requiem become a sod" ("Ode to a Nightingale," 59–60). The narrator emphasizes his "sodlike" character by twice using the word "dust" to describe the muted character of the landscape and of the Henchards ("The grassy margin of the bank, and the nearest hedgerow boughs were powdered by the dust that had been stirred over them . . . the same dust as lay on the road deadening their footfalls like a carpet"

[71]). The silence of the Weydon journey implies that "Fled is the music" and that the "viewless wings of poetry" have literally become invisible or "unnoticed" to use the narrator's synonym; thus the romantic impetus is genuinely and not just tentatively "Forlorn!" in Wessex.

The forlorn character of Casterbridge is hinted at when Susan inquires of a passerby if there is a "little small new cottage just a-builded" (71) nearby. In analogue, she seeks the cottage designed by Wordsworth's Michael and Isabella, a place of domestic bliss. Instead of discovering where she might find Michael's "Evening Star," the symbol of a steadfast romantic faith, she learns from "the pessimist" that "pulling down is more the nater of Weydon" (71) and not "building up" as she had hoped. As we have mentioned, the pessimist is a repressed reference to Carlyle's Mephisto; his "pulling-down" is Carlyle's coinage for the skeptical "de-construction" of one's romantic "nater" and of a romanticized nature of wonder and delight.

Allegorically, she and Henchard are on the dividing line between an "artificial state of society as contrasted with the natural state" ("Characteristics," 13). At Weydon, Henchard will abandon the romantic struggle of those "to whom a higher instinct has been given; who struggle to be persons, not machines; to whom the universe is not a warehouse, or at best a fancy-bazaar but a mystic temple and hall of doom" ("Characteristics," 31). Eventually, Henchard will become a mayoral machine who possesses the earth as his warehouse. He will get his chance to do so at Weydon, a "fancy-bazaar" which is not a mystic temple though the furmity woman's tent is his hall of doom.

When the Henchards arrive at Weydon, they learn that "the real business is done." Henchard's business there will be "unreal" or as fantastic and specular as was Faust's in Goethe's phantasmagoria. Work, the real business of spiritual man according to Goethe and Carlyle, is over and done with; all that remains is "getting away the money o' children and fools," like Susan and Henchard respectively, and "the sale of inferior animals," like Susan and Elizabeth-Jane in Henchard's valuation of them (71).

At Weydon, "peep shows, toy stands, wax-works, inspired monsters, disinterested medical men who travel for the public good . . . and readers of Fate" (72) all ply their trade after the real work has been done. Weydon is a circus of specular and speculative capitalism whose arena aptly forecasts the tenor of life in Casterbridge. The narrator will portray Casterbridge as an arena of social fetishism, parodic relationships, and wax-work pageants of deadly proportions. The Roman arena is the displaced center of the town's square where deadly games of economic survival take place daily. During his reign in Casterbridge, Henchard will be an "inspired monster" whose life provides us with close "readings" in the "Fate" of romantic culture as it enters the age of mechanical reproduction.

The narrator continues to emphasize the difference between the natural past and the artificial present as a sign of his own nostalgia when he describes Susan's search for nourishing food. Mrs. Goodenough is a "haggish creature" and the witch of the modern in Carlyle's sense of a quack Cagliostro (which Hardy misspelt "Cagliostrie" in his 1867 Notebook). Goodenough's invisible hand transmutes the "antiquated slop" of the wholesome grain porridge which Susan sought into a "concoction much more to [Henchard's] satisfaction than it had been in its natural state" (73). Her chemical magic transforms organic nourishment into a mild narcotic which is just "good enough" to put to sleep the little that remains of Henchard's romantic spirit.

Goodenough's tent is Hardy's version of a booth at Bunyan's Vanity Fair read in relation to the social satire of Thackeray's *Vanity Fair*.[5] Hardy's double reading of Vanity Fair produces a deft double writing wherein Bunyan's allegory of a striving but waylaid Christian spirit becomes the scene of a once-striving and, in Carlyle's instance, strident romanticism permanently distracted from its quest toward idealism's heavenly city. Later Wessex romances will place the romantic quest in double jeopardy by satirically portraying the quest for the heavenly city as itself a Vanity Fair of narcissistic delight. To strive after the things of this world is spiritually foolish, yet to strive after the things of the spirit is historically naive. Without a dialectical interaction between idealism and history, there can be no salvation, thus in Wessex there is none.

When he arrives at Weydon, Henchard is a creature driven by a perverse will; he will later be described as a "queer thing" (275) and a "dreadful thing" (270) motivated by "the instinct of a perverse character" (74). His "thingness" emphasizes his mechanical self, while his perversity is best read in terms of Freudian "unlibido" which desires to unbind all erotic ties. His encounter with the furmity woman constitutes the narcotization of his erotic drives as the "primal scene" of the creation of his Casterbridge character. The primariness of this scene is born out years later when she appears at Henchard's trial. Then, she reports that she and the mayor go back some twenty years. To this, one judge remarks: "Twenty years ago—well, that's beginning at the beginning . . . suppose you go back to the Creation!" (274). The irony of his comment is that she has gone back to the beginning of the beginning, to the creationary moment itself. As his comment readily implies, Henchard expels himself from the Eden of romantic possibilities at Weydon. Aesthetically, he leaves the realm of the lyric and enters the realm of case-hardened narratives of self-comportment and self-limitation. Psychologically, he pushes himself beyond the pleasure principle. Henchard is thus an Adam seduced by the tempter within and fallen into the realm of history. When he leaves Weydon, he leaves behind his "young years . . . [those] seasons of a light, aerial translucency and elasticity and perfect freedom; the body not yet become the prison-house of the soul, but . . . its vehicle and implement" ("Characteristics," 2).

Susan is Henchard's Eve, and he names her as such in the furmity woman's tent by proclaiming himself "open to an offer for this gem o' creation" (75). In selling Eve, Henchard falls from innocence and enters the "subjected" plain of history. As one female onlooker to the sale proclaims, Susan has a great "Sperrit," one which anybody could "glory in." The woman advises Susan not to return to Henchard "Till the great trumpet" of Judgment sounds (80), which she will not. Her return eighteen years later sounds the trumpet of Henchard's doom which calls to a close his history as mayor. In allegory, her return inaugurates the apocalyptic time when those who have betrayed love are brought to justice. Significantly, when Susan returns a "brass band" plays beneath Henchard's window.

After he sells Susan, Henchard falls into a sleep so profound that the furmity woman "shook him but could not wake him" (81). A slumber seals Henchard's spirit; his deep sleep signifies the great death that is upon him. Unlike the persona in "Tintern Abbey" who is "laid asleep/ In body, and become a living soul" (45–46), Henchard puts to sleep his living soul only to rise as a pure body in Carlyle's sense of the "earthy" historical man who has no access to spiritual redemption. He will wake and "behold the world as a new *thing*" (82) which indeed it is because he has deprived himself of all I-Thou correspondences which personalize the world. This new world of "thingness" and instrumentalities which will be emphasized in the narrator's extended descriptions of Casterbridge's wares is "silent and still as death" (83). Nothing speaks in it because no thing has a voice, not even the weak, remnant nightingale which was left behind on the road to Weydon.

Beyond Weydon, Henchard will forswear strong liquors which are not grails or "beakers full of the warm south" to him but pollutants which exacerbate his perversity. Henchard is neither Dionysian nor Apollonian in type because alienated from both a divine and inspiring madness as well as from the formative processes which foster representations of the understanding that madness brings. His character is thus a form of *stylo rappresentativo* in Nietzsche's sense of the "completely unnatural" or operatically artificial man who is "equally opposed to the Dionysiac and the Apollonian spirit" because void of "any artistic instinct" (*Birth of Tragedy,* 114).

In order to prevent another embarrassing moment of self-revelation, Henchard swears to uphold the social norms. His new, bookish character is a studied reaction-formation to his drive toward alienation. Afraid of the consequences of complete alienation, he promises to construct a constitutional self. His strong drive toward alienation is restrained by an oath which he seals by kissing "the clamped book" of Urizenic law resting on the "communion table" after which he "made a start in a new direction" (84). His new direction contains his deadly selfhood by "clamping" it down. His oath during which he names himself for the first time in the narrative artificially binds him to a communion from whose natural ceremonies of innocence he has just permanently excluded himself. The new direction he heads is "south-westward": south in opposition to Germanic romanticism's northlands whose values he has just rejected; and west, the direction of death and the horizon opposite to that from which broke Wordsworth's blissful dawn when it was a joy to be alive. In order to sustain himself on his journey downward and westward, Henchard must immediately "strike a bargain with a housewife . . . to prepare him some breakfast for a trifling payment" (85). In a scene which bears comparison to Werther's bliss in Lotte's kitchen or Michael's joy in domesticity, Henchard's first official act as a reformed and clamped-down character is to pay for nourishment that was once freely given him by his wife's "natural piety."

When Susan Newson-Henchard returns to Weydon eighteen years later, the narrator notes that she and Elizabeth-Jane are "not unconnected" to Henchard. His cautious qualification is thematic: Susan is not the original, highly "spirited" presence she had been prior to Weydon, and Elizabeth-Jane is not the daughter Henchard had sold there. Like everything that is Henchard's, both women eventually become his in name only, as a matter of contract. Though his reconstituted Casterbridge family appears to be holy or erotically connected, it is even less so than the one we witnessed on the road to Weydon. In recuperating his family, he recovers the appearance of romance and marriage, which is actually a specular parody of such.

Spectacle and parody are, in fact, what the narrative highlights in the second appearance of the Weydon Fair. Although Weydon seems to be the same place from afar, upon closer inspection we see that, "certain mechanical improvements might have been noticed in the roundabout and highflier [and in the] machines for testing rustic strength and weight" (87). The Carlylean critique in this description cannot, I think, be missed. Henchard is the mechanical "highflier" with whom Susan will eventually remarry. Her second marriage to Henchard is one of convenience and a genteel simulacrum of the (presumably) genuine love affair of her first. When Elizabeth-Jane asks her mother about the "relative" they seek, Susan characterizes him as a man who "is, or was . . . for he may be dead." In terms of vitality and dynamism, he is dead; yet he lives on as a high-flying mechanical man, a public figure who "tests rustic strength and weight" in the Casterbridge marketplace.

When they arrive in Casterbridge, Susan and Elizabeth-Jane encounter a spectacle of civility; it is Carlyle's "World of Knaves" motivated by contractual self-interest we see. We learn from the narrator that the avenues of Casterbridge seem friendly "promenade[s]," yet they are actually "the ancient defenses of the town" (95). In an artificial state of civility, politeness is a mannered way of deflecting aggression. Inside its avenue-fortifications, Casterbridge is all "snugness and comfort," while outside "the unlighted country" appears "strangely solitary and vacant in aspect" (95). The unromantic import of the description is clear: Casterbridge is a snug (or smug) and self-centered place while beyond lies an unenlightened nature in all of its forbidding solitude and emptiness. Neither society nor nature, that is, bears the slightest trace of romantic culture which infused and permeated them both in the earlier century.

In Casterbridge, "ye may as well look for manna-food as good bread" under Henchard's rule because neither spiritual nor natural sustenance can be found. During his "rule of thumb," a term whose oppressive connotations cannot be missed, "There is less good bread than beer" (95). As an agent of the furmity women's adulterating magic, Henchard's midas touch infects all ancient nourishment, commuting it into a profane or "spoiled" concoction. Besides the plaguelike character of the spoiled food, the narrator tells us that Susan's first meal in town is a "temporary substitute for a meal" and not a real meal at all.

Presiding over this realm of substitute refreshments, Henchard appears at a banquet as a darkly clad figure with a "rich complexion" or surface aspect. Framed in a window like a Carlylean "idol" or juggernaut, Henchard is renowned as the "celebrated abstaining worthy" (102), the man who "touches nothing." He has "worked his way up from nothing" (102) and when he loses his work, he will return to nothing. The condition of his stock of "grow'd wheat" indicates that he has gone too far to be saved, except momentarily and by mechanical means. His artificial redemption occurs when Farfrae's apparatus restores his wheat, when he takes on Farfrae as a substitute brother, and when he remarries a weak and "ghostly" Susan. His simulated redemptions are each cast as "mechanical wonders" and mimic miracles which parody the divine intervention of a healing spirit to cure crippling aberrations in one's natural character.

The degree of his exclusion from all correspondences is nowhere made more apparent than when he stands outside the Three Mariners inn whose "interior is so popular" (109) with the Casterbridge community. The three "mariners" of the name perhaps alludes to Coleridge's Ancient Mariner while the inner sanctum or communal common room is a place of song and tradition forbidden to Henchard. On three separate occasions though he stands outside the shutters peering into the warm, congenial interior through "a heart-shaped aperture, somewhat more attenuated in the right and left ventricles than is seen in Nature" (109). The attenuated heart form is a cultural and not a biological figure and is the traditional emblem of eros and romance.

Henchard's exclusion from the realm of eros bears comparison with two instances in Flaubert's *Madame Bovary*.[6] When Madame Dubuc Bovary contemplates Charles Bovary's love for Emma, the narrator compares her to "a ruined man staring through a window at revelers in a house that was once his own" (48). Henchard is just such a strayed reveler looking through the vacancy of his own heart at the communal hearth of Casterbridge. Flaubert further elaborates the sense of this scene when he describes an ambition-ridden Bovary who forgoes his pursuit of a profession to embrace joy. Having abandoned his medical studies and taken to frequenting inns, "every time [Charles] entered the cafe the feel of the doorknob in his hand gave him a pleasure that was almost sensual. Now many things pent up within him burst their bonds; he learned verses by heart and sang them at student gatherings, developed an enthusiasm for Beranger, learned to make punch, and knew, at long last, the joys of love" (12).

The lyrical release Charles finds in the inns, Henchard never finds. He is always shut out from the realm of the heart; his "cultural" heart is as empty as are the heart holes of the shutters. His position beyond the inn's common room suggests further that the values of the hearth can maintain their integrity if and only if Henchard and all he stands for are kept at bay. This interdiction becomes all the more apparent when we recall that the one time Henchard does enter the common room of the inn he transmutes its Sunday psalm feast into a profane concert of curses. When, that is, Henchard finally does sing, eros remains silent and agape becomes aggression.

As the walled realm beyond the pleasure principle, Casterbridge "announced old Rome in every street" (140). It is the "fallen" Rome of the emperors Hardy has in mind, and not Rome of the republic, as the Hadriadic character of the arena reminds us. This Rome is uneasily positioned between the Hellenic and the Christian eras or, in Carlyle's and then Hardy's figurative periodicity, between the dying romantic republican faith and some new faith which is not yet born. As a place of strife, games, and history, the gladiatorial ring outside of town is the displaced thematic center of Casterbridge society. The ring's distance from the actual center is but a metaphor of denial and repression whose near-far ratios partake of the narrator's "from afar-close up" distinctions which reveal the moribund character of seemingly ideal and vital figures and configurations.

Though seemingly picturesque from afar, upon closer inspection the ring is a gruesome circle of deadly spectacles and murderous histories. So terrible are the memories that inhabit the ring that no romantic liaisons can occur there. "The cheerfullest form of [interview] never took kindly to the soil of the ruin" (141) we learn; thus it is the proper place for Henchard to repurchase Susan. Unlike the inspiring ruins of a

The Descent of the Imagination

Tintern Abbey, Casterbridge's ring is inhospitable to romance because its presence recalls a past too vicious to be overcome by nostalgia and too deadly to incite the moral consciousness to anything other than despair. In effect, the ghastly cycle of history as Gibbon imagined it is figured forth in the ring, and no "romantic" in Wessex is strong enough to awake from the nightmare. In this way, the Casterbridge ring is a fierce reminder of the ache of modernism, sometimes called the burden of history, which Hardy will once more depict in the ring of Stonehenge in *Tess of the d'Urbervilles*.

The one modern event recalled by the ring is the torture and execution of a woman in 1705. During this spectacle, her burning heart "leapt from her body." Her history reflects upon Henchard's Weydon execution where his heart leapt from his body significantly when he tore the heart out of Susan. At the ring and from afar, Susan and Henchard seem to have a lovers' assignation. Yet upon closer inspection we see that their tryst is a business meeting. The mock engagement and marriage which ensue recall the mock battles of the Roman arena performed by contract for social gain, yet which were deadly nonetheless. His deal with Susan for the semblance of a family repeats the deal he made earlier with Farfrae to acquire a substitute for his brother "now dead and gone" (117). Henchard demands that both deals be "clinch[ed]" at once "in clear terms" so that each party might be "comfortable in their minds" (133).

We should not leave the amphitheater before noting that it possesses all the characteristics of a Wordsworthian "spot of time." While reading and dozing there (the scene of Wordsworthian quixotic visions), visitors "had on occasion . . . beheld the slopes lined with the gazing legions of Hadrian's soldiery as if watching the gladiatorial combat and heard the roar of their excited voices." The "scene would remain but for a moment, like a lightening flash and then disappear" (142). The recollection of a gruesome event, the flash, and the disappearance of an apparition replay the syntax of a Wordsworthian spot of time, but with a difference. Whereas Wordsworth's spots had a moralizing effect upon the beholder, Hardy's have a demoralizing effect, for they substantiate the dominance of Gibbon's view of history. In effect, Hardy's sense of past and present does not allow for an idealized genius of antiquity to stand as a possible model by which to reform an unidealized modernity. As the ring shows us, the past was as brutal as the present despite the manner in which early romantics and then Carlyle had idealized its gothic character.

Both Wordsworth's and Hardy's transpositions of time zones commence with an unlooked-for apparition of a traumatic event, yet it is only Wordsworth who can imaginatively manipulate the trauma into a therapy for the soul. Hardy cannot do so. Because he cannot, the terror of history remains unredeemed. In the figure of the ring, it is Burke's sublime of terror that reclaims perception thereby abolishing Wordsworth's sublime of moral redemption. Past terrors, traumas, and tortures persist as untransformed memory in Wessex. The failure of imaginative therapies for such terror implies that the very possibility for such acts of overcoming has passed away. If, that is, it was typical of romanticism to imagine eternity peering through time, then at the Casterbridge ring, the historic center of the capital of Wessex, we witness time peering mercilessly through eternity.

Like Henchard, Farfrae is another modern gladiator fighting for possession of Casterbridge. He is a romantic scotsman hailing from the country which gave birth to the romantic impetus in prose and epic with the likes of Sir Walter Scott and Carlyle. In point of character, Farfrae is an economist, a scientist, and an adherent of the modern spirit of progress like many of his famed countrymen. His "character was just the reverse of Henchard's" (185) insofar as it is comprised of both sentiment and reason while Henchard's evinces the absence of both. Unlike Henchard, Farfrae immediately wins the hearts of those in the Three Mariners where he sings of "hame" or home, a concept alien to Henchard. During the performance "The singer himself grew emotional, till [Elizabeth-Jane] could imagine a tear in his eye" (120). The imaginary tear is important for it points up Farfrae's sentimental character. He is not a naive romantic, in Schiller's distinction, but a sentimentalist, one already displaced from an innocent or complete identification with romantic ideals *(On Naive and Sentimental Poetry)*.[7]

In his likeness to and yet difference from romantic man, Farfrae is a romantic simulator whose constitution is directly predicated upon Carlyle's "Characteristics," as we have already noted. He is a compromise formation between head and heart who simulates the whole man of romanticism without reproducing this form of consciousness. When Farfrae first enters Casterbridge, he is poised between Thomas Hope and Friedrich von Schlegel. Given his partly romantic temper and his upcoming romance with Lucetta, he is nearer to Schlegel than he is to Hope, which is why he is presented as a possible redeemer early in the novel. His joy in music and dance is genuine, though it is never excessive and always useful to him. His lyricism is the expression of a sentimental consciousness, and it is this form of consciousness out of which a meliorative romanticism could grow. As a man with a practical yet sentimental nature, he is a kind of second-rate Schiller, a romantic whose "greatest faculty" Carlyle tells us, "was a half-poetical, half-philosophical imagination" (*Schiller*, 192).

The metonymical construction of Farfrae's personality becomes a thematic issue when the narrator tells us that "The curious double strands in Farfrae's thread of life—the commercial and the romantic—were very distinct at times . . . like the colours in a variegated cord whose contrasts could be seen intertwisted, yet not mingled" (232). The narrator's figure is perhaps derived from Carlyle's "Characteristics" wherein the dialectical capacity of the romantic genius is described as a mariner's rope of many strands with one red strand running down the middle which marks it as belonging to the British navy. Farfrae's character is bereft of such a strong central thread which would characterize him as a genuine romantic. Farfrae then is not a romantic genius, but a caricature of such. In him, "Feeling and thought, poetry and rational inquiry [are held in] antithesis, to be 'chosen' between, or to be played off one against the other" instead of seeing them as "antitheses within a disruption; [caused by] the confusion of men haunted by the ghost of mind" in Raymond Williams's estimate of the prevalent form of cultural strife in the nineteenth century (*Culture and Society*, 68).

On a more tropologically sensitive register, Farfrae represents a shift from a predominantly metaphorical intent in romantic writing to a chiefly metonymical one. His character is *like* a romantic's, yet it is not identical to a romantic's. At no time does he achieve the dynamic condition of dialectical selfhood such as Carlyle described it. Rather, he remains a contiguous arrangement of two separate qualities which abide together and do not mix. So conceived, Farfrae's character is a substitute formation arising in the wake of the disappearance of the romantic metaphor of selfhood.

If we recall that Henchard had begun his journey when the century had reached "nearly one third its span" and that Farfrae arrives at Casterbridge eighteen years later, then given the temporal constraints in the allegory, it is evident that Hardy intends Farfrae to portray a mid-century romantic of liberal compromises. In him, compromise replaces dialectic in order to achieve an accord through separation which betrays the romantic hope that the joyous wisdom of poetry, "the breath and finer spirit of all knowledge," would merge with the logic of "getting and spending" and thereby produce an enlightened socio-cultural synthesis.

When in his lyrical phase, Farfrae evinces the "hyperborean crispness, stringency, and charm [of] a well-braced musical instrument" (229). He is "quite a new type of person" as Lucetta describes him, one who is "animated" when he is "thinking of getting on" (231) as well as charming when he is courting. For a demonstration of the efficacy of this new type, we need only recall the drama of Nelly and her lover from whom she is about to be separated because he and his father cannot find work in Casterbridge. Faced with the possibility of a romantic tragedy, Lucetta comments to Farfrae that "lovers ought not to be parted like that" to which he replies: "Maybe I can manage that they'll not be parted" (233). He then goes ahead and "manages" to requite Lucetta's wish that "people should live and love at their pleasure" by "striking a bargain" with the young man who can then remain to work in Casterbridge. Desire and management working together produce a romantic comedy where a tragedy once loomed. In this instance, Farfrae applies his "market mind" (235) to achieve a goal suggested by his "sentimental mind." By so doing, Farfrae satisfies both his dispositions, one of which demands the greatest good for the greatest number (Bentham/Thomas Hope) while the other desires that all partake of sentimental culture (Coleridge/Schlegel). Farfrae's arrangement is "ideal" because he too profits financially and romantically from his action insofar as he uses the young man's romantic attachment to his Casterbridge maid as leverage to employ him and his father at a bargain wage. In this way does a romantic dilemma resolve itself through utilitarian praxis.

Nowhere in the narrative is Farfrae's compromise formation more significantly in evidence than at the arrival of "the new-fashioned agricultural implement called a horse-drill" (238). The machine's name is a hyphenated neologism which contiguously aligns organic and mechanical figures as a means of implying that the "old-fashioned" romance of nature has commuted to a "new-fashioned" romance of artifice. The horse-drill is "painted in bright hues" and looks to be a "compound of hornet, grasshopper, and shrimp magnified enormously" (238). The narrator's description of the simulacra life-forms suggests that the arrival of the horse-drill is a second "genesis" moment during which the earth is repopulated by newly minted mechanical creatures of the land, sea, and air whom it is Farfrae's Adamic pleasure to name. The seed-drill will mime the sower's natural reproductive function, yet it will perform this function more efficiently, just as Farfrae is a more efficient "sower" than Henchard. The horse-drill will organize the organic into an efficient system calculated to reduce the wasteful excesses of natural reproduction; in essence, its arrival announces the age of mechanical reproduction and microscopic joys.

The entry of the horse-drill into Casterbridge is portrayed as a Renaissance *trionfe* to celebrate the triumph of the present over the past, of history over tradition, and of a calculated efficiency over a wanton abundance. The advent of the "vehicle of strange description" (238) is announced by a "rumbling of wheels" and "a fantastic series of circling irradiations upon the ceiling" (238) of Lucetta's salon. The wheels and irradiations lend a hypnotic quality to the mercantile sublime of which Farfrae is the new poet laureate and balladeer. His "inventions" will now legislate the world, and not those poetic instruments which promoted a return to an idealized version of traditional rural culture.

The conjunction of romantic and utilitarian figures continues when the narrator describes the manner in which Farfrae pushes his "head into the internal works [of the horse-drill] to master their simple secrets" while singing "the lass of Gowrie" (240). Farfrae understands the machine because "manufacture is intelligible, but trivial," as Carlyle tells us, adding that "creation is great, and cannot be understood" ("Characteristics," 5). Farfrae understands "manufacture" but not "creation." His assertion that the machine "will revolutionize sowing hereabouts" (240) is correct in its estimate of the totalizing impact of the Industrial Revolution to which his comment covertly alludes. What he fails to see is that much will be lost in this gain. It is Lucetta who reminds him of this loss when she comments that the horse-drill will "kill the romance of the sower" as well as render obsolete the significance of the pastoral metaphor. Implied in her riposte to Farfrae's hymn to progress is that the trope of the sower in the Bible, Milton, Wordsworth, and Keats will become incomprehensible when the reality of sowing changes. To her pointed comment, Farfrae can only reply with the logic of history; he says that " 'it must be so' . . . his gaze fixing itself on a blank point far away" (240). The blank point upon which his gaze fixes (and we note the inflexible, necessitarian tenor of the description) is much more than the uncertain future, it is the blankness of Shelley's "Mont Blanc" seen unimaginatively as the vacant "silence and solitude" of pure process and of nature in its most abysmal form. And it is to this "vanishing point" on the horizon that his progressive vision tends.

Reacting to the horror of Farfrae's modern vision, Lucetta begs him to "forsake the machine for us" (241), meaning for the pleasures of romance. Farfrae ignores her plea because he is enthralled by the iridescent machine, and it is this slight but always evident fascination with the mechanical that suggests that he will lose his balance and slide Henchard-ward toward the purely mechanical and absolutely social.

Accordingly, when we last see him, he recommends that he and Elizabeth-Jane abandon the search for a destitute and despairing Henchard because further efforts "would make a hole in a sovereign" (407). His recommendation places him perilously close to Henchard's frame of mind on the road to Weydon. Farfrae's remark implies that the "curious mixture of romance and thrift in the young man's composition" (348) cannot sustain the equipoise of its own formulation. Lucetta's death and the history of her liaison with Henchard puts an end to Farfrae's romantic aspect. After his wife's death, he is seen to smile "mechanically" while "pursuing his ordinary avocations" because—in a quotation borrowed from Shelley's *Epipsychidion*—"Time in his own grey style taught [him] how to estimate his experience with Lucetta" (376). He does not "insist upon a dogged fidelity to some image" notably romantic, while his failure to so insist excludes him from "the band of the worthy" (376–77), the visionary company from Wordsworth to Carlyle. The Arthurian "hame" of which he originally sang "giving strong expression to a song of his dear native country" transmutes into a rhetorical gesture empty of real content, for "he loved [his home] so well as never to have revisited it" (399) in all of his years at Casterbridge. It is, finally, Farfrae's rhetorical romanticism which bears comparison with Henchard's as he wanders the heath dressed in the garb of the "hame" which he too left in order to become the mayor of Casterbridge.

Because characterized as a compromise formation without invigorating dialectical capacities, Farfrae can maintain but not generate sublime representations constitutive of a poetic faith. Like the mid-century romanticism of which he is emblematic, his character is a holding pattern which gradually loses its grip and slides into a strict, one-sided economism. In terms of the genealogy of mayors, Henchard's misdirected and destructive energies are replaced by Farfrae's efficiency and perspicuity of direction. Such a substitution could never produce a profoundly powerful romanticism, though it does not reproduce so disastrously negative a character as Henchard. Under Farfrae's rule there is more bread available than beer; but society must learn to "microscopically" amplify "minute forms of satisfaction," following Elizabeth-Jane's example, if it is to wrest some contentment from life. The Carlylean critique alluded to in the mechanical metaphor of the microscope suggests that society will never again experience the "natural" amplitude of joys fostered by the romantic sublime with its drive toward ethical perfectionism. This capability was divorced from society during the Weydon moment in its history, "One evening of late summer, before the century had run one-third its span."

In *The Mayor of Casterbridge,* the narrator pits "Northern insight against Southeron doggedness" (186). These northern insights—collectively the line of Germanic romanticism from Wordsworth to Carlyle—lose their claim upon society, though they retain their validity as a vanquished and desirable cultural program. We have not spoken of Hardy's personal interest in such a struggle, Hardy who divorced himself from traditional Wessex life in order to become a professional man of letters, nor have we included in our analysis the portrait of the romantic husband disappointed in his romance with his "pair of blue eyes," Emma Gifford, though we think these matters worth noting in passing. As a biography of regret, *The Mayor of Casterbridge* has much to tell us about Hardy's own ambitious betrayal of his Dorset roots and his eventual sorrow that he ever did so.

Thus far, it has been the unromantic character of Casterbridge and of its mayor that has held our critical attention. In order to complete our analysis though we need to examine the five major spectacles which structure the narrative: Farfrae's and Henchard's northern and southern county fairs, Lucetta's High-Place Hall, the arrival of the royal personage and its companion piece, the skimmington ride with its entailed "spot of time," the waxwork dummy of Henchard floating in the water, and

Henchard's costume drama of redemption at Elizabeth-Jane's wedding feast. Each of these "fairs" re-presents the exchange Henchard made at Weydon; each further elaborates the consequences of selling love in order to purchase a universe of death.

Once relieved of "the pressure of *mechanized* friendship" with Henchard (173, emphasis added), Farfrae is inspired to entertain Casterbridge with a fair. "Fired by emulation" (173) and motivated by the will not to be outdone, Henchard decides that he will also sponsor an entertainment. He can imitate generosity but he cannot initiate it. In this event, the Scot is an original genius with a real desire to give pleasure. Henchard's mimicry is flawed because aggressive, while it is destructive because it establishes a rival where there is none. In effect, rather than respond sympathetically to Farfrae's desire to give pleasure, he responds antipathetically and competitively.

In the construction of each mayor's fairground, we learn much about their respective characters. Henchard chooses an "ancient earthwork" or Roman military camp; Farfrae an arbor among the sycamores of The Walks. To construct his camp, Henchard deploys "a little battalion of men" (174), while Farfrae's pavilion seems to be built magically by nature herself. Farfrae's "cathedral" is "ingeniously constructed without poles or ropes," the vault being made of "closely interlaced" boughs (176). The military character of Henchard's operation contrasts sharply with the easy cooperation between man and nature which builds Farfrae's natural cathedral, a model of romantic communal society.

Within the confines of Henchard's fortress, "boxing, wrestling, and drawing of blood generally" occur, while the people who partake of these heavy-handed amusements seem "heroically gathered in the field" as though marshalled there for some great battle (174–75). Conversely, Farfrae's sycamores provide a sheltered cathedral for music and choral dancing. Costumed as a "wild highlander" who "spins to time" (177), Farfrae is the choral leader who sings a "lyrical ballad," as he did in the Three Mariners upon his arrival.

During Henchard's fair, the wind plays "on the tent cords in Aeolian improvisation." The song strummed is one of terror though, and not delight. The Aeolian harp the narrator has in mind is derived from the negative aspect of Thompson's "Ode on Aeolus's Harp" which Coleridge redeployed in his "Dejection: An Ode." Henchard's Aeolian tent wails "to such a pitch that the whole erection is slanted to the ground," like the smoke from Cain's sacrificial altar, nearly crushing "those who had taken shelter within it" (175), those innocent "Abel Whittles" who are forced by fear to partake of Henchard's circus. Farfrae's fair however generates genuine enthusiasms. His Scotch lyrics and costume capture the hearts of Casterbridge, recalling the rhetoric of Scotland which enthralled a sentimental Victorian England and indeed Queen Victoria herself. Farfrae's fair inspires an immense admiration "for him as one who so thoroughly understood the poetry of motion" (177), a hint by the narrator that he is the upcoming man who has learned how to accommodate poetry to unpoetical historical progress. The narrator's comment further suggests that Farfrae is a sentimentalist who understands the rhetorical use of poetry to further a utilitarian interest in progress.

These contrasts and contests between sentimentality and aggression will intensify when Lucetta Le Sueur Templeman arrives from Jersey. Lucetta moves the combat from a public to a private arena, from the marketplace to the drawing room. By the time that Henchard realizes that he wants to marry Lucetta, he is "getting on towards the dead level of middle age, when material things increasingly possess the mind" (220). Lucetta is one of those material things that possess his mind and whom he wants to possess to adorn his mayoral mansion. Lucetta has all the characteristics of what Hardy would have known as a "P.B." or Professional Beauty. As her Jersey origin implies, Hardy perhaps modeled her upon Lilly Langtry, the Jersey Lilly, who appears beside Hardy in a John Singer Sargent painting of contemporary London figures at the theatre. Lucetta is always the figure of "artistic perfection" whom the narrator describes as "a rare butterfly or cameo" to be appreciated by a collector like Henchard.

Lucetta first appears in Casterbridge as a "veiled maiden" beside Susan's grave. In her veiled appearance, she is a belletristic representation of romantic desire who stands melodramatically over the grave of her rural precursor whose fate she will eventually share as Henchard's "wife." Before coming to Casterbridge, Lucetta alters her name from the "Lucette" of Jersey patois to the more Italian " Lucetta" (219) as a sign of her new aesthetic character. Once installed at High-Place Hall, she surrounds herself with furniture far in advance of Casterbridge's provincial taste, while she is visited there as though Henchard and

Dissembling Henchard: The Mayor of Casterbridge

Farfrae were worshiping an aesthetic goddess whom the narrator compares to a late Renaissance painting of Venus.

Lucetta is *à rebours* or against nature in Huysmans's sense. In this, she is Henchard's ideal mate, for she is as artificial as he is. Like Henchard, she comes from nowhere and settles into the upper registers of Casterbridge society; she can remain there, as he can, just so long as her past remains concealed. For her, as for Henchard, character is a matter of decorum; personality a question of style. Nowhere is this more apparent than when she comments to Elizabeth-Jane, "settling upon new clothes is so trying. . . . You are that person (pointing to one of the arrangements [of clothing]), or you are *that* totally different person (pointing to the other)" (238). The emphasis on the qualifying "totally" should not go unnoticed, nor should the externality implied by the Carlylean metaphor of clothing. In her salon, she lies "on the sofa . . . somewhat in the pose of a well known conception of Titian's [Venus]" (222), whether alone or preparing to receive callers.

Her salon in High-Place Hall is a theater then where she places herself on display. The narrator describes the Hall as "a compilation rather than a design" (211). By indirection, his description points to her inorganic and artificial character. The heraldic emblem of the Hall is a "mask" whose former "comic leer" has been altered into an indescribable horror bearing chipped lips and jaws as "if they had been eaten away by disease" (212). The mask, of course, is a theatre mask which points to the specular character of Lucetta's self-presentation, while the chipped lips point to the venereal disease of history cast as the love of ambition which eats away at erotic discourses (of romanticism) as well as to the prostitution of love, the spiritual price of the cash nexus. The narrator remarks that boys throwing stones have transformed the comic mask (representing the romantic pastoral) into a tragic mask (representing the historic plight of romanticism). In addition to its literary significances, this transforming event recalls the biblical parable of the stoning of the prostitute, a trial and a fable which will be overtly at issue in the upcoming skimmington ride when the criminal element of Mixen Lane casts the first stone of deadly insult at Lucetta for her one erotic indiscretion which originated in an act of charity toward a sick and lonely Henchard.

Lucetta's unforeseen arrival at Casterbridge causes Henchard's "gloomy soul" to effect "an almost mechanical transfer [of] sentiments" from Elizabeth-Jane to her "before [his sentiments] had grown dry" (220). Henchard is attracted to the "artful little woman" who "arrange[s] herself picturesquely" (227) on her divan because he believes that she needs his name to make her an honest woman. This sort of honesty with its implied purity is but a name in Casterbridge and not an intrinsic or integral quality, a matter for the social register rather than of virtuous conduct. Lucetta is an aesthete for whom the question of how to live is a matter of good form; indeed, it is the loss of her good name in the formal sense of reputation that kills her.

When Lucetta learns from the furmity woman's testimony that "at bottom" Henchard is a loveless man who "sold [his] first wife at a fair like a horse or cow" (284), she leaves "gloomy" Casterbridge (276) and marries Farfrae in Port Breedy. Her flight maps the trajectory of the romantic sublime in its desire to evade those gloomy, criminal places in a landscape marked by death. Her wedding to Farfrae at Port Breedy associates her with the lost and wandering romantic mariner Newson whose eventual return begins the partial redemption of Casterbridge, while the name of the chief witness at the ceremony, Mr. Grower, suggests a reinvigoration of various romantic possibilities. Lucetta has genuinely fallen in love with Farfrae and he with her. Their romance will be murdered by "the letter" or character of Henchard's love when her love letters to him are read in public.

In fact, everybody is spiritually better without Henchard, "that infuriated Prince of Darkness" (347). As Abel Whittle tells Elizabeth-Jane, "Tis better for us [work folk]" now that Henchard is gone. Although they must "work harder . . . we bain't afeard now . . . [because there is] no meddling with yer eternal soul" under Farfrae's stewardship. Although he receives "a shilling a week less," Abel "is a richer man" as he says because "what's all the world if yer mind is always in a larry?" (295). Far from being a criticism of Farfrae's parsimony as it is usually understood, Whittle's testimony damns Henchard as a near-literal devil managing a satanic mill at Casterbridge.

The summary spectacle of all romantic engagements begins in Mixen Lane, a Casterbridge slum where "vice ran freely," "recklessness dwelt," "shame [was] in some low windows" and "slaughter [was] not altogether unknown" (328). Mixen Lane, first of all, presents us with a spectacle of a depraved and deprived rural community such as Hardy knew it and Wordsworth did not want to seem to know it, not even when writing about suicides and infanticides. The Lane is, secondly, a place where an "altar of disease . . . might have been erected" (328) rather than a temple of health. We will recall that the prevailing critical metaphor in Carlyle's "Characteristics" was that of disease. The implication is that the disease of mercantilism and the cash nexus has eaten away the moral health of the traditional community. Thirdly, in Mixen Lane white hides black in accordance with the ratios of the parable of the whitened sepulcher. In the lane, "the industry and cleanliness which the white apron expressed were belied by the posture and gait of the [prostitute] who wore it" (329). The Carlylean critique of high culture exemplified by the tragic mask over High-Place Hall is thus extended to all of Casterbridge where prostitution (the buying and selling of "love" and the contractual character of relationship and community) wears the mask of "industry and cleanliness."

It is appropriate then that the spectacle of the skimmington ride should begin in Mixen Lane. The ride itself is "a rough jest" (332) like Henchard's reading of Lucetta's letters to Farfrae as "a practical joke" (324) and like his deadly jest when he tells Newson that Elizabeth-Jane is dead. Jests of this sort substitute for joy with the intended implication that eros (pleasure) has become deadly. The deadly pleasures of the skimmington ride are preceded by Henchard's reception of the royal personage, the *"fête carillonnée"* (336) being a prelude to and prefiguration of the ride. At the fête, Henchard's grotesquely patriotic costume reflects the thespian character of authority itself, which is specular rather than authentic. The historical allusion underpinning the royal visit (Albert's southern "progress" to celebrate the advance of mechanical progress) as well as the snobbery and sycophancy in evidence during the parade are the central characteristics of a "fête" wherein "folks do *worship* fine clothes" (341, emphasis added) and Lucetta is mastered by "a Weltlust" (343) whose delusions of grandeur extend upward to a knighthood for her husband. The French characterization of the "fête" suggests by historical allusion that the republican feasts of liberty, equality, and fraternity have been reversed in a Casterbridge which worships fine clothes and lusts after knighthoods bequeathed for mercantile conquest. Overall, the sense of "hero worship" expressed in the scene is unmistakably contrary to Carlyle's sense of authentic leadership.

Henchard is the central mechanical idol in both parades. The skimmington ride itself is based upon Wordsworth's antilyric of specular London in Book Seven of *The Prelude*. It is as though Hardy is answering Wordsworth's question: "What say you, then/ To times, when half the city shall break out/ Full of one passion, vengeance, rage, or fear?/ To executions, to a street on fire,/ Mobs, riots, or rejoicings?" (7:670–75). The spectacle Wordsworth chooses to depict such a time of discord is London's St. Bartholomew Fair, which, in my reading, is one source of the skimmington ride. It is Wordsworth's "Parliament of Monsters" then which return in Hardy's skimmington ride, itself a "vast mill" of "far-fetched, perverted things/ All freaks of nature, all Promethean thoughts of Man, Wild Beasts and Puppet-shows" which are "jumbled together" to create the "anarchy and din," "barbarian and infernal" of a "phantasma/ Monstrous in colour, motion, shape, sight, and sound" (7:680–720). Wordsworth's phantasma returns as Hardy's skimmington ride. For Hardy as for Wordsworth and then Carlyle after him in his depiction of the phantasmagoria of the French Revolution, this fair is the "epitome/ Of what the mighty city is herself/ To thousands upon thousands of her sons,/ Living amid the same perpetual whirl/ Of trivial objects" (7:722–25).

During the ride, Henchard's character is revealed as a "stuffed figure with [a] false face" (351), while both of the wooden dummies are identified by their costumes ("Why—'tis dressed just as she was dressed when she sat in the front seat at the time the play-actors came to Town Hall" [352]). Each recognition alludes to the specular quality of "the quality" or upper classes and the thespian character of authority in Wessex.

At no time during the ride is its unromantic aspect more closely revealed then when it concludes and the maskers disappear like "the rout of monsters" (356) in Milton's *Comus*. Having completed their profane rites, the denizens of Mixen Lane "Break off [and] run to [their] shrouds within these brakes and trees" (356). When the "rusty-jointed executors of the law" seek to find the culprits, Joshua Jopp is questioned. Jopp's first name alludes to his antitype, the biblical Joshua as well as to "the pessimist" Henchard encountered on his way to Weydon. Jopp's skimmington ride pulls down the facade of Casterbridge respectability with "historical kinds of music" (354) played on a cow horn hidden in his waistcoat (356). The cow horn relates him to his Old Testament namesake, only now it is history and not divine providence which acts as the vengeful lord of destruction. When the magistrate asks Jopp if he has heard anything, he answers: "Now I've noticed, come to think o't, that the wind in the Walk trees makes a peculiar poetical-like murmur to-night, sir; more than common; so perhaps 'twas that?" (355). His reply is pointedly ironic if we recall that the Walks was the site of Farfrae's romantic pavilion or "cathedral" of song and dance and that Lucetta is now Farfrae's wife. Moreover, Jopp's reply mocks the voiced breezes of high romantic poetry by recasting the figure of inspiration as a deceptive alibi of displacement.

The revisionist import of the skimmington ride is intensified when the narrator ironically reports that "Nohow could anything be elicited from this mute and inoffensive assembly" at Peter's Finger, the tavern of Mixen Lane. His "mute and inoffensive" characterization alludes to the unrecognized rural Miltons of Gray's "Elegy," only now their silence is criminal subterfuge. Far from being romantic "folk," the denizens of Peter's Finger *are* the "madding crowd" from which an emergent romanticism once sought to escape by quietly meditating upon the fate of mute Miltons in rural villages.

Bankrupt of his props of character after the skimmington ride, Henchard begins to desire "affection from anything that was good and pure" (361). His resurgent desire starts him weakly dreaming: *"for the first time, he had a faint dream"* (361, emphasis added). He is rudely awakened from his faint dream of a cottage life with Elizabeth-Jane by the arrival of Newson, her real father. By his name and his characterization in the narrative, Newson is the regenerate ancient mariner. He is a trusting, jocular, "overly warm" (334), and "well-be-doing man" (367) who evinces all of the characteristics of a Carlylean romantic. As erotic man, he is Henchard's antitype. When he first arrives in Casterbridge, he greets Henchard "with a profuse heartiness," a liberal warmth which causes "Henchard's face and eyes . . . to die" (366). Newson informs Henchard that a cruel "jest" had disabused Susan of her "belief" in the Weydon marriage. Henchard takes his cue from Newson's narrative and tells another such divorcing jest. He tells Newson that his daughter is "dead likewise." Upon hearing the news, Newson exclaims, "Then what's the use of my money to me?" (368) a question which neither Henchard nor the denizens of Casterbridge would have much trouble in answering. Newson believes Henchard and disappears almost magically; Henchard can "scarcely believe the evidence of his sense . . . [he] rose from his seat amazed" after Newson's disappearance (368). What amazes Henchard is that anyone could be so trusting. Newson's faith is "so simple as to be almost sublime" (369). The near-sublimity of his faith is diametrically opposed to Henchard's disbelief (which is never suspended), while the narrator's qualifying "almost" reminds us that we are still in postromantic times even when confronted with so nearly ideal a character as Newson.

After Newson's departure, Henchard fantasizes a Wordsworthian life of plain living with Elizabeth-Jane. Together they will dwell in a "humble cottage" like that of his romantic namesake, Wordsworth's Michael. Yet his little dream will not be realized because his life is ruled by a self-inflicted curse which damns him to the "leaden gloom" felt by those "who have lost all that can make life interesting, or even tolerable" (370–71) as the narrator informs us in a phrase reminiscent of Shelley's preface to *Alastor*. His phrase refers to those whom Shelley wrote would "languish, because none feel with them their common nature," those who are "morally dead," and who are "neither friends, nor lovers, nor fathers, nor citizens of the world, nor benefactors of their country" (Preface, *Alastor,* 69–70). Henchard is just such a man "without human sympathy." It is only now when his props of character have fallen away that he feels the "vacancy of [his] spirit" (*Alastor,* 69–70), as the narrator is quick to point out.

Bereft of Elizabeth-Jane as he soon will be, Henchard has "nobody to fortify him" in his misery, nor can he summon "music to his aid" (371). As the narrator makes explicit, "[Henchard's] hard fate had ordained that he should be unable to call up the Divine spirit in his need" (371), just as Shelley predicted of those who commit no generous error, as Henchard has not. Because he has not, "the whole land ahead of him was as darkness itself; there was nothing to come, nothing to wait for" (371). In effect, Henchard is condemned in ways which recall Shelley's condemnation of the "selfish, blind, and torpid," who constitute "the lasting misery of the world" (Preface, *Alastor,* 70).

This view of an existence without access to some form of imaginative redemption is forcibly depicted in the scene of Henchard's attempted suicide and its aftermath. The scene, like many others of emblematic import in the novel, is derived from Wordsworth. It is "some floating thing/ Upon the river" that points out Henchard's new course (*Prelude,*

1:29–31), one that will take him back to the heath. Henchard wrongly assumes that the floating thing is a "miracle" (373) sent by Providence to save him. Rather, it is a "materialistic" miracle like Farfrae's chemical process which saved him in the time of his troubles with the overgrown corn. The "miracle" is thus another simulated event, this time in imitation of Wordsworth's tale of the drowned man in Book Five of *The Prelude* (426–59).

Later, when he calls upon Elizabeth-Jane to go and see the figure in the mirroring waters, she returns and tells him that she sees "nothing." Incredulous, he tells her to "go again" and look. She does so and reports that she has seen "a bundle of old clothes" (373). He commands her a third time to "go and look once more," which she does when she finally sees "the effigy." Her three sightings recapitulate in summary form the portrait of character which the narrator has been at pains to depict: first and foremost, Henchard is "nothing"; secondly, he is a costume of selfhood, a "cheap and nasty" tailor's dummy in Carlyle's sense of sweatshop politics, and lastly he is a wooden idol, a criminal "construction" floating upon the black waters of time.

The scene of recognitions at the weir is patterned upon Tennyson's "The Passing of Arthur" wherein Arthur commands Bedivere, the first and last knight, to throw Excaliber into the lake and then return and report the "miracle" that he would undoubtedly witness.[8] Elizabeth-Jane is a Bedivere figure, a first and last follower of the mayor, while earlier Henchard had been compared to Arthur at his round table when in the Three Mariners. Bedivere's genuine miracle is parodied by the wooden miracle witnessed by Elizabeth-Jane, while his lasting faith in Arthur is different from her short-lived faith in her pseudofather's goodness.

When Henchard leaves Casterbridge for the heath, Elizabeth-Jane had "mechanically" promised him that she would not forget him (387), yet as soon as she learns of the "joke" he told to her real father, she decides "to forget him now" (391). His ambitious life has brought him only bitterness, as Carlyle predicted such a life might. Too late he understands that "what he has sacrificed in sentiment was worth as much as what he has gained in substance" (394). His romantic "recantation" is "nullified" because his emergent romantic soul is only "half-formed" while his desire for "amelioration" arises only when his "zest for doing" has passed (394). Henchard finally understands that his existence has been purely specular, "a mere painted scene" as he says, wherein all value depends upon costume instead of culture.

His awareness is given final expression when he "recklessly" (397) decides to attend Elizabeth-Jane's wedding, a genuine ceremony of innocence from which the specular and guilty Henchard is prohibited. By his recklessness, by his being garbed exactly as he had been a quarter of a century before, and by the marriage's occurring on St. Martin's Day, the very day he married Susan, we are alerted to the possibility that the past is now returning in the present in order that we might compare values in accordance with the ratios of Carlyle's critique of "past and present." As it turns out, at this wedding feast a woman will divorce (expel) Henchard from the domain of eros where he now wishes to be included. Henchard purchases a "caged goldfinch" as a way of placing himself "*externally* at any rate, a little in harmony with the prevailing [merry] tone" of the marriage in order not to offend "in appearance" (398, emphasis added). Superficially, Henchard is costumed as a penitent awaiting inclusion into the sacred rituals of the community. He simulates his desire in the hope that his fantasy will become real and historic. The very presence of the goldfinch recalls the "unheard" Weydon nightingale of the prologue. In the sign of the caged bird, the "trite and tiresome" Weydon nightingale returns, only now it does not seem so trite or tiresome but rather symbolizes the romantic redemption it initially did for Wordsworth, Coleridge, and Keats. Ultimately, the bird's death by neglect under a bush, the position of Keats's nightingale, implies that the lyrical presence which went unheard on the road to Weydon has once again gone unheard, only now it represents Henchard's desire for sympathy rather than his will to deny it.

Henchard's return to his mayoral mansion opens a scene of startling romantic contrasts and revelations. In his absence, his house has become a fane to Cupid and Psyche presided over by the erotic Newson where a comedic ritual is under way. As a fetishist, Henchard can see only "fractional parts of the dancers," never the entire body of desire or the complete choral figure. The whole man of romantic myth is not visible to his fragmented sight, his narrow vision. "The gaiety" of the house "jarred upon [his] spirits" which are Alastor-like in their compulsion toward isolation, though from motives antipathetic to idealism. Viewing the bride and groom, "[Henchard] could not quite understand why

Farfrae . . . who had his trials" and "Elizabeth-Jane, who had appraised life at a moderate value . . . should have had zest for this revelry" (401). Their "zest" or gusto is incomprehensible to him, while the sight of Newson's "happy face" spells "[his] complete discomfiture" (401). The totality of his discomfort points once more to the totality of comfort which Newson represents.

Depressed by his alienation from choral joy, Henchard rises to leave the marriage feast, understanding at last the futility of recuperation given the enormity of his crimes against love. When he rises to go, he "stood like a dark ruin obscured by 'the shade from his own soul upthrown' " (401). The dark ruin recalls those dark places in which many a betrayer of love has despaired of redemption, from Satan in *Paradise Lost* to Shelley in his "ruined cell" where he heard "sad dirges" wailed by a "voiceless wind" in "When the Lamp is Shattered" (13–14). Though these allusive readings remind us of the eighteenth-century tenor of Henchard's sublime, the narrator's's figure is borrowed directly from Shelley's *The Revolt of Islam* wherein "some moonstruck sophist stood/ Watching the shade of his own soul upthrown/ Fill Heaven and darken earth, and in such mood/ The form he saw and worshipped was his own" (8:4,2). Like Shelley's sophist, Henchard has worshiped his own formal and delimiting construction called "the mayor of Casterbridge," an ego-narrative which currently lies in ruins, shattered by the counter-insurgent forces of a lyrical necessity which have gathered together to celebrate their victory in the most un-Weydonish affair in the novel, the mariner's wedding feast.

The great pity with which Wordsworth's Michael is remembered ("'Tis not forgotten yet/ The pity which was in every heart/ For the old man" [462–64]) will not be Henchard's. His ultimate demand to be forgotten prohibits the romantic uses of memory as a therapy for the soul that was Michael's lasting gift to culture. Henchard's will toward "disremembrance" is respected "less from a sense of the sacredness" than from a sense "that the man who wrote [it] meant what he said" (410), a meaning which points to Henchard's final awareness of the vacant and profitless character of his life. His final demand not to be remembered is "a piece of the same stuff that his whole life was made of" the narrator informs us, his words "piece," "stuff," and "making" now resounding with the full force of their ironic reflections revealed.

In his death, Henchard deprives his stepdaughter and erstwhile friend of "a mournful pleasure" and an opportunity to gain "credit for large heartedness" (401). His will perversely disinherits his titular "family" of the opportunity to act charitably toward him and to feel the pleasure of such an act, albeit commingled with a certain sadness. Such a commingling of pleasure and sadness would of course reconstitute the Wordsworthian accord between the still sad music of humanity and the joys of sympathy fostered by the corresponding imagination. Ironically, Henchard's "charitable" last will and testament interdicts those Wordsworthian "thoughts too deep for tears" which others may experience at his passing and wish to express. Thus does Henchard end as he began by willfully divorcing himself from love in any of its many forms.

In its concluding moments, the story of a man of character allusively reiterates the struggle between eros and thanatos found in Carlyle's writing. The novel has enlightened us as to the unenlightened character of a mayor whose death (the death of death) permits a weak resurrection of romantic idealism albeit against his wishes. In his absence, desire begins to amplify microscopically small joys in order to bring some warmth to a remarkably cold world. Appropriately, it is Carlyle's "feeble light" enkindled by a "precise recognition of the darkness" which illuminates Elizabeth-Jane's postromantic accord with history ("Characteristics," 13). By seeing just how deadly life has been, she learns to live with the truth of how things are.

[2]

The Woodlanders:
Una Selva Oscura

Noi ci mettemmo per un bosco
che da nessun sentiero era segnato.
Non fronda verde, ma di color fosco;
non rami schiette, ma nodosi e'nvolti;
non pomi v'eram, ma stecchi con tosco.
Dante, *Inferno*

"O for a beaker full of the warm South"
Keats, "Ode to a Nightingale"

"In this world, there are few voices and many echoes."
H. Tennyson, *Memoirs*, cited from Hardy, *Notebooks*

IN THE AUTUMN and winter of 1844, Wordsworth protested the pro-spective incursion of the Lancaster and Carlisle Railway into the Lake District. His protest took the form of an anecdote upon a northern woodlander which he published in *The Morning Post* of October 1844, the import of which he would explain at length in two letters published in December of that year. Not surprisingly, his position was typically "romantic" in its criticism of progressivism, mechanism, and material-ism for which the railroad industry had become an emblem, particularly as it was about to invade his northern kingdom. Rail travel and its effects, Wordsworth wrote, could neither accommodate nor further romantic acculturation. The techniques of the sublime were at odds with the romance of progress, and the two could not be reconciled. To these observations, he added that the romantic tree of life he had cultivated would become an endangered species if concerned citizens did not help him to keep the virgin woods virgin. British culture had arrived at a crossroads, he argued, and would have to choose between the culture of the railway or the woodland; the two could not coexist.[1]

The Descent of the Imagination

The choices and attitudes entailed in Wordsworth's 1844 debate with the railroad were collectively republished at mid-century under the title of *Two Letters Re-printed From The Morning Post*. The booklet, which still goes by this title in Wordsworth's collected works, constitutes a suppressed textual link between Hardy's *The Woodlanders* and the cultural programs and aspirations of the early century for which Wordsworth was chief spokesman and poet laureate. The degeneration of the romantic program and its affects which Wordsworth feared would occur if the railroad's iron tracks penetrated the virgin woods of Kendal and Keswick did occur in mid- and late-century Britain. And it is this degeneration of romantic affects which is the central issue in Hardy's woodland novel. In its tracks, the railroad left a cultural terrain as "iron" and hostile to romanticism as Wordsworth could imagine, and it is this negative imagining that informs *The Woodlanders*.

Though an occasional piece written with specific issues in mind, Wordsworth's *Two Letters* is our best guide to the postromantic concerns of *The Woodlanders* because the document sums up at a late date the originating poet's view on his own achievement as well as articulates his fears for its survival. The specific connection between Hardy's novel and Wordsworth's complaint is to be found in Wordsworth's fable of a northern woodlander which served as an ancedotal prelude to the issues he would discuss in the letters. In the ancedote, Wordsworth praises a Lake District woodlander for his remarkable attachment to an oak tree.[2] For Wordsworth, the woodlander's affiliation with the tree signified his understanding and appreciation of his spiritual and temporal heritage as a woodlander, one which allowed him to live a free life of plain living and high thinking far from the madding crowd. When propositioned by the forces of progress and fashionable tourism to cut down the tall tree growing on his property because it stood in the way of the projected course of the railroad, the yeoman flatly refused. And it is this refusal which ennobles him to Wordsworth who reported his resistance in this emblem:

Near the house of [the Lake District yeoman] stands a magnificent tree, which a neighbor of the owner advised him to fell for profit's sake. "Fell it," exclaimed the yeoman, "I had rather fall down on my knees and worship it." (*TL*, 238)

Framed by Wordsworth's arguments, the woodlander's refusal becomes an emblem for a host of interrelated romantic concerns which pit tradition against progress, the sacred hearth against the profane steam engine, mercantile profits against spiritual profit, the need for roots against deracinating ambition, rural integrity against the emergent fashion of tourism, spiritual placement against displacement and wandering, the sacred idol of "wholeness" against a profane fetish of fragments and partial vision, meditative isolation and contemplation against distracting crowds and thoughtlessness, a timeless and mythic sameness against history and difference, and the desire for a genuinely humane education against the demand for a genteel substitute necessary for "getting on" in the wide world. In brief, Wordsworth suggests that were the woodsman's tree of power cut down, joy would disappear from the woods, the place where this joy had originated.

In *The Woodlanders,* Wordsworth's tree of power is cut down, and with its felling we hear the fall of the Hebraic strain of the romantic tradition in Britain. The resistance to the tree felling evinced by Wordsworth's woodlander is also evinced by Hardy's John South and his sacred elm. Those cultural possibilities which Wordsworth said needed further cultivation in order to thrive are not cultivated in South's woodlands where both naive and sentimental romantics engage in a romantic satire of deadly consequences. What had been a healthy attachment to the tree in Wordsworth's emblem becomes a neurotic dependency in Hardy's reworking of it, one which does nobody any good. Then, too, the felling of South's tree at the command of science and art embodied in the aesthetic doctor Fitzpiers is attributable to precisely those two agents which Wordsworth named as the culprits in the destruction of romantic isolation in the woodlands. The "fellowship of the road and the stream" he wrote, "was put an end to" because "Art interfered with and [had] taken the lead of Nature" (*TL,* 354).

Though a woodland novel about a tree would seem evidence enough to establish the connection between Wordsworth's writing and Hardy's, it seems to me unlikely that Hardy had not read Wordsworth's *Two Letters* which, by 1850, had become a major document in the recent history of British romanticism, one much debated in the press and included in the first published edition of Wordsworth's prose works.[3] By revising Wordsworth's anecdote upon a northern woodlander in a novel about a southern woodlander, Hardy constructs a narrative which implicates, by literary history, Paine's liberty tree in *The Rights of Man,* Burke's tree of tradition in *Reflections on the Revolution in France,* Wordsworth's characterization of Burke as an "oak of tradition" in Book Ten of *The Prelude*, Coleridge's characterization of his "critique" of Wordsworth's poetics in *Biographia Literaria* as the leaves and crown to Wordsworth's "trunk and roots," Carlyle's Igdrasil, Tennyson's "Tree of Fable" in "Timbuctoo," Arnold's stately oak in "The Scholar Gypsy," as well as Hardy's own earlier, and slightly more optimistic, form of romanticism embodied in Gabriel Oak, whose name probably owes its origin to Carlyle's passage on the oak tree in *The French Revolution*.[4] Tropologically then, Wordsworth's oak is incontestably the Jesse Tree of the romantic faith, its roots presumably deep in historical time, its crown spreading into the heavens, a "fairy work of earth," as Wordsworth characterized the ash in *The Prelude,* Book Six. And it is this very significant tree and all of its ramifications which is cut down in Hardy's *The Woodlanders*.

What Hardy found in Wordsworth's *Two Letters* was a thorough and thoroughly suggestive outline of the romantic project as Wordsworth understood it. In the letters, Wordsworth discusses, briefly, the origin of the romantic sensibility in late Augustan forms of literary sentimentality, his transformation of the sublime of terror into the sublime of meditative beauty, the pastoral achievements of the romantic movement, and the programmatic need for meditative walks in familiar woods were nature to continue to bless and be a blessing. In addition, Wordsworth advises the public of the uselessness of tourism as a form of sentimental education and, significantly, his fears that romantic consciousness might revert back to its decorative eighteenth-century origins if society did not take care to cultivate the seed culture he had sown in the early years of the nineteenth century. All of these themes would have been attractive to a Hardy in search of a woodland companion piece to his urban satire, *The Mayor of Casterbridge*.[5]

We will recall that *The Mayor of Casterbridge* began when the century had run nearly one-third its course; thus its companion piece begins, textually, in the mid-1840s when the British railway boom was at its peak and nature was being invaded by genteel tourists in search of romantic sensations. The negative effects forecast in Wordsworth's *Two Letters* are narrated at full length in the Hintock woodlands, a *selva oscura* or dark purgatorial woods in Dante's phrase wherein all that the Lake poet had cultivated either dies (Old South/Winterborne), transmutes back to a sentimental form of consciousness (Grace/Fitzpiers), or survives as a tragically desiccating nostalgia (Marty South). In *The Wood-landers*, the woods are purged of their gentle breezes and inhabiting genius, leaving them ironically "virgin," or abysmal. In effect, Hardy cancels all romantic effects and returns the woods to precisely that point in culture where Wordsworth had found them and redeemed them.

To guide his allegory of romantic culture as it confronts the depredations of history, Hardy consulted the notes he had taken on Arnold's "Wordsworth" which he first read in 1879, the year of its publication. Hardy's notes demonstrate that he was interested in the non-inevitability of romanticism. Romanticism, he copied, was but an "inn" on the highway of time and not a "home" or permanent stopping place as Wordsworth would have liked it to be. And it is the impermanence of all abodes of the spirit which attracted Hardy. Inevitability was a question of "Style [which] takes your fancy" Hardy copied from Arnold's "Wordsworth" (*Literary Notebooks*, 1: 119; henceforth cited as *LN*), of rhetoric and desire. What had seemed self-evident and "natural" at one stage had over time degenerated to a question of style. According to Hardy's understanding, every myth degenerates to rhetoric as time conquers all romances; and in this instance, it was Wordsworth's romance of natural supernaturalism which had been conquered.

Hardy's notes on Arnold's views of mythic slippage are followed by citations he copied from E. W. G.'s "The Egil's Saga" which appeared in the July 1879 *Cornhill* (*LN*, 1: 356). The conjunction of quotations is important for it situates the thematic position Hardy will take when writing *The Woodlanders*. "Iceland," Hardy copied, produced "The finest imaginative works . . . in the thirteenth century. . . . They are called Sagas (legends)." These legends "held the foremost place in the world of letters—The brief luxurious blossom of poetry in Provence & Austria was withering: the bud of more vital promise in Italy & Persia was still unbroken" (*LN*, 1: 119–120). Coming as they do immediately after citations from Arnold's "Wordsworth," the combined notebook entry suggests the thematic core of *The Woodlanders*. It seems that Hardy intended his novel to be a prose poem depicting a culture whose "brief luxurious blossom of poetry in Provence was withering." Withering, then, is the narrative agency of slippage: myth withers to rhetoric, the imagination to fancy, genuine sympathy to a projective narcissism. Grace withers because of her schooling, Giles withers because Grace withers, while Marty withers because Giles does not love her, and it is her shorn and withered figure which opens and closes the narrative.

We will recall in this connection that the presiding mythical dimension of the Hintocks is indirectly derived from Norse or "Icelandic" mythology and that the Norse mythology which is the direct source of Hardy's allusions comes from Arnold's *Balder Dead* as Mary Jacobus has pointed out ("Tree and Machine"). It seems likely then that Hardy's intent is to have "Balder," the beloved of nature, die once more without affording him the possibility of resurrection, as Arnold ambiguously did. By casting his woods as Icelandic, Hardy could depict the withering of the final flower of Wordsworthian romanticism or, what amounts to the same thing, the twilight of the Germanic gods in England.

The Hintock woods are then a gothic region where northern romanticism encounters its southern or "mediterranean" counterpart. The inwardness of the "gothic" romantic is evinced in Old South's "druidic" fantasy or faith, while an oppressive sense of nature as a vast, hostile force is apparent throughout the Hintocks. Into this gothic region come "mediterranean" romantics: Fitzpiers, a Shelleyan type, and Charmond, who married an Italian and who lives abroad most of the year. And it is this mixture of Gothic and Grecian, of Hebraic and Hellenic forms of romanticism that propels the romantic satire of the novel. Grace, whose "education" creates a mediterranean romantic from a gothic romanticist, is the pivotal figure between woodland and aesthetic culture, between, that is, past and present forms of culture. That she chooses aesthetic culture over woodland culture and, ultimately, leaves the woods defines Hardy's sense of recent cultural history, where it had originated, and what it had ultimately come to by 1887.

As a saga detailing the fading of Wordsworth's "Provençal" blossom in ways and from motives which Wordsworth himself had predicted in his *Two Letters, The Woodlanders* is an ideal complement to *The Mayor of Casterbridge.* These two novels constitute Hardy's "Hebraic" phase, while the following two novels, *Tess* and *Jude,* constitute his "Hellenic" phase, being as they are essentially concerned with Keatsean and Shelleyan forms of romanticism. In *The Mayor of Casterbridge,* the narrative focuses its attention on the "snug city," while in *The Woodlanders,* it is the "the unlighted country without" which is "strangely solitary and vacant of aspect" (*Mayor of Casterbridge,* 95) which holds the narrator's attention. The vacancy is "strange" because Wordsworth had populated it with romantic presences which are no longer to be seen or felt there. That is, the strangely vacant woodlands surrounding Casterbridge return as the postromantic Hintocks.

Though we shall have cause for further analysis later, it is worthwhile to mention at this point that the novel opens with a Wordsworthian invention, a peddler out on an excursion. Percomb is in search of Marty's woodland abode in order to tempt her to sell her natural beauty so that he might transform it into an artifice which will protect Mrs. Charmond's beauty from the withering effects of age. The "fall" of hair which Percomb buys from Marty symbolizes her "Fall" from romantic grace. When we first encounter her, Marty is an Eve figure tempted by material necessity to sell the natural beauty of her chestnut hair. Rather than appreciate Marty's beauty, Percomb goes on his excursion to deprive her of it, to transform, that is, her natural beauty into a saleable artifact which will protect Charmond from the ravages of time.

Marty's hair does in fact do this, and a younger-seeming Charmond tempts Fitzpiers away from Grace. It is then the "rape of the lock" for money which begins the play of adultery in the narrative. Marty must sell her chestnut hair to support her father who is disabled by his woodland fancy, an adulterated form of Wordsworthian imagining. His fanciful connection to the tree and his concomitant inability to work constitutes the narrative's ironic critique of Wordsworth's noble woodlander in the *Two Letters*. The sacred freedom symbolized by Wordsworth's woodsman's attachment to his tree has degenerated to a neurotic and debilitating dependency in Hardy's woodlander. Moreover, the freedoms that Wordsworth's yeoman experienced in the Lake District are withdrawn in the Hintocks which are characterized as a harsh manufactory of woodland products.

Percomb's cutting of Marty's chestnut hair begins a narrative concerned with romantic severance. In effect, the scene of divorce in *The Mayor of Casterbridge* is represented now as the scene of tree felling in *The Woodlanders*. Severing, cutting, and dissociating natural and traditional connections and the establishment of artificial liaisons in their place is the business of the Hintocks and the theme of the narrative. Thus Old South's fantasy, a metonymical expression of the romantic intention in metaphor, displays his longing for a beaker of the warm South, in Keats's phrase for the grace of inspiration received at the mythic source of romantic culture in Provence.

The Descent of the Imagination

Having established these continuities of theme, I would like to cite a few particulars regarding Hardy's novel and Wordsworth's *Two Letters* for it is my opinion that Hardy's writing is reactive and reactionary and that the immediate source of his figures and philosophies lies elsewhere in romantic texts. If we keep in mind that Wordsworth was poet laureate at the time of his writing to the *Morning Post* and that in his letters he envisioned 1844 and 1845 as watershed years for romanticism's struggle against the railroad boom and the mechanical modes of connection they implied, then we can gain a sense of the cultural crisis Hardy had in mind when he began to write *The Woodlanders,* forty years after the crisis had passed and romanticism had taken a turn for the worse.[6] The loss of the romantic spirit propelled culture into an "Iron Time," in Arnold's phrase, dominated by mechanical ties and discoordinated, aesthetic sensibilities, and it is this form of culture that invades the Hintock woods.

In the *Two Letters,* Wordsworth argues that improved modes of transportation could only harm the romantic sensibility which depended upon the gradual "organic" growth of the affections between a familiar locale and a creative perceiver. Tourism is not romantic, his argument goes, if the chosen mode of travel is either coach or rail. Railroad travel inhibits the cultivation of correspondences between man and nature; thus the steam engine is an agent of displacement and not placement even though the railway could rapidly carry urban dwellers to the woods. More broadly expressed, the total enterprise of modernity for which the railroad stood is inimical to those transcendental and imminent connections preferred by the romantic self. Improved methods of transportation (as forms of correspondence) Wordsworth argued would cause a degeneration in romantic modes of connection which were essentially peripatetic.

Hardy will characterize Wordsworth's argument by demonstrating the ways in which Grace Melbury's education has harmed her. It is, in the main, the "education of grace" that summarizes the novel's romantic concerns regarding dislocation. Beginning as a native woodlander and the intended of Giles Winterborne, she concludes as Fitzpiers's wife. In effect, Grace becomes a sentimental tourist in her own homeland, while Fitzpiers is always a sensation-seeking tourist in the Hintocks. Their marriage seals the divorce of Grace from the woods.

Wordsworth enforces his argument by pointing out that the sensibility could only become romanticized by staying at home. His argument would have been of interest to a Hardy who was alienated from his Wessex woodlands owing to his ambition to become educated. Moreover, if one had to travel, Wordsworth recommended walking as the preferred mode, for the slow pace encouraged the meditative gaze. If, however, progressive modes of travel were chosen and the perceiving self were too rapidly sent into alien regions for short periods of time, then the soul would not be romanticized. Wordsworth argued further that sending more people more rapidly to distant places would hinder and not help the emergent romantic sensibility. In a society driven by "steamboats and railways" romantic culture would spoil, and when it did, romantic consciousness would wither away and die. The romantic faith was not an essence or an innate given according to Wordsworth, but a view of things that had to be cultivated, and if it were not, so much the worse for culture. This, anyway, is principally what is at issue in Wordsworth's *Two Letters* and what will be at issue in Hardy's *The Woodlanders*.

It is then to Wordsworth and all things Wordsworthian that Hardy trains his attention in *The Woodlanders*. We can begin our examination of things Wordsworthian with John (of the) South who is an oppositional figure to Wordsworth's yeoman of the north. The sacred faith of the northerner in his imaginative connection with nature becomes a neurotic fancy in the southerner. That which Wordsworth's yeoman *had*, Hardy's woodsman longs for. In the Hintocks, the strong, "objective" sense of the imagination as the agent of correspondence becomes a weak, ostensibly subjective agency. In terms of a figural genealogy, what was the imagination in Wordsworth's Lake District has become the fancy in the Hintocks.

John's fancy parodies the Wordsworthian notion of the gradual intertwining of nature with human nature until the two become as "one life." Moreover, the sturdy oak which for Wordsworth was a figure of traditional home and commonsense values becomes the central icon of alienation from those values in Hardy's Wessex. John is alienated from his life-supporting woodland labor and, ultimately, from his life in the Hintock community because of his fixation on the tree. As a figure of alienation and not integration, the tree is a fetish which serves to hide South's emergent horror of disconnection, absence, and vacancy. That

is, his arborial fancy displaces his anxiety of castration, noncorrespond-
ence, and death. That he has such a horror marks him as partly romantic, while his incapacity to imaginatively overcome his terror of vacancy
marks him a weak or failed romantic. John's fantasy identifies his life
with the life of the tree. South imagines that he will live as long as his
tree does in a parodic, because displaced, rendition of Wordsworthian
natural supernaturalism. Together, tree and man seem to mutually support each other; yet the obvious fragility of such an apparent support or
phenomenal relationship constitutes one level of Hardy's critique, while
the mutual destruction of tree and man constitutes another. In effect, it
is South's attempt at romantic correspondence which kills him; his death
is the effect or after-effect of tree felling.

South's tree is a fetish because it represents his desire for wholeness
(for the whole body) in the absence of his being able to perceive it.[7] First
of all, his natural icon is a fragment of the romantic past, a past which
stands for a whole which is no longer conceivable and therefore no
longer possible. His tree fancy alienates him from the "real" woodlands,
which is simply or empirically natural, while it alienates him from the
community of woodland labor as well, of which he was once "tradition-
ally" or integrally a part. Hardy emphasizes this point of deracination
through fancy (as opposed to connection through imagination) by having Winterborne's "life-hold" depend upon South's life which, in turn,
depends upon his tree of life. The felling of the tree causes all to fall
down dominoes style. We will recall that when Giles loses his property,
his "garden plot" seems to disappear like a phantom projected from a
magic lantern slide. Thus, South's woodland fantasy ultimately causes
Giles's woodland reality to become a fantasy. In this way, the insubstantial dispossesses the substantial from its life-hold on tradition and on
independence in a tragic parody of Wordsworthian forms of imaginative
possession.

South's tree of great value interdicts the enabling accord between
perception and apperception essential to the forging of the Wordsworthian sublime. If Wordsworth could see and distinguish the visionary
from the phenomenal dimensions of the real, then it is just this capacity
that collapses in South's visionary mode. The interdependency Wordsworth saw in a multiple yet unitary nature becomes a dependency and a
confusion of values in South's diseased vision. The result of his diseased
vision is that the corresponding yet independent romantic self becomes

merged (confused) with nature in the Hintocks. Merger (confusion) and not correspondence (distinction within relationship) defines the agent of South's limitation and anxiety in contradistinction to the "unlimitation" and elation Wordsworth experienced in the woods. Thus, South's identification with nature in its temporal and ever-decaying condition renders him a "being impaired" rather than (and as a degradation of) Wordsworth's "being unimpaired."

In South's fancy upon a tree we witness the aggrandizement of the destructive rather than the creative element in nature. Instead of man being like nature (cyclical, renewable, and evermore about to be), nature is like man (temporal and decaying only to eventually die). That is, in South we see life and hope and memory colluding to destroy all that these agents created in and for Wordsworth in an ironic reversal of Wordsworthian possibilities. The end result of such a total reversal of romantic fortunes is that Wordsworth's mountain glory becomes Hardy's mountain gloom, in effect returning the Wordsworthian sublime to the site of its origin in and through a figure, the tree, of its origination.

The tree, then, is a synecdoche for Wordsworth's emblem of nature which undercuts the positive values of the emblem. "Old" South is a superannuated romantic trying to reconstitute the way things used to be. To him, the tree represents Nurse nature, as it did for Wordsworth, yet South's nurse no longer has the capacity to heal the wounded spirit. South's fancy of nature tells us that he is unable to face history as the abyss, as vacancy, or as pure phenomenal process. He cannot do what Wordsworth could, separate perception from apperception as well as overcome his idealizing desires and come to grips with the still, sad music of humanity. Moreover, by gazing fixedly upon his tree, South ceremoniously worships the "female phallus," a fantasy object which supplies the "lack" or gap he intuits in mother nature's wholeness. The female phallus, Freud writes, is the supplementary object of the fetishist's desire. No matter how it is represented, the fetishist is always trying to fill a gap or lack in the female body which he perceives as the sight of a horrifying castration (Freud, vol. 21, "Fetishism"). By the long way round, what this all suggests is that South is a weak romantic alienated from perceiving the real woods by his fantasy of an eroticized and potent nature. His inability to overcome his fancy and see the woods as they are constitutes him a "Boldwood" type destructively fixated upon a "valentine" which says "Marry Me." Indeed, South wishes to "marry" the woods and enact a Wordsworthian epithalamium of identity and correspondence, yet his inability to come to terms with the reality of the abyss as history and as alienation prohibits him from engaging in Wordsworthian possibilities of the sublime.

The pseudoidentity which South establishes with his tree is destroyed by Fitzpiers, a doctor-aesthete interested in strange cases of psychic derangement fostered by woodland isolation. Fitzpiers represents science and art as it examines the mind and in its very examination murders to dissect. By having the tree removed, Fitzpiers "modernizes" South's view by showing him the very vacancy he has sought to conceal. In Hardy's understanding, when the romantic faces history, he dies because his idealism will not marry or identify with realism as Coleridge hoped that it would (*Biographia Literaria,* chapter 22). In effect, Fitzpiers shows the romantic that his fancy is just that, and not a genuine imagining, "the *all in each* of human nature" as Coleridge characterized it (*Biographia Literaria,* chapter 18). South is "Old" or archaic and atavistic because he clings to a superannuated fancy as his truth. When the object of his affection is removed, the startling appearance of the vacant sky fills him with the very horror of disconnection he has been at pains to repress in and through a romantic fantasy. His fancy was the sole mode of correspondence remaining to him wherein some form of cosmos could be construed, albeit a weak one. Thus, he desparately clings to his little cosmos of correspondence which he characteristically half-creates in order to perceive.

Like Wordsworth's yeoman, South refuses to live without his sacred tree, yet his insistence is no longer a noble source of freedom but a perverse source of suffering and anxiety for himself as well as his two dependents, his daughter and Giles Winterborne. It is not an increment of independence he achieves by his resolution to worship the tree, but rather an intensified dependency which leads to the debilitation and death of his entire woodland line of descent. Yet so horrible is the thought of the abyss to the old romantic that when his tree is cut down, he dies to prove the truth of his belief. Ironically, the tree finally does become an "emblem of the great apocalypse," only in Hardy's Wessex the terms of such a revelation are reversed. It is no longer "eternity peering through time" that we see, but time and death and severance peering through symbols of eternity. South dies to prove the validity of his life-sustaining connection with nature, his "proof" exhibiting the very irony implicit in his woodland fantasy of survival. The imagination may once have fostered a healthy, therapeutic relationship with nature, but now the fancy is deadly insofar as it reveals to all but the enthralled the very absence it would hide. Interestingly enough, when asked about Old South, Giles tells Fitzpiers that "Others have been like it afore in Hintock" (149), those "others" presumably being the progeny of Wordsworth's northern yeoman who perished before their form of romanticism was cut down by science and an overly introspective and self-serving art.

When demanding that South's tree be cut down, Fitzpiers argues "what's a tree beside a life!" (141). His argument fails to understand the principle of identity between life and nature which fostered those vital correspondences Wordsworth had been at pains to establish in his poetry and Coleridge to argue into truth or "fact" in his prose. Fitzpiers's misunderstanding arises because having been differently educated from South, his "taste" is different. Because he has not been "trained to a profitable intercourse with nature where she is the most distinguished by the majesty and sublimity of her forms," as Wordsworth had (TL, 344), he cannot begin to understand South's obsession in terms other than a debilitating neurosis.

Acting as a member of the "intelligentsia" with the historical prerogative to revolt against the aristocracy, Fitzpiers demands that South's tree be cut down even though Giles warns him that it is Mrs. Charmond's property. Fitzpiers's rejoinder to Giles is that he will "inaugurate a new era forthwith" (149) by cutting down the tree. Thus reason supersedes tradition and demands the institution of a new way of doing things. Though the allusion is slight, in this scene we have an emblem of Burke's complaint against the French Enlightenment. Tradition falls before the axe of reason, only now it is the romantic tradition which is being felled in accordance with Hardy's "forlorn hope" that the lumber of past faiths fallen to superstition would be cleared away by reason and that "poetry . . . the invisible signs of mental and emotional life" would "join hands" with modern science and assume a more enlightened, less superstitious cultural expression" ("Apology," Late Lyrics and Earlier, in Oriel, 57).

Once South's tree is downed, the narrator tells us that "The weakest idler that passed could now set foot on marks formerly made in the upper forks by the shoes of adventurous climbers." His observation gains its most pointed commentary when read in relation to Wordsworth's *Two Letters*. In concluding his assessment of romantic loss and gain, Wordsworth describes the difference between his crossing the Alps before 1805 and then after "the new military road had taken [the] place of the old muleteer track with its primitive simplicities" (*TL*, 353–54). When he crossed the Alps the first time in 1799, he felt as though all he saw "Were the workings of one mind, the features/ Of the same face, blossoms upon one tree,/ Characters of the great Apocalypse,/ The types and symbols of Eternity/ Of first, and last, and midst, and without end" (*TL*, 354). Then, he concludes, "Thirty years afterwards I crossed the Alps by the same Pass: and what had become of the forms and powers to which I had been indebted for those emotions? Many of them remained of course undestroyed. . . . But though the road and torrent continued to run parallel to each other, their fellowship was put an end to. The stream had dwindled into comparative insignificance, so much had *Art* interfered with and taken the lead of Nature" (*TL*, 354, emphasis added). Due to "Art's" interference "it was impossible [for him] to suppress regret for what had vanished for ever" (*TL*, 354).

This fellowship is precisely what is vanishing forever in the Hintock woods. At Fitzpiers's command, the "fellowship" of man and nature no matter how feeble is "put an end to." The regrets expressed for South's passing will be amplified in his daughter's regrets for Giles's death which conclude the tale much in the same vein as Wordsworth concluded his *Two Letters*. Although Giles's stature has "dwindled into comparative insignificance"—and Old South's tree has dwindled from metaphor to metonym—it is still difficult for Marty to "suppress a regret for what had vanished for ever"—the very power of the imagination which Wordsworth felt and saw when meditating upon his first Simplon Pass crossing of the Alps. In effect, the distance of decline measured by Wordsworth's two crossings becomes the ratio of imaginative descent we witness in the Wessex woodlands.

After its felling, "the weakest idler" could go where only adventurous romantics once would have dared to tread. Again, the narrative comment gains its most significant critical emphasis when read in conjunction with Wordsworth's *Two Letters*. In his conclusion, Wordsworth mourns the fact that once "perilous" mountain passes "were gone . . . and instead of travellers proceeding, with leisure to observe and feel, were pilgrims of fashion [hurrying] along in their carriages, not a few of them perhaps discussing the merits of 'the last new Novel,' or poring over their Guide-books, or fast asleep" (*TL*, 354). The invasion of the Hintocks by such "idlers" and "pilgrims of fashion" as Fitzpiers, Mrs. Charmond, and the educated Grace Melbury constitutes another way in which Hardy appropriates Wordsworth's's own criticism of romantic decline in order to portray or realize Wordsworth's worst fears for that form of faith he had inaugurated in England.

After the felling of South's tree, "inaccessible nests could be examined microscopically; and on swaying extremities where birds alone had perched the bystanders sat down" (150). Here, the narrator's use of "microscopic" bears comparison with that of the narrator in *The Mayor of Casterbridge* when he describes Elizabeth-Jane's postromantic conjuring of small joys in Casterbridge. More to the point though, the narrator's metaphor of the microscope revokes the authority of vision by giving priority to the natural eye. In effect, the visionary ratios invoked by Blake's "There Is No Natural Religion" are inverted with the result that natural, rational, and self-limiting man overcomes the synthetic, visionary powers of the poetic genius. But here we must invoke Coleridge to ground our distinctions.

In speaking of *Taste*, Coleridge notes that the "power of the imagination" proceeds by "*meditation* rather than by *observation*. And that the latter in consequence only of the former. As eyes, for which the former has predetermined their field of vision, and to which, as to its organ it communicates a microscopic power." Coleridge then claims that "There is not a man living . . . who has . . . a clearer intuition [of this way of seeing] than Mr. Wordsworth himself" (*Biographia Literaria*, chapter 18, 2:57, emphasis Coleridge's). Coleridge's point is that meditation precedes observation as imagination precedes perception. This prescription for creative perception is precisely what has been reversed in the tree felling. Now "microscopic" observation precedes meditation; perception, imagination. Thus it is no longer the imagination that informs vision, imparting to the bodily eye a "microscopic power," but rather the bodily, empirical eye which closely observes a nature whose distant obscurity once led men like Wordsworth to wonder and to worship.

Fitzpiers recommends that the tree be cut down at night, and so it is. When dawn comes, the doctor pulls back the curtain and says, reassuringly, "It is gone, see" (150). His gesture tears the veil of illusion from this last romantic, leaving him to stare out upon a purely denotative world devoid of imaginative connotations. Fitzpiers's tragic new dawn is to be compared to Wordsworth's blissful dawn when sentimental fancies became powerful and principled acts of the imagination. "As soon as the old man saw the vacant patch of sky in place of the branched column so familiar to his gaze, he sprang up speechless; his eyes rose from their hollows till the whites showed all around, he fell back, and a bluish whiteness overspread him" (150). In a masterful scene of romantic revisions, Hardy presents a figure of the old Wordsworth witnessing the disappearance of his Igdrasil during a night of skeptical inquisitions and artful quibbling over woodland property. The "branched column" of the citation suggests the "Temple of Nature," whose ruin concerned Wordsworth in his *Two Letters,* while the whiteness of South's blind gaze suggests that he has become "as a blind man" to a landscape now vacant of romantic import. Cured by an artful science, South merges with the reality of death from which he fled in vision. His romance ripped from him, Old South is "speechless." His silence interdicts the lyrical "speechfullness" and "full-throated ease" experienced by romantics when in the inspiriting presence of nature. In the absence of that presence, latter-day Wessex romantics grow silent as Wordsworth implied they might when "the sublimity of many Passes in the Alps [becomes] injuriously affected" by the arts of "utilitarian" culture (*TL,* 353). South's final words, "O, it is gone!—where—where?" are pathetic in the extreme; they are meant to express the pathos and regret of a lost and nearly forgotten romanticism which suffuses all of Hardy's writing on the subject. South's question will not be answered until Jude carves "thither" on the stone road sign pointing to the illusive Christminster, the "city of lost causes" where he fancies the "tree of knowledge grows."

To conclude this scene of romantic erasure and defeat, the narrator tells us that South's "whole *system* seemed paralyzed by amazement" (150, emphasis added) when he witnessed the vacancy where his tree once stood. The "whole system" under paralysis is that system which desired that a sense of wholeness be cultivated from diverse aspects of experience and knowledge. It is then the body of an enfeeble romanticism (John's body) which is paralyzed as a prelude to its imminent demise. John does not die immediately, but "when the sun goes down." Allegorically, he dies at the end of the century when the romantic dawn had waned into a twilight dominated by "aesthetic" doctors represented by Fitzpiers who appreciates Shelley yet who cultivates a predatory aesthetics of solipsism. In a sense, South's death marks the beginning of the "modern" period in Wessex, a time dominated by "the ache of modernism" when Arnoldian and Paterian accords and accommodations had failed to bridge the gap between mind and world, culture and nature, and poetry and science in ways that Wordsworth could or could seem to. And it is the conjunction of the old romantic world dying and a new aesthetic form of romanticism arising to usurp its place that informs the tragic drama of *The Woodlanders*.

After South's death, Fitzpiers exclaims, "Damned if my remedy hasn't killed him!" (151). His explication should be read ironically; he is "damned" because his remedy—the remedial effects of his science and art acting upon the imagination—has killed the patient. In effect, modern aesthetical doctors like Arnold and Pater kill off that which they would preserve by their excessive reasoning upon the ways, means, and agencies of the irrational, the inspirational, and the excessively self-expressionistic. That Fitzpiers is a doctor is significant in terms of the connections we have been establishing because Arnold envisioned Wordsworth as "the great doctor" who possessed "healing power[s]" which no others did ("Memorial Verses," *Poems*, 63). Fitzpiers is an aesthetic or artificial substitute for the real, natural "doctor," the poet Wordsworth. In terms of the Arnoldian analogue, he is a negatively parodic Goethe figure, a "physician of the iron age," the sick woodland culture of the Hintocks, who "look[s] on [its] dying hour/ Of fitful dream and feverish power" and says *"The end is everywhere/ Art still has truth, take refuge there!"* ("Memorial Verses," 17–24, 28–29, emphasis Arnold's). Paradoxically, the refuge Fitzpiers offers is death in which there can be no comfort.

All woodlanders long for a beaker full of the warm South, for an infusion of the original romantic impetus which would empower them to revive the ceremonies of sylvan faith that were waning since the romantic dawn in the 1790s. Instead of this grail and the sacred drunkenness it would inspire, they get Old South and his neurotic fancies and an aesthetic physician whose cure kills the patient and whose marriage is an adulterous emblem of the adulterated times into which romanticism had fallen. Had Grace married Giles, as the older generation of woodlanders had once intended, Wordsworth's romantic yeoman with his sacred tree would undoubtedly have returned. Yet their marriage does not occur, and for reasons which we must now explore.

Poetically, the intertextual thread leading from Wordsworth's Lake District to Hardy's Wessex begins in Wordsworth's *The Excursion*, continues on through Arnold's 1879 essay entitled "Wordsworth" in which he presents an appreciation of "The Ruined Cottage," or "Margaret" as he retitles it, and ends with Arnold's "Memorial Verses" of 1850, written to commemorate the passing of the poet laureate.[8] In his "Wordsworth," Arnold cites "Margaret" as an especially "inevitable" poem, and he thought it important enough to include in his *Chosen Poems* of Wordsworth which is introduced by his essay.

Hardy's complex response to the "inevitability" and permanent worth which Arnold found in Wordsworth's "Margaret" is embodied in Marty South, a figure who represents the inevitable impermanence of Wordsworth's woodland romanaticism as her father represented its impairment. In his revision, Hardy follows Wordsworth's assessment of the possible causes of romantic degeneration which were outlined in the *Two Letters*. It is then Wordsworth's suspected sense of the "noninevitability" of romanticism that constitutes Hardy's reply to Arnold, a reply figured forth in the allegory of Marty South and Giles Winterborne, the Margaret and Robert of *The Woodlanders*.

Giles will pass away and then Marty will pine away over his disappearance. By their doing so, they reconstitute in a darker mode Arnold's emblem of romantic loss and nostalgia for a better, more redemptive time which concludes his "Memorial Verses." There, he asks England to "keep fresh the grass" on the grave of an all-but-forgotten Wordsworth, and he will raise the issue once more in his 1879 essay on Wordsworth. The poet whom Arnold implored England to remember in 1850 and of whose greatness he reminded them again in 1879 figuratively passes away in the Wessex woodlands in the 1880s. His passing away completes the descent of one form of the romantic imagination from its moment of origin in the northern woodlands to its moment of decline in the Wessex woods.

As the daughter of Old South, Marty is a direct descendant of an early romanticism whose mid-century cult has grown weak and fantastic. Her "elective affinity" with Giles is of the same character as her father's fancy upon an elm tree insofar as both seek satisfaction by fanciful liaisons with an uncaring other. Both are fixated upon a single object of desire enfigured by an arboreal metaphor (the tree/ Giles the planter of pine trees and the knight of the apple orchard). Yet because she is a third-generation romantic (Wordsworth's woodlander, Old South, and then Marty), Marty lives at a greater distance of time from romanticism's strong center, thus her failure to marry Giles leaves her only one alternative which is to simulate the woodland epithalamium such as that presented in Book First of *The Excursion*. She "imaginatively" married Giles as her father "imaginatively" marries with his tree. Thus she is a mechanical imitation of romantic desire and a figure of Hardyan mimesis but not of Wordsworthian poesis, to invoke Coleridge's crucial distinction between acts of fancy and acts of imagination (*Biographia Literaria*, 2:18). Like her father, Marty is morphologically romantic, not metaphorically so. She is a figure in whom "simulation is master, and nostalgia, the phantasmal parodic rehabilitation of all lost referentials, alone remains" (Baudrillard, *Simulations*, 72).

At the conclusion of the narrative, she remains alone (and she alone remains) in the woodlands miming the romantic relationship between the poet and "the friend" and between past and present which invokes an eternal present of fulfillment. In emblem, she is a parody of romantic redemption which recalls the lost referentials of such redemption, for example those appearing in Wordsworth's *The Excursion*, "Tintern Abbey," and Coleridge's "Conversation Poems," the putative source texts of the dialogic redemptive modality in the greater romantic lyric. Given these sources of character, it is crucial that we read Marty's fate against that of Wordsworth's Margaret in *The Excursion* to measure Hardy's understanding of the effects of time upon the claims and assertions of Wordsworth's form of redemption.

When *The Woodlanders* concludes, Marty alone remains to worship and appreciate a woodland figure whom we might see as the last scion of a race engendered by the northern yeoman of *Two Letters*. Marty's name is a shortened form of Wordsworth's Margaret; in terms of the allegory, she names a fanciful form of imaginative desire, one not empowered to forge actual correspondences but rather condemned to live by fanciful liaisons, shortened forms of the high romantic imagination. In the narrative, she is presented as a fixed (and fixated) "counter" of the fancy, in Coleridge's distinction between the imagination and the fancy, the symbol and the allegory. Indeed, as the narrator last presents her, she is literally an allegorical figure of fancy practicing a "mode of Memory emancipated from time and space" (*Biographia Literaria*, 1:13). She has "received all her materials ready made from the law of association"—she and Giles grew up together and so, in principal, their affections should have gradually intertwined—yet it is just this association and its anticipated results which constitutes the ground of her romantic tragedy (*Biographia Literaria*, 1:13). Contrary to everything Wordsworth thought should be the case, it is her lifelong correspondence with Giles that reduces her joy in actual experience; this, in turn, compels her to construct a fiction of relationship as a compensatory mode to a punishing reality. Ultimately, she will memorialize in fancy a relationship which had been an imaginative failure in reality or history. In this way, she re-presents the drama of her father's "imaginative" failure with his elm tree—his affections too grew and intertwined with the tree because the tree was born when he was. Thus, a narrative of fanciful woodland relationships concludes with a ceremony of remembrance performed by a virgin whose virginity is an equivalent form of romantic vacancy, that unimaginable horror whose sight killed her father.

In terms of *The Excursion*, Margaret's loyally waiting for Robert's return is recast as Marty's perseverance and longing for Giles, her spiritual husband. Then, too, if the complex Hintock genealogies are worked out, Marty is also something of a sister and friend to Giles as Dorothy was to Wordsworth. In this regard, we might note that Wordsworth began "The Ruined Cottage" while he and Dorothy were living in Alfoxden, Dorset, and that the epic is therefore an early form of Wessex poem.[9] Intertextually then, the earlier Wessex poem returns nearly a century later to retell its tale of romantic persistence within historic deprivation, only now it is deprivation which rules in a woodlands bereft of redemptive grace.

At Hardy's disfiguring hand, Marty's desire for Giles becomes a grotesque refiguration of Margaret's sublime love for Robert. On the one hand, Margaret's devotion, humble faith, perseverance, and natural piety are laudable and meaningful. Her fable helps the Pedlar walk "along [his] road in happiness" despite his awareness of suffering. On the other, Marty's devotion to Giles is a punishing romantic fixation comparable to Boldwood's obsession with Bathsheba. Both Wessex fixations parody romantic correspondence, while Marty's satirizes Wordsworth's principle of constancy toward a person and a region with whom one's affections have become gradually intertwined. The rewards of such a principle become punishments in Marty's instance. Nor does our having heard her tale do anything to encourage cheerful happiness despite the knowledge of suffering, the intended moral of Margaret's story.

Marty's history throws into confusion Wordsworth's intent in *The Excursion*, Book First which is to demonstrate how good can come from evil, redemption from suffering. Having no such idealized notions of the Miltonic whence and wherefore of things, Hardy offered none in and through the same figures and dramas which offered such in Wordsworth. In the Hintocks, it is Wordsworth against himself which informs the narrative and constitutes the woodland strife. Otherwise put, it is the skeptical and doubting aspect of Wordsworth which gains the upper hand in Hardy's narrative, an older Wordsworth without access to the empowering imagination living in a sylvan region without correspondent breezes, without the rewards of gentle affections, and without a redemptive natural piety.

Contrary to Margaret's noble endurance, Marty's distorted form of Wordsworthian "sacrifice" condemns her to stand eternally poised in an empty lyric of reminiscence which never had a history. In Hardy's reworking of Wordsworth's Margaret, she becomes a figure of natural piety which does not engage history, though it does have a history. Margaret's marriage and natural piety are retroped by Hardy into Marty's enthrallment to a fetish which conceals as well as discloses her divorce from actuality. In effect, Marty's epithalamium measures her alienation. If Wordsworth's intent in "Margaret" is to square the ways of God with man (of idealism with history), Hardy's intent is precisely the opposite. Marty's suffering squares nothing; her loyalty is purely ideal, while her love is not only unrequited but the very cause of her suffering rather than a source of her redemption.

In *The Excursion*, Wordsworth readily acknowledged that "ambition reigns/ In the waste wilderness." The ambition he had in mind was spiritual, one by which "the soul ascends/ Drawn towards her native firmament of heaven" (*The Excursion*, 4:395–97, henceforth cited as *Ex*). In *The Woodlanders*, Wordsworth's injunction becomes ironic. The emaciated Marty whose prayer concludes the narrative is literally a "soul."

The Descent of the Imagination

She is ambitiously spiritual as a reflex to the punishing conditions of her woodland life, yet the fanciful compensation she enacts in her timely utterance of loyalty to the dead Giles only doubles her suffering and deprivation. She is deformed by her spar-gad cutting and by her need to market her hair to support her fancifully debilitated father. In and through this "descent of the imagination" from Old South to Marty, the historical world of suffering and labor is given center stage and not the poet's capacity to overcome it. Thus, Wordsworth's "plot of garden ground" which inspires heavenly ascents of the imagination becomes "wild" again (*Ex*, 1:54–55) in the Hintocks where we witness the romantic eden "slipping away . . . as if [it] were painted on a magic-lantern slide" (*Woodlanders*, 137). There "Sympathies . . . more tranquil, yet perhaps of kindred birth/ That steal upon the meditative mind/ And grow with thought" (*Ex*, 1:79–81) develop into exotic forms of neurosis which contort the spirit rather than cultivate it, exhaust it rather than refine it.

At the conclusion of *The Excursion*, Book First the Pedlar comments that the "bond/ Of brotherhood is broken" when describing the fallen "elm wood" surrounding Margaret's ruined cottage. Hardy took note of this concluding moment and began his narrative where Wordsworth's left off. Marty's cottage is surrounded by an elm wood, like her romantic ancestress's. South's remarkably tall elm tree and a cottage "in an exceptional state of radiance" (45) are the first things Peddler Percomb sees on his way into the dark woodlands (it is a peddler too who takes us to Margaret's ruined cottage and relates the tale). In the Hintocks, the "creative power of human passion" (*Ex*, 1:75–80) which saves Margaret does not redeem Marty. Unredeemed, she becomes a tragic "Lady Sorrow" antithetical to Wordsworth's contented Lady Sorrow, a figure of joyful melancholia (*Prelude*, 6:555). In Marty, we do not see "dreams and fictions, pensively composed:/ Dejection taken up for pleasure's sake/ And gilded sympathies, the willow wreath,/ and sober posies of funereal flowers/ Gathered among those solitudes sublime" sweetening "many a meditative hour" (550–56), but rather someone in whom the romantic program of contemplation has become a self-punishing defence against a history too painful to recall.

In *The Excursion*, Margaret's deprivation by war brings her a life "abridged/ Of daily comforts." This abridgment owing to strife is the status quo of Marty's woodland life which never is fully "bridged" as Margaret's was when she lived with Robert. Marty's physique bears witness to her having forgone the fullness of life, abridging the years of youthful joy to arrive rapidly at a wizened old age which she will pass mourning over her unreciprocated romance with Giles. Those "carved uncouth figures on the heads of sticks" which Robert whittles to idle away the time return in Hardy's narrative to describe Marty's "deflowered visage" (58) which Giles likens to "an apple upon a gate post" (60). We will recall that "whittling" is Marty's trade and the emblem of her character as are all trades in the Hintocks where work defines the individual. Such a reductionist view is again figured in the narrative when Giles replaces her with a "forked stick" (107), an objective correlative for her body.

The drama of The Woodlanders begins when Marty must sell her hair for two gold coins. Similarly, Margaret's drama begins when Robert must sell his services for a packet of gold coins by enlisting in the military. Robert leaves his coins to Margaret as a sign that he has gone to war; their silent presence on the table speaks volumes to Margaret when she returns to her cottage. The coins return to add poignancy to the opening scene of The Woodlanders where they provide another trace element linking Marty's fate and Margaret's. Marty sells her hair for two "jaundiced" coins which Percomb leaves on her mantlepiece. "The sovereigns were staring at her from the looking-glass," the narrator tells us, the "glass" itself a sign that she has sold her narcissistic investment in beauty in order to support her father's narcissistic investment in longevity. After she has her hair cut, Marty will "not turn again" to gaze in the mirror "out of humanity to herself, knowing what a deflowered visage would look back at her and almost break her heart" (58). In both instances, gold is the sign of romantic loss; it marks the place of a romantic absence whose presence infiltrates the woodlands and renders them an equivalent topos to the city, the usual locus of wasteful getting and spending in Wordsworth's topography of values.

In Wordsworth's poem, Margaret symbolizes her loss to the Pedlar by pointing to a withered apple tree felled in winter (Ex, 1:840–43). Marty's imaginary loss is similarly indicated when she points to Giles who is likened to an apple tree which withers before its prime. Though devastated by her loss, Margaret's faithfulness to her departed lover/ husband is proof to the Pedlar that the "secret spring of humanity/ which, 'mid the calm oblivious tendencies/ Of Nature, 'mid her plants, and weeds, and flowers,/ And silent overgrowings, still survived" (Ex,

1:927–30). Marty's bereavement too will bear silent testimony to the survival of this "secret spring of humanity," yet the import of such a survival has changed over time. Though sexually neuter and deprived of creature comforts, Marty "touched sublimity at points"—precisely those points where her figure coincides with Wordsworth's Margaret—to become an embodiment of "abstract humanism" (438–39). In her abstraction, she is a dark silhouette of Margaret's enlightened endurance. Her neurotic devotion to a dead Giles is a form of necrophilia, a being half in love with death as a way of forgetting or repressing that she is living a life-in-death.

This view becomes all the more poignant if we recall the Pedlar's estimation of Margaret's life. Having retold her tale at full-length, he declares that "all the grief/ That passing shows of Being leave behind,/ Appeared an idle dream, that would maintain,/ Nowhere, dominion o'er the Enlightened spirit/ whose meditative sympathies repose/ Upon the breast of Faith" (*Ex*, 1:950–55). The shows of grief, literally the spectacle of Marty's life, do not appear an idle dream in *The Woodlanders*. Rather, they appear as a nightmare of historical suffering which no form of enlightenment can overcome, though delusion and self-deception can. Margaret's meditative sympathy which springs from the breast of faith returns in Marty as a solipsistic obsession resting within a figure whose "contours of womanhood" are "so underdeveloped as to be scarcely perceptible in her" (438). Hardy recasts Margaret's full breast of faith as a barely perceptible organ in Marty. The breast of faith which is also the classical figure of charity and a source *figura* of romantic joy is recast as an underdeveloped organ incapable of producing substantial nourishment. To this deformation, the narrator adds that the "misty hour" of Marty's final appearance effaces "the marks of poverty and toil" from her figure and makes her appear *"almost* like a being who had rejected with indifference the attribute of sex" (438, emphasis added). It is the narrator's "almost" which marks the critical difference between Wordsworth's figure of faith and Hardy's figure of hopeless persistence. At Giles's grave, Marty fancies herself a wife and widow (there is even a bizarre scene of jealousy enacted between Marty and Grace at the grave) in order to create in fantasy a romantic satisfaction that she has not had in body (in nature) or in history.

The repressed traces of Margaret's marriage to Robert are faintly visible in Marty's grave side prayer when she sexualizes her desire and therein reveals its origin in some other, more romantic life. At Giles's grave, she promises to think of him "whenever I get up . . . and whenever I lie down" (438). She will live with Giles in fancy as Margaret once lived with Robert in history. The fullness of Margaret's life with Robert is fully "abstracted" in Marty's imaginary life with Giles. As an abstraction of experiential joy, Marty is dispossessed of the natural ground upon which her romantic namesake stood. Nunlike in her chaste marriage to an ideal (and there is something of Tennyson's nun-sister of Percival in her), she persists as "a tissue of elevated but abstract verbiage" which Arnold proclaims is "alien to the very nature of poetry" ("Wordsworth," *Essays in Criticism, Second Series,* 49). In this reading, Marty represents all that Arnold thought fanciful, prosodic, and "not inevitable" about Wordsworth's poetry; all, that is, that could be forgotten and discarded from the canon because superficial, airy, and unrealistic. Yet in Hardy's woodlands, it is this character of the Wordsworthian which persists because it is a pure delusion untainted by perceptions of the real, historical conditions whose punishing contours and deformations have been effaced by "the misty hour" of romanticization.

Like Margaret who "loved [her] wretched spot, nor for worlds/ [would] Have parted hence" so strongly was the memory of Robert "fast rooted in her heart" (*Ex,* 1: 911–12), Marty too is rooted to a wretched spot affiliated with Giles. Margaret is "the last human tenant of these ruined walls" (*Ex,* 1:930) we are told, as is Marty if we think in terms of sylvan forms of the romantic tradition and of the poetic tradition of "the romantic couple" such as Wordsworth and his sister had constituted it in "Tintern Abbey." The spiritually enlightened "being unimpaired" despite historical suffering which Wordsworth symbolizes in *The Excursion* by "severed locks" shed "upon the flowering stream" which call to mind "a thought . . . of life continuous . . . that hath been, is, and where it was and is/ There shall endure" (4: 740–57) becomes, at Hardy's deft reworking, a veritable "being impaired" who endures as she was and is, despite her desire to have things otherwise.

The final allusion we will consider concerning Wordsworth occurs in Marty's ultimate appearance in the novel. Marty enters a churchyard and walks to "a secluded corner" (438), a direction and a location which recalls Gray's "Elegy in a Country Churchyard." The implication is that the redemptive voice Wordsworth gave to Gray's "mute Miltons" has returned to its secluded origins and to its muteness. Values espoused in poems like "Resolution and Independence" and represented by Giles Winterborne have returned to the graveyard where Wordsworth found and gloriously resurrected them. No longer do they legislate relationships between man, nature, and human society as they once did in communities like Wordsworth's Quantocks. In Hardy's Hintocks, Wordsworth's romances of rural England are laid to rest. Reading thus, we see Marty as a powerless Urania, the Wordsworthian muse, standing over the "mute" grave of her dead poet or we see Wordsworth himself standing over the grave of his own perished innocence in "There Was a Boy" whose textual source is also located in Gray's "Elegy."

At Giles's grave, Marty swears that "If ever I forget your name let me forget home and heaven" (439). Her conditional oath is just, for indeed to forget the name of Wordsworth would be to forget the textual "home" or center of English romanticism as well as to forego the heaven it promised. Yet it is just this home and heaven which is forgotten in the narrative. The final gesture of dismissal occurs when Grace abandons her ritual visitations to Giles's grave and returns to the fashionable culture of the city after her reconciliation with Fitzpiers, Giles's romantic rival.

In her final appearance, Marty reminds us that the imagination is no longer an agent of metaphysical solace. Her fable does not commute the harsh terms of historical suffering into an emblem for that calm and terrible strength which sustained Margaret in "The Ruined Cottage." At Giles's grave, Marty swears herself in as a belated romantic pathetically holding on to her dead ideals. Significantly, she does so in terms evocative of Arnold's "Memorial Verses," particularly the two closing stanzas wherein the continuance of Wordsworthian forms of overcoming history are put into question. Marty's history can "make us feel" the "cloud of mortal destiny" all right, but Hardy's fable does not help us to "put it by" as Wordsworth's did. Because there just might not be any substitute for Wordsworth's power to overcome suffering, Arnold implores the River Rotha to "Keep fresh the grass upon his grave . . . Sing him thy best! for few or none/ Hears thy voice right, now he is gone" (67–74). This is precisely what Marty "sings" to herself in the country churchyard. When we last see her, she is isolated within a fantasy past become an eternal present in a parody of continuance and overcoming. Marty does see Giles for what he is, as nobody else is able to (Giles's visibility is made problematic in a narrative where he is half seen most of the time), yet as a diminished and distorted form of Wordsworth's Margaret, she survives as as figure of "abstract humanity" antithetical to the *"sublimated* humanity which is at once a history of the remote past and a prophetic enunciation of the remotest future" (*Essay Supplementary to the Preface of 1815,* Wordsworth's concluding paragraph *Prose Works,* 3:83). Histories which depict a sublimated humanity are the materials of redemptive poems like "The Ruined Cottage"; histories representing abstract humanity are not, as Marty's woodland fable is not. What her history does present is an ironic reading of Wordsworth's sublimated humanity, for she does show us "a history of the remote past" which is "a prophetic enunciation of the remotest future." That future will see a return of the remote preromantic past of sentimentality and fancy devoid of imaginative solace, for where we last see her, Marty stands disconsolately in a country churchyard, figuratively where Wordsworth stood half a century earlier when he gave mute Miltons like Giles a voice which, for a while, ruled the madding crowd.

Hardy achieves this revision by backtracking on the path Wordsworth first pioneered in breaking the "bondage of definite form" thereby creating sublime forms of the "enthusiastic and meditative Imagination" ("Preface of 1815," *Prose Works,* 3:35). Thus, if Spencer "maintained his freedom by aid of his allegorical spirit, at one time inciting him to create persons out of abstractions ("Preface of 1815," 3:35), Hardy deploys allegory inversely to create abstractions out of persons. Such characteristic abstractions were Hellenic for Wordsworth because subject to definite form and prone to idolatry. Marty is one such abstraction, and as such is a descendant of Spencer's Una, who, in turn, is the great allegorical ancestor of Wordsworth's Margaret, both of whom exemplify "the highest moral truths and the purest sensations" ("Preface of 1815," 3:34). The point is that where Spencer's and Wordsworth's women are humanized allegories suggestive of the particular in the universal, Hardy's are allegorized humans in which the universal or the type dominates. Ironically, Marty is an allegory of the lyrical spirit. Nonetheless all of these allegorical women are evidence of the continued application of the meditative (Wordsworth) or dramatic and historic (Hardy) imagination upon "its worthiest objects, the external universe, the moral and religious sentiments of Man, his natural affections, and his acquired passions" which are themselves made emblematic in Giles Winterborne, one "worthy to be holden in undying remembrance" ("Preface of 1815,"

The Descent of the Imagination

3:35). It is the vanishing of such commemorative acts which is depicted in the final moment of Hardy's woodland allegory which represents contemporary culture's short memory regarding what was highest and best about its recent past. Thus Hardy's historical imagination depicts the fall and the forgetting of the meditative or lyrical imagination in a woodland allegory whose final figure is generically representative of all that had passed away.

If Arnold's "Wordsworth" and Wordsworth's "Margaret" constitute the sources of Marty's character, it is Arnold's *Balder Dead* that is the immediate intertextual source of the Nordic character of the Hintocks. At one time, the narrator refers to the Hintock night as "an absolute void, or the ante-mundane Ginnung-gap believed in by Marty's Teuton forefathers" (54). At another time, he describes the woods as a "motionless and silent . . . Niflheim or fogland" (141) which enshrouds all those who walk there. In the Hintocks, trees with the "sheet-iron foliage of the fabled Jarnvid wood" (143) make a metallic sound when blown by the wind. To this line of allusion, we can add that Marty is compared to Sif "After the rape of her locks by Loke the Malicious," Percomb being the Loke in question.

Though these allusions could refer to any English translation of the Nordic epics, Mary Jacobus ("Tree and Machine") has shown that they belong to Arnold's *Balder Dead,* and it is this intertextual clue which we must now pursue. There is much in Giles's story which suggests that he is a reworking of Balder, himself a Wordsworthian figure of natural supernaturalism in Arnold's poem.

Arnold's Balder is killed when blind Hider hurls a branch of mistletoe at him. Balder had been promised that nature would not kill him; all animate and inanimate objects swore an oath to that effect save the mistletoe. Thus it came to pass that a nature sworn to protect Balder killed him. His death by a tree recalls Old South's death through the agency of his phantom elm which he fancied had promised to preserve him. South's death inadvertently "kills" or severs Giles's "lifehold" which, in turn, leads to his death by exposure since he cannot enter his one-room shack when Grace is there. Fitzpiers's blindness to the virulence of the elm inadvertently kills the old man, just as Hider's blindness to the potency of the mistletoe kills Balder. Hider's blindness becomes thematically relevant to Hardy's narrative insofar as Fitzpiers, a scientist and decadent aesthete, is blind to the power of romantic magic, those

134

powers wielded by the Nordic gods in question and to the South family to whom Giles is aligned by his woodland property. The narrator once compares Percomb to Loki the Malicious which Hardy spells "Loke," following Arnold's text. After Balder's death, Odin asks the gods to cease to mourn, which they will do. The advised brevity of their mourning is recapitulated in the brief mourning Grace gives to Giles. Hela's dark realm to which Balder descends and the "lonely untrodden" road that leads there is recalled in the dark road leading to the Hintocks. The critical role played by Speipner, Odin's horse, in the attempted rescue of Balder from Hades finds its counterpart in Fitzpiers's erotic adventures on horseback, while the tenth bridge on the road to Hela's frozen realm "which spans with golden arches *Giall's stream*" (1, 148, emphasis added) is perhaps the immediate source of Giles's two names, his surname being derived from the Dorset dialect word for a frozen stream which flows in winter.

These intertextual possibilities to one side, Arnold's "plains of Niflheim, where dwell the dead" (1, 172) define the *selva oscura* of the Hintock woods. There, a dead form of natural-supernaturalism encounters a novel form of aesthetic consciousness, both of which are "lifeless." The "shadow tribe" (1, 174) which dwells there is, overall, antithetical to the visionary company. Reading back from Arnold to his source in Carlyle, we find that Balder was "the white God" which "early Christian missionaries found to resemble Christ" (*On Heroes and Hero Worship*, 23–24). Giles refigures this line of thinking which accounts for the occasional "passion" imagery in a narrative having nothing whatsoever to do with Christianity and everything to do with Wordsworthian romanticism in its Christian humanist phase. The possible resurrection of the romantic god implied by Carlyle and then Arnold, each successive implication weaker than the last, is negated in Hardy's version of the Balder myth. Unlike either Carlyle's or Arnold's Balder, Giles will not be a "once and future" king of the woodlands.

Ghostly Balder's comforting words to his sleeping, sorrowing wife Nanna are paraphrased in Hardy's narrative to become Marty's words to a dead Giles: "Sleep on; I watch thee, dear soul!/ Neither do I neglect thee now, though dead" (1, 292–93). Balder's words themselves recall the closing lines to "Memorial Verses," the implication being that an enduring remembrance of the vital past of the romantic tradition is essential for spiritual survival in an increasingly iron time. Despite Balder's attempt to comfort her, Nanna will be burned with Balder on his funeral pyre. Her self-immolation is tacitly repeated by Marty who dies with Giles, consumed by a self-immolating need for his companionship. Like Nanna, she too desires "To cut [her] thread of life and free her soul" (1, 303) from her body in order to possess in the spirit her god of the woods.

In the Hintocks "the Storm, the Abyss, the Howling, and the Pain" of Arnold's Niflheim cannot be evaded by romantic strategies of sympathy or the sublime. There, nature is the abyss or the void and not an agency offering solace or release. Balder's descent from heaven where he was born to "live in light and joy" to hell where he will dwell in darkness and despair is refigured in the Hintocks where a once-heavenly sylvan retreat has become a hellish place of labor and of suffering. This descent is clearly implied in Hardy's naming his Hintocks after Wordsworth's Quantocks. The branches of the Hintock trees rub against each other and bleed like those of Dante's wood of the suicides. The narrator's numerous descriptions of them so doing countermands the harmonious cast which Wordsworth imparted to his Quantock woodlands. Moreover Giles's ghostly figure flitting about the Hintock trees enshrouded in mist casts him as one of the shadowy tribes of Hela's kingdom that issue "from a lake/ On autumn days" (2, 159). Arnold's autumn kingdom names the season of the soul into which Giles is born. Though a brother figure to Balder in Hades, Giles is a little more dead (the comparison is just in this instance since Giles has no potential for resurrection), a little more winter-born than Balder. As autumn's very brother, Giles represents the last efflorescence of sylvan romanticism in Wessex. After his death, Hardy will leave off satirizing first-generation, "druidic" romantics and focus his attention on second-generation, "hellenic" romantic poets and possibilities.

The "Doom" or "Twilight of the Gods" of which Balder's passing is a mighty portent is thematically central to Hardy's allegory too. The gods who are dying in both Hardy's and Arnold's allegories are the founding fathers of the romantic inspiration, Marty's "Teutonic forefathers," one of whom is surely the Lake District yeoman such as he is portrayed in Wordsworth's *Two Letters*. Arnold writes that with Balder gone the wood is "left uncomforted" (3, 122) because the poetic spirit of light and joy has passed from it. Though there are other "Scalds" remaining in the world to sing, none can versify as Balder could. Only he can "strike/ Another note, and like a bird in Spring,/ [His] voice of joyance minded us, [of] youth,/ And wife, and children, and our ancient home" (3, 140–44). These lines remind us of Marty's closing plaint that "no one can plant as [Giles] planted." Her words recall to mind Arnold's claim that no modern poet could cultivate the sensibilities as deeply and substantially as Wordsworth could. Because no one can, the woods have become a dying, twilight place where shadow-bards sing shadow-songs which mime the substantial songs of the romantic spring.

By his very name of "winterborne," Giles is intended to be a spring of romantic grace which has tragically bubbled to life in winter. The climate of his times is hostile to his form of consciousness, and unlike Wordsworth he is not a strong enough presence to overcome the iron time. In this regard, it is worthwhile to consider the relationship between Giles and William Barnes whose Dorset home was in Winterborne Came close by to Max Gate. Barnes was one of Hardy's favorite rural poets and a man credited with getting Wessex on the literary map before Hardy, though this is not how Hardy saw the question of firsts. In 1886 while Hardy was hard at work on The Woodlanders, Barnes died. Hardy interrupted his work to write an obituary for the Athenaeum. In it, he cites Barnes as "probably the most interesting link between present and past forms of rural life that England possessed" (Millgate, Hardy, 275). Like Barnes, Giles is a link between past and present; and his death signals the breaking of that link.

In addition to Arnold's "Balder Dead," Tennyson's Arthuriad is also at play in the construction of the textual character of Giles's fate. In particular, the seventh idyll, "The Holy Grail," is traceable in the outlines of Giles's heroic life in decline. The numerous, obsessive quests by false and failed questers like Gawain, Lancelot, and Percival which Tennyson depicts in his "Holy Grail" find their equivalent figurations in the central "quests" or intrigues of The Woodlanders wherein Giles, a woodland knight, and Fitzpiers, a peer of the realm, contend for Grace in a misty woods haunted by fancies and projections of romantic salvation. Fitzpiers will have his occasional "wench" like Suke Damson, while Giles and his "sister" Marty will retain the virginal character of Tennyson's Percival and his nun-sister. Giles's failed quest after Grace, the illusive grail, replicates Percival's unsuccessful search for the sacred cup of salvation. Giles is romantically shortsighted and usually portrayed as enshrouded in mist; this obscuring of vision by fog is also the most significant ocular metaphor in Tennyson's "Holy Grail" wherein Percival is blinded by illusions and crippled by doubts on an exhausting quest into regions of fog, hallucination, and failure.

In this connection, we might note that Giles's name in manuscript was Ambrose. Ambrosius, we will recall, is the ancient monk in Tennyson's "Holy Grail" (henceforth cited as HG) who is white-haired and well into the winter of his life when Percival meets him. He has "never . . . known the world without" (HG, 20–21) beyond the cloister walls, just as Giles has never ventured beyond the bounds of the Hintocks. When Giles is sent to meet Grace, he appears to her standing beneath his heraldic sign of the apple tree ("He was standing somewhat apart, holding the tree like an ensign" [77]). This scene of recognitions is reminiscent of Percival's first meeting with Ambrosius who sits apart from the monastic community "Beneath a world-old yew tree, darkening half/ The cloisters" (HG, 12–13). The name Ambrosius is retained in Giles's Ambrosial character which is nectarlike in its identification with cider. The scene wherein Giles listens to Fitzpiers's tales of "Grail chasing" or rainbow-casting distinctly refigures Ambrosius's attentive posture toward Percival as he tells of his delusive quests, while the good sense Giles adds to Fitzpiers's willful relativizing of romantic eros is approximate to the stabilizing wisdom that the monastic sanctuary affords a weary Percival, fatigued after a lifetime spent chasing rainbows of grace.

The intertextual structure of Giles's character is further born out by the relationship between the nun, Percival's spiritual sister, and Marty South, who is Giles's spiritual sister. Both Marty and the nun are "holy maids" whose "knees of adoration wore the stone" (HG, 70–71), one in cenobitic penitence, the other in spar-gad cutting and planting pines. From beginning to end, Marty's fate is neatly summed up by Tennyson's lines upon the fate of the nun who "in [her] earlier maidenhood,/ With such a fervent flame of human love,/ Which being rudely blunted, glanced and shot/ Only to holy things; to prayer and praise" (HG, 72–75). Love's "being rudely blunted" compels both maidens to sublimate carnal desire and become heavenly brides by rejecting "the attribute of sex for the loftier quality of abstract humanism." Abstract humanism in both "idylls" is the result of erotic disappointment. Yet while Tennyson casts the nun's sublimation as laudable, Hardy emphasizes the masochistic and self-mutilating aspect of Marty's ritual of loss which is rewarded by no apparition of grace.

Both "The Holy Grail" and *The Woodlanders* begin with an episode of hair cutting. As the prelude to Percival's quest, we learn that his sister "shore away/ Clean from her forehead all the *wealth* of hair/ which made a silken mat-work for her feet" (*HG,* 149–51, emphasis added). Tennyson's qualifying "wealth of hair" is picked up by Hardy and thematized as Marty's "fall" of hair which is a source of wealth for her. Tennyson's nun undergoes a sexual castration to gain a spiritual power and beauty. Hardy translates this ennobling act into Marty's cutting her hair which rapes her beauty and lowers her self-esteem. She loses her knight's respect, she feels, because she is bald, while the nun gains Percival's respect by making manifest her disregard for worldly beauty. In her disregard for feminine beauty, Marty seems almost like Percival's nun-sister, though the narrator informs us at the conclusion that this is only a seeming. Standing over Giles's grave, Marty "looked almost like a being who had rejected with indifference the attributes of sex for the loftier quality of abstract humanism" (438). She looked, that is, almost like Percival's nun-sister, though she is not completely this figure because her isolation and loneliness are self-wrought and punishing, a fate she must endure rather than a spiritual practice she has accepted that will eventually reward her with a vision of grace or the Holy Grail. It is, ironically, just such a vision (of Grace Melbury) which she feels has deprived her life of romantic grace.

Just as Giles represents the naive romantic past, Fitzpiers characterizes the present and future fate of romanticism as an unprincipled rhetoric of desire. The source of his character lies in Pater's "Leonardo da Vinci" to which we must now turn to disclose its textual specifics.

According to Pater's reading in *The Renaissance,* (henceforth cited as *Ren*), Leonardo is the Italian Faust. Thus it is Pater's characterization that connects *The Woodlanders* to *The Mayor of Casterbridge.* Henchard is the Faust of Casterbridge; he is an adulterous and ambitious demon of the void. In the Hintocks, Fitzpiers is an adulterous wizard-doctor who is a figure of the abyss insofar as he represents the divorce between man and nature. Significantly, one of Hardy's working titles for *The Wood-*

landers was "Fitzpiers at Hintocks" which links Fitzpiers's Faustian character to Henchard's at Casterbridge as a central figure of romantic disruption.

In Pater's aesthetic appreciation of the Italian artist-inventor, Leonardo voluntarily rusticates himself in order to seek "a unique, impression of pleasure" because he has grown weary of the courts (*Ren*, viii). Likewise, Fitzpiers voluntarily rusticates himself in the Hintocks where he seeks "rare things . . . amid the commonplace" (182) having grown tired of the city. Pater's Leonardo leads a "life of brilliant sins and exquisite amusements" (*Ren*, 109), as Fitzpiers does in the Hintocks. "Curiosity and the desire for beauty" are the "two elementary forces of Leonardo's genius," Pater tells us (*Ren*, 109), and it is these two characteristics which Fitzpiers shares with him. Pater notes that within Leonardo "curiosity [was] often in conflict with the desire for beauty" but that the conflict was resolved within his character, thus "generating a union" between the two which in turn created "a type of subtle and curious grace" (*Ren*, 109). This conflict between curiosity and desire characterizes Fitzpiers, too. The narrator describes him as "in a distinct degree scientific, being ready to interrogate all physical manifestations" as well as "an idealist . . . believing that behind the imperfect lay the perfect" (182). As a scientist, he is curious about physical and metaphysical phenomena and as an outsider to the Hintocks he is a curiosity to its inhabitants. His ever-errant desire for beauty does not allow him to establish a stable union with his "subtle and curious" Grace Melbury, though he does marry her. As a sign of his Leonardan curiosity, Fitzpiers will buy Grammer Oliver's skeleton and examine Old South's brain tissue under a microscope to see if he can discover the cause of South's woodland fancy, while his desire for beauty is the source of the conflict between Grace, Mrs. Charmond, and Suke Damson. In the narrative, the three women are cast as The Three Graces, one natural (Suke), one artificial or aesthetical (Charmond), and the last a combination of the artificial and the natural (Grace), though she concludes by consigning herself to the unnatural.

Like the Leonardo in Pater's appreciation, Fitzpiers is "a gentleman fond of science and philosophy, poetry, and, in fact, every kind of knowledge" (69) as well as "a dreamer" (182). Moreover, Fitzpiers is a peer of the realm who reads philosophy and quotes from Spinoza and Shelley to justify his irrepressible, narcissistic form of desire which adulterates the high moral and aesthetic desires of the Wordsworthian imagination. His poetic and philosophic reading tends to excite him to immoral and sensational escapades rather than to quell the desire for such in accordance with Wordsworth's ethical imperatives for a socially responsible imaginative literature.

In his essay, Pater notes that "Raphael represents the return to antiquity" while Leonardo represents "the return to nature" (*Ren*, 109). Like Leonardo, Fitzpiers represents a return to nature. He springs from old country stock whose manor house lies in Oakbury Fitzpiers. Thus his coming to the Hintocks represents a return to his roots as well as the return of the eighteenth-century's "Man of Feeling" to the pastoral topography of his origin one century after he had left it for the ethical landscape of English romanticism. In this reading, Fitzpiers becomes a figure of decadence insofar as he is a figure of the preromantic sensibility returned in postromantic times to the site of its own origins and yet failing to find reinvigoration there.

As a visiting woodlander, Fitzpiers is Leonardo-like in that he is a tourist-observer whose capacity for enjoyment and woodland appreciations stems from the established difference between himself and those whom he observes. The point at issue here is that his form of appreciation is contrary to Wordsworth's which depends upon an identification forged by a deep familiarity between perceiver and perceived. Fitzpiers dreads and avoids such familiarity with either the woods, which he finds alternately dreadful or boring, and with the woodlanders, who are objects of curiosity to peek his interest but not individuals who have anything meaningful to say to him, as leech gatherer and woodsman did to Wordsworth. Significantly, after his marriage to Grace, the woodlanders begin to perceive him as a "compeer" of Melbury's, a reclassification which demotes him from the status of a rusticated Paterian "divinity" (237). His new classification as a "genuine" and "familiar" woodlander depresses him and makes him see the error of this ways in marrying Melbury's daughter. Unlike the Wordsworthian who seeks deeper and more encompassing identifications with woods and friends, Fitzpiers's self-esteem demands that he remain aloof and apart from them. He is thus an example of a "pilgrim of fashion" in Wordsworth's designation (*TL*, 354) who does not understand the character of imaginatively sympathetic relationships, which is one reason why he can readily command that South's sacred elm be cut down.

The Descent of the Imagination

Early in the novel, the narrator characterizes Fitzpiers's experiments as like those performed by Pater's Leonardo who "pore[s] over his crucibles, making experiments with color, trying, by a strange variation of the alchemist's dream, to discover the secret" of "the transmutation of ideas into images" (*Ren,* 112). Doctor Fitzpiers is known as "a weird alchemist-surgeon" (92) by the woodlanders, while the quest for the secret of representation is the object of his experiments on Old South's brain tissue. Grace is first made aware of his presence in the Hintocks by a colored light shining in the night, while his own description of love as a "Leyden jar" projection of an electric rainbow (165) recapitulates the tenor of Leonardo's alchemical "experiments with color." Like Pater's Leonardo who "seemed to [others] rather the sorcerer or the magician, possessed of curious secrets and a hidden knowledge, living in a world of which he alone possessed the key" (*Ren,* 107), Fitzpiers is a "projick" to Grammer Oliver who describes him as a man who "says the oddest of rozums" (90). Fitzpiers too lives alone in a solipsistic world to which only he holds the key, and his isolation is a thematically central representation of the abyss of disjunction into which all imaginative correspondences have plunged.

Though he claims that his solipsistic views come by way of Spinoza and Shelley, Fitzpiers's understanding is essentially Paterian insofar as he sees himself as a sensibility imprisoned within a thick wall of self from which he cannot escape. So thick are the walls of his prison that he "talks to himself" as a sign that he is "a dreamer of more advanced age than . . . men of his years" (182). The narrator's description casts Fitzpiers as both advanced and ancient, just as Pater had cast Leonardo whose ideal mate is the Mona Lisa, a woman "older than the rocks among which she sits" (*Ren,* 125) and a figure of cultural completion and fatigue. As a Paterian figure in the woods, Fitzpiers readily acknowledges that "the whole scope of [his] observation is dwarfed into the narrow chamber of the individual mind; [his] experience, already reduced to a series of impressions, is ringed round . . . by that thick wall of personality through which no real voice has ever pierced on its way to us, or from us to that which we can only conjecture to be without" (*Ren,* 235). He understands that his mind is "a solitary prisoner [dreaming] its own dream of a world" (*Ren,* 235). As such, his mental constitution is antithetical to Wordsworth's which desired to see into the life of things and thereby overcome its prison of selfhood.

The Woodlanders: Una Selva Oscura

It is in and through Fitzpiers then that Hardy assesses the fate of an early romanticism which attempted to pierce through the thick wall of self by deploying sympathy and the imagination to redeem the mind from the suppositions of eighteenth-century skeptical philosophies. The strong connecting links of sympathy between man and nature and man and society are either absent or dissolved in the Hintock woods. There, a romanticism which once was thought to hold the key to releasing the human spirit from its subjective prison through woodland identifications and the bonds of natural piety is reduced to a self-aware form of self-centered confinement ironically reveling in an equivalent form of freedom granted by its total alienation from everything and everybody. In Fitzpiers, the egotistical sublime is diminished to the point of appearing as a sublimated form of predaceous egoism.

Although *The Woodlanders* splices together two allegorical critiques, one of Wordsworth's poetic and the other of Pater's aesthetic, the two are related by difference. Otherwise put, they resemble each other by contrast, and it is through contrast that the overall message of the allegory is communicated. If Wordsworth's theme in *The Excursion* is the ethical necessity of understanding, fortitude, and stability, then in *The Woodlanders* Hardy demonstrates that although an awareness of this ethical necessity had arisen in the earlier century, it had been forgotten over time. Despite Wordsworth's efforts to preserve the "sacred oak" (and Fitzpiers's family, the "family" of his sort of romanticism, originates in Oakbury Fitzpiers), and Arnold's mid-century plea that Wordsworth's message not be forgotten, the tree had been felled by art and philosophy, Fitzpiers's two characteristic interests. Moreover, if we remember Wordsworth's complaint in *The Two Letters* concerning the destructive influence of "aesthetic pilgrims," sentimental tourists, and novel-readers in the woodlands (and we see Grace and Charmond read to each other to stave off the boredom of a landscape Wordsworth once found fascinating), then Hardy's motive for linking the two critiques becomes evident. Fitzpiers is an aesthetic doctor or a doctor of aesthetics who can heal none of culture's wounds nor cure any of its ailments in contradistinction to Wordsworth who had been able to heal and cure both. In his allegory then, Hardy depicts Wordsworth's own fears that the romantic impetus would become weakened and eventually fail if given over to the aestheticians of genteel culture for its continuance and support. In this reading, Hardy's novel satirizes a culture of fashionable novel readers, a form of entertainment disproved of by Wordsworth. In this respect, it is interesting to speculate on the possible connection between Hardy's revision of "The Ruined Cottage" and Book Four of *The Excursion* wherein Wordsworth's Sage desires to "recall" from "long banishment" Saint Giles "to watch again with tutelary love" the English and Scottish kingdoms. Such a renaissance would, in the Sage's estimate, be "a blessed restoration to behold" because it would guarantee the spiritual resurrection of a kingdom "Now simply guarded by the sober powers/ Of science, and philosophy, and sense!" (*Ex,* 4:910–18). Hardy in fact inverts the Sage's plea and deprives him of his hope by depicting a world where the powers of science and philosophy and sense represented by Fitzpiers overcome (and outromance) the woodland Sage's St. Giles who returns only to be conquered by the forces of modernism.

Fitzpiers's "rainbow casting" is a complex refiguration of romanticism's "iris" trope. The metaphor is immediately derived from Wordsworth's 1802 lyric "My Heart Leaps Up When I Behold" which expresses the renowned maxim that "the child is father of the man." In Wordsworth's lyric, the "rainbow in the sky" causes the poet's heart to leap up because it is a figure promising the constancy and continuity of heartfelt connections between man and nature and man and his fellow man. In addition, the rainbow promises a renewed joy despite intermittent periods of gloom, boredom, or sorrow. In reading the poem, we learn that the rainbow appeared when the poet was born; it appears again when he is a man, and it will appear once more, he is assured, when he grows old. Like South's tree, the rainbow has its "roots" on the earth and its apex or crown in the sky; it appeared when the poet was born and it will last as long as he does. And like South's tree, it is Wordsworth's rainbow that is destroyed in Fitzpiers's version of it.

Wordsworth's rainbow and the terms of its stabilizing optimism are reiterated in the more canonically central "Immortality Ode." There, it is a "Hebraic" figure which includes within the tropology of its precedents the rainbow which appears to Noah after the Flood. It is a figure of faith and trust despite historical catastrophe as well as an authoritative signature assuring the continuance of transcendental exchanges between man and more than man.

In *The Woodlanders* all of these Wordsworthian hopes and guarantees are denied in and through their authenticating image of the rainbow. Fitzpiers's rainbow represents a passing sensationalism rather than a steady joy, a variability of object rather than a stability of object, and a termination of transcendental accords rather than a continuance of them within one lifetime and between generations. Contrary to all that Wordsworth had established and which Old South feebly tries to sustain, Fitzpiers believes that "Human love is a subjective thing . . . it is a joy accompanied by an idea which we project against any suitable object . . . just as the rainbow iris is projected against an oak, ash, or elm tree indifferently" (165). In his estimate, desire is neither sympathetic nor lasting, but variable and momentary. His rainbow, unlike Wordsworth's, does not teach a mastery of historical circumstances; rather, it demonstrates what "miserable creatures of circumstance are we all" (165) as he readily admits. By the long way round, Fitzpiers revokes the Pedlar's wisdom in "The Ruined Cottage," which is that despite misery we are not miserable creatures, and articulates Hardy's master allegory of modern Wessex which is the triumph of time.

Specifically, Wordsworth's rainbow symbolizes that "days [are] bound each to each by natural piety." Fitzpiers's rainbow implies that any such binding acts are "romantic" in the very sense of the word from which Wordsworth rescued it in his preface to the *Lyrical Ballads*. Wordsworth is assured that when he grows old the rainbow will return. Did it not, he would prefer to die ("Or let me die!"). Figuratively, this is just what Hardy allows him to do in the Hintocks. There the rainbow does not return as the guarantor of a renaissance of romantic faith; rather it returns as a figure of exhaustion and death representing a culture that is specular and harmful and not substantial and therapeutic. In its revised form, the rainbow represents the very evanescence and eventual disappearance of all strong figures of temporal mastery which leave in their wake figures transparently subject to time.

For Fitzpiers, the Hintocks have "no street lamp or lantern to form a kindly transition between the inner glow and the outer dark" (54). In his world there is an inner glow and an outer dark, but never any well-lit avenues of correspondence between the two. In and through Fitzpiers, the pure white light of transcendental inspiration degenerates into the rainbow light of phenomenal confusion such as Shelley figured it in *Adonais*. On one rare occasion, Fitzpiers is overcome by his sense of a woods unilluminated by the kindly light of the imagination which could connect self to world given a modicum of belief. During this blank interval between rainbow castings, his "sightless" view approximates

Old South's when deprived of his elm and with similar results. Desolate and depressed, Fitzpiers declares, "My God! . . . this is life!" (276). His cry is not a question but a statement answering the concluding inquiry in Shelley's epic of romantic defeat, *The Triumph of Life*. We will recall that the decaying, toothless figure of Rousseau in Shelley's poem originally had been Wordsworth and that Shelley's figure of the decaying woods turns out to be the counterfigure to Wordsworth's decaying, but never-to-be-decayed nature in the "Simplon Pass" passage of *The Prelude*, although Shelley had not read Wordsworth's passage. In the Hintocks, Shelley's decaying and degenerating Rousseau-Wordsworth returns *as* the woodlands themselves and as George Melbury, whose body is compared to the broken and contorted limbs of the Hintock woods. Both Melbury and the woods are broken on the wheel of utilitarianism (as Wordsworth said they would be in his *Two Letters*), while woodland labors are neither kindly nor joyous. Because George Melbury is of Old South's generation, he too is a figure of "Georgian" romanticism, a superannuated Wordsworthian yeoman who willingly sells his tree of great power for great profits. As a dealer in timber, he despoils the woodlands, while the profits of his spoilation go toward ruining the "natural" character of his woodland daughter.

We will recall further that in Shelley's *Triumph of Life* the ghost of Rousseau is depicted as a rotting tree root, a decayed Silenus who says, in so many words, that it were better not to be born than to be born into the rainbow realm of hopeless idealisms which can never materialize in history except as insubstantial, transitory, rhetorical fancies. Shelley's tree-stump Rousseau—a complex inversion of so many romantic Igdrasils—is the foundation metaphor of the Hintocks as a sylvan topos antithetical to Wordsworth's Quantocks. Shelley's *Triumph of Life* is directly implicated when the narrator points out that beneath a grove of trees, "were the rotting stumps of those [felled trees] of the group that had been vanquished long ago, rising from their mossy setting like black teeth from green gums" (378). The felled trees relate to South and his heraldic emblem of the elm; the "group that had been vanquished" refers to the visionary company in properly romantic terms, while the "black teeth" and decaying gums refers to Shelley's Rousseau-Wordsworth who speaks of the decay of nature's lyrical voice and the diminishment of the imaginative intent in romantic metaphor. In effect, Wordsworth's gentle breezes have stagnated into a malaria in a woodlands dominated by new types of romantics like Fitzpiers and Charmond and unregenerate types of woodland yeomen like George Melbury who is forced by necessity to cut down his sacred oaks. Fitzpiers describes his rainbow casting in Germanic scientific terms which recall the Germano-philosophies of Wordsworth and Coleridge. For him, desire is like a "Leyden jar" which projects its electric current onto any proximate object. Although the German source of the Leyden jar fancy broadly relates it to the Germanism of first-generation romantics, it specifically relates it to the electrochemical metaphor in Goethe's *Elective Affinities*. Goethe's premise of an immediate and binding sympathy achieved by seeing into another's life is parodied by Fitzpiers's "affinities" with Suke, Grace, and Charmond, while the mechanical character of his figure of affinity recalls Carlyle's despair at the new mechanical forms of "nexus" which were replacing dynamical connections and interests. We might even see Fitzpiers's Leyden jar metaphor as being on a par with Elizabeth-Jane's "microcsope" of desire, since both compare the generator of desire to a scientific apparatus which mechanically amplifies the real.

To these observations on Goethe's influence, we might add that Fitzpiers's choice of Spinoza as his philosophic mentor is derived from Hardy's reading of G. H. Lewes's account of Goethe's impressions of the Jewish philosopher, excerpts from which appear in Hardy's notes, written in Emma Hardy's hand (*LN,* 1:14, 260). Following Lewes's translation of Goethe's views, Hardy has Fitzpiers evince the "boundless disinterestedness which shone forth in every sentence" (*LN,* 1:260) of Spinoza's, only now such disinterestedness "shines forth" as a rainbow and every rainbow represents a negative figuration of Goethe's and Spinoza's noble disinterestedness. It is then Fitzpiers's ignoble disinterestedness (his carelessness) that interests Hardy. In effect, Fitzpiers's rule of comportment selfishly inverts Spinoza's maxim that "he who truly loves God must not require God to love him in return" (quoted from Hardy's *Literary Notebooks,* 1:14). Appropriately in terms of the descent at hand, Fitzpiers justifies his solipsistic engagements by reading Spinoza and Shelley. As a representative of contemporary aesthetic culture, he exemplifies Hardy's consent to Symond's belief that "As now taught, accepted, & carried out, *are not the processes of culture rapidly creating a class of supercilious infidels, who believe in nothing*" (*LN,* 2:40, quotation from Symond's *Essays Speculative and Suggestive,* emphasis Hardy's). Thus it is Spinoza who leads us to Lewes who then leads us back to Goethe, just as Novalis leads us to Goethe and then to Carlyle in *The Mayor of Casterbridge*.

As Fitzpiers explains, "people living insulated, as I do by the solitude of the place, get charged with emotive fluid like a Leyden jar with electric" (165). His chemical figure replaces Keats's "beaker" of romantic inspiration (of the warm South) and thereby continues the figurations of decline from the organic to the mechanical, the mystic to the scientific and empirical. Moreover, his Leyden jar metaphor historicizes and psychologizes the mystic grail. In effect, it cancels the mythic import which the grail held for questing romantics. Rather than see into the life of things or have visions of higher things, Fitzpiers's grail empowers him to see only the life of his desire cast onto things, notably women, which in turn direct him to those sensationalist escapades that Wordsworth so deplored because inspired by "the fickle tastes, and fickle appetites, of [one's] own creation" ("Preface to Second edition of the *Lyrical Ballads*" [1800], 447). As he readily admits, he is always "in love with something in [his] own head, and no thing-in-itself outside it at all" (165). His admission denies any privileged power or position to the imagination, while the random casting of his "electric" desires parodies the free play of the imagination recommended in Schiller's *Aesthetic Education* and echoed by Coleridge in his *Biographia Literaria*. In his figure of the Leyden jar, the willed cultural mandate to sympathize in order to bridge the abyss of vacancy has degenerated into a willful attitude of narcissistic detachment which emphasizes rather than reduces the abyss between representation and the thing signified.

Hardy's critique in this instance contradicts Coleridge's of Wordsworth in *Biographia Literaria*. There, Coleridge claims that contrary to Wordsworth's assertion that the rural life of independence is all that is really necessary for the development of the great soul, such soul making requires "Education, or original sensibility," or both "if the changes, forms, and incidents of nature are to prove a sufficient stimulant" (2:17). Where one or the other is not present or sufficient, "the mind contracts and hardens by want of stimulants; and the man becomes selfish, sensual, gross, and hard-headed." Thus if education does not act in concert with sensibility, rustic life will be as a picture "to the blind, and music to the deaf" (2:17). In Fitzpiers, Hardy presents us with a portrait of a man for whom nature is just such an unseen picture despite his education. Thus the woodlands are not picturesque to Fitzpiers nor can they educate him to hear their music. The "features" of the woodland "were not familiar to [him]," thus he grows "weary" because they are relentlessly gloomy (174). Though educated and an avowed man of sentiment, Fitzpiers becomes self-centered and sensual in a woods whose gentle breezes do not soften his grossness. In overall effect, Hardy affirms Wordsworth's emphasis on the need for a natural sensibility over Coleridge's emphasis on education, only to darken his affirmation by depicting the disappearance of the last genuine Wordsworthian type, Giles Winterborne. Romantic salvation therefore is just not possible in the Hintocks where education is no substitute for the "tree-grower" Giles, the Wordsworthian yeoman of Hardy's text (Giles "had a marvelous power of making trees grow" [105]).

Though Fitzpiers first casts his rainbow of desire onto Suke Damson, and then engages in a ribald adventure with her which covertly retells Wordsworth's erotic escapade in "Nutting" (Suke's escapades focus upon nutting incidents too), his consort of great value is Felice Charmond. In casting about for a suitable Helen for his Paterian Faust, Hardy had to look no further than Pater's essay on "da Vinci," the source text of Fitzpiers's alchemical character. Felice Charmond is modeled upon La Gioconda who represents for Leonardo the union of art and life, transcendence and time, and the ideal and the real, at least in Pater's account. Charmond comes to represent something like this for Fitzpiers. He would gladly forgo his marriage with Grace in order to possess Charmond; she is his first love and is thus the prototype of all his loves, his model and ideal of woman, his Shelleyan one shape of many names, as he tells her. She is "spiritually" at one with him because she too is an aesthete, and she is his "flesh of the world" (Char-mond) in whom he takes great pleasure (Felice) as her name implies.

Before they arrive in the Hintocks, Fitzpiers and Charmond had met on the Continent, significantly "beside the waters" at a watering spa. He is young and she is older, which gives a certain Paterian flavor to the relationship between artist-aesthete and the older, experienced woman. They are separated for many years and then reunited in the Hintocks where he tells her that she had been the subject of his youthful dreams and the woman he has been searching for all of his life. Her real, imaginary, and then real appearance in Fitzpiers's life is patterned upon Pater's critical interpretation of La Gioconda's role in Leonardo's destiny

The Descent of the Imagination

as the woman of his dreams who, one day, appeared in the flesh as a merchant's wife. Although La Gioconda and Leonardo had "grown up apart," the two had remained "so closely together" that their first meeting seemed like a renewal of their acquaintance (*Ren,* 124). This is precisely the manner in which Hardy casts the reunion of Fitzpiers and Charmond. Like Lady Lisa, Felice is a merchant's wife, and she repeatedly returns to Italy and France. Both countries bear traces of her textual past, for Leonardo worked in Italy and died in France. Moreover, Felice's beauty is artificial and artful; while her need to cosmetically veil her aging beauty is the source of Marty's suffering. Marty has Charmond's rare-colored hair, hence Percomb is sent to cut it and comb it into a fall. Marty's natural beauty is "deflowered" in order to reflower Charmond's withering splendor. Like Leonardo's La Gioconda, Charmond's beauty is produced by artificial means while she needs to remain in an artificially darkened room in order to protect her beauty from the natural light of day.

Because culturally and sexually experienced, the narrator describes Charmond as a woman who "might have been taken for the typical *femme de trente ans*" (289), especially when "she looked her full age and more" early in the morning (289). As a figure of Pater's Lady Lisa, Charmond exhibits the weariness of a beauty "into which the soul with all its maladies has passed" (*Ren,* 125). Her artificial youth recapitulates and parodies Pater's view that Lady Lisa embodies "the fancy of perpetual life, sweeping together ten thousand experiences" (*Ren,* 125). Because experienced, Charmond "sums up" all "modes of thought and life" as does Pater's Lady Lisa. She is a woman of many consummations who is for Fitzpiers the "embodiment of the old fancy, [as well as] the symbol of the modern idea" (*Ren,* 125–26) because she is his old flame as well as his modern love.

Charmond doctors her appearance and thereby attracts the aesthetic doctor. In Pater's account, Leonardo used "artificial means" to protract "that subtle expression on the face" (*Ren,* 124) which was half life and half art. Like Pater's Lady Lisa, Charmond contains in her soul "thoughts and experiences of the world" which "have etched and molded" her into a figure of "Dürer's Melancholia" (*Ren,* 125). She is presented in the narrative as a world-weary figure who feels that she is too "deadly" a consort for the young doctor. The lethal character of Pater's Lady Lisa is exemplified in the "man traps" which hang from the walls of Hintock

House. A mantrap herself, Charmond is "the lady of the rocks" who tempts mariners to stray toward their own destruction, as Fitzpiers, her Leonardo, does. In this regard, we might note that the narrator describes these mantraps as "automatic machines" which produce "sound artistic torture" (421).

Traces of Felice's literary ancestor's portrait appear in her "almond eyes" which the narrator tells us are reminiscent of "those long eyes so common to the angelic legions of early Italian art" (101). Pater's Lady Lisa's "eyelids are a little weary," a weariness which becomes centrally significant in Hardy's characterization of Charmond. Her very name "Felice" finds its textual origin in Pater's essay wherein he imagines a very bored, imprisoned Lodovico Sforza scribbling over and over again on the walls of his cell the motto *Infelix Sum* "in a wistful after-dreaming over Leonardo's sundry experiments" (*Ren*, 122). Lodovico's unhappiness defines Fitzpiers's and Felice's discontent in the woodlands; both feel that they will go "melancholy mad" (*The Woodlanders*, 90) if they are not either dreaming upon some colorful experiment or planning to escape their Hintock prison.

Significantly, the narrator's opening portrait of Felice defines her most important feature, her smile. Felice, we are told, is one of those "women who lingeringly smile their meanings to men rather than speak them, who inveigle rather than prompt, and take advantage of comments rather than steer" (101). The communicative smile, the indirection of activity, the melancholy, and her sense of drifting upon life's currents compactly represent the essential characteristics of Pater's imaginary portrait of Mona Lisa.

Appropriately, the woman who stands between Leonardo and his Lady Lisa is partly Paterian and partly Wordsworthian, while she exemplifies the debate between Wordsworth and Coleridge upon the merits of education in the development of the romantic sensibility. Grace Melbury's character is the convergence point of the novel's double critique. She is a woodlander who once possessed a woodlander's sensibility, and she is a refined appreciator of culture. Her education constitutes the tragic agency in a narrative which could be subtitled "The Education of Grace." In allegory, her character recapitulates the scene of strife between Wordsworthian forms of romanticism that are dying and Paterian forms that are rising in their stead. Thus, her character —the character of Grace—is implicitly a reading of nineteenth-century culture.

The Descent of the Imagination

Grace's return to the Hintocks signals the return of romantic grace to the woodlands which, in Coleridge's estimate, should begin a period of romantic restoration. She possesses all the characteristics necessary for a renaissance of romanticism: independence, sensibility, communal ties, a familiarity with the woods, and education. If she had married the indwelling and indigenous romantic "knight" Giles Winterborne as Grammer Oliver thinks she should, together they would reconstitute the romantic pair along lines approved of by Wordsworth and Coleridge. Because she was raised in the country and educated in the city, she possesses the unique capability to bridge both worlds, thereby marrying past to present. The failure of this marriage to occur either personally within Grace or interpersonally between Grace and Giles constitutes the theme of divorce in *The Woodlanders,* a theme which extends its perimeters to encompass the adulteration of all manner of romantic graces and all forms of socio-cultural redemption fostered by the union of past and present, tradition and imaginative modifications of tradition. Here, as in *The Mayor of Casterbridge,* her mistaking of desire rescinds all that Wordsworth had attempted to marry in his prospectus to *The Excursion.*

Grace's name bears witness to two textual sources. She is a weak revision of Wordsworth's Grace in Wordsworth's mini-epic of romantic heroism *Grace Darling* (1843; henceforth cited as *GD*), and she is a Paterian "Christ" or grace figure in Leonardo's painting of *The Last Supper.* Thus, we find the textual origin of her conflict in Pater's "Leonardo" essay, as was the case for Fitzpiers and Charmond.

The horse which Winterborne purchases for Grace is named Darling. Grace's Darling is later given to Fitzpiers, who jades it on his adulterous rural rides in pursuit of his well-beloved, Felice Charmond. Grace's Darling then points to Wordsworth's epic, *Grace Darling;* the one is an epic of fidelity to romantic values, the other, a tale of infidelity to them. In Wordsworth's poem, Grace and her father comprise the heroic pair; Grace spurs her father on to rescue men drowning at sea on a stormy night. Wordsworth's Grace is a figure of hope to those overcome by waves of despair, while her sea rescue grows in significance if we recall Wordsworth's "Peel Castle" and his deep grief over the death of his brother Jonathan just when he seemed within reach of rescue. Unlike Grace Darling who urges her father to risk life and limb to rescue those who seemed lost, Grace Melbury is dominated by her father's will, while her education makes her indecisive in matters of love, honor, and courage. Her father demands that she become and remain a "lady" despite her occasional desire to become Grace of the Hintocks once more. Her father sees her as a piece of property and an investment in the future by way of elevating his class status. Primarily though, she is intended to redeem him from a past humiliation owing to his lack of education. Rather than a romantic past redeeming an unromantic present (the usual line of argument), in Grace we see the aesthetic present damning the romantic past. This inversion is forcefully brought home when Giles is "drowning" outside his woodsman's hut and Grace will not lift a finger to save him. In terms of the critique at hand, her refined sensibility fails to come to the rescue of the drowning woodlander.

Hardy's Grace is her father's darling in so far as she rescues him from the humiliation he suffered when young. Moreover, she is a class fetish, an object subject to her father's misguided cultural fancies. She is not strong enough to act heroically even when that action would only mean her insisting that her father keep faith with Giles and allow him to marry her. In effect, her education at finishing school renders her a "tourist of fashion" in her own country, one cut off from her romantic past. Rather than engage her woodland aspect once more, she prefers to cultivate Charmond's company, while it is "the possibilities of a refined and cultivated inner life, of subtle psychological intercourse" (216) with Fitzpiers which charms her and compels her to yield to his influence rather than to Giles's.

Like Wordsworth's Grace Darling, Grace Melbury is "pious and pure, [and] modest" (GD, 94), but to a fault, for it is her overly refined sense of reputation that prevents her from saving Giles. Though both Graces are characterized as "meek," only Hardy's is meek and irresolute. In contradistinction to Wordsworth's Grace who "though young [is] so wise, though meek so resolute (GD, 95), Grace Melbury's indecision is a major source of suspense and tragedy in the narrative. Her indecision is the immediate result of her education which divides her energies. Thus, Hardy's Grace has little for which to thank her father. In this way Hardy revises Wordsworth's plea that we "praise the parental love,/ Beneath whose watchful eye the Maiden grew" (GD, 93). Grace Melbury has little to praise her father for, nor is her father's cultivating hand cast as anything other than one more misguided "tree felling" in the Hintocks. In the end, her father's educational blessing curses Giles, the man whose bed his "improved" daughter had been intended to grace, while it damns his daughter to a lifelong marriage of sorrow with the adulterous Fitzpiers.

Wordsworth's Grace practices "natural piety" while Hardy's Grace is well practiced in the affects of culture. We must remember that it is not so much the monetary aspect of her degradation that is the focus of the narrator's attention, but the cultural. We are explicitly told that she does not desire to marry Fitzpiers because she is ambitious in a worldly sense, but because she is an aesthete who requires a life of aesthetic "lubrications" (102). And it is "this rather than any vulgar idea of marrying well which caused her to float with the current and to yield to the immense influence" of the aesthetic figures in the Hintocks (216). Her face "shines like the face of Moses when he came down from the Mount" (109) after she visits Charmond who receives her at noon in a darkened, red-lit room emblematic of her aesthetic condition and Paterian taste. The Hebraic character of the description possesses an increased critical thrust if we compare it to any of Wordsworth's scenes of prophecy and law-giving in, say, *The Prelude,* while Grace's discussion with Charmond concerning the possibility of her writing a new *Sentimental Journey* invokes Wordsworth's criticism concerning sentimental tourists and pilgrims of fashion in the woodlands.

Because she is characterized as a half-caste suspended between her Wordsworthian past and her Paterian present, Grace appears to fade, waver, and become nearly invisible in the Hintocks. Her partial invisibility results from her being suspended between two cultural positions, the natural and the aesthetic, or "stories" in the narrator's metaphor. His metaphor implies both the architecture of society as well as the differences between two classes of cultural discourse. Caught between two discourses, she is a "conjectural creature who had little to do with the outlines presented to Sherton eyes" because she lives an inward life of reflection, while she is also "a shape in the gloom, whose true quality could only be approximated by putting together a movement now and a glance then" (79). In essence, she is an ambivalent and indeterminate presence wavering between a familiarity with the woodlands and an aesthetic alienation from them.

Both Paterian and Wordsworthian discursive domains compete for possession of her character. Eventually, she will swerve away from her romantic "story" and toward a Paterian future with her decadent husband of little faithfulness. Yet while she remains in the Hintocks, she is often compelled to idealize Giles during her "excursions of the imagination" (261) into the woods while recalling her childhood there. These Wordsworthian excursions occur when her refined present is repressed and her rural past is recollected in tranquility. Then, Giles becomes "autumn's very brother" to her. Yet when the other discourse gets the upper hand, she conjures up visions of "a broad lawn in the fashionable suburb of a fast city, the evergreen leaves shining in the evening sun amid which bounding girls, *gracefully clad in artistic arrangements* of blue, brown, red, and white, were playing at games" (83, emphasis added). This is her Paterian aspect which desires well-composed arrangements of fancy (the figure is of a dance) rather than excursions of the imagination and all the heartfelt values such excursions brought with them.

Her double aspect and the direction in which she is finally compelled to go are not without their allegorical implications. Grace's two aspects create of her a figure of cultural history wherein the romantic past lingers on for a while and then disappears into the aesthetic present. Her marriage to the unstable Fitzpiers is a sign in the text of the failure of an aesthetic romanticism to provide a continuous and steady way of reading reality, one which could harmonize its recent past of assertion with the emergent present of suspicion and so forge a coherent tradition.

In this representation, she is a direct descendant of Pater's brief, poetical portrait of the fading face of Christ in da Vinci's *The Last Supper*. The narrator provides us a clue to this source when he notes that Giles's supper was laid out "on a snowy cloth fresh from the press, and reticulated with folds as in Flemish Last-Suppers" (118). Though the Dutch painting motif recalls a rural realism which Wordsworth would appreciate, the specifics of the description allude to art and in particular to Renaissance renditions of the *Ultima Cena*. Pater describes Leonardo's portrait of "Grace" or Christ as "but finished or unfinished" (*Ren, 120*). The incompleteness of the portrait is mirrored in Grace's unfinished, finished character. She is finished because a graduate of a finishing school and she represents the finishing of the romantic tradition in so far as her two aspects combine to produce that Paterian "type of grace" which Leonardo produced by fusing curiosity with beauty (she is first attracted to Fitzpiers out of curiosity). She is unfinished because indeterminate and ambivalent, caught between two worlds. Her indeterminacy portrays a culture caught between a nostalgia for tradition and a desire for cultural advancement. In her unfinished or unresolved condition, she cannot marry past with present, thus the possibilities for continuity fade and disappear in and through her. That is, the romantic face of Grace presiding over the communal feast (and we see the precariousness of her position at Giles's Christmas feast) will fade and disappear as her aesthetic aspect gradually comes to dominate her character after which she will leave the woodlands for "the fashionable suburbs of a fast city" (83).

Like the fading face of Leonardo's Christ in Pater's essay, Grace's character "does but consummate the sentiment of the whole company" (*Ren,* 120). As a former Wordsworthian character become a refined Paterian, "the shape of Grace" (433) measures the ratio of permutation and decay which has altered a woodland romanticism promising stability and renewal. Thus, her face is a composite depiction of the fate of the visionary company, the discipleship at issue in Pater's quotation.

Distanced by forty years from the heroic exploits of Wordsworth's Grace Darling, Grace Melbury represents "but the faintest, the most spectral" (*Ren,* 120) face or aspect of a sentiment and a program that once possessed the woods entirely. She is the derivative, belated Christ of the woodlands whose aspect, like that of Leonardo's Christ, is as "faint as a shadow of leaves upon the wall on autumn afternoons" (*Ren,* 120). Read in relation to Pater's autumnal figure, she is "Autumn's very sister," the aesthetic counterpart to Giles's form of rural romanticism. As the narrative progresses, Giles passes and Grace fades and then disappears, thus are the woodlands returned to the abyss of sentiment and science where Wordsworth had found them in the late eighteenth century.

This return has a marked effect on the narrator's language toward the end of his fable. In his allegory about contending cultural positions, the narrator ultimately establishes his distance from the strife through tautology, a logical form which relates nothing to nothing because it has no related parts. Thus, his language arrives at a condition where it is without either aesthetic capability or the natural grace of a communicative act, the plain speaking of everyday men. In effect, his language is not the exponent of either plain speaking or high thinking, but the baffled expression of a chronicler of baffling times. Toward the end of his tale, when he has made his case about the contest of aesthetic and Wordsworthian romanticisms, the narrator describes moss thus: moss is "like little fir-trees, like plush, like malachite stars; like nothing on earth except moss" (378). If we recall the grand amplifications of Wordsworth's alpine recollections of a pine forest which decays never to be decayed and so constitutes an emblem of the great apocalypse of the Imagination and then place that pine forest next to Hardy's "little fir-trees," we begin to get a sense of the reduction that is at issue. In the Hintocks, moss is an emblem and a figure of an apocalypse of another sort, one contrary to both Wordsworth's and Pater's sense of poetic language. In the narrator's figure, both metaphysical and aesthetic possibilities decay and disappear. Former natural images endowed with remarkable connotations of correspondence are reduced, first, to an empirically denotative register and then reduced even further to a particularity of object and reference which confounds the simplest desire for communication. Seen in the light of romantic aggrandizements of nature, the narrator's tautology bears witness to the decay of all manner of woodland figures. The figure that does remain is barren of aesthetic pleasure—metonyms have been discarded as useless—and hostile to all possibilities for significant redescription. Moss is simply like moss.

The narrator's tautology then negates the most prevalent form of metaphoric intent in the romantic image which is to name being as presence. When successfully executed by the poet, the natural object named is "not a combination of two entities or experiences more or less linked together, but one single and particular experience: that of origination" (de Man, *Rhetoric of Romanticism*, 4). Remarkably, this possibility for being or presence enacted through language is mimed and mocked in the narrator's bald declaration that "moss is like moss." In effect, the romantic metaphor, once a vehicle for the highest of existential possibilities, is reduced to its barest and most absurd form, one without resonance or consolation yet one which retains its former function in a gesture of self-mockery and defeat. This tautology of frustrated romantic intent implies that Wordsworthian metaphorics have passed away, that Shelleyan metonymics are but fanciful substitutes for Wordsworth's poetic assurance, that a sinuous Paterian style is but an embellishment on an empty theme, and that even the base literalism of empirical description ultimately leads to an abyss of insignificance. In his attempt to describe moss, the narrator despoils all registers of language and imagination from the philosophical-metaphysical to the empirical-physical. By so doing, he tersely recapitulates the most prevalent forms of frustration and failure to which the romantic metaphor had been subject throughout the course of the nineteenth-century. The upshot of his brief act of total negation is that all acts of written communication are understood to be metaphorical and to involve a leap of faith, from Coleridge's linking of the grand "I AM" to an infinite number of particular "i ams" to the barest scientific description. And in the absence of such a poetic faith and its leap, language is inadequate to the task of describing even so small and simple a thing as moss let alone so grand and important a thing as the human condition.

Contrary to the most prevalent intent within romantic writing, in and through the narrator's tautology we are pointed to the abyss—to the brute dumbness of things in themselves in which no language game is or can be competently at play. In the diminished figure of "little fir-trees," language falls to the bottom of a scale upon which earlier romantics had once led it upward from the empirical particular to the metaphysically transcendent. And it is by this return to the abyss that the narrator articulates his position of skeptical withdraw—his willingness not to believe—from those discourses he interrogates, be they Wordsworthian or Paterian, woodland or aesthetic forms of romanticism. Moreover, the narrator's tautology condemns all connotative entailments within language to wishful thinking. His leveling tautology renders even the simplest of correspondences subject to disbelief, while natural description becomes an insurmountable task. Thus does the felling of the Wordsworthian tree of power by which I began my interrogation of Wessex romanticism finally appear as a figure for the collapse of poetic language, or what amounts to the same thing, the primary intent of literary culture in the nineteenth century. By tracing the various forms of romantic cultural decline in the Hintocks, we have arrived at the root of the problem: language itself. Thus it is not an aged and despairing Rousseau who represents decay and failure for Hardy, as he did for Shelley, but a narrator who cannot adequately narrate because the world is without the simplest form of faith, the faith that sign relates to reference.

By way of conclusion, I would like to compare one felled tree more with Wordsworth's four-line anecdote upon a northern woodlander in his *Two Letters*. Failing to find a suitable quotation to announce the concerns of *The Woodlanders*, Hardy wrote these parodic Elizabethan lines: "Nor boskiest bow'r/ When hearts are ill affin'd/ Hath tree of pow'r/ To shelter from the wind" (38). Hardy's brief parody all but states that the once-protective woodlands lack the capacity to reromanticize a culture set against itself. In the Hintocks, there is neither aid nor succor for an aging and fantastic woodland culture. Nature is impotent as either nurse or mother, nor can contemporary figures of culture do anything to revive its potential. Read with an ear toward note-catching, Hardy's arboreal epigraph critically revises the concerns and outcome of Wordsworth's *The Excursion* with particular reference to "The Ruined Cottage." Hardy's novel begins in poetry (the epigraph is a poem), continues as a critical supplement to Book First of *The Excursion,* and ends where poetry is no longer possible, with the tautology that moss is moss. Unless hearts first are affined, the emblem reads, the "tree of power" or nature can do nothing to foster bliss, here cast as marriage in the epithalamic phrase of a "boskiest bow'r." The phrase reflects back to the grand claims for cosmic marriages of all kinds in Wordsworth's Prospectus to *The Excursion,* and it is important that we read Hardy's epigraph to *The Woodlanders* as a terse, critical revision of Wordsworth's Prospectus. In this way, the undoing of the stable and enduring relationships between man and man, man and community, and man and nature thematically central to *The Excursion* becomes the central theme of *The Woodlanders.* And it is in this way—or by reading in this contextual manner—that Hardy's novel becomes the last book of Wordsworth's *The Excursion* or the last excursion of the Wordsworthian imagination.

Thus contrary to Arnold's advice in his "Memorial Verses" dedicated to the passing of Wordsworth, that "the end is everywhere/ Art still has truth, take refuge there," Hardy could make no such recommendation. Art is not a refuge, we have seen, but a source of instability insofar as it describes rather than contains the rising tide of confusion. The Hintocks are not a haven for aesthete or nature worshiper; there the cultural elite pine away for the city while the noble woodlander loses his bid for the continuance of his hold on life. Thus the end or abyss whose arrival Arnold felt Wordsworth had forestalled for a generation becomes apparent in a woods where the "Imagination could trace amid the trunks and boughs . . . funereal figures," which mutely project an allegory of its own imminent demise (193).

PART TWO

HELLENIC SATIRES

[3]

Tess of the d'Urbervilles:
Creativity at a Loss for Words

Words are the spirit.
    J. A. Symonds, *Essays Speculative and Suggestive*

The world is only a cerebral phenomenon.
    Leopardi, quoted from Hardy's *Literary Notebooks*

Primal alienation occurs when a text permits of no saving options.
    J. Lacan, *Four Fundamental Concepts*

"ART IS ONE of the conditions of man's realization of himself, and in its turn one of the realities of man," concludes Christopher Caudwell in his *Illusion and Reality* (239), a meditation upon culture and society. His conclusion provides us with a favorable introduction to the fundamental issue of Hardy's *Tess of the d'Urbervilles*, which certainly acknowledges art to be an essential condition of man's reality but does not acknowledge that currently it is one whereby men and women realize themselves, though ideally it should be. It is the unideal, fallen, and historical character of romantic art which is centrally at issue in *Tess*, wherein the many forms of romanticism constitute the tragic agency in Hardy's allegory of beauty.

In Tess's Wessex, Hebraic and Hellenic forms of romanticism no longer possess the imaginative power to unite with intellectual beauty and overcome historical forms of selfhood.[1] Romantic revolt of any sort can no longer overcome the status quo because it has been absorbed into the status quo. As an institutional discourse, culture legitimizes the powers that be rather than promotes liberation from them as it once did. Given this condition, culture inhibits the lyrical spirit of self-realization rather than encourages its productive transgressions. In *Tess*, Hardy will

163

push this and other related reflections "to their logical conclusions," as did Gide in *The Immoralist,* and demonstrate that "culture, born of life" had become "the destroyer of life" because an agent of prescription rather than release.

In *Essays Speculative and Suggestive,* John Addington Symonds wrote *"Literature.* the best poetry is that which reproduces the most of life, or its intensest moments" (*Essays,* 145; abridgment and emphasis Hardy's, *LN,* 2:34).[2] Did we agree with this definition, as Hardy did, then we would agree further that the worst poetry would be that which reproduces or fosters the reproduction of a minimum of life and tamps its most intense, lyrical moments. Such a poetry would arise, in Symonds's estimate, when the figures of an exhausted poetic regime are "brought back . . . when no longer believed in . . . [thus they reappear] as mere . . . artistic artifice . . . Fettering restrictions on creative fancy" (Hardy's citation of Symonds, *LN,* 2:41).

Hardy copied the phrase into his literary notebooks perhaps because it defined the cultural problem in *Tess.* Because words are the spirit, the spirit is thoroughly colonized by language, thus self-expression is implicitly a derivative, parodic, and theatrical manner of articulation for novelist, narrator, and character alike. Tess cannot achieve the character of beauty she desires because she is imprisoned in forms of beauty which do not express the life of beauty she feels, nor can she marry with a significantly strong imaginative spirit who could help her to free herself from language because such strong poets do not exist in her Wessex. Instead of helping her to attain the lyrical release she seeks, that timely utterance that frees the self from the prison house of language, Alec and then Angel dominate Tess with specific forms of beauty which misname her and so misshape her destiny.[3] Each "poet" figure forces Tess to conform to his notion of beauty and truth. Together, poet and "beauty" enact a drama about cultural dominance which Hardy casts as seduction and rape.

Tess is a victim as most writers on the subject would agree, but she is also a figure of beauty in an allegory about the status of beauty in late-romantic Britain. Thus, her life is a fable of art; her tragedy, a drama about repetition and inauthenticity. In leaving behind Wordsworth (a critique of "nature's holy plan" occurs only twice in the narrative) after completing *The Woodlanders,* Hardy began to write satires predicated upon the notions of second-generation romantics in order to complete

Tess of the d'Urbervilles: Creativity at a Loss for Words

his master narrative of Wessex which was to include all early forms of romantic discourse, those written from, roughly, 1800 to 1830 when *The Mayor of Casterbridge* opens. He completes his survey by focusing upon Keats and Shelley in *Tess*, where the emphasis is on Keats, and Shelley in *Jude the Obscure*, which is a retelling of Shelley's *Alastor*. Characters such as Alec and Angel are predicated upon the Byronic and angelic views of Shelley Hardy found in Dowden's *Life of Shelley* and Arnold's essay "Shelley." As interpretations of Shelleyan romanticism, these texts have as central a role to play in the shaping of *Tess* as did Carlyle's prose and Wordsworth's poetry in the shaping of *The Mayor of Casterbridge* and *The Woodlanders*, respectively.

The most prevalent cultural problem in Tess's Wessex is that what had once been liberating, even exhilarating, possibilities have become fanciful postures which complement (and do not critique) the prevailing social mores. Given this narrow and self-limiting cultural climate, beautiful words speak seductive possibilities which always turn out to be empty promises. And it is the empty promise of the romantic word which harms "beauty" or Tess. Another way of putting this is to say that Wessex is circumscribed by cultural narratives which have lost their lyrical capacity for self-expression. Wessex ballads do not lend themselves to lyrical moments of release because the romantic symbol has fallen into allegory. Romantic desire thus parodies itself within reproductions which tragically invert its original intent for authentic self-presence. Tess and her poet–lovers fail to rediscover the original truth of beauty for their moment in time. Instead, each poet–lover subjects her to his misunderstanding of beauty. And it is within their misunderstanding that she must define herself. Beneath all the fanciful impositions which are placed upon her, there arises a cry for difference within sameness. This desired difference could be created by a metaphorics of self that is intent upon shattering the orthodoxies of the ego. Such a shattering would intensify selfhood to the point where it could achieve an authentic purchase upon identity by exceeding the constraints of that name which had been imposed upon it in the name of another's desire.

Because creativity is always at a loss *for* words, identity cannot speak itself in Wessex. Self-expression is the absent character in Tess's story, the character which she longs for and yet lacks. On a more literary historical level, Hardy's novel searches for the poetry of genuine presence within a fallen realm of texts. The specifically cultural character of her quest becomes clearer when we examine the complex intertext which informs the novel.

In the version of *Tess* (henceforth cited as *T*) which appears in the *National Observer*, Tess herself has no name, though Alec refers to her as "my beauty" and "my Big Beauty." Throughout the tale, she is simply referred to as Beauty (*T*, "variants," 502). Far from being nameless (an observation which can only be made in lieu of her having been named "Tess" at a later date in another version), Beauty *is* her name in the *National Observer* version because beauty is the central concern of the allegory. Moreover, her namelessness names both the problem and the solution to Beauty's tragedy. Beauty must always be "nameless" in order that each generation of poets may name it and in so doing define it for the present, yet if that current beauty goes nameless or misnamed, then the present is without an authentic cultural voice.

Naming is of course the Adamic function in poetry from the Bible to Milton. The Adamic function is particularly important to a romantic poetry which sought to name all things anew for a novel or postrevolutionary age which was characterized initially as Edenic. And it is this Adamic function which is at issue and at risk in *Tess*. The narrative draws heavily on Milton's *Paradise Lost* and its Edenic scenes of naming, as well as on Keats's "Dream of Adam" to express its metaphoric concerns about naming and desire, or the desire to name one's desire rather than be named by another's desire. Rather than name "her-self," Tess is condemned to be named by others. Those two others are, in the main, Alec and Angel. They are the two Adams who name their Eve and so make her their "creature" in the biblical sense of wife-creation and in the derogatory sense of whore-possession. Tess's fate is to always be created by the word of some other. Naming is thus the tragic agency of the novel because naming is the manner in which she is "manned" by culture. In all instances of such naming, the designated person is rendered powerless, unmanned. Paradoxically, to be named in Tess's Wessex is to lose one's authentic name as well as one's capability for discovering it. Unlike the perfect and absolutely authoritative naming acts in Milton's Eden, Wordsworth's woodlands, and in Keats's "Dream of Adam" scenario, to be named in Wessex is to want a name, and it is this craving for originality and presence which gnaws at Tess's life as well as at the life of the narrative. Indeed, both are called "Tess of the d'Urbervilles" for this reason.

Tess of the d'Urbervilles: Creativity at a Loss for Words

We will recall in this matter of names that in the epigraph to the novel Hardy promises to shelter Tess's "poor wounded name," thus marrying author to subject is a space marginal to the text. There, beyond a narrative about narrative confinements, the author's "bosom" shall be "as a bed" to Beauty (*T*, 31). In this marginal space, the author desires to do what did not occur in the narrative, marry beauty to self-expression and so recreate an original poetry of presence. Yet what he seeks to do for Tess in the margins he cannot do for her in the text. His inability suggests further that he cannot do it for himself either, that, in effect, we read a narrative about the desire for originality written by an author who desires such for himself. What he wants for Tess, he wants for himself too as an author, a wanting or lack which he replicates in the narrative and which is announced in the epigraph, which is on loan from Shakespeare's *Two Gentlemen of Verona*. What the secondary character of the epigraph implies is that the narrator-author is able to shelter Tess's wounded name in the margins of culture, but he is not able to cure and restore the name of beauty to culture.

We will recall that in *The Woodlanders*, Hardy wrote his own epigraph. Here, he borrows one from the approved canon of literary texts. Thus the marginal space of putative liberation (purity) recalls the terms of Tess's imprisonment by "two gentlemen" figures of culture and cash who, in turn, compel us to consider the tragic possibilities that might arise when romance and the flesh intermingle and contracts are guaranteed on and by the body.

Tess then is Hardy's Big Beauty as well as Alec's and Angel's. The burden of literary history and repetition from which the author would shelter's Tess's "wounded" or seduced name, he himself cannot find shelter from. Their names are mutually wounded in various ways, while the self-expression he wants for her, he also wants for himself. He, the author, is as genuinely dispossessed of culture as is Tess. Both seek an identity, yet both attain no more than character. Hardy's identification with Tess's *wounded name* in the margins of the narrative is his acknowledgement that he *understands* her problem in ways which contemporary culture does not. In understanding his subject—here construed as Tess and authorship—he gains an equivalent form of freedom to that expressed in the greater romantic lyric. That is, by representing his inability to find an authentic voice, he voices something authentic. In understanding Tess who is Big Beauty, he understands the problematic of cultural exhaustion without really seeing how he can solve it. He can trace it on the pure white pages of his manuscript by demonstrating how it is traced on Tess's feminine tissue, but he cannot free her from the impositions of culture because he cannot free himself from such. His pages, like Tess's feminine tissue, are passive; they, like her, reproduce texts rather than produce them, and the act of reproduction is tragically destructive to identity.

Thus, the very method of representing Tess's tragedy is succinctly set forth in the epigraph, which wistfully desires the return of the pure lyrical intent in romantic metaphor. In terms of immediate cultural history, we have a portrayal of Wordsworth's sense of a Hellenic imagination in search of the Hebraic or lyrical imagination, the one imposing the bondage of definite form, the other supplying the agency of release from such definitions (distinctions posited in "Preface of 1815," *Prose Works*, 3:35). As a premise to the narrative, the epigraph states and negates romantic desire by reproducing it. Such a reproduction withdraws what it desires to promote, deletes what it would establish. The desire for purity is harbored in the impure form of a derivative text, while the claim of purity is partially withdrawn in the 1912 preface to the novel (*Melius fuerat non scribere,* 40). In and through a reiteration of the desire for pure presence, Hardy mimes romantic desire without requiting it. He tells us in advance, in epigraph and subtitle, that his literary act shelters a wounded purity. His sympathy for Tess compels us to sympathize with him, for he too seeks a purity he cannot find as the numerous covert intertextual echoes and borrowings demonstrate. Unlike Adam in Milton's Eden or in Keats's "Dream," he cannot produce his desire as real, yet he can sympathize with such a failing and expect us to sympathize also.

Moreover, a sensitive reading of the epigraph suggests that Hardy is rewriting the scene of failure and defeat in Shelley's *Adonais*. In *Adonais*, Shelley redeems Keats from a death suffered at the hands of the cultural elite, or so Shelley believed. In *Tess,* it will be Keats who returns the gesture and redeems an Angel-Shelley who is wounded by the word of culture in its Victorian formulation. Shelley wanted his "poetic bosom" to be a bed for the dead Keats as Hardy wants his to be a bed for the wounded and executed Big Beauty whose truth he has been at pains to relate. A more concrete representation of this thematic relationship of praise and vengeance, eulogy and satire, occurs in the scene where Tess collides with the mailman on the road to Casterbridge. The scene is structured around the verse stanza of *Adonais* in which Shelley wonders where the protective muse or guardian angel had been when Adonais is killed: "Where wert thou, mighty Mother, when he lay,/ When thy son lay, pierced by the shaft which flies,/ In darkness?" (2.10–12). Tess's horse Prince is "pierced by the pointed shaft of the cart" which sped "along these [dark] lanes like an arrow" (*T*, 71), and his destruction eventually leads to hers.

Though we shall have more to say about the comparison later, the point of our remarking upon it now is to suggest that Tess is Shelley's "mighty Mother" of poets who was Milton's and Wordsworth's mighty mother, too. That is, Tess is a further figuration of the romantic Urania; the name of Urania is, after all, implied in her surname of d'*Ur*berville. Moreover, d'Urberville is itself the noble and sublime origin of her provincial Durbeyfield name, while it is in the name of this romantic name that she is taken by both her poet-lovers. As a mark of her inheritance, she pronounces the "ur" syllable in every word she utters, while the narrator tells us that her "ur" syllable is "probably as rich an utterance as any to be found in human speech" (*T*, 52). Indeed it is, for it is the primitive source of all authentic poetry, romantically conceived; the essential "ur" note must resound within all inherited textual patterns if they are to be heard as more than "merely" derivative, decorative, and degenerate.

When Tess's cart is pierced by the mailman, she is carrying a load of honey to Casterbridge, another sign of her ambrosial character, and it is night, the appropriate time for the chariot of the muse of astronomy to be whirling along beneath the stars. She and Aby will have a brief discussion about the stars and about blighted and unblighted planets, fallen and Edenic worlds. Their discussion is predicated upon Adam's and Raphael's in Book Five of *Paradise Lost* wherein Adam questions the archangel about other worlds which, in the astronomical parlance of the day, are called "stars." Moreover, Tess's predawn discussion with Aby enfolds in the matrix of its implications Shelley's elegy to Keats wherein the "soul of Adonais" is said to be "like a star" which has flown free of this "blighted planet" ruled by punishing letters and lettered men or reviewers. Beyond the realm of a cruel literary culture, Keats now "Beacons from the abode where the Eternals are" (55.495–96).

Urania is one such eternal, whose very eternality is called into question in *Tess of the d'Urbervilles*. If Urania is Milton's muse in *Paradise Lost*, Wordsworth's in his prospectus to *The Excursion*, and Shelley's in *Adonais*, it is the descent of this Urania which constitutes Hardy's great theme in *Tess of the d'Urbervilles*. She is the star-soul whose fate is at issue in this phase of the master allegory as Jude's will be in Hardy's next important book to which *Tess* is the companion piece. Tess is the romantic muse of transgressive possibilities who finds no strong poet to inspire to transgress. She is thus confined to history where she dies. She is also love and Venus in search of her modern name, that contemporary expression of desire disburdened of past fables of character. Like Keats in Shelley's view, Tess is wounded and then executed by the letters of culture delivered by "mailmen," those critics of beauty who could not see the authenticity of her expressed desire because their own vision had been narrowed by the letters of traditional culture.

As a Urania figure, Tess represents "the pure spirit" which seeks to "flow/ Back to the burning fountain whence it came,/ A portion of the Eternal, which must glow/ Through time and change, unquenchably the same" (*Adonais*, 38.338–40). This, anyway, is what she dreams of doing. She twice utters this Shelleyan desire when she declares "in a fluty voice" that "our souls can go outside our bodies when we are alive" adding, "A very easy way to feel 'em go is to lie on the grass at night and look straight up at some big star" (*T*, 175). Her fluty voice and her especially attractive mouth characterize her as "the muse," while her formula for imaginative escape is predicated upon Shelley's prayer to Urania in *Adonais* with a glancing reference to Shelley's own position gazing upon the Keatsean polestar in the final stanza of the eulogy to the wounded romantic spirit.

Though the possibility of love and union is held out to her on two occasions, its actuality arises only once, at Bramshurst Court. Potentially, Angel can "raise up dreams with [his] music" and drive away "the horrid fancy" (180) that she is a thoroughly temporal being without even "a portion of the Eternal" in her and thus completely subject to "time and change" in Shelley's phrase, to "time and chance and change" in Hardy's derivation of the Shelleyan phase in "Hap."

Hap is but half of happiness, and it is this halving of the romantic whole (the merger of history and idealism) which concerns Hardy in all of his mature novels. In *Tess*, the defeat of Urania signifies that "Time ruthlessly destroy[s] his own romances" (423) as well as the capability for producing new ones. Just as Tess's surname is a covert form of the romantic muse's, so too her first name is derived by the halving of another muse-ic name. Tess's full name is Theresa and the Theresa Hardy has in mind is derived from George Eliot's revision of the Saint Theresa of Avila myth in the prelude to *Middlemarch*. There, Eliot casts Theresa as the "Ur" figure of inspirational quests. Eliot's Theresa wishes to be a muse of culture and inspire mankind to thoughtful deeds of social perfection. Her current emanation, according to Eliot, is Dorothea Brooke who will try to inspire her philosopher and poet-lovers to sing socially redemptive songs. Yet Dorothea fails where Theresa had succeeded because the times had changed. The coherent sociocultural faith which Theresa could rely on for guidance, Dorothea cannot.

Tess is third in this line of descent. By her full name of Theresa, she is a Theresan figure of high aspirations as was Dorothea Brooke. She seeks the fuller life that Dorothea sought and fails in ways that Dorothea failed, and for similar reasons. Thus, if Saint Theresa's desire marks the origin of such quests, and Dorothea's quest marks the "middle of the march," then Tess's quest is the "end march" or conclusion to the profitable pairing of muse and poet whose marriage constitutes an authentic act foreshadowing cultural renewal.

Significantly, all of the cues for a full understanding of Hardy's critical project lay in the prelude and finale to Eliot's novel, while it is Hardy's persistent denial that he had borrowed anything from Eliot that leads us to suspect that indeed he had. Eliot's opening question in *Middlemarch* (henceforth cited as *M*), "Who that cares much to know the history of man, and how the mysterious mixture behaves under the varying experiments of Time, has not dwelt, at least briefly, on the life of Saint Theresa . . . on that little girl walking forth one morning hand-in-hand with her still smaller brother, to go and seek martyrdom in the country of the Moors?" (*M*, 25), sets the stage for Tess's subsequent departure for that same country where she will experience a martyrdom similar to Theresa's and Dorothea's. Tess's and Dorothea's quests are like Theresa's insofar as all "were the mixed result of a young and noble impulse struggling amidst the conditions of an imperfect social state, in which great feelings will often take the aspect of error, and great faith the aspect of illusion. For there is no creature whose inward being is so strong that it is not greatly determined by what lies outside it" (*M*, 896). In Tess's instance, error and illusion are cast as romantic mistaking, while it is the failure of this most recent form of faith that constitutes the "medium in which [her] ardent deeds took shape" for the worse (*M*, 896). Penetration (seduction/rape) by the cultural word which "lies outside" being and constitutes media is the tragic agency of Tess's life. In her concluding warning in *Middlemarch*, Eliot tells us that external sources will continue to inform "the lives of many Dorotheas, some of which may present a far sadder sacrifice than that of the Dorothea whose story we know" (*M*, 896). As I have discussed in the introduction, Hardy's *Tess* is precisely the story of such a "far sadder sacrifice" than that of Eliot's Dorothea-Theresa in *Middlemarch*.

Though we can but touch on an intertextual web that is immense and, as yet, undisclosed, Hardy's emblem of seduction and rape in *Tess* is partially predicated upon Eliot's sense of tragedy in *Middlemarch*. Both novels are concerned with problems within marriage and with the possible reconstitution of "the home epic" (*M*, finale, 891), though Eliot focuses upon the social aspect of this epic while Hardy concentrates upon the aesthetic aspect. Both Tess and Saint Theresa "soared after some illimitable satisfaction, some object which would never justify weariness, which would reconcile self-despair with the rapturous consciousness of life beyond self" (*M*, prelude, 25), while it is just this "beyond self" that Tess cannot reach. Both novels seek to redefine the problematic of "epos," defined as religious reform for Theresa, social reform for Dorothea, and cultural reform for Tess. Eliot informs us that the "Spanish woman who lived three hundred years ago was certainly not the last of her kind. Many Theresas have been born who found for themselves no epic life wherein there was a constant unfolding of far-resonant action; perhaps only a life of mistakes, the offspring of a certain spiritual grandeur ill-matched with the meanness of opportunity; perhaps tragic failure which found no sacred poet and sank unwept into oblivion" (*M*, 25). Eliot's "life of mistakes" on a quest after "spiritual grandeur . . . ill-matched with the meanness of opportunity" defines the character of Tess's life, while it is her failure to find a "sacred poet" in her latter-day Shelley that causes her to sink into oblivion. Eliot tells us that the "inconsistency and formlessness" we see in "these later-born Theresas" is due to their being "helped by no coherent social faith and order which could perform the function of knowledge for the ardently willing soul" (*M*, 25). Her definition of agency is Hardy's. Tess is deformed by the agencies and effects of an inconsistent cultural knowledge wielded, for the most part, by her poet-angels. Thus it is only when Angel's "inconsistencies rushed in upon him" (422) that he feels remorse for what he has done to her.

Because she is seduced and penetrated by the conflicting codes of culture, Tess is precariously positioned "between a vague ideal and the common yearning of womanhood," or between identity and biology, idealism and history, the "one . . . disapproved [of] as extravagance, and the other condemned as a lapse" (*M*, 25). Like Eliot's Theresa, Tess will wander into the land of the Moors when she journeys to Blackmoor Vale where she too will be martyred for her angelic cultural ideal. Eliot's Theresa is a heroine because she "quickly burned" the "light fuel" of "the many-volumed romances of chivalry" (*M*, 26), after which she sought more enlightened cultural engagements. Tess cannot do this because her guiding Angel has not done this, and she repeats his romances verbatim. Angel's "flame" is not intense enough to burn away the moral romances of his Victorian Hellenism, thus he can find "no life beyond the self" and cannot help Tess to find life either.

In addition to these thematic cues from Eliot's novel, Hardy also grafts the redemptive lesson which Angel must learn before he can be reunited with Tess. The lesson is that "the limits of variation [in women] are really much wider than any one would imagine from the sameness of women's *coiffeur* and the favorite love-stories in prose and verse" (*M*, 26). To "imagine" difference within sameness or variance of expression within a recognizable cultural pattern is the "moral" of Hardy's tale. Thus, it is the absence of Eliot's sense of imaginative sympathy which sees this difference in sameness which makes Wessex so punishing a place for Tess. When transcribed into aesthetic terms, the lesson asks that we learn to recognize covert originality within a copy-culture of apparent similarities, that, in essence, we hear the "ode" or lyric within the parody performance. Paradoxically, Hardy's novel asks us to recognize the need for romantic originality by copying the mandate for such from Eliot's *Middlemarch*.

Although this might at first seem like a self-defeating form of defense, it is to plead no more than Shelley did in the preface to *Prometheus Unbound*. There, Shelley urges his readers to understand that "a number of writers possess the form whilst they want the spirit of those whom, it is alleged, they imitate; because the former is the endowment of the age in which they live, and the latter must be the uncommunicated lightning of their own mind" (*Shelley*, 134). Whether Hardy possesses both "form" and "lightning" or simply "form" is, I think, the essential question which Hardy studies must ask itself, while the derivative and paradoxical context of the demand for originality returns us to the epigraph and the subtitle of the novel. There, Hardy pleads for Tess's purity despite an awareness of her many seductions by the romances of culture. She is thus "a pure woman" and a "wounded name," which is to suggest that she is not pure on the one hand while on the other it suggests that the genuine romantic impetus toward transgression lies beyond language (as it does in *Adonais*) and that a culture which merely reiterates this truth rather than enacting it is indeed "wounded." Thus, the paradox is resolved when we understand that it is the wounded or weakened name of romantic culture that is at issue in the novel and that it is put at issue as an original statement voiced by a weakened romantic.

Finally, it is Eliot's "weight of unintelligible Rome" (*M*, 225) which Hardy refigures as the weight of the unintelligible Wessex world. Eliot's phrase is of course on loan from Wordsworth's "Immortality Ode," just as the prelude to *Middlemarch* refers to Wordsworth's then recently published *Prelude*. For Eliot, unintelligibility is the aftereffect of witnessing a confusing density of cultural material, represented in Dorothea's instance by those buildings, ruins, and monuments which surround her in Rome where the past cannot be forgotten because it constitutes the landscape. Dorothea has no defenses against the density of "impressions" imparted to her by this landscape. Honeymooning amid

ruins and basilicas, palaces and colossi, set in the midst of a sordid present, where all that was living and warm-blooded seemed sunk in the deep degeneracy of a superstition divorced from reverence; the dimmer but yet eager Titanic life gazing and struggling on walls and ceiling; the long vistas of white forms whose marble eyes seemed to hold the monotonous light of an alien world: all this vast wreck of ambitious ideals, sensuous and spiritual, mixed confusedly with the signs of breathing forgetfulness and degradation, at first jarred her as with an electric shock, and then urged themselves on her with that *ache* belonging to a glut of confused ideas which check the flow of emotion. Forms both pale and glowing took possession of her young sense, and fixed themselves in her memory even when she was not thinking of them, preparing strange associations which remained through her after-years. (*M*, 225)

Here lies Hardy's textual authority for Tess's many violations at the hands of a "roman" romanticism, a "vast wreck of ambitious ideals . . . mixed confusedly" with irreverence, misconstruction, and degradation.

Tess of the d'Urbervilles: Creativity at a Loss for Words

They "jar" Tess (the narrator uses this word to speak of Tess's collision with the mailman in a scene of penetration proleptic of her rape in the Chase) and then "urge themselves" onto her instilling her with an "ache" which Hardy rephrases "the ache of modernism" when he places the phrase in his narrator's mouth. The "forms both pale and glowing" which take possession of Dorothea's "virginal" senses become, at Hardy's reworking, "the cloud of moral hobgoblins by which [Tess] is terrified without reason" and which influence her to become a "Figure of Guilt intruding into the haunts of innocence" (*T*, 135).

It is Eliot's "disease of the retina" (which incidentally Hardy borrowed earlier to describe Boldwood's fixation upon Bathsheba's valentine, her "artificial heart") imparted by such a belated landscape "spreading itself everywhere" (*M*, 226) which distorts perception in Tess's Wessex. Her world is a "psychological phenomenon," in a phrase Hardy borrowed from a review of Leopardi's poetry, and a blighted star because perceptions are filtered through romantic ruins. As in Dorothea's Rome, in Tess's Wessex romances are born in time and are subject to the predations of time. Like the ruins of Rome, romantic culture lies in ruins all about Tess although its fragments are verbal rather than visual. In their fallen and chaotic condition, they become "hindrances" to vision (a disease of the retina) "instead of centering [goodness] in some long-recognizable deed" (*M*, 26). Chief among the most recent romances to become subject to time are those which either sought or promised an enduring permanence beyond time and so claimed culture's attention. It is specifically Angel's classico-romantic imagination—his Hellenic fancies which are *roman* in the sense of derivative—which fails Tess and not those earlier, Hebraic forms of romanticism which the narrator quickly dismisses with satire. We might even see Eliot's representation of Rome, a landscape depressingly burdened by time and ruins, as an apt model for Hardy's style in *Tess,* a novel constructed out of the ruins of romantic writing whose icons and momuments lie scattered on nearly every page.

Though she comes to maturity in a fallen culture, Tess seeks what Keats wanted for the muse of English poetry in "If By Dull Rhymes Our English Must Be Chained." She cannot free herself from "dull" and unimaginative ballads. She is Hardy's Andromeda (a Keatsean muse) who is "fetter'd, in spite of loveliness." She cannot fly by herself nor can her weak, second-rate poet escorts "let the muse be free." Because they cannot, Tess is *not* "bound with garlands of her own" nor is the "naked foot of Poetry" shoed with "sandals more interwoven and complete" (all quotations from "If By Dull Rhymes"). The confusion of standards in her cultural moment creates "sandals" which are less tightly interwoven, looser and unfinished. The poetic impetus toward complete self-expression does not overcome old poetic forms in order to produce a new poetry that is vital and contemporary, thus it is constrained to produce an allegory of frustrated romantic desire, in effect using this static literary form to authentically display its own derivativeness and stasis.

Only once in her life does Tess free herself from the formal constraints of culture, and that is when she murders Alec. Her murder is a poetic act, properly revolutionary and romantic. Like the French people during the Terror (and we shall see how Hardy constructs a periodic narrative of her oppression and revolt by using the French revolutionary calendar), she "beheads" her pseudoaristocratic captor, Alec *Stokes*-d'Urberville, and frees her body to speak its desire: frees the body of desire to speak. In this reading, murder is the necessary cultural response to the rape of consciousness by narrative; murder disburdens her of the formal impositions of cultural law and thereby constitutes a moment of poetic freedom. By murdering Alec, Tess exchanges the passive acceptance of cultural dominance for the self-assertiveness of poetic action.

Freed of her past by a violent transgression of the law, Tess becomes the muse who "flies" after Angel who is himself disburdened of his textual past at this time, for reasons we shall presently discuss. Together they flee to Bramshurst Court, an unrented mansion where they will replay the scene of *poiesis* in Keats's "Ode to Psyche." At last and for once Tess becomes her Uranic self by becoming Keats's Psyche while Angel regresses back to his Hellenic namesake which is Eros, the winged god. At the Bramshurst Court of Love, Tess and Angel as Psyche and Eros briefly enjoy the grace of self-expression in an extended fable about the tragedy of not being able to find or sustain an authentic identity. Significantly, this moment of grace remains unnamed, a positive silence in contradistinction to the negative articulations of self which she has been coerced or seduced into accepting and reiterating. And it is here at Bramshurst Court that Big Beauty or Urania or Theresa or Tess soars free above and beyond the fettered allegory of her existence, a short-

Tess of the d'Urbervilles: Creativity at a Loss for Words

lived star of hope—and therefore a Keatsean *figura*—and an unravished bride of quietness.

Keats's formulation of lyrical authenticity is the origin of Tess's command that Angel "call her Tess" rather than this or that figure from the *ars rhetorica* of romantico-Hellenic tropes for the beautiful.[4] As his muse in waiting, she admonishes him to speak creatively if he would be a genuine poet. Too late, he learns to disburden himself of culture in order to produce culture by speaking a poetry embodying the spirit of the present "faithfully supported by its two wings, the past and the future" (Wordsworth, "Essay Supplementary to the Preface of 1815," *Prose Works*, 3:84). Angel's dilemma is summarized in Keats's *Sleep and Poetry* where the creation of "the poet" in modern times is the most thematically relevant issue. If Tess cannot get "poetry," if she must live in Arnold's "unpoetical times," then she would rather have "sleep" (this is Angel's small gift to her at Stonehenge) or death, which she accepts upon awakening once more into Arnold's barren, unpoetical time when the only life is a death-in-life.

In *Sleep and Poetry*, the poet-narrator asks if poetry could ever be forgotten. His answer is "Yes, a schism/ Nurtured by foppery and barbarism,/ Made great Apollo blush for this his land,/ Men were thought wise who could not understand/ His glories" (181–85). Alec's "crime" is foppery and barbarism. He poses as "the country squire," a role new to him, and he expects country women to act as Car Darch and her sister have acted toward him. Thus he barbarically misreads Tess and takes her for another, and she tells him so after the damage is done. Angel's crime too is foppery and barbarism. He poses as the Apollo of Talbothays, a role which is new to him, and he expects Tess to conform to the definitions of purity demanded by a Victorian Hellenism of the moralized sort Arnold traded in. Of both her "poet-lovers" we might ask what Keats asked of the barbaric fops of his day who misunderstand Hellenism or "Apollo's glories," one of whom is Tess: "beauty was awake!/ Why were ye not awake? But ye were dead/ To things ye knew not of—were closely wed/ To musty laws lined out with wretched rule/ And compass vile" (193–97). As second-rate poets, Alec and Angel are one of the "thousand handicraftsmen" who wear "the mask of Poesy" who "go about,/ Holding a poor, decrepid standard out/ Mark'd with most flimsy mottos" (200–201 and 204–6). Subject to their rule, Tess will be compelled to live up to their flimsy mottos and decrepit standards. Her tragedy occurs because "strength alone though of the muses born/ Is like a fallen angel" (241–42). That is, she is enthralled to a weak angel who has forgotten "the great end/ Of poesy, that is should be a friend/ To sooth the cares, and lift the thoughts of man" (245–47).

Tess of the d'Urbervilles then is one of the best readings of Keats that we have, as Jude will be one of the best of Shelley. Tess is seduced and "taken" nine times by the cultural word. Each time that she is (mis)taken by the word, we are presented with a scene of cultural failure in lieu of the expected redemption. She is deformed by the poetic word instead of vitally informed by it. Paradoxically, her problem is that her creativity is at a loss for (because of) words, yet it is just this loss for words which should encourage Tess and Angel to create new and more appropriate names for them (their) selves. Their inability to find new names constitutes the romantic failure and the failure of romanticism in Hardy's fable about the fate of beauty in late nineteenth-century England.

Tess's encounter with the red paint-pot preacher is an emblem of the tragic agency of inscription in Wessex. The preacher writes on nature in a parodic performance of the nature poet who sees into the life of things and describes that which he sees. The preacher's "sermons on stones" mock as they mime the romantic nature poet's program, recalling it in order to negate it. The heart—Tess's heart in this instance—that watches and receives instruction in the woods finds only "barren leaves" there and not those revitalizing awarenesses which poems such as "The Tables Turned" claimed could be found there. Caught between a nature that is an abyss and a writing or scripture that offers no salvation, Tess wanders in a realm absolutely alienating to the spirit. Though his actions speak as loud as his words, the hidden point in the preacher's text—thy, damnation, slumbereth, not—is that Tess's world is dominated by prophets of culture who have "returned to their vomit" (in the undisclosed portion of his apostolic sermon) instead of turning away from the regurgitated figures in search of healthier nourishment.

Each time Tess's mind is taken over by a poet of the regurgitated word, she is as "written on" as are the trees and stones. To structure

Tess of the d'Urbervilles: Creativity at a Loss for Words

this scene of writing on the natural body, Hardy uses Keats's "Dream of Adam" in each and every instance when Tess is taken by the word. Keats's revised Miltonic emblem is the hypogram of the narrative which is repeated nine times in order to structure a fable about creation as destruction and repetition as disfigurement.[5] In principle, Tess seeks what Keats sought, "a Life of Sensations rather than of Thoughts" (*Letters*, 11/22/17), by which we mean a vitality that exceeds dogma. What she finds however is a life of thoughts which confine sensations. Because she is seduced into becoming "the dream of some Adam" or other, she never becomes her own dream which is to say she never articulates her own identity. Poetry has a design on her; and Hardy is in agreement with Keats when he writes that "We hate poetry that has a palpable design upon us" (*Letters*, 2/3/18). It is this "design" which is "traced" on her "beautiful feminine tissue" (*T*, 119) after a barbarous and foppish figure "startles" and "amazes" her, precisely as Keats said genuine poetry should not. In her Wessex, poetry is lethal because it "comes not as naturally as the leaves to a tree," therefore "it had better not come at all" in Keats's estimate (*Letters*, 2/27/18). His estimate sounds the desire for erasure in *Tess* because a genuine romantic revolution does not occur.

Because subject to the Dream of Adam, Tess is an Eve figure. Her problem arises because her Adam "cower[s] under the Wings of great Poets" rather than ascends beyond them inspirited by "a Muse of fire" (*Letters*, 2/27/18) who, potentially, is Tess. Thus Keats's assertion that in "a great poet the sense of Beauty overcomes every other consideration, or rather obliterates all consideration" (12/21/17) tells us, once more, why Angel is not a great poet. Keats's writing again informs the thematic of liberation when Tess seeks salvation in Blackmoor Vale where character can overcome its inherited characteristics and achieve an authentic identity. In the Vale, Hardy refigures Tess as Cynthia and Angel as Endymion. Keats's romantic comedy dominates the scenes in the Valley of the Great Dairies which is a kind of "Maiden Chamber" of innocence for Tess and Angel. Yet because he cannot sustain his love for her beyond the Valley in that "Vale of Soul-Building" called history, Angel loses his opportunity to be authentically romantic and not just romantically so. The comedy of Endymion thus turns tragic because the poet will not marry the Indian Maiden aspect of his Moon Maiden ideal

179

The Descent of the Imagination

and thereby merge romance with reality. Because Angel cannot do so at Wellbridge Manor, the gap between the two realms of representation is not bridged well or bridged at all.

We can see how Hardy incorporates Keats's *Endymion* into the novel by taking a close look at one scene at Talbothays where Tess "went stealthily as a cat through [a] profusion of growth, gathering cuckoo-spittle on her skirts, cracking snails that were underfoot [and] staining her hands with thistle-milk and slug-slime" (*T,* 179) in order to approach Angel. The entire passage is covertly on loan from Keats's *Endymion* where the poet advises us that identity can arise only if we "winnow from the coming step of time/ All chaff of custom" and "wipe away all slime/ Left by men-slugs and human serpentry" (1: 820–21). The slime of custom is precisely what Tess cannot wipe away in her Garden of Endymion, Talbothays, where, significantly, Angel strums a second-hand harp whose "music's kiss . . . impregnates the free winds" as a prelude to its impregnating Tess (*Endymion,* 1: 784).

The upshot of the fanciful (and not imaginative) redemption at Talbothays is that Keats's "System of Soul-making" cannot complete its narrative. Thus no souls or identities are created in Tess's Wessex, a place of undoing (unbeing) rather than doing (being). "Intelligence, mind and heart, and experience" do not "collude to produce Identity" (*Letters,* 2/14/19 and 5/3/18) because an "authenticity of the Imagination" (*Letters,* 11/22/17) is absent. If "what the imagination seizes as Beauty must be truth" as Keats claimed, then what the fancy seizes upon must be fiction, in Hardy's reformulation. In this reading, then, Tess's Wessex is a place where fictions or "idealisms of fancy" dominate. Dominated by fancy, her culture is reproductive and not productive, a topos of forgeries, masks, and theatrical illusions which cannot define the truth of beauty in ways that poets once presumed that the imagination could.

Keats's equation of beauty and truth takes us to the heart of the narrator's model for agency, the "Dream of Adam." All seductions in *Tess* are predicated upon Keats's emblem for the romantic imagination which, he says, "may be compared to Adam's dream [in Milton's *Paradise Lost*]—he awoke and found it truth" (*Letters,* 11/22/17). Hardy inverts these terms, which are Edenic insofar as they refind paradise, to produce an antiemblem of a truly negative capability. For Keats, "the Imagination and its empyrean reflection is the same as human life and its spiritual repetition." What Hardy offers in lieu of this ideal is a historical reflection upon the loss of the Keatsean imagination. Simply, Keats's "Dream of Adam" becomes Hardy's nightmare of culture because repetition is no longer a spiritual reflection.

Tess of the d'Urbervilles is then the story of Eve in post-Edenic times, or Eve on the subjected plain of history. To elaborate his fable, Hardy paid attention to the figural possibilities in both Milton and Keats, and it is to those possibilities that we must now briefly attend before concluding with an analysis of the nine rape scenes which structure the narrative.

In *Paradise Lost* (henceforth cited as *PL*), Book Eight, God tells Adam that he has correctly named his being, thereby "expressing well the spirit within thee free" which is the "Image of God in Man" (*PL*, 8. 439–40). This grace to name oneself authentically is the lyrical capability denied Tess. Unlike Adam's self-characterization, Tess's identity, if that is what we want to call it, is "based upon shreds of convention, peopled by phantoms and voices antipathetic to her" (*T*, 135). These shreds constitute a mental "environment" which is "the mistaken creation of Tess's fancy" and not her imagination (*T*, 315). Tess is then a "mistaken" because fanciful "creation" who names herself wrongly because there are no correct names for her to choose from. These correct names could have been supplied by the Adamic poet to whom Tess would then be a fit helpmate as his muse. That her Adam does not possess "a spirit within" that is free means that he cannot authentically name her or name her in any original way.

Having properly named himself, Milton's Adam is promised by the Creator that he will bring him someone who is "Thy likeness, thy fit help, they other self,/ Thy wish, exactly to thy heart's desire" (*PL*, 8. 449–51). Hardy inverts the creative promise of pleasure in the fulfillment of desire into the pain of thwarted desire. In recreating the Miltonic scene, Hardy listened closely to the sexual overtones and nuances in Milton's writing and he repeats them, sometimes verbatim, in his fable. Milton's Adam is first "overpowered" by his Creator. He is then "Dazzl'd and spent" after which he "sinks down" to the earth where he seeks the "repair/ Of sleep, which instantly fell upon [him]" (*PL*, 8. 455–59). All tragedies wrought by the destructive word in Hardy's narrative follow the Miltonic pattern of seduction and transformation. All victims are surprised by the bearer of some romantic word who becomes their creator; dazzled by his fabular presence and utterance, they are penetrated by "their heart's desire" or a romance, and spent by the penetration, after which they sleep only to wake in a world that is "meaner" as Eden was for Adam after Eve's creation.

If we keep the Miltonic scene of creation in mind we can clear up the quibble among Hardyan critics as to whether Tess was asleep in The Chase and thus innocent or awake and thus complicit in her downfall. We will recall in *Paradise Lost* that Adam enters a trancelike state before he is wounded by the Word. His trancelike state is the undisclosed source of the narrator's ambivalence regarding Tess's state of consciousness at the moment of her taking by her creator. Tess is both asleep (and so subject to fancy) and awake (because aware of what such fancies of "the country squire" can lead to). She is therefore somewhat "taken" or "dazzed" by Alec (and she says as much later on) and somewhat taken or seduced by him. Far from hedging the issue, the narrator's construction appropriately locates the difficult position of desire in a world without access to the imagination. Her trancelike state is emblematic of a life governed by fables which do not correspond to the truth of one's being. In such a culture devoid of imagination, accurate definitions are hard to come by since no one sees into the life of things (others). The overall effect of such an episteme is that one is always dreaming while awake and seduced by fancies which disappoint. That is, "to be taken by" or fascinated in Tess's Wessex is to be "mis-taken" or raped by fancy.

Tess, Alec, and Angel are "taken by their fancy" in all of the ways this phrase might resonate. In this regard, Tess is a figure created by the imagination as it was construed in eighteenth-century associationist psychology. That is, she is a figure devolved from the Coleridgean imagination by which we can measure the extent to which it has degenerated back into its sentimental and pseudo-scientific precedents. This devolution of the imagination finds its precedent in Milton's *Paradise Lost* where the fancy is spoken of as a faculty secondary to reason and beneath inspiration. Fancy, Milton informs us, works by "misjoining shapes." These misjoinders are a "Wild Work" usually produced in dreams which "Ill match words and deeds long past or late" (*PL,* 5. 100–115). Thus Milton's sense of "ill matching" becomes Hardy's sense of seduction and rape by the inappropriate coupling of words to intentions and desires. In effect, nothing is named by such a misconstruction, and it is this void which appears at the conclusion to Tess's fable when she is finally represented by the black flag suspended over Wintoncester. Informed by fanciful misconstructions, Tess "molests" her mind with "wandering thoughts and notions vain" concerning the whence and wherefore of things as Milton stated would be the case and as Wordsworth claimed would not, where the mind is genuinely possessed by the high romantic imagination.

Finally, Hardy's figure of "the wound" in *Tess* is also derived from the scene of creative penetration in *Paradise Lost*. There, the Creative Word comes upon a sleeping, entranced Adam and "op'n'd [his] left side, and took/ From thence a Rib, which cordial spirits warm, / And Life blood streaming fresh; wide was the wound" (*PL*, 8. 465–68). Milton's trope of the wound will be repeated nine times in the novel, beginning with the penetration of John Durbeyfield's consciousness by Parson Tringham's "word" and concluding with Tess's being taken by the word of law at Stonehenge. Characteristically, each penetration by the word in Tess's Wessex is a sorrowful and not a joyful event as it was in Milton's Eden. It is to these nine scenes of seduction/rape that we must now turn our attention.

The inaugural seduction and rape of the nine occurs when Jack Durbeyfield is surprised by Parson Tringham. All other mistakings in the narrative are reproduced in the name of this father who is himself mastered by a poetic romance. Jack is Hardy's "high genitor," as the heroes of Thermopylae were in *Endymion*. Inebriated and stumbling homeward one evening, Jack encounters Tringham who briefly narrates the d'Urberville chronicle. Tringham is a figure of divine authority, a parson, as well as a seducer figure, "the antiquarian of Stag's Foot Lane." And it is his antiquarian lore which masters Jack. Jack will ignore the historic aspect of the narrative to dwell upon its high romantic import, thus opening up a wide rift between his past and his present. His Marlott world is subsequently transformed into a meaner place because his "dream" becomes real.

Impregnated by the parson's lore, Jack is displaced from history into a romance of Elizabethan splendor. In effect, he has "just looked into Chapman's Homer" and seen the fulfillment of his poetical ambition. Jack's Keatsean/ Elizabethan consciousness is duly represented when he later visits the Pure Drop Inn, a tavern whose name resonates with

The Descent of the Imagination

moral and poetical ironies. Having heard Tringham's word, Jack has quaffed a "beaker full of the warm South" and become drunk on romance. His new status, which is fanciful and not imaginative, is signified by his naming himself, as Adam did in Eden, Sir John d'Urberville. The natural suffix "field" in Durbeyfield is replaced by the Frenchified "ville," as a sign of the provençal luxury which his romance has brought him.

When he first encounters the "creative word," Jack is in a "trance" because a drunk. He is both asleep and awake as a sign of his passive receptivity. He is also the first sleepwalker in a narrative which will make full use of this condition as a metaphor of enthrallment. With "drowsed senses" (*PL*, 8. 289) he meets his "great maker" who speaks to him his heart's desire. He idealizes himself with Tringham's chronicle and attempts to realize his novel identity within history, thereby merging the two aspects of representation as Keats thought they might be and as Shelley sometimes despaired that they ever would be. After the encounter, Jack is "spent" by what he has heard. As was the case for Milton's Adam, "a dream . . . suddenly stood at [his] head" (*PL*, 8.292) which tells him that "they mansion wants thee" (8. 269–97). The d'Urberville name is that mansion, his Eden and his Eve. Figuratively and structurally, Jack is the "First Man, of men innumerable ordained/ First father" (8. 296–97) whose "garden of bliss" becomes a world of woe for Tess.

Upon hearing the d'Urberville tale, Jack exclaims "Daze my eyes" (*T*, 44). His exclamation reiterates Milton's "dazzled" which finds its way into Keats's *Endymion* when the romantic hero's "dazzled soul" commingles with the visionary reality of the moon which leaves him "quite dazed/ By a bright something" (1: 594–602). After the bedazzlement, Tringham becomes "the author of all [Jack] seest/ Above or round about" him or "beneath" him as had the Creator of Adam (*PL*, 8. 318–19). Overwhelmed by his vision, Jack falls into a "profound reverie . . . upon a grassy bank by the roadside" where he "luxuriously stretched himself upon the bank among the daisies" (*T*, 46). His postvisionary posture refigures Adam's when "As new waked from soundest sleep/ Soft on the flowery herb I found me laid/ In balmy sweat" (*PL*, 8. 253–55), while the "luxuriousness" of his position sounds the Keatsean note of refinement. Indeed, it is just this luxury in fancy which Keats dwells upon as a substitute for action and any real or actual entitlement to refined luxuries. Touched by the creative word, Jack's "earthy" life is elevated from the dust; his red blood turns blue and Marlott becomes a "meaner" place in light of his newly perceived idea of great beauty. Eventually Jack dies of heart failure and inactivity. Both "diseases" relate his fate to Endymion's, while the actual report of his death by a ring of fat like a "C" tightening round his heart (*T*, 59) is covertly on loan from Keats's "On Seeing the Elgin Marbles" where "dim-conceived glories of the brain/ Bring round the heart an undescribable feud" (9–10). Sir John's "dim-conceived" glories are underwritten by his fiction of the d'Urberville name; the heart constraining "C" is romantic culture in its most luxurious Keatsean formulation.

The second violent penetration in the narrative occurs on the road to Casterbridge when Prince is pierced by the mailman, an authorized carrier of the letter whose "collision" with Tess is one of the darkest sexual puns in a fiction concerned with the phallic capability of the cultural word to pierce and position consciousness. The collision between a mailman and a "female-woman" alerts us to the gender concerns of a narrative which always mark the victim of fancy as passive or female while the impositioning cultural letter is male and active. Women are never active in Tess's Wessex; rather they are powerless objects of the male's fancy, while men who are subject to fancy are "ineffectual" as is Angel or vicious as is Alec. At no time in the narrative does the active or "manly" imagination assert its creative capacity to accurately define and converge with some other in an I-Thou dialectic of equivalence, although a brief simulacrum of this position is suggested at Bramshurst Court. In terms of the gender conflict at issue, the narrative makes its point by subjecting all characters to the domination of the fancy and rendering none of them figures of the capable imagination.

Tess's discussion with Aby or "Abraham" on the road to Casterbridge finds its origin in Book Five of *Paradise Lost* when Raphael and Adam discuss the limits of human understanding regarding "the Whence and Wherefore of Things." Riding in the dark, "Abraham grew drowsy [and] Tess fell more deeply into a reverie than ever, her back leaning against the hives" (*T*, 70). In her trancelike state, subject and object, fancy and history, intermingle and are confused. The result is that the "mute procession past her shoulders of trees and hedges [becomes] attached to fantastic scenes outside reality" (*T*, 70). In this tracelike state such as Adam experienced, Tess will dream of Alec, and her dream will later become real.

As though acting out the unstated content and consequences of Tess's dream, Prince is suddenly penetrated by the "pointed edge of the shaft" of the mailman's running pole which opens a wide wound in his body. Up until now, the narrator has described Tess as Milton's Diana whirling sleepily along in her moon chariot which "by silent course advanced/ With inoffensive pace that spinning sleeps/ On her soft axle, while she paces even" (*PL*, 8. 163–65). Prince's penetration is an overdetermined event thick with phallic references (prince/knight/male/mail/man/shaft/pole). His wounding by the letter carrier associates his body with Tess's, and indeed she follows him "in harness" as the provider for the family. Ultimately, she will have her body "pierced" as Alec's mistress in order to support her fatherless family.

The speeding cart which flies like "an arrow as it always did" (*T*, 71) recalls the invisible arrows of the cultural elite which killed Keats while it associates Tess with Saint Theresa of Avila whose heart is wounded by the arrows of spiritual love shot by an angel. After the collision, "an immeasurable social chasm" opens between her present and past because soon she will be sent to the d'Urberville mansion to claim kin and thereby repair the damage she has caused. Upon impact "a sudden jerk shook her in her seat, and Tess awoke from the sleep into which she had fallen" (*T*, 70). Though this description can and should stand in for the undescribed penetration in The Chase, it is her rude awakening from the dream which is of import, for when she awakes the world is indeed a much "meaner" place. After the accident, Prince's "life blood was spouting in a stream," a description which reiterates nearly verbatim Milton's scene of the wound when Adam's "life blood stream[ed] fresh" irrigating the ground of paradise (*PL*, 8.446). Prince's blood becomes an "iridescence of coagulation" reflecting the dawn in "a hundred prismatic hues" (70), as Eve's beauty did immediately after her creation from Adam's ribpole. The narrator concludes this scene of the creation of Eve by noting that "birds shook themselves in the hedges, arose, and twittered" (71) unmindful of the accident. The unmindful Wessex birds recall a very mindful and sympathetic nature in Eden where "joyous birds" choired Eve and her "prince" into their bower of bliss.

Alec's seduction of Tess in The Chase is the third in the sequence.

Tess of the d'Urbervilles: Creativity at a Loss for Words

Although much of value has been written about this scene, it is important that we remember that Alec is also living out a romance. He is the son of a bourgeois merchant who has purchased a royal name from the encyclopedia of dead names in the British Museum. The narrator makes a point of telling us this history in order to align Alec's story with John Durbeyfield's. Then, too, we might consider that Alec's original surname in manuscript was *Smith*-d'Urberville which more poignantly underscores the bourgeois romance with royalty that is at issue in his character. Alec inherits his father's artificial name and attempts to play the role of the country squire. His play acting is so crudely represented in the narrative that Hardy critics once mistook what was intended to be a wooden performance in a character for a wooden performance by the author. Quite to the contrary, Hardy intends Alec to be as ineffectual a country squire as Angel will be a poet. Both inherit a role in name only, and both harm Tess in the name of that fathering fancy.

In this instance, it is the complex interaction of two fathering fantasies which harms Tess. She is living out her father's fantasy of nobility by claiming kin and Alec is living out his father's fantasy by acting the country gentleman. Together, Tess and Alec "marry" in name only. Their marriage has little to do with romantic correspondences and everything to do with the correspondence of their fathering romances.

Though predicated upon a romance, Alec's role is taught to him by the likes of Car Darch and her sister. He learns from them that maidenly coyness is a ploy used to stoke the erotic character of courtship. Coyness is a fable which excites and attracts the male by conflating innocence (the fantasy) with experience (the history). A confusion of these two realms colludes to create Alec's position toward those women who work for him, women who do not complain of the treatment they receive at his hands, since it is their fantasy that he might eventually marry one of them, at which time they will become as fabulously royal as he is. Thus, Alec's seduction of Tess is predicated upon his Adamic function as country squire to name his creatures as he fancies them and then expect them to live up to his fancy. It is then this pattern of provincial life which accounts for Tess's seduction. After the damage is done, Tess protests that he should not have characterized her according to the stories he has heard about other country maidens but should have tried "to see into the life of things" as it were, a talent which nobody in Wessex possesses.

The Descent of the Imagination

Besides its voicing her function as a Wessex muse, Tess's protest bears traces from Flaubert's *Madame Bovary* (henceforth cited as *MB*).[6] Tess asks Alec "did it never strike your mind that what every woman says some women may feel?" (*T*, 125). This is precisely the narrator's point in *Madame Bovary* when he remarks that Rudolphe Boulanger has "no perception of the dissimilarity of feeling that might underlie similarities of expression" (*MB*, 215). The perception of dissimilarity within sameness is the lacking sense in her Wessex as it is in Madame Bovary's Yonville. Authenticity as both Hardy and Flaubert understand it is a creative position within prescriptions which preform experience. The creative spirit is that "lightning" which Shelley claimed made the difference within texts inescapably "tinged" with echoes from contemporary literature. Not to see this lyrical difference, the difference of tenor carried by the vehicle, is to misunderstand "the pattern" by presuming that life or "the Promethian spark" is only an effect of life-style or narrative.

Although we should accept this interpretation as thematic in *Tess,* it is tempting to consider further that Hardy perhaps intends his audience to understand the terms of such "tragic" and "name-wounding" misunderstandings as a defense of his own authorial practice. In such a recognition lies the key to an affirmation and legitimization of the romantic claims for the ontological priority of spirit. Spirit so defined must exceed those figures which it uses for its expression. This priority of being over language which the narrative claims for the essential Tess is precisely what Hardy wishes to claim for himself despite his remarkably "tinged" and echoic narratives. If, that is, Hardy can get us to understand that *Tess* is about a life struggling to exceed a life-style, then we are in a position to understand that he too is an author in search of authenticity, and, concomitantly, that his narratives are enlivened by Shelley's lightning which reclaims ontological originality from linguistic derivativeness. That is, Hardy does not want us to "mistake" his beauty in ways in which Tess's beauty is mistaken in the narrative; rather we should see the essential originality of his intent despite the derivative character of his art. Yet we have to wonder at this juncture if Hardy's thematizing the case for the failure of romantic originality is sufficiently original to exonerate him from participating in the failure. This is to argue that no matter how creative the portrayal of the failure of creativity, failure still inhabits the work wherein it is revealed.

Tess of the d'Urbervilles: Creativity at a Loss for Words

The Miltonic echoes begin to resound once more when the narrator tells us that The Chase is the "oldest wood in England" (*T,* 116), a prehistoric place of natural origins suggestive of both Milton's Eden and Keats's "old oak Forest" in "On Sitting Down to Read *King Lear* Once Again." Tess hopes what Keats does in that poem, that "When through the old oak Forest I am gone,/ Let me not wander in a barren dream,/ But, when I am consumed in the fire,/Give me new Phoenix wings to fly at my desire" (11–14). She will, of course, be disappointed.

Acting the part of the mounted knight, Alec rescues Tess from her fight with Car Darch. He lifts her onto his horse thereby elevating her in reality and in fancy as Tringham's chronicle had elevated her father in history (he really is the last scion of a noble race as was Hyperion in Keats's "The Fall of Hyperion: A Dream") and in fancy (he is enthralled to a punishing fancy as is the knight in "La Belle Dame Sans Merci"). Prior to this scene, the Keatsean atmosphere of luxury is evoked by the narrator's description of the Trantridge revels. There, country lads and maids seem like "a multiplicity of Pans whirl[ing] a multiplicity of Syrinxes: Lotus attempting to elude Priapus, and always failing" (*T,* 107). The narrator's description measures the distance between history and fancy; his "like" is the metonymical copulative informing this and every other romantic conjunction of history and fancy which "mingles Grecian grandeur with the rude/ Wasting of old Time" ("On Seeing the Elgin Marbles," 12–13). It is by this relentless metonymical distancing that Hardy rhetorically answers Keats's question which asks if it is not "too late a day" to "touch" again the "beautiful mythology of Greece" without dulling "its brightness" (Preface, *Endymion*).

Though it is in advance of when we need to say it, the narrator's metonymical conjunction of history and fantasy is proleptic of the final solution to Angel's dilemma. Like the narrator, he must learn to see romance and reality as supplementary discourses which are necessary and useful for describing experience in its factual and emotional aspects. Thus, contrary to Shelley's evolutionary desire and Keats's dream for merger, it is by separating the two modes of representation that some form of accord between head and heart, history and romance, can be achieved. By sustaining the metonymic distance of "like" and not pushing for a metaphoric identity between the imagination and history, "rude wasting Time" becomes an agent of romance via nostalgia rather than an agent of history which destroys the possibility for idealizations.

The Descent of the Imagination

At the moment of Alec's assault of Tess, a justifiably invisible instance in an allegory about the viewless influences of *Geist,* a mist enfolds the romantic couple as it did in Milton's epic shortly before the creation of Eve. Alec "touche[s] Tess with his finger which sank into her as into down" (*T,* 117), as the finger of the Creator had gently sunk into Adam's side. Tess then "fell into a reverie upon the leaves where he left her" (118). Her position is that in which Adam had been left by the Creator, soaked in a "balmy sweat" lying on a bank in Eden. Having been made over by and into Alec's fancy, Tess's world is a "meaner" place as was paradise for Adam after the creation of Eve. Alec has "traced" his romance onto Tess's "beautiful feminine tissue" which is "practically blank as snow" (119), a scriptural metaphor whose intent is to point up the cultural process at issue as well as to identify Tess's body with "nature," a thing to be written on with the "red paint" of impassioned orthodox views which damn her. Later, Tess will tell Alec that "her eyes were dazed by [him] for a little, and that was all" (125), repeating nearly verbatim her father's words after his encounter with Tringham, the mounted antiquarian of Stag's Foot Lane. Alec is "sorry to wound" her as he did, while Tess's "large and impulsive nature" refuses to accept the rewards of her seduction which would make her "[his] *creature*" (125). She will not be a creature "named" by him, as Adam had named all of the creatures in his garden.

In leaving the "chamber of Maiden Thought" and entering the world of painful experience, Tess follows the Keatsean paradigm for salvation whose telos will not complete its intention in her. The narrator's questioning of the "wrong" done to her is predicated upon Shelley's question concerning the death of Keats by those carriers of the letters of culture, the journal critics. Hardy's narrator asks: "Why it was that upon this beautiful tissue . . . there should have been traced such a coarse pattern . . . why so often the coarse appropriates the finer . . . [and why] analytical philosophy [has] failed to explain [this] to our sense of order" (*T,* 119). The original source of his questioning is found in Shelley's *Adonais* when the poet asks:

> O gentle child, beautiful as thou wert,
> Why didst thou leave the trodden paths of men
> Too soon, and with weak hands though mighty heart
> Dare the unpastured dragon in his den?

Tess of the d'Urbervilles: Creativity at a Loss for Words

Defenseless as thou wert, oh, where was then
Wisdom the mirrored shield, or scorn the spear?
Or hadst thou waited the full cycle, when
Thy spirit should have filled its crescent sphere,
The monsters of life's waste had fled from thee like a deer.

(27.235–243)

Because she has dared the unpastured dragon in his den, she cannot avoid the monsters of life's waste which flood her "fancy" and create her a *"figure* of guilt intruding into the haunts of innocence" making "a distinction where there was no difference" (*T,* 135). Yet this is just what culture always does—makes distinctions where it finds no difference—while it is the kind of difference culture makes that is the subtext to the narrator's complaint.

To erase this figure and its difference, Tess journeys to the Valley of the Great Dairies. The Valley is inscribed under the rubric of liberation from writing and is thus a place conducive to willful acts of amnesia as creative disbelief. Talbothays is determined by legends promising a release via the underdetermination of the literal and the illiterate as the "natural." There, Tess plays the romantic milkmaid to Angel's lyrical swain; both are experienced people "playing" at innocence, and both roles will eventually collapse beneath the weight of history. That their "playing at" does not offer them the final solution of marital merger suggests that genuine salvation cannot be achieved by replaying traditional roles; it can only be achieved by inventing new ones, as Shelley had often written and as he exemplified in his life.

In the valley of the rivers (of life), Tess seeks a romantic revolution which will overthrow the torturous law of the *ancien régime* of romance. Her revolutionary desire is underwritten by the signs of nature (as undifferentiated), of the Elizabethan period (as genuinely creative), and by the French Revolution in its Jacobin phase. Talbothays is prepuritanical, Elizabethan, and "lush" like Keats's pseudo-Elizabethan poetry, and Tess and Angel meet there during a "Thermidorean" summer. We will recall that it was during Thermidor that the more extravagant phase of the French Revolution occurred, and it is this extravagance Hardy invokes at Talbothays. Significantly, the pattern of revolution at Crick's reiterates the pattern of failure narrated by the history of the French Revolution which is also the pattern traced by literary history in England in the early nineteenth century. All of these "allusions" of transgression and defeat collude to cast Talbothays as a place of immense romantic possibilities leading to enormous historical failures.

Angel tempts Tess with his vision of Eden which will sweep history to one side and institute a reign of liberty, equality, and camaraderie. In this, he acts like the revolutionary Shelley of "The World's Great Age" who promises that "The world's great age begins anew" when "faiths and empires gleam/ Like wrecks of a dissolving dream" (5–6). Angel will fail to live up to his revolutionary promise because he cannot sweep past faiths or romances to one side. Rather than culture becoming a "wreck" in a "dissolving dream," his dream of Tess dissolves before the historic fact of her existence, leaving him stranded in a barren and unpoetical time without recourse to either romance or religion. In the context of this reading, we need to recall that Tess enters the Vale only after she abandons the "aristocratic" fantasy of her d'Urberville name. The "one point" on which she "was resolved" is that "there should be no more d'Urberville air-castles in the dreams and deeds of her new life" (*T*, 151). Her rejection of her fabular "First Estate" is roughly equivalent to Angel's rejection of his fabular "Second Estate," his entitlement to clergy. Both willingly join the fabular "Third Estate" at Crick's, a sort of romantic revolutionary collective for them although for Crick and his dairymaids it is simply a way of life. This historical analogy is given further credence by Hardy's having his "angel" espouse Rousseau's pastoralism which seeks the triumph of natural culture over aristocratic culture. Thus when his sentimental naturalism fails, the *ancien régime* returns. After the failure of their romantic revolution, Angel is compelled to restore the ancient order of faith (the morality of the Second Estate) and Tess returns to Alec d'Urberville (the First Estate of the aristocracy).

This pattern is given further credence by the biographic links between Richard Crick (Dairyman Dick) and G. R. Crickmay, the Weymouth architect for whom Hardy went to work in May of 1869 "feeling much lightness of heart" (Millgate, *Hardy*, 115–16). Later in life, Hardy will remark that he was happier at Crickmay's than he had ever been in his entire life. When asked what he would rather have done instead of becoming an author, he readily replied that he would have liked to have remained a small-town architect in Crickmay's service (Millgate, 423). Moreover, Crickmay was the man who sent Hardy to St. Juillot, Cornwall, where he experienced a romantically, and some say sexually, satisfying courtship with Emma Gifford, his pair of blue eyes and future wife.

At Talbothays, the presiding poetic Adam nearly names his Eve to the satisfaction of both. The "waow, waow" voice of the milkers suggests a land where the pre-Oedipal delights of intuitive and absolute correspondences can occur. Blackmoor Vale is a place of "blackouts" where history can be forgotten in the eternal return to the natural, or what is more the case, where the historical return of credibility to myths of cyclical renewal can occur. Crick's is a place where Eden can be refound and where Endymion can unite with his Indian Maiden who is his Moon Goddess in the flesh. Tess's orison to the Vale cues us in to these possibilities. Upon entering the valley, she sings "O ye Sun and Moon . . . O ye stars . . . ye Green things upon the Earth . . . ye Fowls of the Air . . . and Beasts and Cattle . . . and Children of Men" (*T*, 158). Her lyric expresses her need to reinvent her life by reinvoking the Adamic authority of naming one's self as a prelude to naming one's world. Her prelude to renewal is predicated upon Adam's prayer to Eden when first he gazes upon its fair prospect. Seeing its unnamed prospects, Adam prays: "Thou sun, said I fair light,/ And there enlightened earth, so fresh and gay,/ Ye hills and dales, Ye Rivers, Woods, and Plains,/ And ye that move first creatures" (*PL*, 8.270–76). Tess wants to be such a "first creature," one who names rather than is named. In this, she desires no more than Wordsworth did in his *Prelude* as a poetical response to what the contemporary world wanted to achieve by revolution and political contract.

The seduction toward which all Talbothay's flirtations tend occurs in an isolated field. There, Milton's Dream of Adam returns once more to structure the event. Prior to their finding themselves alone, Tess has instructed Angel to "call [her] Tess" and not Artemis or Demeter or "other fanciful names" (*T*, 187). Though brief, Tess's scene of instruction reminds us of her status as a potentially vital muse. At this moment she is not Diana, but "the visionary essence of woman" (187) who points the way toward Angel's salvation as well as her own. Their salvation recapitulates that of the poet and his muse in Keats's *Endymion*. Could Endymion possess the Indian Maiden, he would have the Moon Goddess: could Angel possess his Milk Maiden, he would have his Diana. Moreover, the narrator's use of "essence" in this passage is

The Descent of the Imagination

derived from Keats where it means an imaginative *distillation* of concrete experience. And it is this concrete experience that Angel must embrace if he is to have his dream (of Adam) come true (become real). In the pasture at Talbothays, Angel surprises Tess just as the Creator surprised Adam in Milton's Genesis. She does "not know that Clare had followed her round" (*T*, 209); thus she is surprised to find him there. Angel in turn finds her "in a trance, her eyes open, yet unseeing" (208) as were Adam's when in his visionary/receptive phase as he awaits the realization of his desire. At this moment, Angel sees Tess as a muse or Urania figure whose "mouth he had seen nothing to equal on . . . earth" (209). Her face sends an "aura" over his flesh and a "breeze through his nerves" (208), a description whose allusions to romantic correspondences of joy cannot, I think, be missed. Like Adam—or Wordsworth regarding Urania and Endymion viewing Cynthia—Angel falls under an "influence . . . from the sky" (209). Enthralled, his texts of self-propriety "fell back like a defeated battalion" (it is Milton's fallen angels that are glancingly alluded to here), and he rushed over to Tess whom he "take[s] completely by surprise." She yields "to his embrace, after which her lips parted and she sank upon him in her momentary joy, with something very like an ecstatic cry" (209). The key terms in this scene of salvation are orgiastic, a return of pagan joy and ecstasy. Moreover, Angel's near-intercourse with Tess nearly reestablishes the merger of the poet and his muse, the woman saint and her angel of love.

Could they sustain their joy, the romantic pair would return to the untrodden fields. Yet Angel's pagan moment is held in check for "tender conscience sake" (*T*, 209). His "tender" or genteel conscience will not permit him to complete the act of intercourse and so completely commit himself to Tess. He tells her that he did not "mean [his embrace] as a liberty" (*T*, 209) when this is precisely how he should have meant it, since intention signifies all despite the identity of pattern. His taking her would have "looked like" Alec's taking her, yet it would have been remarkably different.

"Liberty" is the key word in his reply. It is Shelley's "liberty" as well as Keats's and to some extent Mill's. What Angel does not understand is what Arnold did not understand about either Keats or Shelley, that "desires and impulses are as much a part of a perfect human being as beliefs and restraints" (Mill, *On Liberty*, 124). "Strong impulses" Mill tells us, "are but another name for energy," that which we have been

194

calling the lyrical impulse in our analysis. "Energy may be turned to bad uses," Mill notes, as it was with Alec, "but more good may always be made of an energetic nature than of an indolent and impassive one" (*On Liberty*, 124) like Angel's. Hardy's narrative will bear out Mill's wisdom in the chapters which follow the divorce at Wellbridge Manor.

Let me cite Hardy's possible source for the scene of romantic failure at Talbothays, which is Arnold's 1880 essay on "Keats." Typically, Arnold gives priority to "Character and self-control, the *virtus verusque labor* so necessary for every kind of greatness, and for the great artist" ("Keats," *Essays in Criticism, Second Series*, 74). Arnold notes that these two virtues are lacking in Keats, or in the immature Keats who gives priority to "sensations" rather than "thoughts" (73). Basically, then, Hardy is in agreement with Mill and in disagreement with Arnold. Later, he will have his narrator tell us that had Angel been a little more energetic and sensuous, a little more like the "un-Cultured" Keats, the real tragedy of Tess's life, her loss of Angel, would not have occurred. Ironically, and it is this irony that bears the force of the cultural critique, Angel is ineffectual because "cultural" in Arnold's moralistic sense of culture. His character is dominated by "thoughts of beauty," thus he cannot respond energetically to the experience of beauty. At Talbothays then, Angel is Arnold's mature Keats whose "master passion is not a passion of the sensuous and sentimental man, is not a passion of the sensuous and sentimental poet"; rather he is mastered by "an intellectual and spiritual passion . . . the mighty *abstract idea* Beauty" (Arnold, "Keats," 84).

Lacking the passionate spontaneity of the younger Keats, Angel is mastered by an abstract idea of beauty which will not be a joy forever. His failure to take Tess in the pastures suggests the current weakness of the pastoral mode of redemption where love is heroic action. As Mill says, "Where not the person's own character but the traditions or customs of other people are the rule of conduct, there is wanting one of the principal ingredients of human happiness, and quite the chief ingredient of individual and social progress" (*On Liberty*, 120). In Angel, it is the Arnoldian character of abstract beauty that prevents his own imagination and passions from overcoming the past and creating a vital present. Angel's genteel interdiction of the lyrical moment at Talbothays wounds Tess's concrete beauty, for it tells her that she is not strong enough— not a strong enough muse—to inspire her poet-worshiper to release his and her spontaneity. Thus the next stage in her attempt at joyful self-definitions will be to marry in law the poet whom she would have married in pagan joy first.

Yet because they have made their desires known to each other, a breach opens wide between their past and the present, and the world becomes a meaner place for them. "Something had occurred which changed the pivot of the universe for their two natures . . . a veil had been whisked aside, the tract of each one's outlook was to have a new horizon thenceforward—for short time or a long" (*T*, 210). It is the scene in The Chase all over again, only now it is Angel's failure to physically penetrate Tess that becomes the problem as Alec's so doing had been the problem formerly. Angel whisks aside a "veil" as Alec had rent her "feminine tissue." Their "new horizon" recalls the "social chasm" breached by Alec's seduction, while the entire figuration recalls Adam's new outlook after the creation of Eve.

As the narrator describes it, Tess and Angel's moment of intercourse in the pasture is the highest *vatic* moment achievable in Wessex. It is a moment when the "veil" is ripped aside and Shelley's "white light" of beautiful truth is glimpsed through the colored glass of ordinary staining perceptions, that matrix of abstract thought which "makes a difference" and always in Wessex a punishing difference. The frustration of romantic joy at this time measures the depth of romantic despair depicted in *Tess of the d'Urbervilles*. Given the best of all possible opportunities for bodily-spiritual revival, neither Tess nor Angel can avail themselves of it.

At Wellbridge whose very name suggests the marital ironies that will occur there, time destroys Angel's romance of Tess. On the one hand, Alec unlawfully beds Tess and in so doing harms her. On the other, Angel refuses to lawfully bed her and harms her even more. In terms of the romantic allegory (and allegory of romanticism) at hand, Angel's failure to act upon desire is a greater crime than Alec's doing so. In terms of the figural continuities within the master allegory of Wessex, Wellbridge presents us with another Casterbridge divorce which invokes by contradiction Wordsworth's emblem of marriage. It is, moreover, by the matrix of implications involved in the comparison between emblem and antiemblem that we can measure the complexity of the tragedy of romanticism that Hardy has written.

The name of Wellbridge represents the central metaphysical concern

Tess of the d'Urbervilles: Creativity at a Loss for Words

of the British romantic revolution which sought to bridge well the abyss between man and man, man and nature, and, in some form or another, man and spirit. History returns on Tess's honeymoon night to interdict anything from being "bridged well" for her or Angel. Moreover, when Tess arrives at her "mansion," it is Christmas, a time for saving births which inspire the writing of new testaments. Such new testaments—in effect, idealized histories presaging hope and redemption—do not get written at Wellbridge because Tess speaks a real history which places her self within time and not beyond it. As a historical being she cannot be an idealized being, an impossibility which itself marks the distance in time between early and late romanticism in nineteenth-century Britain. Coming to him as she does with a history and not with a romance, Tess recalls the fallen world from which Angel seeks to escape by marrying his fantasy of her.

At Wellbridge, natural beauty and the poet cannot overcome culture in its moralized, abstract, and Arnoldian character. Angel cannot overthrow the fictions of the *ancien régime* because he is too committed to their conservative ethos; his Hellenism, like Arnold's, is too Christian. As a Christian Hellene, he cannot "lyricize" Tess's ballad of "the fallen maiden" and create a new poetry as a novel form of consciousness and experience. Rather than legislate his world through new forms of consciousness, he is legislated by the world's culture. Thus, he judges Tess in accordance with the "vulgar morality" of the moment—which desires Hellenism as a decorative rhetoric yet demands Hebraicism as society's rule of conduct—instead of "the affections of the heart" as Shelley recommended poetic spirits should (Preface, *The Cenci*).

During their honeymoon, Milton's Dream of Adam returns once more to structure a scene of transformation without renewal. After Angel confesses his transgressions to her, she "surprises" him with her "sin," the "intelligence" of which "had not yet got to the bottom of him" when he "looked vacantly at her, to resume [listening] with dazed senses" (*T,* 297). His imaginative Mont Blanc has become "vacant," and the view of vacancy "dazes" his senses. The world next becomes a "meaner" place paradoxically filled with Shelley's absolute sense of "silence and solitude." Tess's historical "narrative had effected a terrible and total change in his life, in his universe" (*T,* 298) as did Adam's vision of Eve, first positively and later negatively. Because Angel's "cell of Fancy" has been penetrated by biography, "the essence of things changed" (*T*, 297). Essence for Angel is not Keatsean, the distillation of concrete experience and therefore historical, but a matter of abstract ideas, and therefore idealistic. Hearing the tale of her history, Angel's projected "double" (*T*, 291) or intellectual beauty disappears and "difference" appears: the difference between romance and reality, idealism and history. Rather than "two angels" marrying as "pure spirit with pure spirit intermixing" as they do in Milton's heaven, two historically real beings face each other on the subjected plain of history. Angel wants a Tess who matches his romance of himself, thus when a woman appears who is actually like him (he had had an affair in London), he cannot recognize her historic identity because he refuses to recognize his own.

In denying Tess, Angel effectively denies his own sensuous nature. As Angel rightly says after hearing Tess's history, "forgiveness does not apply to the case. You were one person; now you are another. My God —how can forgiveness meet such a grotesque—prestidigitation as that!" (*T*, 298). Indeed, it cannot in a world where cultural practices define essence and where to be is to be perceived. In essence, there is no one to forgive, no other Tess who stands over against the historical presence which has just supplanted his romance.

Although there is certainly something of Keats's poet facing Memnosyne in "The Fall of Hyperion: A Dream" in the scene where Angel faces a historic Tess, at heart Angel's horror at hearing Tess's real story is predicated upon Arnold's horror at reading Dowden's *Life of Shelley* which had been published in 1886. The ineffectual because cultural Angel Clare is the product of Hardy's critical retroping of Arnold's immoral and so ineffectual Shelley whose "real" history first appeared in Dowden's *Life*. We know that Hardy read Dowden's *Life* in 1894, but we do not know if he read it then for the first time (Björk, *Literary Notebooks*, 2: 64). I suspect that he did not. There can be little doubt as well that Hardy had read Arnold's "Shelley" in 1888 when it first appeared. Arnold's essay is a critique of Dowden's *Shelley,* and it is almost certain that if Hardy had not read Dowden's biography, then Arnold's review of the work would have led him to it. Arnold claims that Dowden's *Shelley* reveals two aspects of the poet, the one an idealist whom he can appreciate and the other a Byronic libertine who disgusts him. It is surely Arnold's split view of Shelley—Shelley the libertine and Shelley the ethereal poet—which informs Hardy's creation of Alec and Angel in order to construct a critical allegory of Arnoldian culture divided against itself because unwittingly committed to "the vulgar morality" even when recommending "sweetness and light" and "flexibility." Arnold's Victorian romanticism then defines Angel's tragic character while it is this form of Hellenism that Hardy satirizes in *Tess*.

Briefly, the "problem" Arnold saw in Dowden's *Life* was that it created two Shelleys; a historic Shelley who was a damnable libertine and an idealistic Shelley who was admirable enough although ineffectual. Arnold had come to know and admire the angelic Shelley through the discreet and protective recollections of T. J. Hogg and Mary Shelley, and it is this "angel" whose bright image had been placed in jeopardy by Dowden's history of the "real" Shelley. Dowden's *Life* disabuses Arnold of his beautiful romance just as Tess's history disabuses Angel of his. Both "poets" are horrified by the libidinous truth of the historical revelation; both figures of Hellenic culture quail before the "grotesque prestidigitation" or specter raised by a historical narrative. For Arnold as for Angel, it is regrettable that "the time had come" for such truths, in Arnold's words, "but come it had" ("Shelley," *Essays in Criticism, Second Series*, 153). In both instances, the advent of historical truth has destroyed an idealized portrait or beautiful appreciation. For both Angel and Arnold, the historical truth destroys the romance; in effect, both would rather muse upon their romance of great beauty than take Hardy's full look at the worst.

Arnold concludes his review of Dowden's *Shelley* with the "liberal" sentiment that it would have been better had Dowden not revealed the truth about the real Shelley. This consideration informs the concluding chapter of "The Consequence" wherein Tess agonizes as to whether or not to reveal her history to Angel. Read as an Arnoldian problem, Tess's dilemma suggests that culture cannot accomodate historic truth despite culture's avowed practice of flexibility fostering imaginative sympathy and seeing things as they really are. The failure of such an accord between culture and history constitutes Angel's, Tess's, and Arnold's problem; it is this problem which Hardy redescribes in his novel, while it is the ultimate conquest of time over romance and law over Tess that inform us of Hardy's view as to which agent of truth would ultimately win the day.

After looking into Dowden's *Shelley*, Arnold set out to write an essay that would evaluate the damage and recuperate his exploded ideal of an angelic Shelley. Arnold solved the problem by willfully suppressing the historical Shelley and dismissing the odious aspect or specter from his memory. This is what Angel tries to do by abandoning Tess and commanding her not to write to him. Arnold's inability to "forgive" Dowden, the biographer, for spoiling so fine an ideal becomes Angel's inability to forgive Tess for spoiling so fine a romance by recounting the truth of her life. In Angel's rejection of Tess, we see that "sweetness and light" is dominated by moral conventions precisely as Shelley hoped romantic forms of Hellenism would not be for much longer. Arnold's career and late revisionist stance toward romantic Hellenism demonstrate the failure of Shelley's program for social and ethical health through love, and it is this failure which constitutes the irreparable wound in Tess's life. Thus, Tess's Arnoldian "Prometheus" fails to merge with his Asia, with the expected result that the "world's new age" does not begin, although the possibility had arisen at Wellbridge.

What this intertextual reading amounts to is a demonstration that Angel's character represents Hardy's quarrel with Arnold, whom Hardy claimed "split hairs" too finely (*Life and Work*, 224). Hardy embodies his criticism of a "hair-splitting" Arnold by splitting Arnold's Shelley into two characters. Angel is Arnold's "beautiful and lovable Shelley" of romance, while Alec is Arnold's "ridiculous and odious" Shelley of biography ("Shelley," 126), which is one reason why Hardy criticism has so often seen Alec as a Byronic character. The Angel of sweetness and light "delights" Tess, while Alec "disgusts" her, as Dowden's libertine Shelley did Arnold. In splitting "Shelley" in two, Hardy reproduces as an external struggle (it is Alec who defines Tess's agon with Angel) what was initially an internal struggle within one personality. Hardy's objectification in this instance does no more than refigure such characters as Donald Farfrae, the romantic-pragmatist, and Grace Melbury, the Wordsworthian-Paterian, as two characters thereby evolving his style of debate with a decaying and fragmented romanticism which once promoted "the whole man" as a unified and unifying cultural ideal. When Hardy sets out to write *Jude,* he will revise Arnold's Shelley once again and reconstitute the two aspects of the poet back into Dowden's one personality, half sensualist, half idealist.

Following Tess's "narrative" (*T,* 297), Angel must face facts although, like Arnold, he wishes that the "time for such truths had never come" ("Shelley," 122). In effect, the romantic "honeymoon" between fable and history has ended for Angel as it had for Arnold. Because the time has come, Arnold is forced "to review his impressions of Shelley" ("Shelley," 125) as Angel is forced to review his of Tess in order to see if fact cannot be squared with imaginative fact, which it cannot. Having wrestled with the problem, Arnold triumphantly claims that "[his romance of Shelley] subsists even after [he] has read the present biography" (125). This is the position toward Tess that Angel will eventually assume after his visit to Brazil. For Arnold, the poetical Shelley will "subsist with many a scar and stain [but] never again will he have the same pureness and beauty which he had formerly" ("Shelley," 125). Arnold's view of the fallen Shelley also informs the narrator's view of Angel after he denounces Tess. Thus, Angel will "subsist with many a scar and stain" now and after Tess's death precisely because he has asserted the moral priorities of Saint Paul and the Bible over the imaginative imperatives of Hellenism's sweetness and light.

Arnold's failure to understand the temperament of the passionately revolutionary Shelley informs Angel's failure to cope with Tess. Like Shelley, Angel falls upon the thorns of life—here cast as historical truth —and bleeds. Like Arnold too, Angel has "to find a sure and safe ground for the continued use and authority of the Bible" (*God and the Bible*, 8) despite an announced commitment to Greek joy. Arnold's fear (and Pater's) that such a commitment could get out of hand will later be figured in Alec's conversion to Angel's "creeds" when he encounters Tess at Long Ash Barn. That Angel fails to practice the flexibility that Arnold preached critiques the limits of Arnoldian flexibility, a limit defined in his essay on "Shelley" as well as in his earlier essay on "Keats." By presenting a satire on Victorian romanticism in general and on Arnold's *Essays in Criticism* Second Series in particular, Hardy suggests that it is Arnold rather than Shelley who is ineffectual when it comes to surmounting the conventions of the past in order to create a new and vital ethos for culture.

To this central consideration which applies Shelley's evolutionary historicism as a corrective to the ethical impasses in Arnold's culture, we might add that Arnold's essay on "Shelley" provides us with a remarkably accurate reading of Angel's indecisive character. Arnold's essay opens with an anecdote which "so far as he knows has not appeared in print hitherto" ("Shelley," 121). The unpublished anecdote which Arnold publishes for the first time is this: Mrs. Shelley asks a friend for advice on schools to which she might send her son. The friend counsels her to "send him somewhere where they will teach him to think for himself" ("Shelley," 151). Mrs. Shelley violently objects to this advice saying, "Teach him to think for himself? Oh my God, teach him rather to think like other people!" (151).

Arnold's preludic anecdote is the source or "mother text" of Angel's problematic character. He cannot marry Tess because he thinks too much like other people and not enough for himself. Arnold of course implies that the better course would have been not to send the young Shelley to the institution recommended by the friend, and he assumes that his readers will think so too after they have perused Dowden's *Shelley*. By way of responding to Arnold's assumptions, Hardy creates an "angel" who demonstrates why such assumptions are damaging to cultural health. It is, specifically, Angel's inability to become passionately involved with Tess which inhibits the free play of his thought over conventional matters, and the narrator is quite specific on this point. Were Angel a little more like Alec, he says, then he would let nothing stand in the way of his possessing Tess. Thus, the Keatsean solution in *Endymion* can only occur if the two "Shelleys" are joined within one character. That is, Arnold's misunderstanding of the value of the complete Shelley becomes Angel's tragedy of incompleteness. After he publishes *Tess,* Hardy will proceed to extend his satire by exploring the problems such a "complete" character would have in Arnoldian culture; this, in effect, is the history of Jude's struggle with Oxford-Christminster, a culture which is fancifully but not actually flexible and imaginatively sympathetic to contemporary society.

Having seen the "real" Shelley, Arnold is inclined too to cry out with Mrs. Shelley: "My God! he had far better have thought like other people" ("Shelley," 150). The exclamation and its import are echoed by Angel when he sees his romance in the harsh light of biography. Then, he too cries out: "My God—how can forgiveness meet such a grotesque —prestidigitation as that!" (*T,* 198). Neither Arnold nor Angel comes to terms with the "grotesque prestidigitation" of history; neither can take Hardy's "full look at the worst" by which he generally means Shelley's view of history in *The Triumph of Life,* and neither can allow any Hellenic "sweetness and light" to enter their ethical ken as more than an intellectual fancy or decorative romance. Read in terms of its textual precedents, Angel's horror at Tess deflects the force of Arnold's moral outrage back onto Arnold himself. Rather than Tess being *sale* or *bête* as Arnold claims Shelley is, it is Angel-Arnold who is seen as abusive and illiberal in his judgment of Tess. In our seeing an "impaired" and "insane" Angel (these are the terms of disapprobation which Arnold leveled at Shelley), we also see a flawed and ineffectual Arnold "beating his luminous wings in the void." The sort of purity which Arnold expects of Shelley is the sort which Angel expects of Tess; this, we should add, is not the sort of purity which "atheist" Shelley expected of the neo-Hellenic mentality. Then, too, it is specifically a Shelleyan plea which Tess levels at her unforgiving Angel when she says: "In the name of our love, forgive me" (*T*, 298).

The sixth seduction of the narrative occurs at Long Ash Barn where Tess meets Alec once more. The name of the barn adequately describes the burnt-out character of Tess's postromantic Wessex, a place without expressive freedom or "sweetness and light" although the textual authority for enacting these Hellenic virtues is there. Long Ash Barn is to be compared to the Carlylean Great Barn in *Far From the Madding Crowd* in order to gauge the distance Hardy has come from a tentative assent to vital forms of romanticism to a complete denial that they could ever become viable cultural practices. The Great Barn at Weatherbury is a cathedral of nature and tradition, a place of work and worship, and not like Long Ash, a place of reiterated scriptures and vulgar Hebraic moralities. Besides the decline from comedy to tragedy it measures in the Hardy canon, the line of descent from the Great Barn to Long Ash traces the decline of romantic culture from its "comic" past to its burnt-out hour in the decadent eighties, whose premises and practices are represented by Alec after Tess converts him to Angel's rational Hellenism.

When she meets Alec in the barn, Tess is Angel's "angel" or messenger, a text-puppet who has gotten his creeds by heart in a parody of what it means to have heartfelt beliefs. She is an obedient and passive being with an external or scriptural character. Her objective subjectivity places in jeopardy all subjectivities in the novel by constituting them as ballads in search of a lyrical expression they never find. The irony of her character cuts even deeper once we realize that the sort of texts she has got by heart promote a liberation from creeds and testaments, from texts themselves. Her angelic creed at this moment is constituted by a combination of Huxley's plea for a separation of mind (image) from nature (abyss) and Voltaire's skeptical tracts of rational enlightenment

(*T*, 401–2). Ironically, she recites these liberationist tracts as a means of keeping herself enthralled to her Angel, while her reciting them to Alec leads to the incarceration of her body and the debilitation of her will.

In this reading, Tess "represents" or dramatizes Angel who comes freighted with liberating creeds he cannot listen to. She represents him in the sense that she reiterates his words and in the sense that she is not aware of the implications in what she says. Ironically, Angel's inherited romanticism keeps Tess negatively "pure" in Mill's sense because it "remain[s] as it were outside the mind, encrusting and petrifying it against all other influences addressed to the higher parts of our nature; manifesting its power by not suffering any fresh and living conviction to get in, but itself doing nothing for the mind or heart except standing sentinel over them to keep them vacant" (*On Liberty*, 103). Her literate vacancy reproduces Angel's, while her reciting Angel's creeds to Alec liberates him from Parson Clare's creeds as they could not Angel.

One level of satire represented by her position is that she is an orthodox romantic liberationist freighted with creeds which are not "realized in the imagination" (*On Liberty*, 103). Thus, the means of escape which lie at hand incarcerate the self and "stand sentinel" over "her higher nature." The vacancy which results is the scriptural equivalent of the unimaginative, despite her intelligible reiteration of the powers and capabilities of love and imagination. At this moment, Tess is a figure of Victorian romanticism which could reiterate "appreciations" of Shelley's poetry and reformist aspirations without acting upon their inherent wisdom. A second level of satire lies in the apparent textual construction of her character and of Angel's. Angel's character is a second-hand construction, but Tess's is third-hand and third-rate. He reiterates what he cannot act; yet she reiterates what she does not understand. Surely there is no small amount of submerged self-revelation here for a novelist who constructs his narratives by reiterating past cultural manifestos adrift in the *zeitgeist* but who will not act upon them himself? Moreover, at this stage of her tragedy, Tess represents a culture that can appreciate a Shelley or a Voltaire but that will not stray from God and the Bible. Arnold should act upon his preachments, the satire reads, and England should be alert to Arnold's inconsistencies. Then, too, we might consider that Tess's repetition of Angel's Hellenic creeds articulates her love for a romantic poet who has failed her, yet whom she hopes will return

Tess of the d'Urbervilles: Creativity at a Loss for Words

if she "sticks to the letter" of his manifestos. In effect, she keeps hope alive by reiteration, as Hardy does regarding Shelley's romanticism. Whatever the case, the character of Tess's reiteration points to her status as a "Daughter of Memory" rather than of the Imagination, a status that emphasizes her passivity and subjection to time rather than her ability to overcome it. Read this way, Tess is the proper muse for Wessex; she is a temporal Urania of reiteration who parodies past programs of redemption that she cannot enact. She repeats faithfully poems she has memorized instead of producing new poems; thus she transforms self-expression into a theatrical event peopled by actors and actresses who have memorized their lines but who do not know their import.

As agents of culture and religion at Long Ash, Tess and Alec are pure figures of speech. Their textual interaction presents us with an emblem of the tragic agency of the novel. At this time, Alec is a second-hand Angel Clare because he has become the "spiritual son" of Parson Clare. His conversion to religion equals in form and function Tess's to Angel's Hellenic creeds, which are an orthodox religion to her rather than a means of liberation from orthodoxies. In a self-evident play of texts, Tess converts Alec to Angel's Hellenism which liberates his desire (as it did not Angel's) which, in turn, leads to his retaking Tess at Sandbourne, an aesthetic retreat whose very name suggests the ungrounded character of its aestheticist life-style. Alec's possession of Tess at Sandbourne depicts Arnold's and Pater's worst fears regarding the "mistaking" of pagan joy for pure hedonism in a culture of licence.

In the scene of textual exchange at Long Ash, Tess's words act as Alec's creator-muse thereby recalling the Miltonic Dream of Adam once more, always with reference to Keats. After he is recreated by Tess's "angelic" words, Alec seems "like a man awakening from a luring dream" (*T*, 402). He claims that Tess "tempted [him]" and tells her that her mouth is as "maddening" as "Eve's" (402). After this Miltonic scene of creation, his "old self" seems to have returned; yet this is not entirely the case, for every advance in the narrative represents a stage of literary history wrought by a textual transformation of a former stage. The libidinal "country squire"—a kind of bourgeois imitation of the whig Shelley—is not reinstated after Tess converts him to hedonism. Rather, a Paterian aesthete appears where a passionate preacher of Hebraic texts once stood.

The Descent of the Imagination

In terms of literary history, Arnold's hedonist Shelley returns as an aesthete of the decadence. The aesthetic note begins to refrain when the narrator tells us that after Alec's conversion, Tess's "Cyprian image" suddenly "appeared upon the altar, whereby the fire of the priest had been wellnigh extinguished . . . as in the legend" (*T*, 384). The "legend" to which the narrator cryptically refers is a Paterian fable such as "Persephone and Demeter" which recounts the return of exiled Grecian gods and goddesses as patrons and practitioners of aesthetic delights. By way of appreciating her Cyprian image, Alec remarks: "I though I worshipped on the mountains, but I find I still serve in the groves!" (*T*, 402). Alec's new understanding charts the descent of the romantic imagination from its northern, Hebraic position to its southern, Hellenic position which then declines even further to become the decadent literary life-style promoting style as life in the eighties and nineties.

In order to liberate himself from Parson Clare's views, Alec finds a "freer way of taking, a possible modification of, certain moral precepts" as had Giordano Bruno in *Gaston De Latour,* Pater's final word on the subject of the lower pantheism published in the *Fortnightly Review* of 1889, just in time for Hardy to peruse it while writing *Tess*.[7] Tess provides Alec with an argument by which he can energize his "primitive ideas, [those] with [an] earlier and more liberal air." Her words provide him a rationale for permissiveness just as his role as "the country squire" had provided him with such at Trantridge. Created by Tess's angelic words, Alec's lost dream of Tess becomes real and his erotic "Eve" returns. A wide abyss then opens between his *fictional* past as a preacher and his *fabulous* present as a "worshiper" in the groves. Soon after, Alec "returns to this ancient 'pantheism' after the long reign of a *seemingly opposite* faith" (*Gaston,* 142, emphasis added).

Alec's fabular Hebraic "faith" is as seemingly opposite to his fictive Hellenism as was Bruno's genuine Hebraic faith to his genuine Hellenism. The narrator repeats Pater's subtle distinction which is no distinction at all when he comments that Alec's conversion is the effect of "a careless man in search of a new sensation" (*T*, 403). Like Bruno, Alec shifts narratives, from the Hebraic to the Hellenic, and like Bruno, the desire within the narrative is the same despite a different patterning or articulation of it. Though there is certainly some parodying of English culture's Hellenic and Hebraic dialectic in Alec's conversion, what is of thematic importance is the presentation of the purely superficial charac-

Tess of the d'Urbervilles: Creativity at a Loss for Words

ter of cultural discourse at the present time which can be put on and shrugged off like garments. Whereas Bruno's shifts were profound, Alec's are merely decorative. And while we might condemn his superficiality, it does present us with half of the solution to Tess's dilemma, which is to see all conventions as "styles" rather than absolutes with transcendental legitimacy. Alec sees the import in Angel's creeds which Angel does not, and acts upon them in a way that Angel should have and, incidentally, Shelley did. In this sense, he supplies the right response in the wrong situation because Tess does not love him.

The seventh scene of seduction by texts occurs in Brazil when Angel is transformed into a "Citizen of the World" by the "large-minded stranger." The stranger helps Angel to see the relativity of all cultural values—a relativity explained, significantly, in the romantic terms of the Swiss landscape of mountains and vales (*T,* 422)—after which he can make a philosophy for himself which suits his temperament, one that need not exclude a nostalgia for past romances. The man of liberal views is a mounted Tringham figure who penetrates Angel's consciousness with a late eighteenth–century ideal which romantics from Shelley to Mill had tried to revive as an essential element of liberal culture. In keeping with the Miltonic analogue, Hardy means Brazil to be an Eden where Angel can see "the way things mostly are & always have been" as opposed to how culture had fancifully construed them (*Literary Notebooks,* 2: 6). If we follow the clues provided by Hardy's surviving notebooks, we can construe the Brazilian tropics as an antithetically natural foil to Wordsworth's ethical nature as well as to Arnold's moral Hellenism. Brazil as Eden is not a place where the romantic imagination saves the wandering sinner through a vision of vengeful mountains rising to crush the transgressor; rather, the primeval forests are a Huxleyan region where the mind as a repository of cultural representations is understood as distinct and apart from the world or reality in itself. In Brazil, "all things are simplified" (*Literary Notebooks,* 2: 6) rather than exaggerated, sublimated, idealized, or personified. In this Eden of the abyss, Angel sees that all conventions are productions of the cultural word, not absolutes. Therefore he can shape things the way he wants them if he can willfully enact what he says he wants. In effect and by way of the Miltonic-Keatsean paradigm, Angel learns how to dream like Adam and realize his own desires.

In other words, Angel learns Mill's lesson that history and romance

The Descent of the Imagination

"derive their utility from the deficiencies of the other" (*On Liberty*, 110). Ideally, they are complementary discourses which need not be antagonistic. All along, Angel has been characterized as a "promising intellect combined with a timid character" (*On Liberty*, 95). Given his timid and intimidated character, he does not possess "the resources of ingenuity [which attempt] to reconcile the prompting of his conscience and reason with orthodoxy" (*On Liberty*, 95). In Brazil and thanks to the aid of "the large-minded stranger," Angel ingeniously reconciles history with romance by becoming a typically "split personality," such a Donald Farfrae, who accepts his duality as a compensating form of romanticism's whole man. From the moment that "[h]is inconsistencies rushed in upon him like a flood" (*T*, 422), his salvation begins, for this is the moment of a genuine historical awareness which emphasizes the chaos of the ego's selfhood as a reflection of the chaos of scriptural possibilities in the world, as the world. During his moment of historical enlightenment, contradiction interdicts his fantasy "character of perfection." In the interim, his repressed desire for Tess begins to speak because his narrative of perfection has been silenced. He begins to understand that he has dwelt in Mill's "deep slumber of decided opinions" (*On Liberty*, 95), a condition Hardy had allegorically presented at Wellbridge when Angel sleepwalks and buries Tess (his beauty and his life) in the abbot's coffin.

After much "thought and discussion" with the large-minded stranger, Angel "throws himself into the mental position of those who think differently from" him, those of a more "cosmopolitan mind" (*T*, 422). He then "substitutes one partial and incomplete truth for another" because he now understands the "difference between the political value and the imaginative value" of facts (*T*, 423). In temperament, he is well on his way to becoming an aesthetic historian such as Hardy understood that Paterian profession. According to Pater, the aesthetic historian comprehends the distinction between that which "comes from the world without" and that which "comes from the vision within" (Pater, quoted from Hardy's *Literary Notebooks*, 2:17). Because Angel has gained the ability to separate romance from reality, he can accept reality as it is rather than as he would like it to be and thereby make it something closer to what he would like it to be. Tess's d'Urberville name which had been a sign of her decadent will becomes "a most useful ingredient to the dreamer and the *historian* of decline and fall" (emphasis Hardy's from the *Graphic* edition). As a "dreamer and historian," Angel is a

208

nostalgia artist musing upon ruins much as Gibbons did in Rome. In effect, Angel becomes a historian of the fall (or Tess's fall) who recuperates loss with nostalgia. By so doing, he accepts history as an agent of romance rather than a destroyer of it. It is thus under the sign of decline and fall that time becomes a "romantic" agent. Time might "ruthlessly destroy his own romances" (*T*, 423) as the narrator tells us quoting Shelley's "Epipsychidion," but in the wake of that destruction nostalgia restores in parable that which was removed in reality.

Given his incipient nostalgia, the "historic interest of [Tess's] family" acquires positive value for Angel. Her name is no longer a decadent thing, but a romantic thing, a ruin or an abbey fraught with picturesque and sentimental associations which artfully transmute the oppressive facts and barren truths concerning the faiths and empires which built them. Angel learns "that the new fragment of [romantic] truth is more wanted, more adapted to the needs of the time than that which it displaces" which is factual truth and conventional estimates of value (*On Liberty*, 109). By accepting romance as a supplementary discourse to history, Angel gives "both elements . . . their due," the romantic "d'Urberville" name and the historic character of a "particular" d'Urberville whom he has married. By so doing, he makes poetical a barren time by comprehending the pastness of the past and thereby freeing the present to speak its mind. That is, Angel becomes a figure who no longer accepts the cultural dominance of the past and who can then create a poetical present suitable to his desire.

Once emancipated from the burden of history, Angel recalls Tess's image. His recollection conjures a "vision" that "sent an *aura* through his veins" (*T*, 423) that he had felt at Talbothays when he had nearly achieved romantic enlightenment. As a figure of Adam in Eden, Angel in Brazil will next dream of embracing his vision in the flesh. To do so, he will have to become his own "Creator-Word" and then become a co-conspirator with Tess. Together, they will overthrow the *ancien régime* of aristocratic culture and by so doing clear a space for self-expression. Before this revolution can occur however, Tess has to free herself from Alec. She gains her liberation by murdering him with a knife, returning phallus for phallus and heart-wound for heart-wound. By the law of the double negative, Tess returns her self to its pure, uninscribed state by forcibly erasing all textual impositions from her "feminine tissue." After she kills Alec, Tess becomes an outlaw who exists "on the road" be-

The Descent of the Imagination

tween all confining and defining discourses in a "space" of self-expression free of language. Figuratively, her murder places her in a Brazil of her own, a primitive, undetermined region where the body has not yet been colonized by tyrannical narratives. In this unwritten space, she becomes an Eve figure who is no man's fancy and who fancies a man of her own in Angel.

By killing Alec, Tess picks up where she had left off at Talbothays during her "Thermidorean" period of erasure with its concomitant possibilities for transgression. She arrives at this place once more by following the self-threatening knowledge in Angel's words, for it is he who had told her at Wellbridge that "If [Alec] were dead it might be different" (T, 313). At Sandbourne, his words incite a Jacobin revolution of terrible revolt whose historical subtext is decapitation, castration, and the "horrors" of gender inversion.[8] The violence she turns against Alec reflects the violence his phallic romances had turned against her. Her murder of Alec liberates her from the enthrallment of her "conqueror" Alexander while it is also a form of therapy which relieves her of the burden of history (the recent past) and thereby replaces her in a virginal past (the remote past of Marlott). In allegory, the death of the recent past of culture clears the way for the return of the remote and authentic romantic past of liberty and love.

This occurs because in taking up the knife against Alec, she effectively severs her body from all discursive impositions. Freed of all influence and textual positions, she becomes a muse existing where all romantic muses should exist, beyond discourse. As a muse, she inspires her poet-angel to timely utterances of lyrical release. Together, they produce a paradise. In her opening Adam's side, that is, Tess realizes her own Edenic desire by reclaiming from the male (God/Word) the right of primogeniture and in so doing returning myth to biology, culture to history, romance to the body.

Following the Miltonic paradigm, Tess assumes the creative "finger" of God and removes from her sleeping Adam a creature of great beauty who will bring her great joy and everything she desires. That creature born of Tess is Tess herself. Tess dreams of her desire to kill Alec before she actually murders him as Adam had dreamed of Eve. Her death wish induces in her a "temporary hallucination" (T, 475) like Adam's trance in Eden. She then inflicts upon Alec a "wide wound with blood streaming fresh" (PL, 8. 465–67), and we see the blood stream on the ceiling of Mrs. Brooks's parlor. Afterward, Tess awakens from the trance to discover that her dream of freedom has become real. The world next becomes a "meaner" place for her because, on the one hand, she anticipates a future romantic delight which will render her past romance sordid and ugly, while on the other she is an outlaw without legal freedoms. Her transgression is criminal according to the old testaments of the cultural and social order, but "saintly" and "Saint Theresan" according to the creative imperatives of cultural production.

Though it is somewhat incidental to the narrative, we should note that Tess's self-creation occurs in Mrs. Brooks's boarding house and that the proprietor's name alludes to Dorothea Brooke of *Middlemarch*. Tess's story is above hers, as it were, a continuation or the next story after Eliot's in the sequence of narratives about failed and frustrated attempts by heroines to free themselves from culture's Causaubons. Tess's murder begins a brief crusade which will result in her eventual "martyrdom" for the romantic faith in the "country of the Moors," the land of the philistines and barbarians of culture and society. Romantically conceived, her knife is the "key to all mythologies" in the sense that it is the tool which unlocks the present from its incarceration by the past. Her knife is the agent of lyrical release and so the technical equivalent of the large-minded stranger's discourse which liberates Angel. The stranger's death "sublimes" his words just as Alec's death "sublimes" Tess's desire to liberate desire. Although it may strike some as a curious formulation, in *Tess* murder as a form of lyrical release is the solution to seduction and rape as a form of narrative confinement.

On the road to Bramshurst, Angel and Tess meet absolved of their sociocultural "souls," those fables of self which inhibit self-expression. When Tess "flies" after Angel, he does not see her as a "Diana or Faustina or Cornelia or Lucretia" as he once did, but as "a human figure running," a biological "form" which he describes as "a woman's" (*T*, 473). Her flight characterizes her as a muse figure, but it is the muse of the body's desire which is figured here, a "being" which is disburdened of painful memory and in search of authentic satisfaction. Angel's recognition of the body in its primitive "simplicity" is the prelude to their lyrical moment of intercourse at Bramshurst where they will *not* reenact the Miltonic paradigm of the "Dream of Adam/The Creation of Eve" and by their omission reconstitute the imaginative paradise of the romantic imagination.

The Descent of the Imagination

Bramshurst is a "court" of love as Keats imagined it in his "Ode to Psyche" as well as a "Tennis Court" where Tess and Angel reenact the French scene of liberationist oath taking. The ode to renovation and renewal occurs there because "no living soul [arises] between them" (*T*, 476). Disburdened of their surfeit of soul which is a surfeit of text, Tess and Angel are headed "nowhere in particular" (476), meaning that all narrative expectations have passed away. They become "intoxicated" with each other's pure presence instead of with a prescriptive image. By going nowhere in particular, they arrive at an "empty mansion," a phrase which recalls Milton's Creator's description of Eden, yet whose "emptiness" suggests that it is dispossessed of the Word. The narrator suggests the Edenic condition of this scene when he describes the unrented mansion as a "happy house" (482). The Court then is the "house beautiful" of romantic culture where genuine enactments of metaphor, copulation, and dialectical integration result in desirable correspondences predicated upon elective affinities both real and imaginary.

Love briefly returns to Wessex at Bramshurst and with it the entire complex of romantic cultural possibilities entailed in the emblem of marriage. During Tess and Angel's stay there, the rooms remain "in darkness" for they have entered the realm of Dionysus from which form derives its content, shape its intuition of substance. The reverse has been the case up until now, for parodic Wessex has been a punishing, Apollonian region where form dominates desire. In the dark space, the Keatsean "ellectric fire [sic]" of pure vitality burns away the dross of past narrative romances, thus permitting "existence" to silently speak it desire. At Bramshurst, Tess and Angel enter Keats's Chamber of Maiden-Thought as a prelude to their emergence into the vale of soul-making which, for them, will be a vale of tears. In their Bramshurst chamber of innocence, they "see nothing but pleasant wonders, and think of delaying there for ever in delight" (Keats, *Letters*, 5/3/18). There, Angel finds "rest at last" after which he and Tess remain "in great quietness" for nearly a week (*T*, 478). Both remain quiet because beauty is truth once more and fanciful images of romance are kept at a distance. There, Tess becomes Angel's "unravished bride of quietness," while their mating enacts a mystical (because bodily) marriage of desire with desire.

At Bramshurst "by tacit consent," Tess and Angel "hardly once spoke of any incident of the past" (*T*, 480). If words as the spirit have been the problem, then silence is the solution. In order to structure this moment

Tess of the d'Urbervilles: Creativity at a Loss for Words

of erasure and redemption, Hardy turned to Keats's "Ode to Psyche," traces of which remain embedded in the scene. The inaugural question to Keats's poem, "Surely I dreamt today, or did I see/ The winged Psyche with awaken'd eyes?" (5–6) applies equally to the revelations that occur at Bramshurst where romance and reality, desire and the body, merge. Like Apuleius's version of the trials of Psyche which inspired Keats's poem, Tess's life recounts the trials of beauty at the hands of Eros, figuratively a winged Cupid or, in Hardy's version, an Angel Clare whose punishing commands Tess follows to the letter.

By allusion, we can compare the comic culture represented by Apuleius's *Golden Ass* and the romantic culture of Keats's odes with Hardy's tragic culture where beauty is executed and not enthroned. As a Psyche figure, Tess's search for genuine eros refigures Keats's "system of Spirit creation" which leads the "intelligence" to "the sense of Identity." Identity so construed can only arise if the self can overthrow its enthrallment to the past and live creatively in the present (*Letters*, 2/14; 5/3/19). Self-shattering is the road to identity in Keats, and it is this road which leads Tess and Angel to Bramshurst.

A close inspection of the literary architecture of Bramshurst Court reveals its near-relation to Keats's "Ode to Psyche." The "crimson damask hangings" (*T*, 478) of the bed chamber are on loan from Keats's ode where the poet promises that "Dryads shall be lull'd to sleep,/ And in the midst of this wide quietness/ A rosy sanctuary will I dress" (58–59). To enter Bramshurst, Angel must "clamber in" through an open "casement" after which he lets Tess "in after him." This scene of entry is patterned upon the ode wherein Keats promises that "there shall be for [Psyche] all soft delight" once the "casement" is "opt at night,/ To let the warm Love in!" (64–66, 67). In a spirit similar to Keats's poet-persona, Hardy's narrator promises to be Tess-Psyche's "voice, thy lute, thy pipe, thy incense sweet." He is her "priest [who will] build a fane/ In some untrodden region of the mind" (49–50), notably Bramshurst Court. His promise is reiterated by Hardy in the epigraph to *Tess* which closely parallels in diction and intent Keats's vatic promise to Psyche.

One of the working titles for *Tess* had been "Too Late Beloved." The phrase alludes to Keats's ode where the poet apostrophizes beauty as "O brightest! though too late for antique vows,/ Too too late for the fond believing lyre/ When holy were the haunted forest boughs" (37–38). Keats's nostalgia for some sacred past of poetry summarizes the central longing of the novel and of Hardy's latter-day Wessex in general. It is the disappearance of such "haunted forests" that obsesses and troubles Hardy as it does Keats, while it is the acceptance of history as a premise to nostalgic idealizations that constitutes the solution for Hardy as for Keats. Like Psyche, Tess has come "too, too late for the fond believing lyre" of her Angel—or any would-be romantic—with his belated, "second-hand harp" or romantic texts which have become purely formal reiterations rather than genuinely revolutionary and inspirational instrumentalities. Rather then her eventual elevation into the company of Olympians by a strong, overcoming Eros, Tess will descend into the inferno of modernism where Shelley's "riddles of death Thebes never knew" prevent the romance of overcoming from being regarded as anything other than a quaint fancy.

Yet the Bramshurst Court of Love is the singular exception to the rule of cultural law in Wessex. In this unrented space where the romantic past is not "rent" or torn to shreds, the self can speak with authority and become "unrented" or whole. In the empty mansion Tess becomes the "latest form and loveliest vision far/ Of all Olympus' faded hierarchy" ("Ode," 24–25). There, she reigns "unrent" or pure until the faded hierarchy returns and repossesses her, (mis)placing her back into the power of "The President of the Immortals" who initially had been "Time, the Arch-satirist" in the Graphic version of the novel (Tess, Textual notes, 500). When the caretaker stumbles upon Tess and Angel, she sees "a stream of morning light through the shuttered chink [fall] upon the faces of the pair" (T, 481), just as Keats's poet did when he "wandered in a forest thoughtlessly,/ And on the sudden, fainting with surprise,/ Saw two fair creatures, couched side by side" ("Ode," 7–9). Tess and Angel lay "wrapped in profound slumber; Tess's lips being parted like a half-opened flower near [Angel's] cheek" (T, 481–82). The sleeping Bramshurst pair are in the same position that Keats finds a Psyche and Cupid who "lay calm breathing on the bedded grass/ Their arms embraced . . . their lips touched not, but had not bid adieu/ As if disjoined by soft-handed slumber" (15–18).

At Bramshurst then, we are asked to imagine the unimaginable, the return of the lyric impetus. Though embedded in a satire about fictions, Bramshurst offers us a scene of difference which stands over against the other nine seduction rapes by narrative in the narrative. This difference, however, is what has been desired all along in a narrative structured on sameness. Figuratively, the Miltonic "Dream of Adam" is not invoked at Bramshurst so that the difference of difference might silently speak. In terms of the Wessex project, Bramshurst's unrented mansion is equivalent to the marginal space of the satirist whose position is different from that which he parodies. His satires critique that which they repeat in order to negate that which they are committed to display as derivative. By such an act of irony and reiteration, the satirist gains an equivalent form of liberation to the erasure he desires but cannot find. In this view, Bramshurst is undoubtedly the most optimistic topos in all of Hardy's major fictions because it signifies or names a place where the possibility for an equivalent form of romantic authenticity returns. And it is from this space of equivalence that the satirist can leave off writing and the poet can begin to speak.

From the silence of love at Bramshurst, Tess and Angel travel toward the silence of death at Wintoncester, stopping along the way at Stonehenge, a place of cultural beginnings which have hardened into absolute conclusions. At the Henge, Tess will be reinscribed into the law as an outlaw, which defines her status as having no status at all. In its stony circularity, the Henge is an emblem of narrative closure which admits of no escape, as well as of the ruined character of the sacred "druidic" past from which both first- and second-generation forms of romanticism sprang. The ring's stony circle suggests repetition without saving distortions within a cultural closure deprived of redemptive alternatives. At the Henge, Tess-Prometheus is rebound to rock of the Caucasus where she awaits the black vultures of "The President of the Immortals" (*T*, 489) to come and pluck her liver or "life"—or as Shelley recasts it, her heart—from her once more.

Stonehenge is constructed from an ensemble of three literary anti-Edens: Gethsemene, where the Son of Man is betrayed by a kiss; Eden in Book Eight of *Paradise Lost* (for the ninth time in the narrative), and the fallen Eden of Book Twelve of *Paradise Lost* wherein Eve is sent a saving vision by the Creative Word in compensation for her death by sin which is the origin of history. Tess will be denied this saving vision by her Angel and thus will die as the Son of Man, a woman born of man's word and condemned by his sociocultural narratives. The scene of the Henge recalls further the trope of the eolian harp with particular reference to Coleridge's "Dejection Ode." Unlike the joyous harp which figures so strongly in Wordsworth's poetry, Hardy's Henge is a dark

The Descent of the Imagination

conceit which wails a monotonous "booming tune" of terror, its very structure rendering "the black sky even blacker" (*T*, 482). The harp of the Henge is thus a "spot of time" which does not effect a compensating vision of redemption; its presence signals the return of Burke's sublime of terror which obliterates the romantic sublime of joy.

Having recently merged with his muse, Angel possesses the insight to correctly name the stony circle as a "monstrous place" over which "stiff breezes blew" (*T*, 482) as they did before Wordsworth had characterized the winds as gentle and gracious. The "gigantic one-stringed harp" (483) is a "Temple of the winds" (484) in the novel version of *Tess*, while in the *Graphic* version the Henge is a "Hall of Pandemonium," a place to which the romantic "angels" of enlightened revolt have fallen and become petrified. In Tess's Wessex, the giants of an enlightened romantic revolt have fallen and petrified into Hebraic orthodoxies and decorative ruins. What is needed is a revolt of the Titans against the Olympians, but there are not such Titans remaining in Tess's world. Stonehenge thus represents this fallen condition insofar as it is a gigantic figure of permanent defeat and imprisonment whose epic proportions match and cancel the literary effects of romantic epics of revolt from, say, Blake's *Jerusalem* to Shelley's *Prometheus Unbound*.

We can begin to understand just how drastic a negation is at issue here by reading the scene beside Coleridge's "Dejection: An Ode." Lying as they do in erotic and imaginative despair, the generative concerns of Coleridge's ode align it to the themes of *Tess*, while the generic relation of Coleridge's ode to the courtly "plaint to a lady" is synonymous with Hardy's narrative "plaint" to Tess. In his ode, Coleridge writes mournfully of "Reality's dark dream" which is apprehended by an awareness of the abyss between sign and reference, sense and sensibility, imagination and nature. In stanza seven, Coleridge interrupts his meditation upon the bleakness of a world without genuine imaginative correspondences in order to interject a brief tale concerning "a little child/ Upon a lonesome wild,/ Not far from home, but she hath lost her way / And now moans low in bitter grief and fear/ And now screams loud, and hopes to make her mother hear" (94–135). Coleridge's little girl lost returns to the scene of loss and dejection as Tess. Like her predecessor in type, Tess is lost upon a lonesome wild not far from her mother's home. As she tells Angel, "One of mother's people was a shepherd hereabout . . . so I am at home" (*T*, 484). All along, Tess has struggled to (re)find the mother within her who is her "home" or true center. In other words, she needs to give a voice to the narcissistically inclined ideal ego which has the potential to shatter the misprisoning ego ideals of the father. That Tess's mother was a shepherd who worked near the Henge suggests further that Tess is a daughter of the romantic pastoral tradition. Failing to (re)find the romantic mother within herself, she returns in defeat to the scene of her origin, thereby closing the circle where it originated on Salisbury Plain in poems such as Wordsworth's "Guilt and Sorrow."

All pastoral utopias become Gethsemenes at the Henge where a redemptive beauty is betrayed by a kiss. Tess's "I am ready" reiterates the Son of Man's single utterance in the Garden of the Rock. In the Wessex Gethsemene, Tess and Angel enact the biblical scene of betrayal as the betrayal of the romantic redeemer, which for Keats and for Hardy is beauty and its effects on consciousness. While Tess sleeps, Angel "kneels down beside her" (*T*, 484). When the agents of law come for her, Angel reenacts Peter's defense of his Christ: "Springing to his feet, [he] looked around for a weapon, loose stone, means of escape, anything" (486). Because Adam's dream has damned her, Tess can only find the equivalent of peace as "a lesser creature than a woman" (487). Her salvation lies neither upward in some hypothetical empyrean nor inward in explorations of a subjectivity so thoroughly colonized by cultural narratives as to be absolutely alienating. For Tess, salvation lies downward toward the body of desire which lies beneath and before the hermeneutic circling of culture's testamental gardens of stone.

This last scene of the taking of Tess reiterates the essential features of all eight others wherein Eve is taken by Adam's fancy and characterized in accordance with his wishes which are demands. At the Henge, Tess sleeps on the altar stone. There, she is surprised by the word of law whose dark figures daze her by their sudden approach: "What is it Angel?" she asks, "Have they come for me?" (*T*, 487). Her forced taking by the law opens an "immeasurable social chasm" between past and present, thereby dissolving the redemptive authority of Shelleyan and Keatsean love which she and Angel had experienced at Bramshurst. Hardy renders his final allusion to Milton even darker by superimposing Book Twelve of *Paradise Lost* onto Book Eight in order to construct a scene of continuation (of the same) and conclusion (of difference), of repetition (Tess is reinscribed into the law) and finale (Tess is dead). We will recall that, despite all she has done, Milton's Creator sends Eve a kindly "dream propitious presaging some great good" to comfort her before she enters the "subjected plane" of history. Eve has fallen asleep with "sorrow and heart's distress/ Wearied" (*PL*, 12. 610–15) as has Tess, yet no dream of hope comes to Tess because culture has forgotten how to dream comforting dreams which prophesy a joyful outcome to history's sorrowful narratives, which is the Word's prophecy to Eve. The absence of dreams at this point in the narrative—and we will recall that Tess asks Angel for a dream presaging the great good of their meeting again in some unspecified future (*T*, 486)—implies that she now faces reality's darkest dream which is not to have any dreams at all.

Deprived of every comforting fancy, Tess regresses from being half in love to becoming fully in love with death. She accepts her incarceration by narratives which say again to her what they have always said, "die." Because all representations of life have been death sentences to her (to her self), she desires to die as a means of achieving an equivalent pleasure to that which is denied her. Taken once more and for the last time by narratives, Tess is sentenced to death in a court proceeding that is not represented in the narrative. In this way, her sentencing represents the literal truth of her tragedy, how it occurred (invisibly) and why it occurred (by ruling texts). The unstated pain of the Court of Law is thus the contrapuntal emblem to the unstated pleasure of Bramshurst Court, the one a place of sentencing which annihilates the romantic couple, the other a place where all sentences and their determinations are erased thus promoting the merger of the romantic couple.

Just before she is taken, Tess's angel refuses to promise her a small fancy of redemption. Tess hears his denial and accepts it, finally realizing perhaps the absolutely alienating character of her culture. She asks Angel "do you think we shall meet again after we are dead? I want to know." Angel in turn "kissed her to avoid a reply at such a time." Tess understands the kiss as a "no" (*T*, 486). His kiss betrays her final imaginative fantasy of reunion which kindness would have given her but which reason withholds. His reasoned refusal alerts us to the resurgence of romantic failure in his character. Rather than a well-balanced Angel Clare who understands the place of fancy within history, we see a realist and a skeptic who refuses to utter any fanciful comfort to the distressed mind. In effect, Angel recapitulates the final imbalance we have seen emerge in characters like Donald Farfrae who once had achieved a balanced view of reason and romance. Moreover, in Angel we see the rationalist, atheist Shelley denying the irrationalist, myth-making Shelley. Thus, Angel can tear down old faiths fallen into superstition, but he cannot construct any new myths to replace them—even though he will soon have all that he would need to do so: the love of a heavenly muse (Tess) as well as that of an earthly or corporeal muse (Liza-Lu).

After her execution by hanging, Tess is figuratively suspended on the "stiff" breezes at Wintoncester, the original capital of Wessex. Originality has been the romantic problem at issue in her life and so it is appropriate that she die in the original capital, thereby closing the account and ending the quest. The black flag which alerts all onlookers to her death is also a palimpsest which represents the agency of her death. Moreover, the very lineaments of the city over which it/she flies betray the tragic conflicts of her existence, for Wintoncester is at once imaginative and rational, ancient and modern, idealistic and historic. There, cathedrals exist side by side with "red brick buildings, of a modern construction, the whole contrasting greatly by its formalism with the quaint irregularities of the Gothic erections" (T, 489). From on high— which is presently the narrator's and Angel's position—the concerns of the narrative as well as the figurative contours of the narrative spread out beneath the gaze. Past aspirations (the spires) are petrified and interspersed between "modern constructions" which are linear, practical, and unpoetical. Seen in "an isometric plan," the city resembles the "plan" or map of the narrative wherein imaginative aspirations reside beside but do not merge with reasonable possibilities, where the past of romantic aspiration is petrified and the imaginationless present is horizontal, linear, and purely historical. The compartmentalized character of the overview represents the divorced condition of the imaginative reason in Wessex, while the overview of such divorcements represents, finally, the "subjected" plain of recent cultural history such as Hardy viewed it.

Mergers do not occur in Tess's Wessex where the imaginative reason is the one thing necessary but missing. In seeking to revive lyrical aspirations toward the genuine beauty of self-expression, Tess has sought to locate a space in which to erect those "quaint irregularities" of self within a highly formal sociotext "of a modern construction." Significantly, Tess is condemned for her "quaint irregularities," in the narrator's final allusion to Tess's sex and her crimes of passion. Instead of a sustained lyrical joy, Tess finds only "a formalism . . . bespeaking captivity" (*T*, 489). Form bespeaks captivity by speaking for the self and thereby prohibiting the self from uttering its fondest desires.

In Wessex then, the future of poetry is not immense, as Arnold had claimed it would be, because the religious impetus which is the poetic spirit cannot practice what it preaches. Culture in the hypothetical totality of its written formulations is an "ineffectual angel beating its wings in the void," that void being the night sky of Shelley's *Adonais* minus its polestar of poetic inspiration, continuation, and redemption. As Tess says, the present and the future will be dominated by horrid fancies unless angels of culture "can raise up dreams with [their] music and drive all such horrid fancies away" (*T*, 180) which they cannot. Keats's form of beauty/truth is executed at Wintoncester, and she and her poet-angel will not meet again at an unspecified future time. Thus "Heaven's light," or the muse Urania, does not "forever shine" as "Earth's shadows fly," as Shelley had predicted; rather, "Life [or history], like a dome of many-colored glass,/ Stains the white radiance of Eternity (*Adonais*, 52. 460–462). It is the story of this "staining" of beauty which we have witnessed, while it is the putative purity of Shelley's white light by which Hardy half-heartedly qualifies Tess as pure in an afterthought to the novel. His afterthought articulates his nostalgic glance backward toward those strong poetic originals of the romantic past whose texts now lie in ruin.

Curiously though at the very conclusion of a narrative which reiterates the essential concerns of *Paradise Lost*, Angel gets what he wants: a virgin Tess or a paradise refound. As Angel and Liza-Lu turn to view the black flag of execution, the narrator invokes the Miltonic scene of remorse and exile from Eden. Angel and his new Tess recall the fallen Adam and Eve as they look back on their lost paradise before stepping forth into history. He is described as an emaciated Christ; she is "half-girl, half-woman—a spiritualized image of Tess" (*T*, 488). Though there is certainly an echo of *Endymion* here too, what we witness is an emblem of Hardy's belated romanticism: a weakened poet with his "unformulated" new beauty who is "slighter [than Tess] but with the same beautiful eyes" (488). Both are shadows of their former selves (or the self to come in Liza-Lu's instance) with "faces . . . [which] seemed to have shrunk to half their natural size" (488). Together they enact a miniature version or vision of marriage and redemption which satirizes

Tess of the d'Urbervilles: Creativity at a Loss for Words

the typically romantic "ending" which, according to the law of genre, must state or imply redemptive possibilities. Liza-Lu is Angel's "sister-in-law"; her position ironically undercuts the hopeful possibilities of their union because it is a matter of law, and genre law at that. In terms of structure, their "redemption" or this scene of redemption is conventional and a weak replication of the strong redemptive scenes which typically conclude the romantic epic.

Weakly walking the last mile together, Angel and Liza-Lu evoke only to mock the redemptive possibilities of the romantic epic. Hardy's enfeebled conclusion is but a shadow of the great success Wordsworth achieved in "Tintern Abbey," where past and present merge in the figure of the poet and his younger sister who enact a ritual of recuperated joy which overcomes the burdens of time. Hardy's conclusion burdens such romantic epiphanies with time. We are, typologically, in history or outside the garden. Moreover, Angel and Liza-Lu exemplify Hardy's historical revision of Shelley's transcendence, the "one shape of many names" (*Laon and Cynthna*, 1, 27:3) insofar as Liza-Lu is another name for Tess. There is no transmigration of souls here, only a biological similarity whose "immortality" is a predicate of material reproduction, as it is for Keats's nightingale, while it is an immature form of Tess which returns to marry a weakened Angel. If indeed they do marry. We will recall that we never see Angel and Liza-Lu marry, we only see them wearily head in that direction, toward that possibility and that promise. Because their weariness is tonally Swinburne's from his "Garden of Persephone," the modern Eden of entropy, we must wonder about the future of a poetry consigned to mechanically reproduce its former glories in accordance with a promise promoted by that strong former beauty whose glory has passed away.

In the end then, we are given an emblem which suspends romantic endings in a parody about romantic conclusions which have become "classical." The expected promise of joy and hope is reproduced in weary, weak, and immature figures. In this covert fashion, the problem in the narrative returns once more to conclude the narrative. The parodic cast of Hardy's finale inevitably draws our attention to the narrator's failure at achieving a genuine and authentic comic conclusion, though he provides one to show good form. He knows what he wants and knows how to reproduce it, yet he does not know how to produce it. If he did know, he would be a genuine romantic. Otherwise stated, he knows what he lacks and knows how to reproduce that lack, but he does not know how to overcome it.

In this regard of form without substance, the narrator speaks for Hardy whose "bosom" is "a bed" for the weary name of a wounded beauty. Like Angel, Hardy will wearily go forward and write *Jude* by reconstituting Angel's two Shelleyan aspects as Jude's problematical character, while Tess or Liza-Lu will become Sue Bridehead (Sue is one of Tess's names in manuscript; Tess, Liza-Lu's former name). Because his critique of culture has reached for, but not reached, romantic authenticity, Hardy's *Tess of the d'Urbervilles* offers no solutions for an overly orthodox and scripted culture. Instead, it formally reproduces the desire to be romantic as a novel form of literature which is more than half in love with death.

[4]

Jude the Obscure:
Shelley's Modern Prometheus Once More

---

*Sterne says that if he were in a desart [sic] he would
love some cypress.*
Shelley, "On Love"

*Not a having and a resting, but a growing and a
becoming is the character of perfection as culture
conceives it.*
Matthew Arnold, *Culture and Anarchy*

Becoming obscure is becoming clear to and in itself.
Friedrich Nietzsche, *The Will to Power*

"THE LETTER KILLETH" reads the epigraph affixed to the title page of Hardy's *Jude the Obscure,* and much has been made of the phrase borrowed from Paul's *Corinthians.* Since *Jude* was first published, the Pauline phrase has served as a beacon pointing the way to the social concerns of the novel which were outlined for Hardy in J. S. Mill's *On Liberty,* in particular his chapter entitled "Of Individuality, as One of the Elements of Well-being." As Hardy rephrased Mill's theme, Jude Fawley is an idealist whose form of individuality is killed by the letters of convention, those terrible orthodoxies of society at large which curtail the liberty of vision and love. This much, and it is a great deal, has been illuminated by the Corinthian phrase.

Yet in spite of the ambivalence entailed in Hardy's deft Corinthian clue, there remain obscure letters in need of illumination if the complete allegory of Jude's character is to be read in the fullness of its tragic desire. The obscure letters which kill Jude by their irresistible luminescence are the scriptures of the British romantic tradition, those "Corinthian" and arabesque figures whose capacity for mystification offers a sublime clarity to the romantic self in quest of those transcendental

223

significances achieved when desire exceeds demand. Jude is a romantic idealist in Mill's sense, but a *weak* idealist who "excludes[s] one-half of what is desirable," which is concrete history or rational perception, in order to single-mindedly pursue his vision of great beauty. Instead of a successful romantic who, in Mill's definition, possesses "great energies guided by vigorous reason, and strong feelings strongly controlled by a conscientious will," Jude is a captivated narcissist unable to overcome his enthrallment to sublime literary forms of culture and thereby dialectically engage history, community, and individuals in wholesome relationships (all quotations from "Of Individuality," 135).

Locked in Blake's "Crystal Cabinet" of glorifying self-delusion, Jude's romantic self is at once monstrous and Promethean, grotesque and heroic. "Punishing" is the word which immediately comes to mind. The romantic agencies in his life, which are always literary and textual, create of him a simulacrum of the suffering hero and victim of an earlier time. Jude lives tragically because romantically by following the figures of the romantic faith "to the letter." His fate in narrative thus narrates the fate of romantic consciousness in history at the close of the nineteenth century. That is, he lives out in history the monstrousness of a severely conflicted and contradictory form of idealism which continues to fail nearly a century after it had stated its case and attempted to redeem the world.

Because his character "characterizes" past romantic forms which come to life in the present in order to test the waters once more, Jude is always belated, always behind the times, even when he gazes into the future. He is a figure of the past (of past figures) inhabiting a contemporary landscape. Ironically, his future lies in the past as the temporal oxymoron of Christminster suggests. Like the city which reflects his desires, his subjectivity is a haven for lost causes and abandoned ideals. His character is thus without social force, though it is not without a nostalgia for social power. Thus, Jude is both ghostly and statuesque, sublime and beautiful in his monumental reproduction of romantic consciousness.

The genesis and effects of Jude's monstrous and belated Promethean-ism constitute the most pressing problem in Hardy's final novel about culture and dominance. Culture is the agent of Jude's redemption and damnation. He is culture's creature and yet his fate within culture "at the present moment," in Arnold's phrase, is monstrous.

Read with its suppressed Shelleyan heritage fully reinstated, *Jude the*

Jude the Obscure: Shelley's Modern Prometheus Once More

Obscure is Hardy's retelling of *Frankenstein*. That is, Jude is a figure of the Shelleyan desire for revolt and renovation who is born into a cultural moment which encourages such a desire as long as the prevailing social order is not upset, altered, or revolutionized. In effect, Jude is "brought to life" by a poet-creator, inspired as he is by visions of Christminster in its many fantasy forms. Jude labors to achieve his visionary goal and thus legitimize his claim to letters, yet he is rejected by the institutions of culture as they are historically represented in their totality by Christminster as it actually is. His visionary aspirations are *virtually* but not actually condoned by the presiding institutions which dominate culture from Christminster, and it is this virtual recognition which is the source of the drama in novel about a life lived in and through letters.

In Hardy's allegory of romanticism in eclipse, the university itself represents the universe of cultural discourses which frustrate Jude's cultural desires, which are legitimate but not legitimized. Thus when he attempts to gain admission to the university, he is rejected outright by the dons of his parenting culture, even though culture at the present time espouses modified forms of Shelley's republican program for enlightened change or "flexibility," as Arnold would have it. The upshot of this conflict between the romantic self in its early phase and romantic culture in its mid-century formulation is that Jude suffers as does Frankenstein, the monster whose maker rejects his claims for love and home, fearing as he does that the monster might reproduce and overwhelm civilization.

Jude is thus caught in a double bind; his form of consciousness can offer him no lasting satisfaction in and of itself nor will he find a home in Christminster. This double alienation creates him a nostalgic figure of romantic revolution whose life in letters constitutes Hardy's critical response to a postromantic culture whose elitism and aristocratic presumptions continue to dominate society, albeit its published sentiments are often poetic and liberal.[1] In this way, the original aspirations of the poetic past are pitted against present conditions, or, in terms of the most significant lines of intertextual influence, Shelley is pitted against Arnold. Both figures of early and mid-century romantic culture desire that men know "the best that is known and thought in the world," and both imagine the quest after perfection to be the most significant cultural activity for contemporary man, yet it is only Shelley who offers society these views as revolutionary.

The Descent of the Imagination

Jude's quest for culture within a domain of institutions and representations dominated by Arnoldian culture renders him a ghost of Shelley's
program who returns, like Hamlet's father, to challenge the inactivity
and bad consciousness of the son, whom Hardy casts as Matthew Arnold. Ironically, by striving to attain his place in culture in accordance
with current and past programs of cultural acquisition and preservation,
Jude insures his alienation from all forms of culture both high (Arnoldian) and low (Wordsworthian). Jude begins his life in culture by rejecting his natural Wessex home; thus he alienates himself from Wordsworthian forms of inspiration and stability, from folk tradition and rural
culture, as a means of heading "Thither" toward Christminster. After
this initial alienation (which repeats Shelley's rejection of Wordsworth's
conservatism), Jude engages Shelleyan figures of desire in his quest for
Christminster, collectively the name of the romantic quester's desired
goal. In his attempt to achieve that goal—or realize it—he will learn
that flexibility is what culture preaches but does not practice, that, in
fact, his city of light is a dark and stony place of institutional power held
by an aristocratic and elite clerisy.

In my reading of the cultural strife that informs *Jude,* the republican
authenticity of Arnoldian culture is measured against Shelley's authentic
republicanism. In Hardy's fable, Arnold's cultural program of reading
and flexibility in the 1880s is represented as a rhetoric without substance
because culture enforces the order of things rather than critiques them
with any "real" or political force geared toward change. *Jude the Obscure*
is thus another Hardyan exercise in past-present comparison where a
specific romantic past is pitted against the cultural present which is
envisioned as a muted, socialized version of that more powerful and
glorious past.

Like the deformed creature of Mary Shelley's novel, Jude is inspired
or "brought to life" by Shelley's poetry. Hardy brings his novel to life
by reading Shelley's works and then replicating their conflicts in an
allegorical narrative representing that form of consciousness. Mary Shelley's allegory of her husband's monstrous Prometheanism is thus analo-
gous to Hardy's novel which also presents a critical reading of Percy
Shelley's poetry and politics, what they were about and whither they
could lead. Jude's monstrousness is a refiguration of Shelley's overreach-
ing character; his loneliness and alienation are Shelley's, while his generous errors are Shelley's too. Moreover, both Mary Shelley's novel and

226

Jude the Obscure: Shelley's Modern Prometheus Once More

Hardy's are allegories of art which are reaction formations (or critical readings) of Shelley's romanticism.

More specifically, it is to Shelley's *Alastor* and *The Triumph of Life*, those mini-epics of noble failure and generous erring, that Hardy turned in order to structure and inform his last novel which is concerned with the triumph of time over romantic idealism. Primarily, *Jude* (henceforth cited as *J*) defines its themes and forms in relation to Shelley's *Alastor* and *The Triumph of Life*, while it invokes passages and contentions from Dowden's *Life of Shelley* and Arnold's essay "Shelley" in order to contemporize its inherited matrix of Shelleyan texts. As we shall see, the fable of Jude's life closely follows the narrative of Shelley's *Alastor*, while Jude's fate in society replicates to a large extent Arnold's ethical assessment of Shelley in his critical review of Dowden's biography. Thus, the curve of Jude's life is structured upon Shelley's works as well as upon contemporary views of those works. This is so much so that we might read the novel as a representative critical account of Shelley's life and works near the turn of the century.

Like Arnold's "beautiful and ineffectual angel beating his wings in the void," Jude's lifelong pursuit of culture is as ineffectual as was Shelley's pursuit of a romantic revolution which would make a social difference. In this matter of pursuits, Jude's quest is best defined by Shelley when he writes that idealism is motivated by the need to seek that "invisible and unattainable point to which love tends; and to attain which it urges forth the powers of man to arrest the faintest shadows of that, without the possession of which, there is no rest or respite to the heart over which it rules" (Shelley, "On Love," 474). Shelley's definition of the quest is repeated in so many words by Arnold when, in *Culture and Anarchy*, he describes the "character of perfection as culture conceives it" as "not a having and a resting, but a growing and a becoming." Arnold's character of perfection is Shelley's poetical character; thus both forms of desire find their just representation and critique in Jude's pursuit of Christminster. Jude's quest is informed by Shelley's "On Love"; driven thus, he seeks to "arrest shadows"—and we see him arresting them at Christminster—while he acquires these shadows or visions by "reading," that form of cultural acquisition which, in *Literature and Dogma*, Arnold described as the very being or essence of culture itself. Driven by love to practice reading, Jude is infected with the restlessness of "becoming," rather than the rest or stability of "having," as his form of the ache of modernism (*J*, 399), a malaise whose symptoms constitute the cultural problematic of the novel.

Hardy positions his last novel between these early and mid-century formulations of culture in order to demonstrate that Shelley's tragic idealism still offered a formidable critique of Arnold's views on the character of cultural perfection. To effect this critique, Hardy casts Arnold's quest for cultural perfection as a Shelleyan "Pursuit of the Well-Beloved," to invoke the title of that brief fable of culture Hardy wrote in the interim between *Tess* and *Jude*. Significantly, *The Well-Beloved* provides an allegorical account of the romantic concerns of the more apparently "realistic" novels which precede and follow it. Like Joycelyn Pierston of *The Well-Beloved,* Jude pursues his well-beloveds in the form of three "shadows" which he seeks to arrest: Christminster, Arabella, and finally Sue. His well-beloveds are, one and all, "airy children of his brain" (Shelley, "On Love," 473) which are monstrously out of touch with the times or, in the instances of Arabella and Sue, projections of his desire and not actual historical beings which he can recognize as such.

As past forms of aspiration returned to the scene of conflict, Jude's mental figures are dead letters which ultimately kill his spirit, although it is just these figures which have brought it to life. Though Jude imbues fragments of the past with an artifical life, each figure is as petrified and corrupt as the statues and gargoyles he attempts to restore at Christminster. Thus Jude's character is a "Frankensteinian" creature constituted of a composite body of decayed romantic texts which bear him into a life of loneliness, alienation, and obscurity in the frozen wastes of the present, unpoetical times.

Jude's class standing as an artisan-copier and not an artist-sculptor casts him as a "reader" and not a writer of culture. His appointed task is to trace the past and in so doing restore it to the present. What this suggests is that Jude lives within secondary and belated regimes of representation which dominate his consciousness and compel him to live a form of life which can offer him nothing but the pleasures of alienation, the joys of self-absorption, and, ultimately, the sorrows of total obscurity. The source of his "thirst" for this form of domination is defined in Shelley's essay on love. Like Shelley, Jude absorbs figures of cultural delight "in correspondence with this law that the infant drains milk from the bosom of its mother" (Shelley, "On Love," 473). In order to represent Shelley's sense of this desire, Hardy depicts Christ-minster as a glowing, white breast on the horizon, while Arabella hatches eggs on her body and Sue characterizes herself as an Epipsychidion mother-wife figure from whom Jude drinks a nourishing intellectual beauty. Like Shelley too, Jude's desire is never wholly turned toward Wordsworth's "mother" nature as a "nurse" form. Always, he is turned toward the fantasy of a literary "breast" whose visionary narratives nourish and sustain the questing self which seeks to restore the glory of the remote past in the proximate future.

In characterizing Jude as a Shelleyan type, Hardy presents us with an allegorical portrait critical of romanticism's narcissistic tendencies. This is to do no more than Shelley did in *Alastor,* a poem intertextually at play throughout *Jude.* Like the Alastor-poet, Jude is turned away from the concrete world of the father and toward a nurturing mother culture. Because nature appears cruel to him and the world of man, or the "real Christminster," vulgar, gross, and frivolous, Jude progresses by re-gressing to "a fixation on either the archaic, grandiose self-configuration or the archaic, overestimated, narcissistically cathectic object [a parent imago]" (Schapiro, *Romantic Mother,* 13) as Shelley often did. Regression is the source of Jude's "archaic" character which is obscure because it replicates an obscure form of the romantic sublime which sought rapid social change rather than encouraged gradual social compromise. Wordsworth would understand Jude's narcissistic enthrallment as "monstrous" because so entirely self-absorbing and unrealistic. Such enthrallments must be overcome if a strong, authentic romantic con-sciousness were to emerge from literary fantasies and engage the "still sad music of humanity." Only such a balanced consciousness could be politically effectively, while it is just this balance which Jude lacks.

Given his depressing early childhood—his mother dead, his father possibly hanged, his Aunt Drusilla daily proclaiming the wisdom of Nietzsche's Silenus—Jude splits his ego along lines suggested to Hardy by Arnold's essay on Shelley. He divorces history from the imagination and then lives in ahistoric fantasies of overcoming. Divorced from na-ture, time, and reason, Jude is "an ineffectual angel" in pursuit of a paradise of high culture; thus does he relentlessly beat his luminous wings in a void which is poised and waiting to engulph him. His ineffectual life thus puts on trial Arnold's recuperative method regarding Dowden's biography of Shelley while it critiques Shelley's defensive

The Descent of the Imagination

inwardness. We will recall that Arnold desired to forget the real history of the libertine Shelley in order to preserve his angelic fancy of Shelley. This motive becomes instrumental in Jude's repression of history in order to create himself "a divinity," as he names himself when comparing himself to Sue (Sue is the divinity; he is like Sue).

Jude's Christminster is "both defensive and compensatory"; it provides him with "a fantasy of an ideal, omnipotent self [which] compensates for severe oral frustration, rage, and envy, and the fantasy of an ever-giving ever-loving accepting parent [which] compensates for the depriving realistic one" (Schapiro, 14). History (as class standing) has deprived Jude of advantages; his imaginary view of culture will supply them to him. By imagining himself a "son" of Christminster loved by his mother, Jude transforms history and melancholia into idealism and elation. Yet his imagining is fanciful: the institutions of culture are only geared to promote such fantasies; they do not supply the realities of their republican pronouncements. Like Arnold regarding Shelley, Jude alters in parable that which he cannot change in history and thereby compensates for whatever is the truth of the case. Conversely, whenever Jude's "romantic mother" seems to disown him—that is, whenever he sees the shape of things as they are—he becomes suicidal. Unobscured by fanciful projections, the historic world becomes a "dark reality" whose equivalent term is death (Shelley, "Hymn to Intellectual Beauty," 1. 48).

The source of Jude's "power" is his terrible thirst after Shelley's intellectual beauty or culture, that "awful *loveliness*" which, for him, is awful (punishing) and awful (inspiring). Jude's character is at once sublime, as was the Alastor-poet's, in its aspirations, and grotesque insofar as he lives in a world of deforming excesses. In this regard, we might note that the sublime is the grotesque insofar as both are "grotto" forms which depend upon the indefinite and the excessive for their figuration. Hardy takes full advantage of this ambiguity in his presentation of Jude's sublimely grotesque life. The upshot of this double figuration is that Jude's character is informed by a type of consciousness which we might call Shelleyan while his history criticizes the ineffectuality of a certain manner of cultural elitism which we might call Arnoldian. Overall, the character of Jude's perfectionism presents a complex portrait of romantic idealism at the turn of the century which is as much an appreciation of its revolutionary aspirations as it is a depreciation of its conflicting pronouncements and inability to rationally regulate behavior by balancing the imaginary with the reasonable. Read in this context, *Jude the Obscure* represents Hardy's final estimate of a romanticism that is found to be wanting: wanting in the power to engage society in a dialectic of change and renovation, and wanting in its ability to deliver a lasting personal satisfaction to the individual. In Shelley's estimate, romantic desire acquires its power from "wanting"; its drive is an effect of dissatisfaction, thus as soon as the "want or power is dead," the quester "becomes the living sepulchre of himself" ("On Love," 474). Immediately before his death at Christminster, the narrator represents Jude as "a living sepulchre of himself," a motiveless subjectivity which no longer wants anything, so total are its disappointments. Because constitutionally romantic, Jude's alternatives are either to live and to "want" or to stop wanting, become powerless, and die. His life in allegory thus unfolds between wanting and dissatisfaction and death, or, as we have cast it, between a frustrating idealism and a damning history.

Jude will pursue one "well-beloved" after another only to appear finally as an exhausted form of cultural striving or wanting, as Shelley's "sepulchre" of the romantic self which has exhausted its power to want. Alive, he is an allegory of the monstrous power of romanticism in its Promethean phase; dead, he is an emblem of history, or of the history of romantic discourse now become "beautiful," classical, and statuesque, an art form without political force. In his last appearance, Jude is depicted as the beautiful and statuesque cadaver of sublime forms of culture that have passed from the world because they could not engage with the world and effect the renovation forecast in *Prometheus Unbound.* Like Shelley's Prometheus, Jude does not cease to hope, yet unlike Shelley's romantic god, Jude does not win. Thus, the narrative of his idealistic life ultimately comes to represent the history of idealism which, in Shelley's "Works" appears as *Alastor, Prometheus Unbound,* and then *The Triumph of Life* or time over idealists. Otherwise construed, Jude's Christminster cadaver depicts "the century's corpse outleant" of Hardy's "Darkling Thrush," a century repleat with cultural programs and aspirations which amount to a beautiful but ineffectual corpus of texts.

No doubt there is an element of self-accusation on Hardy's part in his depiction of Jude's monstrous Prometheanism. Like Jude, Hardy had deracinated himself from traditional Wessex culture in order to pursue the culture of letters. The irony of his pursuit lies in our awareness that by turning his historic past into a literary artifact, Hardy gains in parable the "home" that he had lost in actuality. First and foremost, it is always Hardy's alienation from Dorset that is on display in Wessex. Then, too, by all current biographical accounts, as a returned native Hardy lived a lonely and isolated life in Dorset as a figure of culture.

Yet if there is something self-accusatory on Hardy's part in his presentation of Jude's deracinating ambition, there is also something defensive in his presentation of the aspirations of the autodidactic self. This defensiveness finds its most appropriate form or pretext in the structure of noble folly in Shelley's *Alastor* which Hardy invokes in *Jude* to elicit pity and a concomitant sympathy for a tragic desire which his successful engagement with culture and high society does not immediately warrant. Hardy admired Shelley's idealism, yet he cautiously toned down his youthful republicanism and turned away from his desire to be a poet until he had acquired a sound financial estate and the lucrative reputation of a famous author. Moreover, his concession to the business of writing popular novels compelled him to keep in check his strong bent toward social satire and sarcasm. It is to Shelley's *Alastor* then that Hardy turns in order to narrate his own "life in letters" as Jude's in order to demonstrate to what end an unrestrained idealism could lead. In effect, the narrative of Jude's life justifies Hardy's conservative wisdom while it displays his youthful revolutionary desire. *Jude* is thus the story of a man who does not concede, written by one who did. Such a story is Alastorish; the protagonist is both foolish (not to be followed) and noble (to be followed). The novel thus succeeds in the complex ways that Shelley's *Alastor* succeeds as an ambivalent response to a particular form of socio-cultural aspiration.

The difficulty of reconciling the laudable with the foolish, the poet with the fanatic, and the idealist with the rationalist in *Alastor* returns to constitute the burden of interpretation in *Jude*. In *Tess,* Hardy had turned to Keats's letters and to *Endymion* to guide him as he wrote his allegory of truth and beauty; in *Jude,* he turns to Shelley and to *Alastor* which Keats "revised" when he wrote his *Endymion.*[2] Thus by backtracking the literary history of textual engagements between Shelley and Keats represented by *Alastor* and *Endymion,* Hardy advances his exploration of romantic culture. He erases Keats's solution-text in order to rewrite Shelley's problem-text. In effect, *Tess* "undoes" Keats's resolution in

Jude the Obscure: Shelley's Modern Prometheus Once More

Endymion which then frees Hardy to return to Shelley's *Alastor* in *Jude*. *Jude* is Hardy's reworking of *Alastor* with all of its difficulties left intact. This is so much so, that we might recall the history of contradictory interpretations of Shelley's poem and apply those views with equal justice to *Jude*.[3] Or, we might imagine *Jude* as one more contribution to the perplexity generated by *Alastor* and in this way include Hardy's novel as one text more in the history of the romantic problematic. The perplexity evinced by most interpretations of *Alastor* are instructive insofar as they admit that romantic culture in its early and mid-century "Hellenic" phases amounts to "a chaos of principles" in Jude's words, as Jude's own life does, and that this "chaos of principles" constitutes culture *as* anarchy which is the single most important way it is characterized overall in Wessex.

Having rejected Marygreen and all of its Wordsworthian implications, Jude sets out in search of "the highest and best that is thought in the world," as did his predecessor in type, the Alastor-poet. Like his predecessor, Jude will meet with an "Arab Maiden," or Arabella (the beautiful Arab) in Hardy's reworking of the name of carnal/domestic desire. Jude will eventually divorce himself from his romance with "Abby" in order to pursue once more the abbey of Christminster culture by becoming a licentiate in the church. When this pursuit fails, he "thirsts for intercourse with an intelligence similar to himself" and "images to himself the Being whom he loves" (Shelley, Preface, *Alastor*, 69). This "being" is Sue "Bride-head" in Hardy's reworking of the name of Shelley's intellectual beauty, the "Veiled Maiden." Jude "images" her before he sees her—this is the textual motive behind the play of Sue's photograph in the narrative—and falls in love with his image of her which is not and will never be fully her self. In this respect, Jude is a combined figure of Alec and Angel (who, we well recall, are created by Hardy's reading of Arnold's splitting of Shelley into carnal and ethereal aspects) while Sue is a reworking of Tess (whose name was Sue in one of the drafts). What this amounts to is that Jude will have an idealistic aspect and a carnal aspect, yet like all of Hardy's compartmentalized romantics, he will never be able to marry or merge his two halves. He can have it one way or the other, never both ways at once. Such a merger or marriage would effectively recall the whole man of a strong and viable romanticism and make Wessex a different place from what it is.

Ultimately, Jude's desire for the satisfactions of the whole man compels him to force Sue to enact the narrative of *Endymion;* when the time becomes ripe, he forces his Moon Goddess to become his Indian Maiden. In effect, he compels the Veiled Maiden to act like the Arab Maiden. His desire for Sue's incarnation ultimately kills her spirit by forcing a purely intellectual beauty into history where, historically, she cannot long survive. Thus the most optimistic and "pagan" moment in the novel when Jude and Sue live as husband and wife in "the Elsewhere" recalls only to rescind the romantic comedy of Keats's *Endymion:* to have the Indian Maiden is not to have the Moon Goddess, while to force the Moon Goddess to become the Indian Maiden is to kill the goddess's divine light or, what amounts to the same thing, to compel her to abandon her form of consciousness.

Time in Shelley's sense of it in *The Triumph of Life* returns in *Jude* as "Little Father Time" whose "grey manner" concludes the brief Endymion comedy and ends the Wessex Alastor-poet's quest after vision and love. Moreover, Little Father Time kills the "next generation" or Jude's children, thereby calling to a halt the spiritual evolutionary process within history. Little Father Time not only kills the poetry in Jude's life, but he suspends the generation of romantic poetry itself and thereby ends (or implies an ending to) the eternal return of poetry to history such as Shelley had optimistically construed it in his "Defence of Poetry." It is specifically because Little Father Time does not understand either vision and love or passion and its outcome that he murders Jude's children and then kills himself. His act is tacitly apocalyptic and thus a perversion of the joyful apocalypse witnessed in Shelley's *Prometheus Unbound* which begins with the flight of the Chariot of the Hours. In Hardy's reworking of Shelley's figures, the arrival of Little Father Time marks the conclusion of the joyous time in the Elsewhere. His death will initiate an inverse biblical apocalypse; it spells the end of a glorious time and the beginning of history. In this way, Little Father Time's death calls to a close Shelleyan schemes of historical evolutionism and perfectability, while it signifies Jude's final awakening from his complete enthrallment to pure culture into "pure" or concrete history, a time without vision or love.

If one of the ways which Shelley sustained his poetical vision was by affirming Keats's romanticism in *Adonais,* then Hardy undermines both forms in *Jude* and thereby ends this sequence of cultural appropriation and transmission. In this way, Jude is a "last" last romantic and not a plea for the restoration of past forms of romanticism. Unlike Keats, Jude does not ultimately dwell in the realm of the Eternals but in history; when we last see him he is a cadaver and not a "star." His life in allegory is an allegory of literary history as one of the regimes within cultural history; his death is the terminal point of that history, or intended to be so, and not a point for further departures or resurrections as Shelley had cast Keats's death perhaps in reference to his own.

Moreover, in *Jude* Hardy critiques the Arnoldian critique of the libidinal and the idealistic aspects of Shelley's character as Dowden had presented them in his biography. As *Jude* demonstrates, both aspects are "ineffectual" if they are not integrated. Arabella loves Jude's body; Sue, his sensibility. Like Arnold, neither woman can accept "all of him." Conversely, because he cannot see this—see the reality of their limited desires—he permits his passion to destroy Sue's intelligence, while it is his Shelleyan "vegetarian" sensibility which initiates his divorce from Arabella once the romantic element in their relationship subsides and the light of common day returns.

We should note in this regard that Arnold's derogatory epithet for Shelley, "ineffectual," is itself derived from Shelley's prologue to *Prometheus Unbound* and that it is Shelley's sense of the ineffectual as the unaccomplished that partly informs Hardy's sense of failure in Jude's life. In the concluding paragraph to the preface to *Prometheus Unbound,* Shelley writes:

> Whatever talents a person may possess to amuse and instruct others, be they ever so inconsiderable, he is yet bound to exert them; if his attempt be *ineffectual,* let the punishment of an unaccomplished purpose have been sufficient, let none trouble themselves to heap the dust of oblivion upon his efforts; the pile they raise will betray his grave which might otherwise have been unknown. (136)

Jude the "Obscure" is thus readily translated into Shelley's terms as Jude the "Ineffectual" or the unaccomplished. In Shelley's determination, Jude's failure of purpose is sufficient punishment for his form of striving and for his inability to overcome his enchantments and "live" when he is afforded the opportunity, which he is on three separate occasions. His "obscurity" or "oblivion" constitutes the historical and social register of the fable while his death in isolation from all that he loved repeats the warning of Shelley's *Alastor* (henceforth cited as *Al*) without reinstituting its plea for leniency.

The curse of the ineffectual in the preface to *Prometheus Unbound,* or

The Descent of the Imagination

its gist, is repeated by Jude on his deathbed when he quotes from the Book of Job. His asking that no man remember his name, that the "day perish wherein [he] was born" (*J*, 485) requests that no one "heap the dust of oblivion upon his efforts" which would only serve to "betray his grave." Jude's oblivion is thus "graveless" and not intended to mark the spot of the idealist's passing where the cult might once again revive. That is, the absolute punishment of obscurity which Shelley imposed upon himself if his cultural programs did not succeed is carried out in *Jude* as a way of finally or historically judging Shelley. Hardy does not "heap the dust of oblivion" upon Shelley's grave as Arnold had in his "Shelley." Rather, in allegory (which leaves Shelley out of the picture), Hardy determines Shelley's fate in accordance with those ratios Shelley himself had set in the preface.

Jude dies in precisely the textual position in which the Alastor-poet perished: unknown, dissatisfied, and obscure. The difference between the two death scenes is a difference of time. Hardy does not glorify Jude in the way that Shelley glorifies the Alastor-poet's death. When at Christminster for the last time, Jude's sensibility approximates that of the Alastor-poet who can "no longer know or love the shapes/ Of this phantasmal scene, who have to thee/ Been purest ministers" (*Al*, 696–97). In fact, during his last visit Jude will name his Christminster ghosts "stupid fancies" (*J*, 472) and condemn his quest as foolish. Yet unlike the concluding praise Shelley heaps upon the Alastor-poet, that "Nature's vast frame, the web of human things,/ Birth and the grave are not as they were" (*Al*, 719–20), all of these realms, indeed all the world, are exactly "as they were" before, during, and after Jude's arrival on the scene of longing. Nothing has changed; society is the same and culture is the same despite Shelley and despite Jude. It is then this final swerving away from the paradigm of *Alastor* which constitutes Hardy's debate with Shelley's valuation of the narcissist's quest and advances his estimate of just how much of a difference culture had actually made on the real, historical condition of men's lives since Shelley's day.

The terrible waste which Shelley portrayed in *Alastor* is depicted once more in *Jude,* but with an added increment of folly and futility. What had been noble for Shelley's generation had become pure folly by Hardy's day despite a good deal of cant to the contrary. This is partly because Shelley attempted to establish a form of culture which would critique the prevailing society and its mores, whereas by Hardy's day

culture had become complicit with society; rarely was high culture a
critical force of any power, while its published pronouncements concerning the need for change served mostly as a containment strategy for
the Anglican establishment. Hardy emphasizes this past-present comparison by having Jude die on Remembrance Day. Above all, it is those
early, revolutionary forms of culture we are asked to remember, only to
recall further that they have failed to duly liberalize and republicanize
society.

As the epigraph to part four tells us, "Save his own soul [Jude] hath
no star" to guide him. His star-soul is a figure of Shelley's early romanticism as well as Swinburne's latter-day transformations of such vital
figures into exhausted, aesthetic forms. In fact, we might best see
Jude's consciousness as a confused ensemble of romantic "stars" which
guided three generations of poet-prophet-questers through the "dark
reality" of time in the hope that its illumination would alter history. It
is the conclusion of this star's flight which is depicted in Jude's history,
a narrative about the fate and trajectory of the lyrical republican impetus.
In terms of content, Jude's romantic character or lamplike soul is a
complex composite of stellar romantic texts which arise with the youthful Wordsworth's "reflex of a star" in *The Prelude,* which becomes
Shelley's "lone star" in "To Wordsworth," and set with Swinburne's
"star" from "The Prelude" in *Songs Before Sunrise* from which Hardy
borrows the epigraph to part four. It is this descent of the romantic
imagination from Prelude to Prelude or from the dawn (Hesper) to dusk
(Vesper) which has been Hardy's great theme in Wessex and which he
concludes in *Jude.*

The star first appears in Wordsworth's *The Prelude* as a "reflex . . .
that fled, and flying, still before [him] gleamed/ Upon the glassy plain"
(1: 425–52). The "flying" figure guided by the star is, of course, the
figure of the poet with a capable imagination. By following his star, he
redeems society from an ice age or "Iron Time," in Arnold's phrase, by
figuring forth a culture of hope and joy. The skating figure is an emblem
of the Wordsworthian imagination which finds excitement in "something evermore about to be" in a world of possibility fit for man.
Moreover, the star's reflection on the ice projects the poets's youthful
aspiration that heaven and earth could be bound to one another in a half-
created, half-perceived moment of vision which is real.

Those "first-born affinities that fit/ Our new existence to existing things/ And in our dawn of being, constitute/ The bond of union between life and joy" (1: 555:558) are absent in Jude's life. He is orphaned young as was Wordsworth, yet instead of sublimating nature into mother nature, he turns away from "Marygreen" whose Wordsworthian signature is apparent, and toward "reading." In the eighties, Arnold had declared that, "culture is indispensably necessary and culture is *reading*" (Preface, *Literature and Dogma*, xxvii, emphasis Arnold's). It is this method of cultural praxis that Jude follows to find enlightenment; by reading he constructs his inflated parental imago or "home," Christminster. Thus when he is alone in Christminster, he speaks to texts, in effect, speaking to himself, to his self as text.

Significantly, twice in his life Jude's guiding visions will disappear and he will attempt suicide by walking out onto the frozen waters where he attempts to break through the ice. Both suicide attempts refer us back to Wordsworth's scene of ice-skating in *The Prelude*. Jude's frustration, rage, and alienation are the obverse emotional reflex to Wordsworth's joy, contentment, and cosmic sense of affinity with man, nature, imagination, and community. Unlike the strong inspiration which Wordsworth felt when young, Jude is "weak-lunged" (*J*, 490) and capable only of a fanciful inspiration, in Coleridge's sense of fancy. Jude never actually corresponds to anything or anyone, though he fancies he does. His romantic projections are comparable to Fitzpiers's parodic form of Shelleyan love; both forms of desire are the effects of "reading" and of isolation. Like Fitzpiers, Jude casts his desire onto things; he never sees into the life of things as Wordsworth's strong imagination could, or claimed it could, nor does he ever "see things as they are" in Arnold's recommendation concerning the one thing necessary for overly enthusiastic romantics. Jude's drive to possess his vision is equal in force, persistence, and brutality to Boldwood's. Like Boldwood in the instance of Bathsheba's valentine, Jude becomes fixated on Sue's "sweet saintly self" whose character he then projects onto her as a way of seeing "how she is." Thus, in need of someone to love, he fancies her to be identical to himself. His fancy of identity presents Hardy's satire on the romantic self which now can only "fancy" an elective affinity which previously it could sympathetically imagine. Jude takes a fancy to Sue, that is, and thus tragically mistakes the truth of her being.

Five years after completing *Jude* if his dates can be trusted, Hardy wrote that "Rationalists err in one direction, as Mystics err in the other"

(*Life and Work*, 190). His comment indirectly applauds the imaginative reason as a balanced norm of consciousness, while it is the inability of this form of consciousness to arise and dominate history that constitutes the drama of Wessex in general, and of Jude's life in particular. In Hardy's Wessex, image and history never merge or dialectically interact to produce the romantic symbol, while it is the concrete processes of history which gradually erode the cultural preserves of the romantic symbol, leaving in time's wake a nostalgic aestheticism which produces impotent fancies as "symbolic" outlets for bereft desires. This is the form of romance which Jude unwittingly cultivates by reproducing the lost referentials of an earlier faith now fallen into ruin and chaos. His is formally and reproductively romantic, not energetically and productively so.

Jude thus errs in the mystical direction because he does not engage the rational direction. Moreover, he desires acceptance, not revolution or social change, although his acceptance by Christminster would have signaled social change. Rather than applaud a solipsistic idealism as Shelley did, Hardy amplifies the critical element which Shelley had softened in the preface to *Alastor* and in the poem itself. Jude's romances condemn and inspire him (the terms are equivalent within the ambivalence of the text and its lineage), while his struggle is viewed as praiseworthy, monstrous, and punishing, as it is in Shelley's *Alastor*.[4] Jude's "generous error" creates of him a Joseph the Dreamer and Don Quixote figure as Sue correctly characterizes him, and her description is not completely affectionate. The source of her figure is found in Book Five of Wordsworth's *The Prelude* where the poet narrates his dream of the "Arab Quixote" (5:50–16). Unlike Wordsworth who could "overcome" such idealistic enthrallments which arise, significantly, through reading, Jude remains subject to all of his lettered enchantments because they constitute the sole terms of his self-esteem and value.

Like Wordsworth in *The Prelude* and Shelley in *Alastor*, Hardy too gives "a substance" to "this arab phantom" and "fancies him a living man" who is "crazed/ By love and feeling, and internal thought/ Protracted among endless solitudes" (*The Prelude*, 5:143–47). In keeping with the prevalent posture of romantics toward this phantom, Hardy seems to "reverence" his "semi-Quixote" perhaps because he too *once* shared "that maniac's fond anxiety," which is apocalyptic, and desired to "go/ Upon like errand" (*The Prelude*, 5:159–60). Yet like Wordsworth, Hardy desists from going on the quest, and it is from this position of wise resistance that the narrator of *Jude* conceives his fable of praise and blame. The narrator himself supplies the balance between history and fantasy or reason and mysticism that is lacking in Jude's conception of things. Thus, the novel itself provides a model of the balance that is absent in the subject of the novel. Moreover, reading *about* Arnoldian "reading culture" and the impasses it can lead to in an elitist culture supplies the social critique for that method of cultural acquisition, just as reading about Shelleyan quests after narcissistic delight provides the necessary admonition concerning the dangers implicit in that form of madness.

We will recall that Wordsworth had confessed to quixotic temptations when he wrote that "Me hath such strong entrancement overcome/ When I have held a volume in my hand . . . Shakespeare, or Milton, laborers divine" (*The Prelude,* 5:163–65). Like Wordsworth's Arab-Quixote, the Alastor-poet is "Obedient to high thoughts" and seeks visionary knowledge written on the walls of ruins. Wordsworth overcame the enchantments of his reading, while Shelley did not. Thus Jude turns away from the "still sad music" of Marygreen and the vulgarity of the real Christminster in order to cultivate evasive entrancements whose covering figures he encounters in his reading. In Arnold's estimate, Jude "does a good work" by reading and self-education (*Literature and Dogma,* xxvii), yet the prevailing institutions of culture are not ready to reward him for such a divine labor. His desire for reading, which is his passion for culture, originates in the schoolroom, and his desire has many names —Phillotson, Arabella, Sue. Yet contrary to Arnold's declaration that nobody wastes his time who reads, Jude's life becomes a waste of time (and is finally wasted by Time) because he reads books but not the world, not things as they are, but as he imagines they should be. His life is thus a "Folly" or Fawley in Hardy's pun on the surname, while his folly finds its source in his "fall" from the grace of genuine historical being by ignoring what is persistently the case, that culture is elitist and class-bound and not republican and open.

In Hardy's allegory of the fall, Jude eats from the "tree of knowledge" (one of his figures for Christminster [*J,* 66]) by reading about culture in school; thus does the prison house of literature grow round him. Yet the fruit or "treasure of refined things" in George Eliot's designation, is forbidden him by the god of culture whose most recent testament was

Arnold's *God and the Bible*. As Eliot writes as a case in point, the working classes "must submit themselves to the great law of inheritance" by which she means that they do not have the knack or tradition of handling ideas and therefore should desist from trying to use them. It is "the endowed classes" which have inherited the know-how to handle the "precious material of life" or culture (*Felix Holt,* 421); thus, according to Eliot it is only logical that the upper classes should continue as the high priests of culture and that they should continue to receive the financial support to do so.[5]

Because he romanticizes Phillotson's life in culture, Jude becomes a "lost Man" who "on visionary views would fancy feed,/ Till his eye streamed with tears" (Wordsworth, "Lines: Left upon a Seat in a Yew-tree," 44–46). He is lost and tragic because, like Wordsworth's hopeless dreamer or John Durbeyfield or Angel, he cannot permit his romance to "fade into the light of common day" ("Intimations of Immortality," 5. 76). This reading, which aligns Phillotson to Tringham as the instigator of the romantic tragedy, is counterbalanced by Shelley's sense that such "romances" or ideals ideally should overcome the light of common day or dominate history and thereby produce the world's new age. Thus in *Jude,* Shelley's will to continue (or resume) the enlightened revolt of the late eighteenth-century French intelligentsia against the aristocracy is pitted against Wordsworth's (re)acceptance of the *ancien régime* after 1815.

It is no scholarly secret that Hardy derives Christminster, the "home of lost causes," from Arnold's lyrical description of Oxford. Albeit this intertextual link is well known, the implicit ironies of its imagining have not been drawn out for the cultural dissonance they contain. As the center of Arnoldian culture, Oxford-Christminster is the home of lost causes, all of which come under the general heading of British culture. Though this allusion is clear enough and significant in terms of the novel's literary historical thrust, there is yet a repressed historical referent which Mary Shelley's *Frankenstein* can help us to release.

When Victor Frankenstein and Clerval travel to Oxford, the narrator tells us that as they entered the city, their "Minds were filled with the remembrance of the events that had been transacted there more than a century and half before. It was here that Charles I had collected his forces. The city had remained faithful to him, after the whole nation had forsaken his cause to join the standard of parliament and liberty" (*Fran-*

kenstein, 157). The "lost cause" that is housed at Oxford is that of Charles I and the royalists, of oppression and tyranny, of aristocracy and elitism, and it is this "lost cause" which we are also *asked* to remember on Christminster's Remembrance Day as Frankenstein and Clerval do when they arrive at Oxford.

In this regard, it is surely not without some irony that Mary Shelley names Oxford the city of lost causes which Percy Shelley thought *should* be lost if the "World's New Age" is to begin. To this irony, we might add one irony more by recalling that Shelley himself had been expelled from Oxford in 1811 for writing *The Necessity of Atheism* and it is just this necessity which is the source of Jude's and Sue's alienation from the Wessex community. It is then Arnold's fantasy of Oxford which is satirized, and not embraced, in *Jude*. At Christminster, Hardy shows us Mary Shelley's royalist Oxford, an inpregnable bastion of elitism which dominates culture. Jude, a Cromwellian enthusiast or "protestant," fights to gain entry to the royal treasury of culture, a Camelot belonging to the high born or the wealthy. The Master of Biblioll College to whom Jude applies for advice concerning admission passes on to him George Eliot's advice to the working classes in Felix Holt's "Address." He tells Jude that he should see his class interests as class duties and then go about them, leaving culture to those who are born to it. In a collusion of cultural ironies, the Master speaks for the master race. He speaks "ex cathedra" for Biblioll College, Hardy's reworking of the name of Oxford's Balliol College by way of an allusion to Arnold's *God and the Bible*.

In this regard, we might see Jude as an artisan who, empowered by his *enthusiasm* for reading, attempts to enter the capital of staid High Anglican culture, its Vatican or Canterbury as it were. Jude is a puritan of culture—Bunyan is among the textual constituents of his earliest imaginings—whose form of *Geist* or religion is an alternative representation of his class drive toward dominance or, at least, bettering his condition. He seeks to infiltrate the High Anglican retreat of Arnoldian culture which refuses him entry. The dominance of culture is thus as much at issue in Jude's struggle as it was in Shelley's against High Anglican Oxford and its repressive culture, only in Jude's day one would presume that things had changed thanks to writers like Shelley. The deciding factor in Jude's struggle is that culture is society—and high society at that—the two do not constitute a system of checks and balances, of law and "flexibility" as Arnold wrote they should, but rather collude as one inflexible law expressed on two different discursive registers. Only in Jude's fantasy is Christminster a "home of lost causes" which are not truly lost but are able to be refound. Only in nostalgia are the ideals not lost; in history, the battle is over. The historic Christminster then is a place where the forces of Charles I and Matthew Arnold continue to reign against those of Parliament, the people, liberty, and Shelley.

Jude's failure to arrive at Christminster further implies that Wessex culture is constituted within what Raymond Williams has called a "deadlock society," one in which patience and caution are preached to the masses without providing them a means of escaping from the viciousness of their plight (*Culture and Society*, 109). Jude demonstrates his "good faith" toward high culture and its fear of revolution from below by replicating its ecclesiastical-aristocratic past. Acting as a caretaker of cultural forms, he copies the cultural past as a premise to producing the cultural future, a stage at which he never arrives. By copying, he is a conservator or a conservative of culture, as were Arnold and Eliot. He works to preserve the "treasures" of the past as Eliot recommended culture should in Felix Holt's "Address," while he interdicts Eliot's advice that workers should desist from acts of appropriation since they had little or no experience in the matter of "reading" and figuring things out.

Within this maze of reference and cross-reference, it seems that Hardy partially constructs Jude's fate in culture by having him follow Eliot's and Arnold's advice, only to demonstrate why their advice was indeed correct, but not for their stated reasons. Acting in good faith toward high culture, Jude acts in bad faith toward republican culture; he replicates the figures of the old faith and so lives in the past, a ghost speaking to ghosts and a serf or servant seeking to imitate his masters in the hope that they will invite him to take a seat at their table. Ironically, his love of the past reinstates those cultural forms and institutions which stand in his way. Jude is thus always busy reproducing those cultural forms which prevent him from inventing, originating, or cultivating his own form of culture. In Shelley's estimate, "Time's worst statue[s]" remain "unrepealed" because no "glorious Phantom" bursts forth "to illume [the] tempestuous day" of Jude's Wessex ("Sonnet: England in 1819," 14–15). That is, by replicating past cultural icons, Jude denies contemporary culture its productive potential. He is thus not a glorious phantom of romantic revolution, but a weak reflection of the imaginative potential of an earlier day now nearly completely contained in the prison house of letters. As such, he is the final lamp of the romantic lyric which is tamped and then shattered by the orthodox and conservative vestiges of romantic, republican culture whose "classical" or statuesque aspects he worships and reproduces.

Because Jude *reproduces* romantic desire within England's lowest class, his history offers us a special understanding of culture at the turn of the century. Primarily, Jude's cultural desires condemn him to a life in allegory which appears allegorical or "lettered" because displaced to a class not natural to the desires they articulate. The final paradox at issue in his life—and in Hardy's satire—is that by affirming culture Jude critiques culture; by reproducing culture according to its rules or grammar of reproduction, he demonstrates its psychic effects, which are dislocative and not comforting, and its hidebound character, which is resistant to change albeit it speaks ceaselessly about change and improvement. The confusion at which Jude finally arrives in "these uprising times" (*J*, 398) emphasizes the confusions which saturate culture yet which were not immediately apparent owing to the strongly reasoned and sympathetic essays and addresses wrought by prophets of culture such as Arnold and Eliot. That is, Jude colludes in their mystifications in order to display their contradictions.

Jude the Obscure renders apparent the contradictions within late-nineteenth-century cultural discourse by representing or personifying its mandates on a lower social level than they were intended to be practiced. Jude's confusions are indicative of Hardy's in the face of a cultural episteme thick with models of liberal comportment and programs for social improvement, but thin on action and institutional change. What Jude "wants" ultimately is what Hardy had once wanted, which is what Arnold wrote that every "young writer" wants, "a hand to guide him through the confusion, a voice to prescribe to him the aim which he should keep in view" (Arnold, "Preface to Poems, 1853," *Poetry and Criticism* 208). Yet this helping hand and guiding voice are precisely what Jude does not find in a culture which is not intended for the likes of him—and so, finally, he asks to be judged on "intention" of aim rather than "result" (*J*, 398). Jude's star-soul cannot guide him because culture is no guide. In Jude's Wessex, it is culture itself which constitutes

Jude the Obscure: Shelley's Modern Prometheus Once More

"the confusion of the present times," a bewilderment which is the result or effect of "the multitude of voices counseling different things" (Arnold, "Preface to Poems, 1853," 208). In *Jude,* Hardy demonstrates that *any* foray into the culture of reading—let alone an autodidactic engagement by an individual from the lower classes—could only replicate the confusion.

Thus, culture is Jude's tragic fate, reading his siren and temptress. Hardy achieves this cultural critique of "the letter" whose songs "killeth" by following Arnold's advice in his "Preface to Poems, 1853". There, Arnold writes that "Failing [sure guides], all that can be looked for, all that indeed can be desired is, that [the writer's] attention should be fixed on excellent models; that he may *reproduce* at any rate something of their excellence, by penetrating himself with their works and by catching their spirit, if he cannot be taught to produce what is excellent independently" (Arnold, 208–9). Here is the source of Jude's cultural labor as a copyist, as well as Sue's as an ecclesiastical designer. Jude's problem is that he cannot be "taught to produce what is excellent independently," and the narrator twice comments upon his inability for a sustained "true illumination," once at Christminster (*J,* 131) and then again at Melchester.

At Christminster, Jude loses his purchase on the true illumination "that here in the stone yard was a centre of effort as worthy as that dignified by the name of scholarly study within the noblest of the colleges" (*J,* 131). He loses it owing to "the stress of his old idea" which is Shelleyan in its desire for intellectual beauty and Arnoldian in its mandate that cultural ephebes must read. At this point, the narrator's comment is remarkably reiterative of the older Hardy's estimate that he had missed an opportunity for an authentic and comforting life as a small-town architect in a "stone yard" which was a little "center of noble effort" equal to any scholarly pursuit (*Life and Work,* 478), while the class notation in the narrator's estimate of a true illumination implies an independence and authenticity which Jude's aspirations toward high culture do not.

In keeping with Arnold's advice in the preface to his 1853 volume of poems, Hardy reproduces the textual past as a sign of the absence of any strong inspiration which could produce a different textual present (Arnold, "Preface," 208). Thus the really surprising thing about the novel is that there are no surprises in it, especially not if we keep Shelley's

Alastor in mind. In principle, the novel is not novel; it reproduces a specific textual past and depends upon our recognition of its belatedness for its novel significance. Moreover, Jude's form of romantic consciousness is not an index of freedom or self-expression; rather, it denotes the essential dimension of his incarceration in and by culture. Form, which culture after Kant conceives of as the nonmimetic component essential to the freedom of the human spirit, is mimetic in *Jude;* Hardy represents Jude's desire for freedom as a formal dimension which then paradoxically denotes the absence of such.

Thus, far from colluding with Arnold's cultural assumptions, Hardy's authorial aim in *Jude* is to contradict them by writing "A true allegory of the state of one's own mind in a representative history . . . [as] the highest thing one can attempt in the way of poetry" at the present time (Arnold, "Preface to Poems, 1853," 208–9). Such allegories were *precisely* the genre Arnold declared writers should not attempt. Allegories of the state of one's own mind were "assuredly not" the "highest problem of art" Arnold decreed in his 1853 preface. And it is against his decree that Hardy defines his protest by writing *Jude.*

Significantly, Hardy finds his authority for going against the Arnoldian grain by grounding his claim for allegory in Shelley's preface to *Alastor.* There, Shelley writes that his "poem . . . may be considered as allegorical of one of the most interesting situations of the human mind," namely enthusiasm and imagination "inflamed and purified through familiarity with all that is excellent and majestic" (Preface, *Alastor,* 69). It is curious just how closely Arnold's definition of what not to do approximates Shelley's definition of what he had done in *Alastor,* a curiosity which becomes intertextually meaningful within the critically reproductive context of *Jude.*

The point of this comparison is to suggest the complexity of presentation in Jude's posture toward Arnold's cultural program. *Jude* (the novel) is "classical" because distanced from the state of mind it represents and "romantic" because Jude (the character) is engaged in the vicissitudes of romantic subjectivity in its narcissistic phase. Hardy endows Jude with Shelleyan aspirations which must be worked out or through within a culture dominated by Arnoldian ethical classicism as it is represented by the "real" Christminster of Oxford. Given this transposition of past and present, Hardy replicates Arnoldian premises and precepts in an un-Arnoldian form, as an "allegory of the state of one's own mind within a representative history." The representative history at issue is romantic literary history, or culture in its past (subjective/ nostalgic) and present (objective/historic) state. Thus, like Arnold, Jude is a "nostalgia artist" whose delusions are revealed because we have access to the history of his mind and his conflicts with Christminster, real and fanciful. His form of mind is centered in the past of cultural aspirations which he ironically casts as future possibilities and thereby disregards present impossibilities. Jude is always looking toward the horizon of the past (the temporal oxymoron of Christminster) which situates his consciousness at the scene of French revolutionary vigor at the turn of the century or in 1815 when the will toward enlightened leveling revived in Shelley and the Marlow circle. Yet despite this positioning of the subject, Jude is a copier or conservator of present forms of power, represented collectively by Oxford-Christminster. What Jude finally comes to understand—and what we finally come to understand by reading Jude's life in culture—is that romantic forms and possibilities have already been tested by time during the century-long debate between culture and society. Rather than an increment of liberality and flexibility, the century has covertly restored and conserved its old orthodoxies and traditions, biases and class stratifications. Culture has constructed nothing remarkably new nor has it deconstructed anything old and shaken. Thus, Jude's subjectivity is objective (a genre piece), while the allegory of his plight recapitulates the historic status of romantic culture as a dead end, though mystifications of possibility remain as a residual rhetoric.

Eventually, Jude learns that the "thither" he carves on the milestone to Christminster is the prevailing rubric for romantic deception which requires that "something ever more about to be" in order to insure that nothing ever "is." His thither of hope ultimately surfaces as his disease of unrest which makes him "after all, a paltry victim to the spirit of mental and social restlessness, that makes so many unhappy in these days!" (J, 399). Cleverly, Hardy recasts Dante's "so many, I had not realized [spiritual] death had undone so many" in Jude's citing of the most prevalent form of cultural death "these days," a phrase which recalls Arnold's "at the present time." Moreover, Jude's assessment correctly equates mental unrest with social unrest: ambition in the marketplace is the alter ego of Christminster ambition, while high culture, like high society, discourages any upstarts from entering the ranks of the profitably blessed.

In this regard, we might note that one of the working titles for *Jude the Obscure* had been "The Simpletons." Hardy's title is on loan from George Eliot's "Address to Working Men, by Felix Holt." There, Eliot defines the working class as either "Roughs who have the worst vices of the rich . . . or else mere sensual simpletons and victims" (417). Jude is a both a "rough"—a Wessex peasant whose early cultural dreams are saturated with intimations of luxury—and a simpleton and victim in his sensuality. In his public confession at Christminster, he sums up the advice of Eliot's "Address" when he states that "It takes two or three generations to try to do what I did in one" (*J*, 398), in essence agreeing with Eliot's call for gradualism. He claims further that his "impulses—affections—vices perhaps they should be called," and Eliot had called them such, "were too strong not to hamper a man without advantages" (*J*, 398). In principle, Jude agrees with Eliot that culture cannot be adequately appropriated without "advantages," yet the position from which he consents to her views and the history of why he so consents constitute Hardy's critique of Eliotic culture as an elitist institution that has lost touch with its original mission as Shelley had defined it, which is to level the *ancien régime* and republicanize England.

To return to Shelley in order to conclude our introduction, we should note that the "thither" which Jude carves on the Christminster milestone is on loan from *Alastor* too. There, the poet asks "O stream!/ Whose source is inaccessibly profound,/ *Whither* do thy mysterious waters tend? / Thou imagest my life" (502–5, emphasis added). Shelley's question applies directly to the romantic questions at issue in Jude's obscure life. The milestone measures the distance romanticism had come since Shelley's time, while the stone itself is at times overgrown with moss just as Jude's Christminster life is at times subjugated to the natural, cast as the sexual, the biological. Moreover, the milestone is symptomatic of both Shelley's Alastorish aspirations and Arnold's character of cultural perfection. Both discourses image a life which aims at a limitless horizon, both are "milestones" along a route without a discernible end, and both institute a wandering after lost causes or homes defined in idealistic terms. In sum, the rubric "thither/whither" represents desire's desire, which is to desire rather than to have.

In order to confirm this reading, we need only turn to Wordsworth, for unremarkably Shelley's "whither" is on loan from Wordsworth's "Intimations of Immortality." There, the poet asks forthrightly: "Whither has fled the visionary gleam?/ Where is now the glory and the dream?" (56–57). This is the central question which Hardy *reiterates* in *Jude,* a question which by the 1890s entailed Wordsworth's, Shelley's, and Arnold's pronouncements about culture. At best, these Christminster gleams have become "lost causes" or obscure motives and nostalgic fancies whose most debilitating legacy is that their transcendental affect obscures history; at worst, they represent monstrous and nightmarish forms of life whose unrest is undying and whose promised wider horizons have become frozen, solipsistic wastes.

As a nearly transparent reading of Shelley's romanticism, Hardy does not deflect Jude's fate from the discursive destiny of the romantic subject. Jude strictly reiterates all the textual moves predicated in Shelley's *Alastor,* its ancestor text, and in this way engages Wordsworth as well. As a reiterative form of romanticism, *Jude* highlights the authorial problem central to Hardy's Wessex where self-expression is repetition and individuality is burdened by time, a fate which produces caricatures and allegories rather than characters and naturalistic novels. Yet as we have affirmed in other chapters, the reproductive fate of his fictions fully engages the reproductive destiny of culture, and so aptly defines "the highest problem of an art which imitates actions" in contrast to Arnold's critical view that allegory could not adequately do so (Arnold, "Preface to Poems, 1853," 208–9).

In the beginning as his beginning, Jude inherits Phillotson's cottage piano. Phillotson is an Arnoldian character, a poet turned pedagogue whose pedagogy authors Jude's fate. Like the Arnold who abandoned an overly enthusiastic romantic poetry in order to write instructive essays on culture, Phillotson abandons the village of Marygreen and his cottage piano to study at Christminster-Oxford. As Phillotson's spiritual son, Jude assumes the instrument and instrumentalities of Phillotson's abandoned enthusiasms, symbolized by the cottage piano. He too will turn away from Marygreen and its rural music and toward high culture's music and those lyrical visions inspired by reading. In effect, Jude becomes entranced by the abstract character of Phillotson's concrete ambition; moreover, his fate begins, allegorically, where Shelley's did when he turned away from Wordsworth's druidic romanticism in order to inaugurate his own Hellenic form of culture. In effect, Coleridge's and Shelley's insistence on the necessity of letters is depicted as a turning away from Wordsworth's cult of the natural sensibility.

Jude's first "proper good notion" for getting *Geist* is to store the cottage piano in his aunt's "fuel house" where it will fuel his romantic enthusiasms (*J*, 47). Later Jude will become a rough musician, yet he never writes the music he plays nor is he sufficiently skilled to rekindle the spirit of the scores which move him. He becomes a good hand at reading scores (as Hardy became a "good hand" at the serial novel) who never understands the music business, which is a professional, mercantile institution (as Hardy came to understand the business of letters). Thus, when Jude meets the composer of "At the Foot of the Cross," he does not see that the composer is not a poet but a discontented businessman who has decided to enter the wine trade because it is more lucrative than trading in music. Culture, represented collectively as Christminster, is a business like trading in wine; its Dionysian enthusiasms are no longer appreciated, though its Apollonian forms can be lucrative products in the marketplace.

Genealogically, Jude begins his life in signs where the sign is severed from its classical grounding at the moment of the French Revolution.[6] Ironically, he reproduces the revolutionary moment one hundred years after the Revolution and roughly sixty years after its cultural effects waned in Britain, if we take Carlyle's writing in the 1830s as the first symptom of slippage as Hardy did. Jude is a peasant who seeks the rewards of culture in a society which seems to offer him such if he only read. His desire for cultural transcendence and a transcendent culture is the equivalent of his desire for class transcendence. What Jude does not see is that getting *Geist* is like "Getting On" for Ruskin or like "Getting and Spending" for Wordsworth. Over time, the difference between cultural value and mercantile value has collapsed. Jude's youthful intuitions are "proper and good" as the village blacksmith tells him, yet what he does not see is that culture is no longer a republican affair but a business proposition. Abstracted because absent, Phillotson becomes the obscure object of Jude's desire. The teacher is thus transformed into a figure of romance who offers possible but not actual transcendence. Actual culture, to which Phillotson himself will fail to gain access, is as aristocratically bourgeois as was Alec's d'Urberville name. And it is in that name—or the character of that name—that Jude suffers, as Tess did. In both instances, the romances of romantic culture are collectively the tragic agency responsible for the catastrophe, those lost causes of the lost.

Jude appears to escape history by fleeing into Keatsean "realms of gold" predicated upon reading and hearsay. His fancies never marry with history, rather they impart to history a kinder, more parental aspect. His form of romantic consciousness is cast as self-deception, thus the fable of his life is not metaphorically romantic presenting a genuine return of transgressive possibilities, but metonymically so because representing a simulacrum of such possibilities. Jude is "like" a romantic idealist—like the Alastor-poet in fact—he "re-presents" that which had already been presented enthusiastically by romantics such as Shelley. Thus the novel itself is a form of writing trapped in parodic replications of romantic forms as a sign of its unremarkable character.

Unlike Shelley's claim for his age as one which would be "memorable . . . in intellectual achievements" because he "lived among such philosophers and poets as surpass beyond comparison any who have appeared since the last national struggle for civil and religious liberty" ("A Defence of Poetry," 508), Hardy could only claim for his age a belated and diminished character which, in turn, is exemplified by the character of his writing. If, that is, Shelley could confidently boast that in his age and in his person "Poets . . . [are] mirrors of the gigantic shadows which futurity casts upon the present" ("Defence," 508), then in Jude we witness Hardy's confession that novelists could only mirror or copy the gigantic shadows which the romantic past casts upon the present.

Our awareness that Hardy was reading Shelley's poetry as well as Dowden's Life of Shelley while writing Jude would be sufficient reason for seeking analogical pretexts to Jude's plight in the canon of Shelley's poetry and prose. Besides his immediate dependence upon Shelley's works while writing Jude, Hardy was involved in an extended flirtation with Mrs. Florence Henniker which had its impact on the text. Florence Henniker is the "Florence" of Sue Florence Bridehead. Mrs. Henniker was the daughter of Richard Mockton Milnes who had visited Oxford to exonerate Shelley's name. Hardy placed great faith in his "Shelleyan" relationship with Mrs. Henniker, as his letters to her attest (One Rare Fair Woman); thus he could not understand why the daughter of one so closely connected to the Shelley heritage and so imbued with Shelleyan creeds of free love would not desire to consummate their affair, as Mrs. Henniker did not (Millgate, *Thomas Hardy*, 338). Hardy's disillusionment at her refusal is the historic source of Sue's "failure" as a type of Veiled Maiden. Henniker's weak Shelleyan character becomes Sue's; Henniker's miming of Shelleyan possibilities for romantic transgression becomes Sue's demanding that Jude see her "as exactly like" the intellectual beauty in Shelley's poetry. Read in the light of biography, *Jude* is an instrument of Hardy's revenge upon Mrs. Henniker for not fully practicing what she preached. As Sue Florence Bridehead, Mrs. Henniker becomes a representative figure for all weak "Epipsychidions" who dissemble a Shelleyan love to which they are not wholeheartedly committed.

Rather than a social tract on marriage reform as it has often been misconstrued, despite Hardy's admonishment that it not be so understood (Preface, *J*, 40), Jude's relationship with Sue depicts a Shelleyan tragedy wrought by the mutual shattering of "the ideals of the two chief characters" (Preface, 40). Read in the light of biography, *Jude* depicts the shattering of Hardy's idealization of Mrs. Henniker whom he had imagined as his romantic muse and counterpart. After their affair had come to a disappointing end, he wrote that he could not believe that "one . . . pre-eminently the child of the Shelleyan tradition" had "allowed herself to be enfeebled by a belief in ritualistic ecclesiasticism . . . mechanically adopted" (Millgate, 339). Hardy's letter should stand as a gloss indicating the motives behind Sue's default. Henniker's decorative and, to Hardy, coquettish dissimulation of romantic liberty coupled with her staunch fidelity to her husband become, in Hardy's allegory, Sue's cowardly return to Phillotson in order to "mechanically adopt" and perform the "ritualistic ecclesiasticism" of a traditional marriage.

The saga of Sue Bridehead is then not the fable of a "new woman," but rather a critique of the Arnoldian emphasis on duty rather than on "doing as one likes," a mandate clearly opposed to Shelley's emphasis that one should do as one desires if one's affinities are elective and one's reasons are just. In effect, Hardy pits "Laon and Cythna" against *Culture and Anarchy* in order to demonstrate the negative effects of the Hebraic aspect of an ostensibly Hellenic culture. Albeit there is an element of Hardy's misogynistic belief that "we can trust to imagination only for an enfranchised woman" (Millgate, 339) because women are "The

Weaker" (*J*, 211) sex, essentially Sue is a decorative and debilitated simulation of the young Mary Godwin Shelley. Like Mary Godwin, Sue is a figure of the French enlightenment—Jude will call her "quite Voltairian"—while her tomboyish character and early romance with a university student-turned-London journalist characterizes her as literary and bohemian. Her two middle names, "Florence and Mary," are intended, I think, to satirize Mrs. Henniker as a "Florence" who is not enough a "Mary" Godwin Shelley, her nobler predecessor in type. In this reading, the combined form of "Florence Mary" becomes a temporal sign of degeneration within the feminist romantic temper (as indeed the name of Mary Shelley had become by Hardy's day). As the line of descent from "Mary" to "Florence" suggests, at one time the desire for vision and love could produce poetic couples like Laon and Cythna and historic couples like Percy and Mary Shelley; currently this desire inspires only the rhetoric of release in tragic romantic pairs like Jude and Sue or frustrating *liaisons dangereuses* in couples like Hardy and Mrs. Henniker.

In seeking a profession for Jude, Hardy went to Dowden's *Life of Shelley* from which he extracted this note: "*Sculpture*. The ideality of the art of Sculpture—each object presenting beauty or passion in an immortal abstraction from all that is temporary & accidental—appealed in a peculiar degree to Shelley's imagination" (*Literary Notebooks*, 1: 69). In accordance with Dowden's assessment of Shelley's taste, Hardy has Jude work as a second-rate sculptor or stone mason. Jude will speak to "immortal abstractions" or Christminster ghosts from which "all that is temporary or accidental" has been leached. Hardy's intention in characterizing Shelley's taste as Jude's proclivities is to present Jude as "like the Poet in Shelley's 'On a Poet's Lips I Slept'," an emblem of "pure fancy" in flight from the "Prosaically accurate" Wordsworth of "Peter Bell" (*LN*, 2:35). We see Jude on such a "flight" when he rides the Wessex roads in his baker's cart absorbed in his reading. During his rural rides he becomes so abstracted from the countryside that he seems to "sleep upon a poet's lips" and thus becomes a danger to the community at large as the police officer warns him. His form of romanticism is, in fact, a danger to the community because it removes him from the concreteness of genuine engagements with humanity and with time-honored forms of humanity embodied in local traditions, as Wordsworth knew following Burke's critique of French radicalism in his *Reflections on the French Revolution.* Though it is a latent irony in the text, it is precisely Wordsworth's prosaic engagements with natural forms, rural traditions, and community that could provide Jude the necessary balance of the concrete, were he not blind to them because sleepwalking in realms of literary gold.[7]

If Shelley's view of sculpture informs one register of Jude's abstracted character, it is Schopenhauer's view of Rome that informs another. Hardy copied this excerpt from Schopenhauer into his literary note-books: "the genius of the Greeks, . . . translated by their sculptors into statues . . . expired in Rome; the cycle of their psychological concep-tions had been exhaustively presented through this medium [of sculp-ture] (*LN,* 2:34). At Christminster, Hardy refigures the expiration of the Greek genius in Rome as the exhaustion of the romantic genius in England. Christminster is like Schopenhauer's Rome, and George Eliot's for that matter as she depicts it in *Middlemarch,* insofar as it is a city where a once-flexible and inspired form of culture has ossified into a sculpted orthodoxy, itself in need of a "romanticization" or lyrical shattering. Instead of shattering those forms, Jude restores them and thereby suspends the problem rather than solves it. Moreover, Schopenhauer's city of fallen signs is reproduced as Jude's Christminster consciousness, a "roman" form of romanticism. High culture is imperial in Jude's England; it dominates his consciousness, and it is mostly rhetorical and decorative. The faith it once promoted is as "dead as a fern leaf in a lump of coal," to deploy Hardy's figure, and not alive with organic possibilities. Jude restores these forms instead of innovating new shapes of a powerful self-expression, and in this way, his insurgent heart is that of a simpleton and a victim.

As we have been suggesting all along, Jude's character may be satis-factorily glossed by Shelley's *Alastor* and the preface to *Alastor.* Both preface and poem outline the idealistic concerns of the novel which "may be considered as *allegorical* of one of the most interesting situations of the human mind" (Preface, *Alastor,* 69, emphasis added). Hardy derives his sense of Jude's obscurity from his reading of the fate of Shelley's poet-quester who dies in an obscurity so profound that art itself cannot describe the loss. That Hardy's art can and does describe the loss is another sign of the classical character of Jude's sublime and the historical character of his fate.

Jude is an "adventurous genius" who, like the youth in *Alastor,* flees

Jude the Obscure: Shelley's Modern Prometheus Once More

"reality's dark dream," the "brown depression" symbolized by "the Brown House" and Troutham's concave field, into bright visions. Jude uses sublime images to transform his "revulsion of" the natural and communal world into a "desire for" the Christminster world of porcelain luxuries. Just as the Alastor-poet's "self-centered seclusion" is ultimately "avenged by the furies of an irresistible passion," so too the direct path of Jude's journey to Christminster will be broken by his passion for Arabella and then Sue. Jude wants to "drink deep of the fountains of knowledge" as does the Alastor-poet, yet he cannot get to such a fountain because he is poor; thus he drinks "shallowly" and in so doing personifies Eliot's lower classes who are not the "natural" inheritors of culture. Jude's essential flaw is that the "magnificence and beauty of the external world [does not sink] profoundly into the frame of his conceptions" (Preface, 69), thus it is appropriately "Father Time" or concrete history in conjunction with "the external world" or biology that brings about his final downfall. Eventually Jude will "thirst for intercourse with an intelligence similar to" his own as did the Alastor-poet before him. Afire with this thirst, he will "image" a "Being" who is like him and project his image onto Sue, his "Veiled Maiden" or "Bride-head." Sue is Shelleyan insofar as she is Jude's cousin and something of a sister to him, since both were raised by Drusilla, yet she is first and foremost "the vision in which he embodies his own imaginations" (Preface, 69). Because she "unites all of wonderful, or wise, or beautiful, which the philosopher, or lover could depicture" (Preface, 69), she becomes his third "teacher" or Christminster phantom.

Like the Alastor-poet's tale, Jude's fable is about "homelessness" or alienation. This problem is defined by Shelley when he notes that although a swan "hast a home . . . a mate . . . and joy," the idealist-poet "lingers" alone despite "a voice far sweeter than [the swan's] dying notes/ Spirit more vast than [the swan's], frame more attuned/ To beauty." Like the poet, Jude too will waste his "surpassing powers/ On the deaf air . . . the blind earth, and heaven/ That echoes not [his] thoughts" (*Alastor*, 280–98). No institution or woman actually echoes Jude's thoughts, although he will echo theirs. Despite the appearance of correspondence and elective affinity, Jude is always alone in history, always in solitude, always homeless despite the prevalence of a rhetoric guaranteeing him hearth, home, and sympathetic companionship.

Jude lives for "vision and love," and it is by their agency that his spirit is ultimately exhausted, as was the Alastor-poet's before him. Culture is the tragic agent in his fable, as it was in Shelley's *Alastor,* and not labor or "the hard grind of reality" as Jude claims. In Jude's life we see the final "departure" of the culture of vision and love, an exodus which had begun in Shelley's *Alastor* (360–68), while the question central to *Alastor,* "who shall save?" (357) remains as unanswered and obscure as ever, despite a century-long response to the question by writers such as Arnold and Eliot. The exhaustion of the Alastor-poet's quest is repeated by Jude, who dies from consumption and exhaustion after the failure of his last "quest" to recover Sue. To conclude his Alastor-novel, Hardy refigures the Alastor-poet's deathbed scene as Jude's. Both scenes describe the "blackness of [a] heaven" no longer illuminated by bright dreams and both present us with "An image, silent, cold, and motionless,/ As [the] voiceless earth and vacant air." Like the dead Alastor-poet's, Jude's "wondrous frame" now has "No sense, no motion, no divinity"; thus, he appears as "a fragile lute, on whose harmonious strings/ The breath of heaven did wander—a bright stream/ Once fed with many-voiced waves—a dream/ Of youth, which night and time have quenched for ever,/ Still, dark, and dry, and unremembered now (*Al,* 660–70). Jude dies unremembered on Remembrance Day, and he dies "dry" and thirsting for water. Ironically, as Jude lies dying it is *his* "heart" which "burn[s] to the socket" and not those of a more worldly cast, like Villbert and Arabella who are romancing each other, and Christminster at large, which is enjoying a boating regatta. But this is Hardy's way of emphasizing his difference from Shelley, for as his retelling of the Alastor myth is brought to a close, high romances of transcendental idealism return to their vulgar source in romances plain and simple.

Jude's fate in culture officially begins in school and with books which offer him a form of inspiration equivalent to Wordworth's nature. In the beginning as his beginning, Jude turns away from Marygreen, in effect refusing to engage in Wordsworthian forms of satisfaction and redemption. Hardy's fable begins by depicting Jude firmly under the tutelage (or subjection) of Phillotson who, at this time, is a kind of Matthew figure as he playfully appears in Wordsworth's "Expostulation and Reply" and "The Tables Turned." We learn in the opening "argument" of the novel that "everybody [in the village] *seemed* sorry" that "the school-master was leaving" except Jude who was genuinely sorry. Jude "grows double" in Phillotson's schoolhouse because he learns to desire the "dull and endless strife of books" ("Expostulation and Reply," 2 and 9). He learns, that is, to live in culture and not in the world. His split or doubled personality, at once a fantast and erotolept, evinces an inability to integrate nature as culture and reading as culture. Thus, he desires to leave the country—and all that it represents—for the city, a place where literary culture is gotten and spent. Jude does not want "Nature be [his] Teacher," as Wordsworth recommended it should, but scriptural culture or Phillotson and Christminster.

When he gazes into the village well which is "as ancient as the village itself," he sees "a shining disk of quivering water" and not the water itself, nor does he see "the lining of green moss near the top, and nearer still the hart's tongue fern" (*J*, 49). The hart's tongue fern alludes to Wordsworth's "Hart-Leap Well," while the well itself in its natural aspect is the source of a profound Wordsworthian grace. Because he is blinded by his form of enlightenment—symbolized by the Shelleyan sun—Jude misses the opportunity to feel the bonding of "natural piety" with others. Instead, he thirsts for "sunlight" and correspondences with bright things "thither" from his village, preferring sermons written on stones to those spoken by babbling brooks.

Jude's vision of the shining disk at the bottom of the well is our first clue to his Shelleyan sensibility; its shimmering presence is derived from Shelley's *The Triumph of Life* where Rousseau-Wordsworth glimpses a "shape all light" in the reflected "sun's image radiantly intense . . . on the waters of the well that glowed like gold" (346–47). Jude's cultural inspiration begins where Shelley's did, by turning away from Words-worth, that "lone star" whose light had dimmed in the early part of the century when the poet betrayed his commitment to liberty and reform ("To Wordsworth"). Moreover, Jude will die burning with fever and thirsting after "water," the real grace of a simple life which the village well once offered and which he experiences briefly in the "Elsewhere."

For Jude, school is not the "prison house" it was for Wordsworth, but a palace of art. Those boys who "seemed sorry" but are actually glad, are, collectively, the youthful spirits of *The Prelude* or the boy whose death Wordsworth mourns in "There Was a Boy." For the Marygreen boys, summer is a time of joy because one's spirit has been freed from "That burthen of . . . the unnatural self," or scriptural culture (*Prelude*, 1: 20–21). The "Dear Liberty" and cheerfulness that the Marygreen boys look forward to in Phillotson's absence, Jude mourns. For Jude, breezes do not become "corresponding" until they are infused with "an auxiliary light" coming from Christminster where he imagines his pedagogical saint of culture walks in glory.

Jude's childhood is inspired "By solemn vision, and bright silver dream" like the Alastor-poet's, yet he is not "nurtured" by "Every sight/ And sound from the vast earth and ambient air" as Shelley's poet is (*Al*, 60–70). Jude's "Great Mother" (*Al*, 2) and "Mother of this unfathomable world" (*Al*, 18) is Christminster and "her" female substitutes, and not the culture of nature. Later, when he meets Arabella, he will become more "natural" or "sexual," in Hardy's naturalistic interpretation of Wordsworth's conception of nature. To Arabella, Jude is "as simple as a child" (*J*, 81), and she entraps him with a fantasy of motherhood. By giving in to nature and abandoning culture, Jude's life becomes Wordsworthian for a while. He will settle down in Wessex and attempt plain living. Eventually, he will pine away for high thinking as he comes to see that nature stands in the way of his original form of desire, as it did for Shelley's Alastor-poet and Wordsworth's Arab-Quixote, albeit it brings him brief periods of joy when he submits to low or common romances and acts naturally, sexually.

In this regard, we might consider that both Sue and Jude eventually believe that "It was Nature's intention, Nature's law and *raison d'être* that we should be joyful in what instincts she afforded us" (*J*, 413) that has deceived them. Sue's pronouncement suggests that it is their trust in Wordsworth's nature which has brought them to grief. Accepting his views on "Nature's intention," they abandon their Shelleyan quests and engage in plain living and high thinking away from Christminster. Eventually, though, "fate" gives them a "stab in the back for being such fools as to take nature at her word" (*J*, 413). Sue's assessment implies that the two most prevalent forms of romantic culture are tragically contradictory to each other and that the fate or "Alastor-spirit" which has hunted them down is Wordsworthian in character rather than Shelleyan. Furthermore, her estimate of their tragic destiny reiterates the conflict between Wordsworth and Shelley in *Alastor*, and by so doing it revokes Keats's solution to Shelley's problem in *Endymion*. In Hardy's allegory, the poet-wanderer (Jude) and his intellectual beauty or Moon Goddess (Sue) decide to act naturally and live domestically. Such a resolution is no solution at all according to Sue because "Nature's holy plan" is a tragic destiny for certain forms of romantic consciousness.

Specifically, Sue's charge rescinds Wordsworth's claim that "Nature never did betray/ The heart that loved her; 'tis her privilege,/ Through all the years of this our life, to lead/ From joy to joy" ("Tintern Abbey," 122–24). This is the "plan" or promise that Sue claims "fate" has stabbed them in the back for following. As in Shelley's *Alastor* where the value of Wordsworth's nature is recognized and then rejected by those committed to pursue "intellectual beauty," Jude and Sue renounce their commitment and follow nature's holy plan at the cost of foregoing their pursuit of letters. When they meet initially and court in Christminster's precincts, they are a Shelleyan couple; she is his sisterly/ wifely intellectual beauty, he, her adoring idealist-worshiper. Beyond Christminster however, in "Aldbrickham and Elsewhere," Jude and Sue reconstitute the lifestyle of the early "romantic couple," as a kind of Dorothy and William in love who engage in "plain living and high thinking." Yet it is just this "natural," domestic lifestyle which Sue and then Jude eventually hold responsible for their tragedy.

Thus we might read Sue's ultimate return to Phillotson and to "Duty" as an allegory of Wordsworth's turning away from his trust in nature and reform and toward ecclesiastical forms of culture after 1815, a devolution which Shelley deplored as a return to cultural philistinism. Appropriately, Jude's complaint against Sue's returning to Phillotson recapitulates Shelley's complaint against Wordsworth's conservatism in "To Wordsworth." Like the Shelley of 1816 in regard to Wordsworth, Jude all but says to Sue right before she leaves him: "One loss is mine/ Which thou too feel'st, yet I alone deplore./ Thou wert as a lone star, whose light did shine/ On some frail bark in winter's midnight roar . . . In honoured poverty thy voice did weave/ Songs consecrate to truth and liberty,/ Deserting these, thou leavest me to grieve,/ Thus having been, that thou shouldst cease to be" ("To Wordsworth," 5–8, 12–14). In the novel, Hardy's reconstructs this scene of abandonment in Jude's final complaint against Sue. Echoing Shelley, Jude says: "That a woman-poet, a woman-seer, a woman whose soul shone like a diamond— whom all the wise of the world would have been proud of, if they could have known you—should degrade herself like this! I am glad I had nothing to do with Divinity—damn glad—if it's going to ruin you in this way!" (*J*, 426).

Earlier, Hardy had initiated his satire on Wordsworth's poetics by depicting a young Jude gleaning information about Christminster from the gossip of tramps, carters, and quacks, those leech gatherers, beggars, and soldiers who wander the roads of his Wessex. Jude extracts only the "choicest impulses" from their (mis)information and constructs a saving vision from his weave of fables. For example, he learns the direction in which Christminster lies from a "tiler, glad of any kind of diversion from the monotony of labor" (*J*, 60). Jude will "romanticize" the information when he suggests to the tiller that the glowing dome of Christminster looks like "the heavenly Jerusalem" (*J*, 60). The tiler agrees with Jude, adding that he "never would ha' thought of it" himself (60).

Jude's scene of instruction inverts the priorities of Wordsworth's quest for knowledge in children and leech gatherers in order to satirize Wordsworth's method. Indeed, Jude, the child, is father to the man insofar as he poeticizes bald information and thereby transforms fact into something like Wordsworth's "breath and finer spirit of all knowledge" (Preface, Second Edition of *Lyrical Ballads*). Yet in Hardy's refiguration, it is the "natural man," a tiler of the soil, who is taught a different way to see by the addition of a scriptural metaphor to his plain perception. Thus, the satire of Jude's romanticization of Christminster reveals the mechanism behind Wordsworthian wisdom gathering; in effect Hardy unveils the rhetoric of romanticism by demonstrating that it is the product of a "schooled" sensibility which ventriloquizes its desire through humble people and bored natural men. In Jude's scene of instruction, that is, we see Coleridge's critique of Wordsworthian "plain speaking" in chapter 17 of the *Biographia Literaria*.

Hardy sustains this parody when he depicts Jude's numerous meetings with the trade "volk" who service Christminster. By climbing to "the highest rung" on a workman's ladder (*J*, 60), Jude inhales the *Geist* in the ambient air. Atop the ladder, Jude is a self-made Jacob figure who has climbed the golden staircase to gaze upon his Heavenly Jerusalem. Appropriate to his Shelleyan form of character, he ignores the "utility" of the workman's ladder in order to follow in "the footsteps of Culture"

Jude the Obscure: Shelley's Modern Prometheus Once More

("A Defence of Poetry," 507), nor does he consider the "wooden" character of his visionary support which is not without its class import. Jude continues to collect shreds of information about Christminster by interrogating two carters who supply him with an outrageously absurd account of the theological and academic life there. After their recitation, one carter tells Jude: "Well, 'tis only what has come in my way . . . I've never been there, no more than you" thereby negating all that he has said previously. Repressing the carter's admission of ignorance in order to possess his knowledge, Jude proclaims that Christminster "would just suit" him (*J*, 66). It suits him because it is him, an image of his desire and not of history. His romance with Arabella will suit him in a similar manner as will his romance with Sue. The actual Arabella has little to do with the woman Jude loves; she exists as a construct of his fancy, while he is compelled to marry her owing to a fable or lie of pregnancy which is without concrete, historic truth. Sue Bridehead will also suit him because she too will exist as a fabular being absolved of history and abstracted from her body, while it is only when the body and then history interfere with his visionary quests that his romance collapses. In all instances, Jude must refuse history in order to possess his dream.

Energized by suitable misinformation, Jude takes to studying the outdated grammars of ancient languages. His books fall under the double rubric of the belated; they present dead methodologies for learning dead languages. Like the Alastor-poet, he hopes that by reading ancient tongues, "The fountains of divine philosophy" will not "flee his thirsting lips" (*Al*, 72) and like his poetic ancestor, he too desires to be "obedient to high thoughts." Tragically, his subjection to Arnold's principle of reading "the highest and best that is thought in the world" condemns him to be consumed by a yearning he cannot satisfy, nor will the prevailing institutions of culture help him to slake his thirst.

While reading his ancient texts, Jude "Visit [s]/ The awful ruins of the days of old" (*Al*, 107–9) and imagines the he will be the one to restore these ruins. He first attempts to approach Christminster by asking Villbert the wanderer to bring him grammar books. Villbert is the first Christminster "Doctor of the Theatre" (*J*, 490) whom Jude meets on his quest in specular culture. Villbert's "golden ointment, life-drops, and female pills" are guaranteed "to cure all disorders of the alimentary system, as well as asthma and shortness of breath" (*J*, 68). His quack cures are approximate forms to Jude's "romances" which are also benign deceptions predicated upon rhetoric, artifice, and desire. Significantly, his "golden ointment" derives its name from the Song of Solomon wherein the poet chants his love for his mistress and the believer hymns his love for his church. Obliquely, the double referent of romance and religion points to Hardy's two lost faiths, the one religious, the other poetic, a double loss thematically central to poems such as "The Impercipient" and "A Sign Seeker." More immediately though, the double referent forecasts Jude's upcoming romance of religion as a "golden ointment" for his disesteem and lower-class status while it describes his romance with Sue who is a substitute form of religion for him—or, as he first sees her—an ecclesiastical copyist. Moreover, the bogus form of all golden ointments of culture suggests the quacklike character of those who offer such cures to the unsuspecting poor.

As a first form of Sue, Jude imagines Christminster as a "vague city veiled in mist" (*J*, 61), and he addresses the form "as a lover would his mistress." As the place of knowledge, Christminster is Shelley's "Veiled Maiden." The narrative continues to track Shelley's poem by having the poet-quester thirst first for knowledge in the "ruins" of ancient cities after which he becomes the student-admirer of two women. Our awareness of the derivative character of the plot undermines our sense of the project as original, yet such an undermining of one sense of originality constructs another in its place. By presenting Jude's romantic readings within a critically distanced narrative, Hardy reveals the sublime to be a rhetorical form wherein figures of desire conceal figures of history in order to produce symbolic meaning. This authentic revelation of the rhetoric of the sublime distances the sublime from its effects while it opens a dimension of historical difference between source and copy text wherein the author can lay claim to an originality suitable to his contemporary understanding of culture.

By revealing the mechanism or ruse of *hypsos*, the narrator defuses the power of romantic figures and prevents them from becoming captivating once again, though they might remain attractive. Such a suspension indicates an awareness of the problems within romantic culture and its evolved forms. Hardy presents this problem by framing his fable of a pre-Oedipal or narcissistic sensibility within a narrative which is post-Oedipal because mediated by a narrator with a historic sensibility. The overall effect of this structure suggests a resolution to a problem which is never resolved, for the two registers of frame and tale never merge. Thus the easy authority of the imaginative reason or "whole man" is alluded to structurally yet it is never made manifest within the structure of representation. In this regard, Hardy's novel is a *theoretical* and *historical* project insofar as it recognizes the saving solution to its proffered dilemmas, yet it cannot in good conscience represent it because history had not.

The narrator obliquely refers to Jude's form of captivation when he informs us that Villbert's pills are said to cure a "shortness of breath" after which he notes that Jude develops "a stitch in his side" (*J*, 69) by running after the wandering doctor. Ironically, he must run himself breathless in order to procure the pills which are supposed to cure his breathlessness. By racing after the bogus doctor, he catches the disease which only the doctor can seem to cure, which is the point. By chasing after a series of "quack" doctors such as those who man the bastions of Christminster culture, Jude exhausts himself seeking "the character of perfection" in contradistinction to the narrator who invigorates his authorial powers by narrating the chronicle of Jude's exhaustion.

When Jude first sits down to read the Christminster grammars which Phillotson sends him, he takes the books "to a lonely place, and [sits] down on a felled elm" (*J*, 71). Intertextually, the elm recalls to mind Old South's fallen romantic icon which, in turn, leads us back to Wordsworth's "Ruined Cottage." Primarily though, Jude's position recalls the scene of poetic vision in Shelley's *Triumph of Life* where the poet is laid to sleep on the felled trunk of an old chestnut. There, he experiences a disillusioning vision of the history of romanticism from Rousseau to Wordsworth. Jude too experiences his first great disillusionment with the culture of reading as he sits beneath a felled tree. Glossing over his "historical" texts—historical because out of date and because grammars of dead languages—Jude enunciates his disappointment through the narrator's voice: "this was Latin and Greek then, was it, this grand delusion! The charm he had supposed in store for him was really a labour like that of Israel in Egypt" (*J*, 72).

Aside from Hardy's astute comparison of charm and labor to culture and dominance, we might note that Jude's grammars teach him the process of "turning the expressions of one language into those of another." As a metaphor for romantic effects, his grammars teach him to

The Descent of the Imagination

"turn" or trope literal and historic representations into sublime symbols by obscuring the actual with projections thrown up from his narcissistic reservoirs of desire. Disillusioned by the immense effort he sees it will take to trope history into culture, he wishes that "he had never seen a book . . . that he had never been born" (*J, 72*). In fact to "see a book" is to be born for Jude's lettered form of character, while to see one's idealized character as a "gigantic error" as Jude does for an instant is to incite the death wish or, "to wish [oneself] out of the world" as Jude presently does (*J, 72*). Still, Jude will not face history, and within a matter of weeks he has reinvested culture with narcissistic desire as his form of tragic flaw or "gigantic error."

It is, of course, Shelley's "generous error" that is recast by Hardy as Jude's "gigantic error," while it is Shelley's sense of "vacancy" which Jude must avoid at all times. He must, that is, project a totality of signs to cover and hide the totality of death. This need to live within vision or signs causes him to see Troutham's "work ground" as the ground of history, a place of ugliness and violence because devoid of a redemptive love. Yet, as the narrator informs us, other rural naturals had found only "love matches" in Troutham's field. There, "every inch of ground had been the site, first and last, of energy, gaiety, horse-play, bickering, weariness" (*J, 53*). Again, it is Wordsworth's natural culture which depresses Jude, and in this way too his life recapitulates that of the Alastor-poet.

The narrator describes Troutham's field as brown and concave, thus it is the antithetical figure to Christminster's "field" of light which is a convex dome. In the field, Jude "stands work on its head" by feeding birds he is supposed to shoo away. He thereby turns labor into a Shelleyan form of "love" culture by gesturing his denunciation of Wordsworth's youthful adventures in bird hunting (*The Prelude*, Book First). Jude's mental inversion is made concrete when Farmer Troutham picks him up by his feet and spins him around until he is dizzy in a scene reminiscent of Dickens's *Great Expectations* when Magwitch inverts Pip in a gesture proleptic of the effect his wealth will have on the young boy.

Although Jude gains a sense of self-esteem and self-aggrandizement by his cultural inversions, the narrator does not ennoble Jude's idealizations. Rather, he presents Jude's evasion of work as a recognizably *flawed* form of romanticism which is why the novel is a critical reading of romantic culture and not a call to reinstate its possibilities. When speaking for Jude—which, incidentally, the narrator does so often that the confusion of voices we hear approximates the dialogic collapse in *Alastor* which suggests, in turn, that an older, worldlier man is recounting a view of his youthful, poetic self—the narrator tells us that "As you got older, and felt yourself to be at the center of your time, and not at a point in its circumference . . . you were seized with a sort of shuddering . . . all around you there seemed to be something glaring, garish, rattling, and the noises and glares hit upon the little cell called your life, and shook it, and warped it" (*J*, 57). Jude's "little cell called your life" recalls Milton's "Cell of Fancy" in *Paradise Lost* as well as Keats's "Chamber of Maiden Thought" replete with images of narcissistic delight. Preferring always the maiden or untried life, Jude lives in a "cell of fancy" on the circumference of time, a figure marginal to history and to social endeavors whose labors he inverts in the mirror of his cultural reproductions.

At night, Shelley's time for "weaving dreams of joy and fear" ("To Night"), Jude pauses to worship the moon by reiterating a Horatian ode. Because he divines meaning from texts rather than reads their historical context, Jude cannot understand that the Horatian ode he quotes in praise of Diana had been written as a rhetorical gesture composed for a public occasion; the poem he reiterates is not an authentic prayer or even a religious text, but a means of pleasing Caesar and getting on in Rome. Although the scene of Jude's lunar laudation bears some comparison to Endymion's moon worship immediately before he encounters the Indian Maiden (and Jude will soon encounter Arabella), the more immediate analogue occurs in *Alastor* when the poet "lingered, poring on memorials/ Of the world's youth, through the long burning day/ Gazing on those speechless shapes when the moon/ Filled the mysterious halls with floating shades/ Suspended he that task, but ever gazed/ And gazed, till meaning on his vacant mind/ Flashed *like* strong inspiration, and he saw/ The thrilling secrets of the birth of time" (*Al*, 123–28, emphasis added). By gazing on the moon which in Shelley's symbology governs the realm of fancy, Jude experiences something *like* genuine inspiration. The secondary or fanciful character of his inspiration is given emphasis when the narrator describes the "shiny goddess" to whom he prays as looking "softly and critically at his doings," critically because perceptively, with the rhetoric of his desire revealed, softly, because nostalgically, with a wistful regard for the sunlight of the imagination that once inspired such acts of pagan faith.

Jude next encounters Arabella, his Arab Maiden of carnal temptations which are also allurements to domesticity. Like her Shelleyan ancestress, Arabella takes "Time from duties and repose to tend [the poet's] steps" (*Al*, 132). She is "enamored" of her poet before he is taken by her in keeping with the Shelleyan analogue, and she will return to her poet on more than one occasion during his life, as do the Arab Maidens in *Alastor*, sometimes to "call him with false names/ Brother and friend" (*Al*, 268–69).

Married to a real wife and mother, Jude could escape his enthrallment to Christminster, his imaginary wife and mother. His marriage to Arabella thus inverts the paradigm of values in Shelley's *Alastor* where the poet does not marry and so never tests Wordsworth's virtue of capitulating to experience. In becoming the father—or in imagining that he will— Jude momentarily escapes the lunar world of imaginary reproductions and enters the socialized world of symbolic productions. The irony in his fatherhood and its available opportunities for redemption arises when Jude learns that his romance has "fathered" a lie instead of a real child. With the help of much theatricality on Arabella's part, Jude "gets" or projects upon her body a romance of the Arab Maiden, thus the child she is supposed to bear is appropriately cast as a fable of entrapment Villbert suggests to her as a "cure" or "golden ointment" for her love sickness. This delusion of engagements effected by an engagement of delusions will be the case with Sue too. Little Time, the fabular child who does not appear in Jude's first marriage, uncannily appears in his second marriage to return it to fable, for it is by his hand that Jude learns that his casting Sue as his Epipsychidion or double has been yet another grand illusion of identity. Little Time's fabulous character is instrumental in dissolving Jude's first romance with Arabella, while his concrete, historical presence dissolves his second romance with Sue as a premise to the dissolution of all romances and romanticisms which fall victim to "Time's . . . own gray style" (*Epipsychidion*, 55).

When Jude first encounters her, Arabella introduces herself thusly: "Arabella Donn. I'm living here" (*J*, 82). Could Jude accept "living here" with her instead of "thither" with his fancy he could break with his Christminster enthrallments. Seeing Jude reading as he walks the Wessex roads (a form of abstraction for which he has become renowned), Arabella understands that she must translate herself into a romance in order to entrance her Arab-Quixote. Jude's romance with Arabella will work its way through various courtly fantasies until artifice shows itself as deception rather than enlightenment, after which the woeful real reappears and he must engage once more his protective Christminster visions.

Like her Arab Maiden namesake, Arabella is "a fine, dark girl" with "a rich complexion of a cochin hen's egg" (*J*, 81). She is Arabian too in her Cleopatra-like figuration; like the Nile, she hatches life upon her body and tempts Jude from his noble activity which, at the time he meets her, he fancies as the pursuit of aristocratic luxury. She is thus the "Abby" who distracts him from Christminster "Abbey" where he imagines himself a bishop with an income of £5,000 a year (*J*, 79). When he first encounters her, he feels himself "drifting strangely" toward her. Her strange attraction and his "drifting," coupled with her Circe-like character as a pigswain, her sexual experience, and her ability to artificially conjure a dimpled smile, constitute Arabella another Hardyan figure of Pater's "experienced woman," Mona Lisa. Like Pater's Lady Lisa, Arabella is an expert at "strange potions," those liquors which she prepares in Wessex bars, while her nickname, "Bella Donn" echoes the poisonous character of Pater's deadly courtesan, the *bella donna* of the romance tradition. Like Pater's Lady Lisa, Arabella lives beside the waters; she and Jude meet on the bridge over the stream where she washes her father's pig meat. Moreover, as Lady Lisa, Arabella represents Jude's "old idea" of Christminster in a "modern form."

It is then "Medea's wondrous alchemy,/ Which whereso' ever it fell made the earth gleam/ With bright flowers, and the wintry boughs exhale/ From vernal blooms fresh fragrance!" which Arabella employs to romantically enthrall Jude (*Al*, 672–75). Rather than an elective affinity, her "correspondence" and subsequent marriage to Jude is the result of a calculated risk on her part, the outcome of a conventional romantic plot. Having only a "general impression of her appearance" after he first encounters her, Jude resumes his "lonely way, filled with an ardor at which he mentally stood at gaze. He had just inhaled a single breath from a new atmosphere, which . . . had somehow been divided from his actual breathing as by a sheet of glass" (*J*, 82–83). As the narrator is quick to point out, Jude's "idea of her" is more important than she is in and of herself; it is her atmosphere which intoxicates him as

Christminster's had done previously, and not anything real, concrete, or actual about her. Arabella then is another name of the form of Christminster, a point the narrator further emphasizes when he describes Jude's ardor for her as seizing him "as a violent schoolmaster a schoolboy" (*J*, 48). His description reiterates Jude's enthrallment to romances of high culture in Phillotson's night school, structurally the primal scene wherein Jude originates his romantic character. She is his second "teacher" or don, and he will talk "the commonest local twaddle to Arabella with greater zest than he would have felt in discussing all the philosophies with the Dons in the recently adored University" (*J*, 88). As a Christminster figure, Arabella is a precursor to Sue Bridehead, the "Veiled Maiden." Both Sue and Arabella are "teachers"; both are aspects of Shelley's "one shape of many names"; both are "veiled" by artifice, and both are profoundly implicated in a play of representation and desire wherein difference is misconstrued as sameness.

Significantly, actual difference returns to Jude and Arabella through a series of unveilings wherein the historical is revealed. Of primary interest in the play of artifice is Jude's discovery that Arabella's dimples are as false as is her fall of hair. During the pig killing, he, in turn, reveals to her just how inadequate to the tasks of "real" life he is. That renowned scene of killing is proleptic of Father Time's killing of Jude's children and then himself; both hangings "suspend" romance and inaugurate the reign of history in its violent and predatory aspects. Jude next learns that his and Arabella's "child" is a fable, after which they part company. After leaving Arabella, he is once more confronted with "reality's dark dream" and so he fixes his gaze upon Christminster again and reinvests it with narcissistic desire, even though "he sometimes felt that by caring for books he was not escaping the commonplace nor gaining rare ideas, every working-man being of that taste now" (*J*, 112). Despite momentary glimpses of historical truth, Jude must create an illusory difference where he finds none in order to preserve his form of individuality.

The phantasmal, parodic rehabilitation of all Shelleyan referentials recurs when Jude becomes enthralled to Sue. With her, Jude seeks "intercourse" with an "intelligence" similar to his. In order to find identity, Jude simulates likeness, thus "[h]e images to himself the Being whom he loves" and loves himself in the imagining (Preface, *Alastor*,

69). He first sees Sue in a photograph, a sign to us that she will exist as a mechanical reproduction or copy of his form of desire. Seeing her working in an icon supply shop, he imagines her to be "Conversant with speculations of the sublimest and most perfect natures" (Preface, *Al*, 69) when she is only laboring for a living. Typically, Jude sees neither the labor nor the supply side of her craft but imagines her to be imaginatively engaged, poetic, angelic.

Viewed in the light of his misunderstanding, he declares that Sue is engaged in "a sweet saintly business" (*J*, 135). He does not see the contradiction in his oxymoron of a "saintly business," nor does he comprehend the paradox in her simulating the letter of joy as a form of labor (she copies the word *hallelujah* when he first sees her). His initial misunderstanding will be carried out—or worked through—in his relationship with her. Thus, through misconstruction and projection, Jude imagines Sue as his Veiled Maiden who "unites all of wonderful or wise, or beautiful which the poet, the philosopher, or the lover could depicture" (Preface, *Al*, 69). After having wandered through "Araby/ And Persia, and the wild Carmanian waste" (*Al*, 140–42), or in terms of the narrative "hard times," Jude encounters "A vision" of "a veiled maid" who "Sate near him, talking in slow solemn tones" (*Al*, 150–53). During his first days in Christminster, her vision "haunts" him as a sign that she has become a substitute form of his textual Christminster ghosts, while the scene at Melchester when she is dressed in his clothes reconstitutes as surface the scene of the Alastor-poet's identification with the Veiled Maiden. Regarding her then, Jude "saw in her almost a divinity" (*J*, 199) because that is how he needs to see himself.

Needing someone like himself to reflect his fantasies back to him, Jude imagines that "Her voice was like the voice of his own soul/ Heard in the calm of thought" (*Al*, 153). When Jude is overcome by "waves of pedal music" from a church organ whose sounds "ensphered [he and Sue in] the same harmonies," he is confirmed in his belief that they are counterparts. He then fancies her a "delight" who has "much in common with him" (*J*, 139) just as he did when he became ensphered in Arabella's "atmosphere." Although "not altogether . . . blind to the real nature of the magnetism" (*J*, 139) which is sexual, he prefers his delusion of a veiled maiden whose "music long,/ Like woven sounds of streams and breezes, held/ His inmost sense suspended in its web/ Of many colored woof and shifting hues" (*Al*, 154–57). Sexually as well as intellectually, Sue is unlike Jude, yet part of the "veil" of her veiled character is the rainbow of desire which Jude casts upon her in order to create a fanciful sameness by repressing an actual difference.

In between courting Sue the copyist and copying gothic forms, Jude addresses a gallery of imaginary portraits of the Christminster genius as though they were alive. Alone at night, Jude "found himself speaking out loud, holding conversation with them as it were, like an actor in a melodrama who apostrophizes the audience on the other side of the footlights" (*J*, 127). The narrator's description of the specular character of the act tells us that Jude practices a melodramatic and parodic form of imaginative address. His "epiphany" is transparently an act of memory, and not of inspiration; it reflects, it does not create; it addresses respectfully, it does not debate and master. The scene we witness is technically an allegory of lyrical desire which is distanced from any presumption of depicting an actual realization of that desire. Genuinely lyrical acts of self-expression are creatively forgetful of their implictly derivative character, as Jude's dramatic monologues are not, not for Jude and not for the narrator who annotates the address.

The satire continues when Jude attempts to establish a residence in Christminster. Then "Necessary meditations on the actual . . . compelled Jude to smother high thinkings under immediate needs" (*J*, 130). The "necessity" the narrator has in mind in Shelley's totalizing trope for those forces which militate against perfectionism, while the phrase itself recalls Wordsworth's "plain living and high thinking" only to emphasize that plain living interdicts "high thinking" rather than contributes to it. Faced with immediate needs, Jude begins to perceive "the defective real" of Christminster. Instead of a glowing dome, he now sees "the cruelties [and] insults . . . inflicted on the aged erections" (*J*, 130). As a romance, Christminster is "an unravaged bride of quietness," as a reality, however, the city is "a rotten historical document" (130). Jude restores this "rottenness" by imbuing it with a dignity it once had. As a lesser form of sculptor, he replicates the frozen past in order to preserve it in an unoriginal and uncreative present.

The narrator describes the stone yard in which Jude labors as "a little center of regeneration." In search of grand modes of redemption, Jude does not see the possibilities for "little" acts of redemption which are available to him here. He cannot see, that is, that *this* is Christminster culture too. In the stone yard, there "were forms in the exact likeness of those [Jude] had seen abraded and time-eaten on the walls. These were the ideas in modern prose which the lichened colleges presented in old poetry" (*J*, 131). The narrator's view of Christminster is specifically Shelleyan. In "A Defence of Poetry," Shelley writes that the prose of the world would become poetry as time wore away the rough edges of particularity, leaving in its wake a vision of essential truths and eternal principles. Time in this aspect "makes immortal all that is best and most beautiful in the world" by calling our attention to "the vanishing apparitions which haunt the interlunations of life" ("Defence," 505). Thus it is by "the blood of the mediator and the redeemer Time" ("Defence," 506) that Christminster's rotten history becomes poetic; Christminster the city, that is, will become "Christminster" the ideal when washed in the blood of Shelley's redeemer Time.

The narrator reiterates Shelley's assertion concerning temporality and ideality when he notes that Christminster's buildings "had done nothing but wait, and had become poetical" (*J*, 131). To his agreement, he adds the admonition: "How easy to the smallest building; how impossible to most men." His entailment reiterates Arnold's complaint regarding Dowden's biography of Shelley, while it suggests that historic man would never again become poetical and heroic since no sordid detail of any poet's life would ever be eroded from the record and forgotten.

As a copyist of the gothic imagination, what Jude does not see is that his romantic "medievalism . . . was as dead as a fern-leaf in a lump of coal", and that "other developments were shaping in the world around him in which Gothic architecture and its associations had no place" (*J*, 131). Because blind to the present as he copies forms of the past, Jude does not see the "deadly animosity of contemporary logic and vision towards so much of what he held in reverence" (*J*, 131). As the emblem of the fern-leaf aptly displays, Jude's imagination is highly formal and inflexible in its romantic desires, while it harbors a dead impression of an "organic" poetry that once grew lush and powerful in the world. Moreover, the narrator's figure inverts Pater's gemlike flame on two registers: Pater's figure for the capable imagination combines form and heat and light; Hardy's figure conjures a vision of an extinguished flame of life imprisoned within an opaque gem. The implication of this black figure of death wherein the organic has quite literally turned to stone over time is that romantic culture has itself become a rigid orthodoxy in need of shattering. Jude's imagination (and Hardy's imagining Jude) is like the fern-leaf in the coal, an Apollonian form of past organic life which offers an archeological reading of a certain regime of the imagination within literary history.

The Apollonian note is sounded again when Jude first sees Sue copying the word "alleluja" onto "the dead-surface paint" of a "piece of zinc, cut to the shape of a scroll" (*J*, 135). Her aesthetic labor reproduces gothic forms of joy as surface appearances, while the scene of her labor provides us with a kind of apocalypse in itself. As Jude's "Intellectual Beauty" and muse, she will shatter his gothic faith with Voltaire's skeptical enlightenment and Shelley's notions of liberty. He will liberate himself by singing her "Ode to Liberty" and then use his new-found liberty to do as he likes with her, much to his and her regret. Sue has gotten by heart the liberal creeds of her Oxford "angel"—a Shelley figure—and like Tess, she will recite his views verbatim to Jude with *dramatic* conviction but without a deep commitment to them or an awareness of their implications. Given Sue's talent for convincing performances, she will convert Jude from "the Shelley who thinks too much like other people" into the "Shelley who does not think enough like other people" in Arnold's characterization of Dowden's Jekyll-and-Hyde Shelley ("Shelley," 121). Moreover, Sue's conversion of him to a liberal creed replicates the scene of conversion between Tess and Alec at Long Ash barn, and with the same results.

In an allegorical enactment of Shelley's "Philosophical View of Reform," Sue casts herself as an agent of the "forces of liberty" which oppose "the forces of despotism" (Cameron, "Social Philosophy of Shelley," 512). As a son of Christminster Jude's Hebraic temper represents the "forces of despotism." Sue's victory over his gothic temperament leads to her final defeat which imprisons her first within her body (motherhood) and then within convention (marriage). Summarily represented, history defeats Sue's idealistic, textually constructed self. Allegorically, she is first presented as Jude's "star" in whose "smile" his cultural life is transformed (*Triumph of Life*, 418–19) and as the "teacher" muse from Shelley's "To a Skylark" and thus the third "don" whom Jude encounters on his pilgrimage. Yet she is last seen as a faded glory who walks "Beside [his] path" as "silent as a ghost . . . Through the sick day in which [Jude] wakes to sleep" (*Triumph of Life*, 430–33), a figure of time's conquest over romantic, republican aspirations.

Sue is an aesthetic figure for Jude, an artifact or fetish which possesses the power to "polish" or refine his rude village character. When he first encounters her, he sees her as an "ideal character about whose form he begins to weave curious and fantastic daydreams" (*J*, 136). The narrator's description immediately calls to mind Pater's essay on "Leonardo" which played so decisive a role in determining the themes of *The Woodlanders*. Sue names herself an epicurean, and although she is also epicene in character, she becomes a refiguration of Arabella and a Paterian Mona Lisa, thanks to Jude's compulsive rainbow casting. When she flees from the training college, she will "rise beside the waters," as does the Mona Lisa in Pater's description, and come to Jude dripping wet after which he will worship her as Leonardo did La Gioconda. In this respect, we should note that the narrator describes Sue as lively, but not beautiful ("a painter might not have called her handsome or beautiful" [*J*, 136]), just as the Lady Lisa is not typically beautiful though she does inspire the painter's imagination. Like the Shelleyan psyche he is, Jude will "add beauty to that which is most deformed" ("A Defence of Poetry," 503) and thereby create an erotic delight where he found only a "Bridehead" of erotic indifference. As "the old fancy and the symbol of the modern idea" combined into one ("Leonardo," *Ren*), Sue becomes Jude's Christminster (of ideas) and Arabella (of flesh). Moreover, she announces herself as a figure of "the modern idea" in her love of the railroad station as a substitute cultural center to the cathedral, while she claims to be more ancient than Christminster itself in her paganism (*J*, 187).

Pater's writing continues to inform the narrative from this point forward. Jude's desire for Sue is described in terms of the mechanics of the Leyden jar which projects its static electricity onto a suitably proximate object. From the moment Jude sets eyes on her, "the emotion which had been accumulating in his breast as the *bottled-up* effect of solitude and the poetized locality he dwelt in insensibly began to precipitate itself on [her] half-visionary form" (*J*, 136). My critique in chapter 2 of the ironies and revisionary ratios informing the mechanical character of Fitzpiers's Leyden jar affinities applies with equal force to Jude's erotic attachment to Sue, while the narrator's mention of "solitude" as half the motive for Jude's infatuation further reminds us that Jude's character is a parabolic restatement of the Alastor-poet's and that Hardy's narrative is an allegory of an allegory in which time makes the difference in the figure.

The Descent of the Imagination

The Cyprian note is sounded again when Sue purchases her idols of Apollo and Venus from a Paterian "God in Exile," a "foreigner with black hair and a sallow face" (*J*, 140), a Greek or Italian selling copies of past faiths as decorative objects of romance. This distinction between a genuine renaissance of the Hellenic spirit and the decorative rhetoric of the Hellenistic spirit is dramatized by Sue's engagement with the idols. With her plaster forgeries firmly in hand, she enacts a fanciful pagan love which dares not speak its name. Her hedonism is abstract and specular, for she fears the body, her own and Jude's. Like the love letters she writes to Jude which distance as they embrace, her passion for letters far exceeds her desire to commit herself bodily to the programs she espouses.

As her subsequent history makes clear, Sue's idols have clay feet. After she procures her plaster "treasures" (a designation that recalls Eliot's word for culture in *Felix Holt*), the "white pipeclay rubs off on her gloves and jacket" (*J*, 141). The narrator's description suggests that there is something of the hypocrite or whitened sepulcher about her pagan character. She buys her icons in a private moment of daring, but she has not the force to carry her revolt undisguised through the market-place. Her lack of courage is further insinuated when she disguises Apollo and Venus under the names of Peter and Magdalene. Her disguise forecasts the shift in allegorical forms of consciousness that she will later undertake as historic circumstances bring pressure to bear on her ersatz Hellenism. Like Peter, she will deny her Shelleyan new testaments of love and like Magdalene she will end her life as a repentant prostitute. As did Magdalene in fable, Sue will fill "all the places of her joy . . . with torn hair" as a sign of her repentance and whoredom (Epigraph, *Jude*, Part Sixth). Eventually, the "Pale Galilean" will conquer her equally pale Hellenistic idols. The fable of her ambivalence points up the weak character of her revolt, and in this sense she is emblematic of "the modern woman" as Hardy understood her, while it emphasizes the purely formal and rhetorical character of both Hebraic and *Hellenic* faiths in Wessex.

Sue's decorative revolt is but another form of flawed romanticism. She buys or accepts figures of culture and then seems "almost to wish that she had not bought the figures" (*J*, 141). Given her epicurean and epicene sensibility, she can only amplify "the merest passing fancy," such as her plaster icons, into "a great zest" (*J*, 143) in the manner of an actress becoming involved in a role. Zest or gusto or an enthusiasm which offers "a quickened sense of life" are the key terms for the effects of her form of romance (quotation from Pater's conclusion to *The Renaissance*). Yet her enthusiasms are specular and theatrical and cannot bear the punishing weight of historical existence. Untested by circumstances, her fancies are but Burke's "wild gas" of revolutionary ardor[8] which leads to the debacle of the "Terror" when Time hangs her children. Following the Terror, her humiliation and defeat lead to the "restoration" of the *ancien régime* when she returns to Phillotson.

Cast as an aesthetic designer, a romantic duplicator (the picture she gives to Phillotson she also gives to Jude "and would have given to any man" [*J*, 217]), and a copier of sacred texts from the Bible to Shelley, Sue is a forger of enthusiasms. Once under her spell (or his spell of her), Jude models his views upon her designs for life. He reiterates her romances, sometimes verbatim, and thereby shows himself to be a romantic simulator whose reference is always another reference without authority, authenticity, or creativity. Craving "intellectual sympathy . . . in [his] solitude" (*J*, 146), Jude agrees with everything Sue says, even when his current form of culture is at odds with hers. In the early stages of his courtship, he becomes enthralled by the illusion of correspondence and begins to construct a parodic "elective affinity" where there is none at all. He will engage in a specious intellectual sympathy with her in order to promote his desire for real or physical sympathy.

The narrator satirically presents Jude's first attempt to forge an identity from difference in his portrayal of the debate over the model of Jerusalem. Sue notes that the mock-up is "a very imaginary production" (*J*, 309). Jude's agreement with her textual definition articulates a pretence of sympathy which is also textual: he wants to be her Alastor-poet. telling aside "(although he did not)" (*J*, 156). Jude intentionally mistakes Sue's meaning to promote a romantic accord, while in and of itself, Sue's meaning contradicts Shelley's understanding of the redeeming character of history or time which is that it erases abrasive particulars and thereby creates poetic abstractions: those beautiful romances worthy of worship. More importantly though, the narrator's aside tells us that Jude's imaginative identity with Sue will be fanciful and poetic insofar as it will ignore the particulars of her existence in order to affirm his "myth" of her, which is that she is like him. Jude will model his subsequent relationship with her—his imaginary Jerusalem—by claiming to understand her meaning, when he does not.

The Paterian sensibility emerges once more in Hardy's retelling of the Alastor-myth during the outing to Wardour Castle, a Wessex palace of art. Before the outing, Sue tells Jude that she has "lived too much in the middle ages . . . but [that] is played out now." To this pronouncement of exhaustion she adds that "I am not modern either. I am more ancient than medievalism, if you only knew" (*J*, 187). Her self-definitions are borrowed directly from Pater's imaginary portrait of La Gioconda in which he claims that the painting expresses the fancy of a subtextual unity of "spirit" beneath all ancient and modern expressions of beauty. For Jude, moreover, "every detail of the outing was a facet reflecting a sparkle" (*J*, 189), a description which invokes Pater's figure of the gemlike flame. The figure appears once more when the narrator tells us that the event "formed the basis of a beautiful crystallization" (*J*, 189) when Jude ponders its erotic possibilities. By courting Sue while he seeks to become a licentiate in the church, Jude ignores "the life of inconsistency he was leading," expecting perhaps that all disparities will dialectically resolve themselves into an aesthetic experience of great beauty, a gemlike flame.

Like the Alastor-poet, Jude feels "Lost, lost, for ever lost,/ In the wide and pathless desart of dim sleep" (*Al*, 209–10) once Sue, his "beautiful shape," leaves him to marry Phillotson. Deprived of his fancy, he becomes suicidal, seeking release in "black and watery depths . . . where every shade which the foul grave exhales/ Hides its dead eye from the detested day" (*Al*, 225–28). For Jude, reality has but two forms, both of which had been figured forth by the Marygreen well. Reality is either "shimmering" or the black pit of the abyss. Yet thanks to Phillotson's "large mindedness" (*J*, 302), a qualifying term which recalls Angel's savior in Brazil and aligns Phillotson's character to J. S. Mill at this point in the narrative, Sue is given her liberty to live with Jude. When she goes to live with him, she tells him that she is "quite unfitted by temperament and instinct to fulfill the conditions of the matrimonial state" (*J*, 303). She desires to live with him as his intellectual beauty, an abstract ideal and mental Epipsychidion. Like Christminster, she must remain in the distance in order to remain "real" and to maintain the reality of her idealizations. She pleads with Jude for a new form of marriage, one based upon camaraderie, by insisting that "My nature is not so passionate as yours" (*J*, 303). Jude, however, does not understand "her feelings" (*J*, 308), yet he insists that he does, just as he had insisted that he "knew her meaning" regarding the model of Jerusalem when he did not.

Having fancied her his double, he presumes that she must feel as he does and want what he wants. Curiously, and it is a curiosity worth considering in terms of Jude's putative heroism, Sue's complaint against Jude reiterates Tess's against Alec. Both men become punishing Adam's to their Eve's who recreate her in their romantic image. Like Tess, Sue protests that although things seem romantically inclined toward physical intercourse, there is no inclination on her part for such. Jude remains deaf to her plea for difference and thus mistakes his fanciful blindness for imaginative insight.

Once again, Shelley's poetry becomes instrumental in their affair when Sue recites lines from Shelley and asks that he say she is "exactly like" the description of intellectual beauty presented in the poetry. At this point, the narrator becomes explicit about the process of character construction at issue in his narrative. Self-definitions for Wessex romantics are textual; expressions of self are reiterations of texts, thus personal dramas are also textual conflicts. Specifically, Sue names herself "a Being . . . too gentle to be human," a visionary form first and a woman second (*J*, 309). Jude's agreement with her textual definition articulates a pretence of sympathy which is also textual: he wants to be her Alastor-poet. By agreeing with her in parable, he hopes to eventually possess her in reality. Ironically, Jude capitulates to her demand that she be seen as the "spirit of freedom" and unconventionality in order to gain her trust and then violate the terms of that trust by demanding that she act in a more sexually conventional manner. In effect, he names her an enlightened feminist radical in order to domesticate her.

During the moment when there is "not a soul between [them]," a phrase which recalls Tess and Angel at Bramshurst Court, Jude "conquers" Sue (*J*, 332). He does so by threatening to return to the "tent" of his Arab Maiden, Arabella, unless Sue becomes a substitute figure for her in his bed. Sue then "ran across [the room] and flung her arms round [Jude's] neck" (*J*, 332) in response to his threat. Her embrace recalls to mind Shelley's *Alastor* when the "flowing limbs [of the Veiled Maiden] beneath the sinuous veil of woven wind . . . Outstretched, and pale, and quivering eagerly" (*Al*, 177–79) embraced the poet. Like the Veiled Maiden, Sue "drew back a while,/ Then, yielding to the irrepressible joy,/ With frantic gesture and short breathless cry/ Folded his frame in her dissolving arms" (*Al*, 184–88). Although her enthusiasm is lukewarm and her desire never quite eager, Sue completes the intertextual allusion by declaring his victory in Shelleyan terms, announcing that "The little bird is caught at last" (*J*, 353). In effect, she proclaims that the intellectual beauty or skylark has been grounded in time, a grounding that will have tragic effects on the character of her idealism.

Having temporarily resolved the problem of body and mind, world and idea, and thereby created a little rendition of Shelley's *Prometheus Unbound*, Asia marrying her Prometheus, Jude and Sue live in the historic "Elsewhere," an antithetical place to "Thither." In the Elsewhere, they can "have" or possess—as they possess each other—because they have abandoned their quest after becoming. In Aldbrickham, a town in the historical Elsewhere to culture's great beyond, Jude and Sue enjoy a moment of "Greek joyousness" because they have erased time by forgetting "what twenty-five centuries have taught the race" (*J*, 367). By forgetting their ghostly Hellenic and Hebraic culture and its scriptural heritage, they enjoy a bodily reality that has no history; thus, beyond the pale of the killing letter, they can know some happiness as Tess and Angel knew it in the unrented mansion of Bramshurst. Elsewhere is a place which exists before written history. There, Jude and Sue can escape Time's Chariot as it is characterized in *The Triumph of Life*. That is, they live beyond time in an ahistoric region of bodily delight which is described, mythically, in the concluding verse stanzas of *Prometheus Unbound*. By returning to their Wessex roots as artisan villagers, they overcome their Arab-Quixote mentalities and become domestic and ordinary. In terms of the allegory at hand, they defer to Wordsworth's advice and overcome their enchantment to epic literature (*The Prelude*, 5: 160–165).

During their time in the Elsewhere, Little Father Time comes to stay with them. He arrives from Australia, the land down under, as a sign that he embodies all that romantics have suppressed in order to assert the priority of correspondence. In allegory, Little Time represents the abyss of temporal difference. Moreover, Little Father Time's explicitly allegorical character tells us again that *Jude* is "allegorical of one of the more interesting conditions of mind" (Preface, *Alastor*, 69) called romantic idealism, if we had not already seen that this were so, while his qualifying nomination of "little" marks his difference from Shelley's Big Time or redeemer Time which is an agent of poetic aggrandizement ("A Defence of Poetry," 506).

Little Time is a figure of rationalist, materialist history—or necessity —who cannot see the value of romance. He is the rationalist who errs, Hardy wrote, in the other direction to mystics. Little Father Time does not father "new and wonderful applications of the eternal truth which time contains" within its historic particulars and so act as "a mirror which makes beautiful that which is distorted" ("A Defence of Poetry," 485). Instead, he "destroys the beauty and the use" of idealizing time by seeing only the particular and the historical. It is, after all, Sue's "discourse with the boy" that causes the tragedy (*J*, 410); she tells him the facts of life but fails to explain the romances of life that are also involved, thus he misconstrues the nature of love and fails to see the beauty of Sue's conception, here cast as her next child, the holistic result of both romance and reality.

Time arrives by railroad, a mechanical "chariot" alluding to Shelley's Chariot of Time in *The Triumph of Life* as an oppositional vehicle to the Chariot of the Hours in *Prometheus Unbound*. As a miniature form of Shelley's grand *trionfe* (and the minimal figuration is thematic), Little Father Time will pull in tow Jude's three "love" children, while his suspension of himself (of time) places in brackets all further genealogical transformations of the romantic figure.

As a figure of difference, divorce, and death, Little Father Time is Henchard writ small. His appearance returns Christminster romances to Casterbridge realities such as we have described them in Chapter Two. As "little Judy," he is also the child who is father to the man, for he represents all that Jude tries to forget or repress in and through figures of narcissistic aggrandizement which are infantile. Little Time comes with a key and a ticket as his ensigns; in terms of the allegory at hand, he supplies the missing "key" to romantic failure in Wessex. Jude's fancy distorts experience in the direction of the romantic mother (narcissism's gaze), while Little Time distorts it in the direction of the castrating father (history's word of denial). Because the two forms of representation are at odds, the imaginative reason cannot (re)compose the whole man who is, after all, the product of a successful resolution of the Oedipal conflict within culture. Jude always acts in impractical ways;

The Descent of the Imagination

Time always acts practically. Together, they could revitalize Wessex; at odds, each commits suicide, killing himself by his own hand out of a pressing despair which only the other can relieve.

As the *clef* to Hardy's romantic *roman à clef*, Little Time is an unenthusiastic figure; he says "yes without animation" and his "attempts at smiling fail" (*J*, 342). Time's walk is a "mechanical creep which had in it an *impersonal* quality—the movement of the wave, or of the breeze, or of the cloud" (*J*, 334, emphasis added). Unlike the high romantics for whom wave, breeze, and cloud were personified as strong *presences* voicing significance, Little Father Time stands for everything that is antithetical to the romantic desire for presence and correspondence. He represents the It which stands in opposition to the the romantic Thou. He categorically "depersonifies" poetic presences and intimations of immortality and correspondence as a sign of his time-bound character. In him, nature as mother devolves to nature as pure process, that vacancy of death so abhorrent to all forms of English romanticism.

As an antithetical figure to romantic discourse, Little Father Time represents the hidden germ of failure within romanticism. Appropriately, his appearance calls to a close all Wessex explorations of romanticism which had begun with Henchard. His death "suspends" Hardy's master narrative of Wessex which extends from Henchard's divorce to Little Father Time's refusal of love and vision. Deprived of an understanding of the I-Thou relationship which transforms impersonal history into a comfortable habitation for the mind (Bloom, *Ringers in the Tower*), Little Time's appearance signals the return of the totality of I-It relationships wherein mind is uncomfortably situated in a world hostile to its fondest desires for "home."

Little Father Time's "preternaturally old" (*J*, 347) sensibility indicates that all manner of idealizing rhetorics are about to collapse back into their discursive origins in the late eighteenth century. His character and his actions "desublimate" all that had been sublimated and thus made sublime, while he defamiliarizes all that had become familiar and defensible forms of metaphysical and aesthetic correspondence. As the narrator trenchantly informs us, a "house" is not a "home" for Little Time to whom all things made familiar by romantic discourse are misunderstood, unfamiliar, illogical, and thoughtless.

Jude and Sue liken Little Time's face to "the tragic mask of Melpomene." Their comparison suggests that he represents the tragic wisdom which they have ignored in their comedic pagan fantasy in the Elsewhere. Absolved from time, they are content; upon time's return, their ideal marriage collapses. The rhythm of the novel thus follows the rhythm of Shelley's canon, wherein *Alastor* is followed by *Prometheus Unbound* which is then followed by *The Triumph of Life*. That is, Jude's Alastorish wanderings in search of Christminster lead him to the pagan paradise or utopia of the Elsewhere. This paradise collapses when Time or history returns to the scene of idealizations to triumph over them.

Little Father Time is thus a Moneta figure whose tragic wisdom tests the idealist's self-understanding against the record of history in order to determine whether he is a poet or a fanatic, genuine artist or genuine fool. If the romantic dawn brought with it a zest for life—metaphorically, the desire for more life—Little Father Time carries in train "the universal wish not to live" (*J*, 411). Jude's overflowing eros fills vacant historic space with a fantasy of presence; Time's erotic lack empties this space of its images, which are "ghosts" anyway and not strong imaginative conceptions which could confound Time's wisdom. Jude's narcissism overdetermines experience, while Time's "realism" underdetermines experience, thereby negating the romantic's visions of grandeur (excess) and leaving only intimations of history as process. Otherwise put, Little *Father* Time castrates the child in Jude, cutting him off from his romantic mother Sue as a form of Christminster. He, in turn, cannot survive the loss of his narcissistic attachment to Sue who nurtures his enthusiasm at the cost of her ideals.

As an agent of castration, divorce, and the word of death, Time bears Jude into history and not out of it as Wordsworth's child did. If "poetry defeats the curse which binds us to be subjected to the accident of surrounding impressions" (Shelley, "A Defence of Poetry," 505), Little Father Time defeats poetry and calls down this curse onto Jude's life. Deprived of poetry at Time's machinations, Jude is no longer the "inhabitant of a world to which the familiar world is a chaos" ("a Defence," 505), but the inhabitant of the chaotic world of time, chance, and change. Shelley's phrase is the source of Jude's proclamation that although he began life with a few good principles in hand, his mind has fallen into a "chaos of principles" over time. The historic world which lurks behind his covering visions is chaotic because poetry has "withdrawn" its "figured curtain" from the "scene of things" and left apparent "the common universe" which, for Jude, is "life's dark veil" ("Defence," 505). Little Father Time then is a Shelleyan figure of poetic disruption and erasure who stands as a threatening shadow to all the light and heat cast by the flaming figure of the capable (romantic) imagination.

The castrophy which Time will precipitate begins when Jude returns from Elsewhere to Christminster because "it is the center of the universe" for him. Jude is compelled to return even though he understands that culture "hates all men like [him]—the so-called self-taught" (*J*, 391). He is not wrong. In his accusation, we hear Eliot's "Address" and Arnold's classed cultural views as well as Hardy's resentment of those views. When Jude arrives at the "city of many memories," he and Sue tread its walks while "receiving the reflection of the sunshine from its wasting walls" (*J*, 391). The narrator's allusion establishes Christminster as a sort of Tennysonian Camelot, the visionary "center" of the mid-century's cultural glory which is now passing, though its social power remains. Over time, Christminster's "once clear call" has become "thinner," more suspicious in its republican intent, and specular in its possibilities for effecting real change, as have the "horns of Elfland faintly blowing" in Tennyson's "When Splendour Falls on Castle Walls," the probable source of Hardy's brief allusion.

When Jude arrives at Christminster, he delivers his "Christminster Sermon," which engages the central question in Keats's "The Fall of Hyperion: A Dream." Keats's poem opens with the statement that: "Fanatics have their dreams, wherewith they weave/ A paradise for a sect . . . bare of laurel they live, dream, and die" (1, 1–6). Keats's phrase aptly describes Jude's character and his fate: bare of laurel, he will die obscure. The question concerning romantic culture which that character and fate ask is whether he has lived as an authentic poet whose poetry "alone can tell her dreams,/ With the fine spell of words alone can save/ Imagination from the sable charm" or as a "Fanatic" whose fancies are delusory and self-destructive. Jude echoes Keats's dilemma when he says that it is difficult to judge whether he has lived "wisely" or for a "freak of fancy" (*J*, 398). Keats is again heard when the narrator casts Jude as the "Pale Omega of a withered race" ("Hyperion," 1, 288–90), perhaps with an unintended pun on Jude's Christminster logos "Whither," a once-mighty god now "shaking with palsy [and] weak as a reed" ("Hyperion," 1, 425) whose "fallen house" is the last temple of the "golden age" of romantic discourse.

Jude the Obscure: Shelley's Modern Prometheus Once More

Remarkably, Hardy concludes *Jude the Obscure* by placing Shelleyan optimism and perfectionism under the restrictions of Keatsean doubt in order to reconstruct a genuine scene of romantic skepticism from the chronicle of a naively aspiring idealist. Intertextually, it is Keats who questions Shelley in *Jude the Obscure* in order to revoke Shelley's own strong view of Keats in *Adonais* and by so doing give precedence to the skeptical and disillusioned Shelley of *The Triumph of Life*.

The echoes and fragments from Keats become dense toward the conclusion of Jude's fable. Earlier, at the Kennetbridge Fair, Arabella had noticed that Jude is "charmed by [Sue] as if she were some fairy!" (*J*, 361). Later, at Christminster, Jude calls Sue "a sort of fay, or sprite— not a woman" (*J*, 428). In both instances, she is characterized as the fay in "La Belle Dame Sans Merci" who promises fulfillment only to frustrate and disappoint the knight-quester. Sue in turn names Jude an Alastor-figure, a hopeless "Quixote" and "Joseph the Dreamer" whose dreams are "fanatical." Together they have created a "sect" for two which both finally recognize to have been predicated upon selfishness rather than selflessness. As his "Veiled Maiden," Sue has remained inaccessible; she withholds herself from her poet and by so doing completes the Shelleyan allegory of an elusive intellectual beauty. Following the deaths of their children, Sue disabuses Jude of his last illusion—that they are counterparts—by naming him a "seducer" (*J*, 418), after which Jude realizes that he has been fanatical and not poetical in his insisting that he possess her.

In Hardy's deft use of the available biographical material and commentary on Shelley, he presents Jude as a Shelley figure who reads Dowden's *Life of Shelley* and sees the historic results of his womanizing and then momentarily consents to Arnold's disapprobation and disgust at the facts. Thus, whatever sympathy we might have with Jude's desire for sexual gratification constitutes a critique of Arnold's Hebraic assessment of Shelley's pagan libertinism. Assessing his life through Sue's eyes, Jude sees himself as rapacious and "ineffectual," proclaiming to her: "My God [and she is his god] how selfish I was! Perhaps—perhaps I spoilt one of the highest and purest loves that ever existed between man and woman!" (*J*, 430). Condemning Jude in ways in which Arnold condemned the libertine Shelley, Sue leaves him and returns to Phillotson who, we have noted, is a figure of Arnoldian culture.

In his defense, Jude accuses Sue of being "not quite so impassioned, perhaps, as [he] could wish" because too much the Keatsean "sensitive plant" (*J*, 420). Unlike the successful poet-quester in *Endymion*, his Indian Maiden and Moon Goddess never do merge into a Paterian gemlike flame. Although Sue's "soul shone like a diamond" (*J*, 426), it was all light and no heat. Sue continues to act a harsh "La Belle Dame Sans Merci" when she tells Jude that "however fondly [their affair] ended, it began in the selfish and cruel wish to make your heart ache for me without letting mine ache for you" (*J*, 429). To this insult she adds injury when she tells him that she "never deliberately meant to do as [she] did," meaning sleep with him; she "slipped into [her] false position through jealousy and agitation" (*J*, 428) which, of course, he had provoked in order to seduce her. Jude then invokes Pater once more when he tells Sue: "Your heart does not burn in a flame" (*J*, 429). In effect, he accuses her of being an overly Apollonian character, a romantic impersonator or designer without force or passion, or, if we invoke Nietzsche, without a genuine relationship to being. In the wake of these exchanges, their romantic comedy of formal affinities dissolves into a tragedy of historic differences.

During the course of his life in allegory, Jude returns to Christminster three times, perhaps as a temporal allusion to Tennyson's *In Memoriam*. His last visit occurs on Remembrance Day, a kind of "in memoriam" celebration during which he recalls those fading texts whose figures once meant so much to him. Moreover, his return is accompanied by the ringing of bells (*J*, 401), an allusion to the peel of bells which accompanies the three Christmases of *In Memoriam*. In Tennyson's celebratory conclusion to his recuperative remembrance of things past, the "whole creation moves" under one principle and one God (Epilogue, *In Memoriam*, 144). Hardy will echo and rescind Tennyson's celebratory epilogue by having Jude overhear a fatuous debate upon the "eastward position" of altars and then exclaim, "Good God—the eastward position, and all creation groaning!" (*J*, 411). When Jude dies, "Hurrahs!" will resound throughout the city as they did for Tennyson's Galahad when he entered the Heavenly Jerusalem, yet with a reverse effect. The great gain of Galahad's successful quest inverts to the great loss of Jude's quest, for Jude is not an aristocrat as Galahad was, nor was he entitled to a place in the university as Tennyson was. Thus, the Christminster "hurrahs" are contrapuntal to Jude's dying curse, although the shouts do arise from the home of the blessed. Jude will remain on the earthly and earthy or lower-class side of the waters imprisoned in Time or history.

At Christminster again, Jude perceives the source of his visionary light to have emanated from "a circular theatre with that well-known lantern above it, which stood in his mind as the sad symbol of his abandoned hopes" (J, 396). Jude's quest within a specular culture has been like that of Blake's "The Mental Traveller," a poem which Bloom notes is comparable to the total structure of Shelley's poetic canon from *Alastor* to *The Triumph of Life* (*The Visionary Company*, 361–2). The well-known lamp above the theatre which had once been Jude's Adonais-star of hope, now appears as a figure of a spectral culture which is rhetorically hopeful and not actually so. The theatre's lamp, moreover, alludes to Shelley's brief poem of romantic disillusionment, "When the Lamp is Shattered." When Jude last visits Christminster, his "lute is broken" and the glories of his rainbow are shed. He sees "up close" as it were that the glow of Christminster has always originated in a theatre. All along, then, it has been this form of deception and artifice which has inspired his life. Culture is an aristocratic form of entertainment and not an authentic arena of republican change.

In concluding his quest, Jude communes one last time with his Christminster ghosts. On his last visit, he reviews "those spirits of the dead" which he now sees "in a different way" as "stupid fancies" (J, 474, 472–73). Thanks to the brutal therapy of Time (or Little Father Time), Jude has gained a historical perspective on his form of idealism. His affinity for the letter of culture finally appears as an enthrallment to "murky shades." In particular though, two ghosts catch Jude's attention: "Fancy!" he exclaims, "the Poet of Liberty [Shelley] used to walk here, and the great Dissector of Melancholy [Burton] there" (J, 473). In one sentence, Jude sums up the tragic dynamic of his character. "Fancy" has been the agent of his creative and destructive misperceptions, the Shelleyan "West Wind" of his life as it were. Moreover, his naming Shelley and Burton in the same breath tersely recapitulates the active and reactive polarities which have energized his form of deception. As an abandoned child, Jude's early life was gloomy, melancholic; to flee from his depression, he embraced liberal and liberating fancies by taking culture at its word, following its mandates to the letter. In flight from his gloomy "spots of time" at Marygreen, Jude uses culture as a reaction formation to counteract his depressing circumstances. As a critique of this form of consciousness, *Jude the Obscure* is then both an imaginary portrait of redemption and an anatomy of melancholy.

In his last days at Christminster, Jude comes to understand what Shelley seems to have understood all along but to which he gave a particular emphasis in his last poems: that "No voice from some sublimer world hath ever/ To sage or poet [adequate] responses given— Therefore the name of God and ghosts and Heaven,/ Remain the records of their vain endeavour,/ Frail spells—whose uttered charm might not avail to sever,/ From all we hear and all we see,/ Doubt, chance, and mutability" ("Intellectual Beauty," 3. 25–31). Armed with this awareness of futility, Jude liberates his consciousness from its enthrallment to visions. By so doing, he assumes the skeptical position that Shelley did in *The Triumph of Life*. He therefore dies an authentic romantic because he is able to articulate the self-threatening knowledge lying at the heart of his own idealism, his "awful Loveliness."

Ultimately, he sees that his life has been shaped by the "poisonous names" by which his "youth [had been] fed" ("Intellectual Beauty," 5:53). As he lies dying, the "hum" of the organ faintly buzzes in his ears and then fades away as a sign that the religiocultural sentiment is passing with him. His defeat demonstrates that the future of poetry is not immense, as Arnold predicted it would be, and that unpoetical times would continue to dominate history, as Shelley hoped they would not. Lying alone on his "couch of fever" like the Alastor-poet before him, the narrator shows us that "Heartless things/ Are done and said i' the world" (*Al,* 690–91) such as Arabella's courting of Villbert and the summer season's bursting into a magnificent bloom. On his deathbed, Jude is "half-elevated" as a final sign of the fanciful or half-imaginative posture he held in life and of the problematical character of his heroism. Moreover, the "Hurrahs" of the Christminster regalia and the blooming summer season tell us that Shelley's prefatory prophecy to *Alastor* is under revision, for it is Jude who dies with his heart "dry as summer's dust" burning "to the socket" (*Al,* 70) and not those less inclined to idealizations and idealistic quests.

In the end, it is Jude, and not the Christminster populace, who feels "the vacancy of spirit" wrought by a "selfish" and "blind" life. For him, the "loneliness of the world" finally appears when his illusions of grandeur and of elective affinity disappear, leaving only a preternaturally old questing self who is immediately headed for "a miserable grave"

Jude the Obscure: Shelley's Modern Prometheus Once More

(Preface, *Al*, 70). On Remembrance Day, that is, Hardy asks us to recall Shelley's closing lines from *Alastor* and then to note by the comparison that "Nature's vast frame, the web of human things/ Birth and the grave" (*Al*, 719–20) are exactly as they were before Jude's quest began.

Unlike Shelley who could enthusiastically claim that "his age will be a memorable age in intellectual achievements" ("Defence," 508), Hardy wrote for and about a derivative age which looked back in admiration to the achievements of Shelley's "memorable age" and wondered if those achievements could be surpassed rather than merely reproduced. Unable to reactivate "the power of communicating and receiving intense and impassioned conceptions respecting man and nature" ("Defence," 508), Hardy's postromantic culture spent the "accumulated power" of its literary heritage reproducing past metaphors as a means of sustaining its inheritance and maintaining the status quo. It is, finally, the spirit of this age that is made manifest in *Jude the Obscure*.

Plagued by "Riddles of Death Thebes never knew" as Hardy wrote in an unacknowledged quotation from Shelley in the Preface to *The Dynasts*, Wessex chronicles the historic fate of one riddle more, the romantic problematic. The decline and fall of the romantic empire into time condemns Wessex romantics to be but impercipient sign seekers and potential visionaries whose desires are curtailed by culture and society rather than encouraged by them as Shelley had hoped. In its particular dependence upon Shelley's *Alastor*, *Jude the Obscure* is an emblem of Hardy's relationship to and understanding of the generational strife between a conservative Wordsworth and a radical Shelley, which he replicates by taking Shelley's part as his own and giving Wordsworth's part to Arnold. As *Jude* readily attests when read in light of Shelley's relation to Wordsworth, Hardy saw clearly the difficulties which had arisen between a cultural program of enlightened change and a cultural praxis enforcing a conservative stasus. As *Jude* attests, Hardy saw with clarity the obscurity into which romantic desire had fallen over time as well as the obscurity in which it had always traded as an unresolved interrogation of republican possibilities within postenlightenment culture. It is then this clarity regarding recent and remote literary history in Britain which Hardy brings to novel writing, a clarity which renders the romantic program somewhat less obscure but not less problematic.

Notes

Introduction. Disenchanting Wessex: Hardy's Trading in Romantic Signs

1. It is not unusual for Hardy critics and scholars to point out possible and probable analogues to and sources of his works from all periods in literary history including romanticism. Yet none makes the case I do for conscious forgery and its thematic and stylistic results. Nor do any offer a "romantic" reading of Wessex. Those studies which did help to me in my search for probable and possible sources and analogues are: William Rutland's *Thomas Hardy: A Study of His Writings and Their Background* (1938); Richard Purdy's *Thomas Hardy: A Bibliographical Study* (1954); Carl J. Weber's *Hardy of Wessex* (1940); J. O. Bailey's *The Poetry of Thomas Hardy* (1970); and F. B. Pinion's *A Hardy Companion* (1968). To these studies in annotation and literary history, I should add *The Collected Letters of Thomas Hardy,* ed. Purdy and Millgate and Lennart Björk's *The Literary Notebooks of Thomas Hardy,* an invaluable source to Hardy's reading from 1867 to 1927, and Michael Millgate's informative (though protective) biography *Thomas Hardy* (1985). It has been my ongoing assumption that had Hardy, his second wife, and Sir Sydney Cockerell not burnt most of his drafts, notes, copybooks, and chapbooks this study would have been written quite some time ago.

2. I am neither unaware nor unappreciative of David DeLaura's perceptive analysis of "the complex contemporary matrix of Hardy's fiction—especially the 'modern novels' " in " 'The Ache of Modernism' in Hardy's Later Novels." My sense of a "latter-day Wessex" approximates DeLaura's sense of the "modern" Wessex of the "later" novels, while the matrix to which he refers I define as the intertextual weave of romantic sources, analogues, and contentions in Wessex. What DeLaura sees as Hardy's complex response to Matthew Arnold, I understand as Hardy's response to a cultural form to which Arnold himself had responded. In many instances, Arnold is indeed the figure in the foreground, but it is always English romantic writing which constitutes the supporting background to the narrative matrix.

3. Because many types of intertextuality currently flourish in the literary mar-

ketplace, it is important that I distinguish my sense of this notion and method from others. As I understand it, all distinctions among intertextual methods are, in the main, differences of scope. I am not immediately concerned with Julia Kristeva's or Roland Barthes's notions of an intertextuality infinitely expanding or "drifting" beyond the margins of any specific text, although this view is of course valid. Rather, I have sought to understand Hardy's novels as a focused response to a specific character of text, notably romantic writing in the early nineteenth century as well as responses to this form of writing in the mid- and late nineteenth century. It is not then the manner in which every "text echoes another text into infinity, weaving the fabric of culture itself" (Plottel, "Introduction," *Intertextuality*, 2:xv) which interests me, although I am not opposed to such an aesthetics of drift. Rather my interest lies in exhuming and examining Hardy's reading of an English romanticism whose texts supplied him with what Michael Riffaterre might call a catalog of subtextual "hypograms" *(Semiotics of Poetry)*. It is the argument of this book that Hardy drew his key themes and figures from this catalog.

4. Critics who work on *The Dynasts* inevitably must confront the problem of Hardy's textual forgery. Moreover, the literature on *The Dynasts* is rich in suggested and confirmed sources and analogues appearing in Hardy's novels, poetry, and prose. This is why a critically alert reading of themes, forms, sources, and method of composition in *The Dynasts* is perhaps our best introduction to Hardy's writing in general. See, for example, Walter Wright's *The Shaping of the Dynasts* (1967), particularly "The Influence of Others," 1–55, and Chester A. Garrison's *The Vast Venture* (1973), particularly "Sources, Influences, and Analogues" (26–61).

5. Hardy owned a copy of *The Works of Friedrich Schiller; Early Dramas and Romances* (1873) as well as Bulwer-Lytton's *The Poems and Ballards of Schiller* (1873), but I suspect that it is from Carlyle's *The Life of Friedrich Schiller* (1825) that Hardy obtained his Germanic quotations.

6. In *The Vast Venture,* Chester Garrison cites numerous instances of forgery and near-plagiarism in *The Dynasts*. Typically, Garrison excuses Hardy of all wrongdoing immediately after he raises the issue by citing other critics who have made similar claims and also pardoned or excused Hardy. Reading a good deal of this sort of passive assertion, one gets the impression that Garrison, as a case in point, does and does not want to say something about the secondary character of Hardy's art. It is more than likely that Garrison feels he is attacking Hardy's integrity by imputing forgery. He probably feels this way because he as well as Hardy are subject to a romantic aesthetics of originality; suggestions, therefore, of unoriginality dilute all claims to authority and authenticity. At times, Millgate engages in the same sort of apology, particularly after he has described some relevant "source" of character or incident. See, in particular, *Thomas Hardy,* wherein Millgate notes that "Hardy's plots may be invented or borrowed" only to drop the issue or excuse it in a paragraph-long corrective interpretation to the evidence at

hand. Another such instance occurs when Millgate comments that "the significance of the sketch map [of Wessex] is not (despite a teasing allusion deleted from the *Early Life*, to the map in *Treasure Island*) . . . a guide to buried biographical treasure" (201). Indeed, it may not be, but that does not discount the possibility that it might well be a guide to buried literary treasure despite Hardy's claim that "nobody guided him to Wessex" (Björk, *LN*, 1:381).

When discussing matters of "influence" on the epic-drama, such as Hardy's incorporating sections from Tolstoy's *War and Peace*, Garrison balks at implicating Hardy in scandal. After much apology and excuse making, he finally concedes that "an artistic creation can never be original in every respect" (66). He goes on to insist that "*The Dynasts* is the artistic creation of Thomas Hardy. To view it otherwise is to minimize unjustly his creativity" (67). While we do not dispute that *The Dynasts* is indeed the artistic creation of Thomas Hardy, as is Wessex, we do think that there are issues of forgery here worth investigating and discussing, issues brought to our attention in many instances by reputable critics who insist that Hardy's "habits of defensive secretiveness" (Millgate, 201) are not worthy of theoretical consideration.

In this regard, it is interesting to note that the literary historians of *The Dynasts* were among the first to seriously question the integrity of Hardy's writing, see for example Hoxie Fairchild's "The Immediate Source of *The Dynasts*," *PMLA* 67 (March 1957): 43–64.

7. As Barthes defines it, second-degree writing is an aesthetics of reading which rejects "denotation, spontaneity, platitude, innocent repetition [and] tolerates only languages which testify, however frivolously, to a power of dislocation: parody, amphibology, surreptitious quotation. As soon as it thinks itself, language becomes corrosive" (*Barthes on Barthes*, 66). It is this corrosive attitude of a romanticism thinking itself which I have sought to describe in characterizing Wessex as a second-degree writing.

8. My understanding of the term "Victorian romanticism" is largely derived from Edward Bostetter's excellent *The Romantic Ventriloquists* (1975). Like his immediate precursors in Victorian romanticism, Hardy came to realize that romantic writing deployed "a syntax of [idealism] that proved inadequate to the demands placed upon it" (Bostetter, 5), yet unlike his precursors, this inadequacy appears in Wessex without apology.

9. The Hardy-Eliot relationship has been the focus of one study, Lina W. Berle's *George Eliot and Thomas Hardy: A Contrast*. Berle's study misses the relevant point of association though because she contrasts information that should be compared. Eliot's name had been linked to Hardy's since January 1874, when a reviewer in the *Spectator* guessed that the author of the then anonymous *Far From the Madding Crowd* was none other than George Eliot. In his *Life and Work*, Hardy covers the traces of this relationship by "generously" conjecturing "as a possible reason for the flattering guess, that he had lately been reading Comte's *Positive Philosophy*, and writings of that school,

Notes

some of whose expressions had thus passed into his vocabulary, expressions which were also common to George Eliot" (100). It is denials such as this that I seek to interrogate in my study. Despite the claim of "public domain," surely Hardy had read Eliot and surely she had influenced him. Yet throughout his life, Hardy stubbornly refused to acknowledge any aesthetic influence from Eliot, once going so far as to write to Samuel Chew to correct Chew's assertion of such influence in *Thomas Hardy: Poet and Novelist*. It was not Eliot's Warwickshire folk who resemble Wessex peasants, Hardy claims, but Shakespeare's clowns. His correction removes a near-influence a safe distance away from forgery by placing it in the public domain of quotable material. For an account of the Hardy-Eliot relationship such as it stands today, see Björk, *Literary Notebooks* 1: 381.

10. Jean Brooks's *Thomas Hardy: The Poetic Structure* (1971) is the first book-length study of specifically "existential" dilemmas in Wessex. Although her "close readings" of specific works are remarkable, she does not situate the problematic she finds within any specific literary history or textual heritage, as I do. It is after all but a short step from Schopenhauer—whom Hardy studied—to Nietzsche, whom Hardy read, or from Hegel to Pater—whom Hardy read with attention—to Sartre, Derrida, and de Man. These steps or continuities within a specific scope of aesthetic investigation become thematically interesting once we establish Hardy's "existentialism" as but one further permutation in an on-going problematic set in motion as a response to Kant's aesthetics. In effect, Brooks's reading of existential Wessex becomes more valuable the better we are able to situate Hardy within romantic literary history, those texts to which Brooks's study inadvertently points.

11. Criticism and scholarship have not sufficiently explored Hardy's reliance upon Keats. Hardy's aesthetic debt to Keats is large as I will demonstrate in my chapter on *Tess*. Hardy read and took notes from biographical and critical material on Keats as it appeared in newspapers, journals, and books between 1885 and 1906. He copied into his notebooks the cancelled passages from Keats's *Fall of Hyperion* along with a critical assessment which affirmed his own view that "in the very height of the Romantic movement Keats has detected the germs of [its] decay" (Björk, *Literary Notebooks*, 1: 262–64). Hardy's lifelong interest in Keats is recounted in Millgate's *Biography*, while Björk informs us that in his copy of Brenneke's *The Life of Thomas Hardy* (1925), Hardy writes "false" next to Brenneke's assertion that Keats is one of "the few great English lyricists who do not seem to have held the slightest interest for Hardy" (Björk, 1:291, n. 416).

12. Frank R. Giordano's *"I'd Have My Life Unbe"* (1984) examines the sociological implications of Hardy's desire to "unbe." While I find Giordano's reading of interest, my reading presumes only to examine Hardy's debate with being and nothingness within the discursive polarities of a romantic culture whose representations are always half in love with death and half in love with love.

Notes

1. Dissembling Henchard: *The Mayor of Casterbridge*

1. Hardy read deeply in Carlyle whom he understood as "a poet with a reputation for a philosopher" (*Life and Work*, 233). He owned the People's Edition of Carlyle's works (1871–74) in thirty-seven volumes. Edward Blunden claimed that "Hardy's love and exact memory of Carlyle's work was a mixed blessing" (223) for reasons that need not concern us here. Given the possibilities implied in the above information, I find it surprising that there is no full-length analysis of Hardy's relationship to so influential a conduit of German romanticism into English culture. For a detailed listing of the Hardy-Carlyle relationship such as it has been treated by scholars and critics, see Björk 1:254–56.

2. Here as elsewhere, my understanding of the death drive is derived from Jean Laplanche's decisive analysis of Feud's writing on the subject, a synopsis of which appears in his *Death and Life in Psycho-Analysis* (1976). Laplanche's sense of the struggle within Freud's *oeuvre* between two different concepts —eros and thanatos—defines my sense of the strife within Hardy's allegory of a romantic culture in dire straits. Henchard is a "discontinuist" and a "functionalist," in Laplanche's sense of the "character of all modalities of the negative" (5) which are repressed at first (as they were in Freud's writing up until 1920) and then come to the center of the system from which they were once denied access. In my reading, I have interpreted this surfacing of an about-face in three ways: Hardy finding his themes in the gaps of romantic writing, Henchard representing the radical negativity of the sign torn free from all signifying contexts, and Hardy's representing Henchard as a Wordsworthian spot of time, the one "moment" which the imagination has to overcome with an awesome sense of connectedness in order to vitalize or "personalize" the world.

3. *Jouissance* is of course Lacan's term for the effect of joy produced by the fantasy of primal connection to the mother. To supplement my own readings in Lacan, I have read with attention Anika Lemaire's *Jacques Lacan* (1977) and Ellie Ragland-Sullivan's *Jacques Lacan and the Philosophy of Psychoanalysis* (1987). As a revisionary thinker who attempts a synthesis of Freudian psychoanalytical thought with Anglo-American clinical observations, Lacan's writings offer us remarkable readings of the romantic self. In my brief Lacanian reading of romantic man in Wessex, I have understood Jude as one who fails to "accede" to psychic castration in childhood and so forecloses "the signifier of death and separation" but retains "that psychic sense of wholeness which is on the side of immortality," or at least vague intimations of such. Henchard conversely lives by castration or "difference—the Father's Name functioning to break up the identificatory fusion with the Other" or M(Other) (Ragland-Sullivan, 199). Turned away from his narcissistic reserves, Henchard has no access to *jouissance,* Lacan's refinement upon

Notes

the pleasure principle, as the source of the fantasy of wholeness. Henchard thus rules Casterbridge as an embodiment of the law of thanatos, of castration, of severance; thus he is "the scourge of an idealizing, unitary Eros" (Ragland-Sullivan, 139).

4. Hardy's interest in phantasmagoria as history and as reverie stems from his reading of Carlyle's *The French Revolution*. *The Dynasts* is Hardy's continuation of Carlyle's French history, and it is as much a phantasmagoria as Carlyle's. Carlyle's phantasmagoria, in turn, is derived from his reading in German romanticism, which Marilyn Butler has summarily characterized as a "literary generation" that saw "life as dream, miracle, theatre" owing to its alienation from society and power in the 1770s (*Romantics, Rebels, and Reactionaries*, 74). Putting to one side issues involved in the sociology of romantic alienation and inwardness, it is interesting to note the similarity between Carlyle's phantasmic reading of French history and Wordsworth's in Book Seven of *The Prelude* where the Reign of Terror is covertly described as the "phantasma" of an anarchic London. Hardy, of course, would have been familiar with both. In Hardy's writing, the phantasmagoria always depicts the condition of men and women confined to the "real" irreality of an existence characterized as a "psychological phenomenon." For an astute historical and critical study of the phantasmagoria and its epistemological implications all of which are relevant to Hardy's view of history, see Castle's "Phantasmagoria."

5. Hardy's relationship to Thackeray's writing deserves more attention than it has received. I suspect this inattention is due to the current critical misunderstanding of Hardy's project of novel writing. Hardy is first and foremost a satirist. He begins by writing satires of romantic culture (*The Poor Man and the Lady*) and ends there (*The Dynasts*), although we do not yet see Wessex in this way. Moreover, his writing is satirical in the Latin rhetorical sense of a "salad" or mixed composition of high (poetical) and low (journalistic) writing.

    Both Macmillan and Morely were quick to pick up on the Thackeray-like character of Hardy's writing. Macmillan compared Hardy's first novel to Thackeray's, noting that while Thackeray "meant fair," Hardy *"meant mischief"* in his satires on English society (Millgate, 110). Morely, too, saw a certain "rawness of absurdity" in Hardy's early attempts at satire and urged Hardy to study "form and composition, in such writers as Balzac and Thackeray," which the insecure novice most certainly did (Millgate, 110). Hardy recommended Thackeray's *Vanity Fair* to his sister (*Life and Work*, 40), while later on he singled out the first thirty pages of that novel as "wellneigh complete in aesthetic presentation along with other magnificent qualities" (Orel, 121). In his notebooks, he copied citations concerning the perfection and profundity of Thackeray's art; see especially Björk 1:374–75.

6. There is to date no full-length study of Hardy's debt to Flaubert which I suspect is significant. A clue to the extent of this debt appears in Hardy's *Literary Notebooks* that contain extended assessments of Flaubert and the

French scene of writing. Given Pater's high opinion of Flaubert and Hardy's high opinion of Pater as well as Hardy's deep reading in French writers from Balzac to Zola, it seems more than likely that the presence of Flaubert is, to date, an undisclosed vein to be mined in Wessex.

7. Although there is no direct evidence that he did so, it seems unlikely that Hardy had not read Friedrich Schiller's *On Naive and Sentimental Poetry*. Hardy's notebooks evince his continual interest in Schiller and in all things romantically German, an interest which he cultivated by reading deeply in Carlyle—including his *Life of Schiller*. Citations such as the following are not unusual in Hardy's notes: "One of the chief poetical names of the Continent since the death of Moliere . . . Schiller" (Björk 1:118). On one occasion, Hardy copied this estimate from the *Cornhill Magazine* of 1881: "*German poets*—Schiller & Goethe gave the crowning grace to Germany's poetic glory—little poetry before them—little since." Hardy's citation concludes with this quoted exclamation by the writer of the article, "Alas! the day when we, too, may no longer need them [the poets]" (Björk 1:141). The disappearance of poetry in Henchard's life explores allegorically what such a "day" would be like.

8. Although Tennyson's influence on Hardy has been sporadically mentioned in studies by Bailey, Brooks, Millgate, and Wright, while a list of allusions has appeared in Pinion (208–9), to date there is no critical study of the relationship. I find this strange insofar as Tennyson was poet laureate during the time that a young Hardy set out to apply himself to the craft of poetry. Hardy may have even written an essay on Tennyson in 1859, the year when the first of *The Idyls of the King* appeared in print (Millgate, 71). There is an inordinately large amount of citations from *In Memoriam* in Hardy's "romance," *A Pair of Blue Eyes*, while the narrator of *Tess* alludes to Tennyson's *Idyls of the King*, a thematic relationship which has caught the eye of one critic (Weissman, "*Tess of the d'Urbervilles*" [1975]). References to Tennyson abound in Hardy's *Literary Notebooks* and in his *Life and Work*. Hardy's autobiography is perhaps partly modeled upon Hallam Tennyson's biography of his father; both books provide a highly edited fragmentary record of a life compiled with the help of a relative and published under the relative's name.

2. *The Woodlanders: Una Selva Oscura*

1. For a complete history of Wordsworth's dispute with the railways, see Wells, "Wordsworth and the Railways." All of Hardy's published writings on the Dorsetshire yeoman align his thinking with Wordsworth's in his *Two Letters*. Like Wordsworth, Hardy did not want the Dorsetshire yeoman to fell his tree of tradition, yet unlike Wordsworth, he understood why he might want to or need to. Though Wessex yeomen lose their rural individuality and picturesqueness by uprooting themselves, "they are widening the

range of their ideas" by so doing and thereby "gaining in freedom" (Hardy, "The Dorsetshire Labourer," in Orel, 181). Who after all would better know the advantages and freedoms of deracination than Hardy? In a speech he delivered in September, 1912, Hardy poignantly asked: "Where is the Dorchester of my early recollection—I mean the human Dorchester—the kernel—of which the houses were but a shell?" (*Life and Work,* 380). The emergence of this shell from a once entirely human way of life is precisely what Wordsworth had tried to prevent in his contest of letters with the Kendal and Windermere railway. Thus, Hardy's complaint that "We [in Dorsetshire] have become almost a London suburb owing to the quickened locomotion" of the railways aligns his view of what did happen to Wordsworth's sense of what would happen were progress to come to rural England. Yet unlike Wordsworth, Hardy readily admitted that "though some of us may regret this, it has to be" (*Life and Work,* 380). Whereas Wordsworth was in a position historically to resist the onslaught of mechanical progress, Hardy was not, for the battle had been lost (indeed, even Wordsworth had lost his case against the railway). Interestingly, in his 1883 article "The Dorsetshire Labourer," Hardy explicitly compares the Wessex yeoman to a tree (Orel, 181) while he notes that the increase in the "nomadic habit of the labourer" has fostered "a less intimate and kindly relation with the land he tills" (181). This of course is precisely Wordsworth's complaint in his *Two Letters.* In this connection, we would note that Hardy's clear sense that "Domestic stability is a factor in conduct which nothing else can equal" (Orel, 182) not only aligns his views with those of Wordsworth in the *Two Letters* but evinces his essential agreement with the theme of "The Ruined Cottage" segment of *The Excursion.* The "custom of granting leasehold for three lives [which served] the purpose of keeping the native population at home" ("Dorsetshire Labourer," 183) is dissolved when Giles's lease is not renewed by Mrs. Charmond. This issue of "liviers" or leaseholders then is moral, in Wordsworth's sense of it in "The Ruined Cottage" (it is Giles's ruined cottage which precipitates his tragedy), while Giles's dependence on Old South's lease-hold relates his plight to that of Wordsworth's Quantock yeoman.

2. The tree which Wordsworth used as his emblem for rural independence and tradition was itself famous by the time he wrote about it. As early as 1789, James Clarke had described the sixty-year-old oak on the Birkett property as a "real curiosity" (*A Survey of the Lakes of Cumberland, Westmorland, and Lancashire*). In the nineteenth century, owner and tree were identified in William Knight's *The English Lake District* (Edinburgh: William Paterson, 1878). Knight is the editor of the *Works* of Wordsworth owned by Hardy. More suggestively, Knight is the name of the scholar-writer in *A Pair of Blue Eyes,* published in 1873 immediately following Hardy's most "pastoral" novel, *Under the Greenwood Tree.* Given Hardy's penchant for combing gazette and journal articles for curious events to add poignancy, suspense, and significance to his narratives and given his persistent interest in

Wordsworth, it seems more than likely that he would have read about Birkett's and Wordsworth's oak.

3. Wordsworth's protest over the invasion of his woodland kingdom by sentimental tourists had created quite a stir; it gathered around it vehement accusations of snobbish elitism from critics writing for such divergent publications as the *Spectator*, one of Hardy's favorites, to the *Examiner*, the *Pictorial Times*, the *Westmorland Gazette*, and the *Whitehaven Herald*. So virulent was the outcry that Wordsworth complained that his letters to the *Post* had brought upon his head a "torrent of abuse" (*Wordsworth's Letters: The Later Years*, 1241; henceforth cited as *WLY*). Despite their notoriety, the *Two Letters* was acclaimed by Henry Crabb Robinson to have "a permanent value" above and beyond the occasion for which they were written (*WLY*, 1242, 1248–49) because the pamphlet presented the elderly Wordsworth's final thoughts on the nature of nature and on the romantic sensibility. Wordsworth was seventy-five when he wrote the letters and had been poet laureate for one year, since 1843. As the elderly statesman of an English romanticism approaching a mid-century identity crisis, Wordsworth's *Two Letters* were of inestimable value, and it is that value which would have made the pamphlet attractive to Hardy.

4. When asked to contribute to a symposium in the *Fortnightly Review* of August 1887, seeking to discern "Fine Passages in Verse and Prose," Hardy wrote "I think that the passages in Carlyle's *French Revolution* on the silent growth of the oak have never been surpassed by anything I have read, except perhaps by his sentences on night in a city" (Orel, 106–7). Though it exceeds my present concerns Carlyle's influence on Hardy is apparent in the "slow and silent" growth of Gabriel Oak as well as in the central tree metaphor in *Under the Greenwood Tree*.

5. For an early attempt at mapping Wordsworth's presence in Hardy, see Casagrande's "Hardy's Wordsworth: A Record and a Commentary" (1977).

6. My sense of Wordsworth is that he is Hardy's strong antagonist. Hardy's encounters with the northern poet extend, in notebook entries, from Arnold's "Wordsworth" (1879) and his buying the collected works in 1896 to his reading Walter Raleigh's *Wordsworth* in 1901, the year of its publication. Given this long-term interest, I gather that Hardy intended to rival and usurp the Lake Poet's authority, or, at the very least, to demonstrate that Wordsworth's clarity had passed into an irrecoverable obscurity. Published nearly one hundred years after Wordsworth's strong period, *The Dynasts* is Hardy's "prelude" which outlines the confusion of "the poet's mind," rather than its growth to coherence. Hardy's *The Dynasts* shows us a poetic "mind" which neither grows, develops, nor comes to understand itself; rather it projects the phantom notions of romantic culture onto the specular stage of history. In allegory, all of the hopes and possibilities outlined in Wordsworth's *Prelude* collapse in Hardy's *The Dynasts*.

7. The basis for my interpretation of Old South's tree fetish is Freud's "Fetishism" (1927) and "The Splitting of the Ego in the Process of Defense" (1940).

In this reading, South's tree of life is a weak compromise formation between what he needs to see as a romantic and what he knows is true as a realist. As a fetish, his tree figure maintains his posture of denial while it invests him with an ironic longevity whose very fragility nearly worries him to death. That is to say, that although his tree of power supports his life, it is also the source of a deadly anxiety. Furthermore, South's tree represents romantic presence as deception and its absence as recognition. According to Freud, the fetish is the "female phallus," that image which stands in the way of a terrifying recognition of absence, of castration. It is specifically this phallic form of mother nature which I find of interest in the play of the romantic signifier in Old South's impotent fancy of power. Hardy's thinking on the character of the fetish as a religious symbol decayed to the status of a neurotic fancy was undoubtedly informed by his reading of Comte, from which he extracted this note: "Fetichism [sic]—the universal adoration of matter" (*Literary Notebooks*, 1:66). In a telling conjunction of textual notes related to the fetish, Hardy copied: "We cannot return to the state of thought about the world, out of which primitive myths sprang" (*LN*, 2:42) and "The soul [is seen by primitives] in the reflection" on the water (*LN*, 2:45), this last item taken from a review of Frazer's *The Golden Bough*. What these three entries amount to is a thematic summary of John South's tree fetish which is intended to portray matter adored as a reflection of one's self in an attempt to revitalize the assuring correspondences which culture had forged in the name of myth and symbol.

8. A detailed bibliography of the complex Hardy-Arnold relationship appears in Björk, *Literary Notebooks*, 1:256–59.

9. For a history of the various publications of "The Ruined Cottage," see Jonathan Wordsworth, *The Music of Humanity: A Critical Study of Wordsworth's "Ruined Cottage"* (1969).

3. *Tess of the d'Urbervilles:* Creativity at a Loss for Words

1. My understanding of the Hebraic and Hellenic phases of romanticism and what is at stake in each phase as, first, a reaction to the French Revolution and then as a reaction formation to that initial reaction is derived from my reading of Marilyn Butler's *Romantics, Rebels, and Reactionaries*. I imported Butler's critical periodicity into my study well after the initial drafts had been written because her sense of cultural history outlined the satirical shifts I had already located in Hardy's mature novels. That Hardy "reads" romanticism as Professor Butler does suggests to me that there is a good deal more to investigate regarding Hardy's quite astute views on romantic culture.

2. John Addington Symonds's influence on Hardy's late narratives has not received the critical attention it deserves, perhaps because Symonds is no longer the literary lion he once was. Hardy and Symonds had become personal friends by the eighties and the two frequently corresponded on

Notes

literary/cultural matters. In the spring of 1891, for instance, we find Hardy reading and commenting upon Symonds's *Essays Speculative and Suggestive* which had just been published albeit containing material which had appeared during the eighties. Hardy's surviving literary notebooks bear extensive quotations from Symonds's *Greek Poets*, some of which have an impressive bearing on the Hellenic aspects in *Tess*. For example, Hardy took a special interest in Symonds's view that *"the final dictum of the Ion of Plato is inspiration, not art"* (*Literary Notebooks*, 1:19, emphasis Hardy's). In my reading of *Tess*, Symonds's assessment translates into the need for the lyric impulse to dominate narratives patterned by "art," technique, or genre law. Tess's beauty comes to harm because none see the "difference" or inspiration within the pattern or "art" of self-presentation. Furthermore, Hardy noted with interest Symonds's comment in the *Cornhill Magazine* of 1879 that "The *Italians* reserve for the passionate art-workers (in contradistinction to those conscious of their methods) the phrase *con furia"* (*LN*, 1:19, Emma Hardy's hand, Hardy's emphasis). The gist of this second quotation is the same as the first; conscious methods need to be practiced *con furia* if their productions are to exceed mere copywork. Both citations accord well with Mill's view that energy needs to inflame inherited cultural forms, otherwise those forms would be deadening while they suggest the aesthetics of Pater's "gemlike flame." Lastly, Angel's reconciliation with Tess accords well with Symonds's view of the Greek way of life: "Greek philosophy of life—what Clough described as a 'stoic-epicurean acceptance' of the world" (*LN*, 1:65). This is the philosophy Angel learns in Brazil, after which he can stoically accept the truth of history and then become an epicurean of Tess's d'Urberville name as the name of nostalgia. In short, Symonds's view that only *"impassioned revolutionaries"* (*LN*, 1:124, emphasis Hardy's) could overcome cultural complacency—a view which favors Shelley over Arnold—establishes the ground for Hardy's satire on culture in *Tess*.

3. Tess's search for "her" identity—or the identity of the female—has been written about by Jean Brooks in *Thomas Hardy: The Poetic Structure* (1971), Penny Boumelha in her *Thomas Hardy and Women: Sexual Ideology and Narrative Form* (1982), and Mary Jacobus in "Tess: The Making of a Pure Woman" which appears in Susan Lipshitz's *Tearing the Veil: Essays on Femininity* (London: Routledge and Keegan Paul, 1978). Each of these studies is excellent in its own way. My reading joins theirs insofar as I understand Tess to be a figure of beauty who is a victim of culture. I take issue with these studies insofar as they cast Tess as the only victim, when, as I read the sexual ideology in the narrative, both males and females are "victims" of cultural narratives which compel them to mis-take one another. By the time her story concludes, Tess is dead, Alec is murdered, and Angel is emaciated. My point is that it is the hypothetical totality of ways of relating which is at issue in the narrative. In this regard, we should take into account Hardy's claim that he did not intend to write a novel about "the woman question," while he did intend to write an allegory about art. It is also an

Notes

irony worth pondering that the author of an acknowledged feminist classic was himself classically oppressive toward both his wives and compulsively immature regarding young women. What I am suggesting is that a close reading of Hardy's biography and of his portrayals of "the Weaker" sex (*Jude*, 194) in his novels would find no champion of feminism in his life and works.

4. Neither criticism nor scholarship has adequately explored the extent of Hardy's reliance upon Keats for themes and forms in his narratives. Specifically, it is Keats's romances and romantic epics which helped in the shaping of *Tess*. As his literary notebooks sufficiently demonstrate, Hardy read all things Keatsean as they appeared in newspapers, journals, and books. He copied into his notebooks the cancelled passages from Keats's *Fall of Hyperion: A Dream* as well as extensive critical commentaries on Keats's poetry. Of special interest is one such note which reads "in the very height of the Romantic movement Keats has detected the germs of decay" (29 March 1905, *LN*, 1:262–64). I suspect that Hardy's interest in this note lies in its affirmation of his own views concerning the short-lived character of English romanticism as an idealistic but flawed literature. Thus, it is the Keatsean germs of decay which are cultivated in his Wessex satires of literary circumstances. Furthermore, in his copy of Brenneke's *The Life of Thomas Hardy* (1925), Hardy writes a definitive "false" next to Brenneke's claim that Keats "is one of the few great English lyricists who do not seem to have held the slightest interest for Hardy" (Björk, *LN*, 1:291). Taking into account these and other clues in the Hardy canon, I think there can be little doubt that Hardy would have read the 1883 H. Buxton Foreman "definitive" edition of Keats's *Poetical Works and Other Writings*, those "other writings" being in the main Keats's epistolary account of the making of a romantic poet. It is Keats's letters which I have used to guide my understanding of romantic failure in *Tess* because I believe that Hardy used them to guide his writing of *Tess*. Hardy's long-term interest in Keats is recounted in Millgate's *Thomas Hardy* (1985), while a relatively complete list of criticism's engagement with the Keats-Hardy relationship appears in Björk, *Literary Notebooks*, 1:291, n. 416.

5. In his discussion of the hypogram in *The Semiotics of Poetry*, Michael Riffaterre claims that any poetic "text is in effect a variation or modulation of one structure—thematic, symbolic, or whatever—and this sustained relation to one structure constitutes the significance" (6). In *Tess*, the hypogram which underwrites the narrative is derived from Milton's Dream of Adam in Book Eight of *Paradise Lost* and Keats's revision of it. By dint of such an understructure, *Tess* is always alluding to its absent "parent" texts, which constitute a lost center of authority, while it is the narrative's sustained relation to its literary inheritance in Milton and Keats which constitutes the novel as postromantic and wanting the lyrical originality and authority of other texts.

6. In addition to my discussion of Hardy's relationship to Flaubert's writing in

Notes

chapter 1, there are sufficiently remarkable similarities between *Tess* and *Madame Bovary* to suggest that Tess is an Emma Bovary figure. Both novels are concerned with the status of romantic culture as a recent acquisition of the middle class. The luxury and danger of romanticism is central to Keats's canon, to Flaubert's writing, and to Hardy's *Tess* and *Jude*. Moreover both Hardy's and Flaubert's novels are self-referring; they are novels about novel writing, novel reading, and character formation by narratives. Both heroines are passive vessels of romances which eventually lead them to their deaths. Alec evinces the same class and class-character as Rudolphe Boulanger, a connoisseur of women and a bourgeois, "gentleman" farmer. Emma's "taking" by Rudolphe is textually similar to Tess's seduction by Alec; both women are seduced after a horseback ride which "elevates" them from their provincial peers. Both acts of intercourse "dazzle" the women's eyes, while afterward an "enormous chasm" of difference opens between each woman's past and present. Flaubert writes it this way: "Nothing around them had changed and yet to her something had happened that was more momentous than if mountains had moved" (*MB*, 182). Hardy writes it in the following manner after Angel and Tess embrace in the field at Talbothays: "there was not a sign to reveal that the markedly sundered pair were more to each other than mere acquaintances. Yet in the interval since Crick's last view of them something had occurred which changed the pivot of the universe for their two natures" (*T*, 210). The terror of boredom invades both Tess and Emma's lives when they realize that existence is a "series of identical days" in Flaubert's phrase, "numbers of tomorrows just all in a line" in Hardy's (*T*, 180). Like Tess, Emma Bovary "longed to fly away like a bird, to recapture her youth [of religious ecstasy] in the *immaculate* reaches of space" (*MB*, 332, emphasis added). Emma's "immaculate reaches" of pure romance and religious ecstasy are the *locus classicus* of Tess's "Theresan" purity and the purity of the romantic muse. Then, too, both women die by the word of romance.

7. The Hardy-Pater relationship has not been given the attention it deserves despite occasional forays into the territory. The most complete account of this relationship is rendered by F. B. Pinion in his *Art and Thought of Thomas Hardy* (Totowa, N.J.: Rowan and Littlefield, 1977, 179–82), but his assessment is hardly adequate. Pater's writings appear frequently in Hardy's *Literary Notebooks*. Hardy seems to have read everything Pater wrote as it was published, an avidity which bespeaks keen interest. Of particular significance to my discussion are Hardy's notes on Pater's "Style," an essay which appeared in the *Appreciations* of 1889 while Hardy was drafting *Tess*. At that time, Hardy copied that "All progress of mind consists for the most part in differentiation, in the resolution of an obscure & complex object into its component aspects" (*LN*, 2:17). Angel resolves his romantic dilemma through such an analysis which allows him to differentiate history from romance, while Hardy's sentimental characters are always "componential" constructions. We need think only of Farfrae or Grace Melbury. Moreover, Pater's

discussion of "Classic and Romantic" in "Style" was sufficiently interesting
to Hardy for him to copy large portions of it into his notebooks. For our
purposes here, we might note that Tess seeks "romanticism" as Pater defines it as "the union of strangeness & beauty . . . [which is] successful . . .
& entire" (quoted from Hardy's *Literary Notebooks, 2*:17, 18, 19). This union
characterizes her goal and defines the success she never finds.

8. Although it is difficult to encapsulate in a note what amounts to a manner
of writing about the French Revolution, English characterizations of the
Revolution in, say, Burke and Paine invoke the Terror in metaphors which
imply decapitation and castration while the struggle between past and present, tradition and originality is often cast in covertly Oedipal terms. The
"gender inversion" which I have mentioned refers to incidents which were
particularly terrifying to Burke when, during the early 1790s, women who
dressed like men (or men who dressed as women, the record is not clear on
the matter) attacked the established powers that be. In this regard, decapitation or castration figures centrally in Hardy's *The Woodlanders* as the metaphor of South's tree felling. The felling of the tree of power is a traditional
metaphor deployed by conservatives such as Burke and Wordsworth to
signify the severance of a community from its roots or tradition. Tess's
wielding the knife against the psuedoaristocrat is a summary emblem of
revolt against a particular tradition or *ancien régime*. Her transformation from
a passive female to an active woman who is the agent of her own destiny
invokes the ratios of reversal in Blake's "The Tiger," while it is the fearful
symmetry of her act—knife for phallus—which casts her murder as a
legitimate form of revolt which, when satisfied, returns her to a calm
beauty. For a remarkable investigation into figures of decapitation, castration, and gender conflicts in romantic revolutionary politics, see Ronald
Paulson's *Representations of Revolution (1789–1820)*, particularly Paulson's
chapter on "Burke, Paine, and Wollstonecraft: The Sublime and the Beautiful."

4. *Jude the Obscure:* Shelley's Modern Prometheus Once More

1. The anxious regard of the English essayist and novelist toward low or
working-class culture is admirably discussed by Raymond Williams in *Culture
and Society 1780–1850*, while the best "materialist" reading of the Hardy
canon is George Wooton's *Thomas Hardy: Towards a Materialist Criticism*.
According to Williams, during the nineteenth century culture meant Oxford
and aristocracy, while respectable literature evinced only a patronizing regard for the masses when it was not covertly hostile or clandestinely anxious
about the gradual enfranchisement of the proletariat. A posture of resentment arises when Burke's "spirit of the nation" becomes national culture, as
it did during the course of the nineteenth century, beginning with Coleridge's
clerisy and proceding on through Arnold's culture. The confusion and

collapse of significant distinctions between culture and state, both of which were characterized as aspects of an organic society, curtailed the appropriative desire of aggressive individualists like Jude. It is the curtailment and containment of individualism that is centrally at issue in Jude's life where culture would approve of his desire but would neither permit nor provide him adequate outlets whereby he could express and cultivate his desire for a cultured life.

Hardy's relationship to Arnoldian culture is adversarial in part owing to Hardy's lower-class background. Hardy spent his youth aspiring to "Christminster," which he finally succeeded in entering by the late 1880s. In one way, Jude is a fable of Hardy's fate if he had not "arrived," while Jude's written protestation on the college walls that *"I have understanding as well as you; I am not inferior to you; yea who knoweth not such things as these"* (*Jude*, 168) should be read as an expression of Hardy's resentment. What I am suggesting is that there is a love-hate relationship between Hardy and Arnoldian culture which is fired by his early alienation from a class-dominated culture as well as by his affiliation with republican politics when a young man. Hardy was, after all, the son of a working man and an autodidact who had to depend on secondary—and oftentimes second-rate—means of acquiring *Geist*. In this regard, we might recall that Hardy is, in some way or other, always writing about "The Poor Man and the Lady" (Jude is immensely attracted to "the lady" in Sue), and that his early attempts at writing produced social satires whose attacks on the upper classes were so sharp that both Alexander Macmillan and John Morely advised the young writer to temper his prose attacks which were too radical and "meant mischief," in Macmillan's estimate (Millgate, *Hardy*, 110). It is the class consciousness of the social satirist which is at work in *Jude*. This is so much so that Jude Fawley may be seen as a final form of Hardy's hero in *The Poor Man and the Lady*, Will Strong, while his tragedy recounts the defeat of the cultural desires of this strong republican will, as Millgate has suggested (Millgate, 111). Hardy does, in fact, take his title for *Jude* from the *General Epistle of Jude* in which he had underlined these words in August of 1871: "having men's persons in admiration because of advantage" (Millgate, 139). The advantage here is not specifically social, but rather the cultural advantages entailed in being well-born.

In this reading, it is perhaps worthwhile to note that Jude's self-affirmation and self-degradation in and by Culture suggest that Hardy thought culture should be defined along lines established by the likes of William Morris, as "a quality of living" and not as "ideas" or "reading." Putting to one side the contradictions involved in Morris's thinking on the matter, Jude's tragic life in letters tends to affirm Morris's wisdom, while the novel itself implies that in a genuinely republican society, "the cause of Art is the cause of the people" as Morris had declared in *Art and Society*. *Jude* is then a lower-class reading of the politics of culture which are found wanting in comparison to Shelley's cultural politics as stated in, say, "The Mask of

Notes

Anarchy" and the "Ode to the Men of England, 1819." In *Jude,* Hardy
represents his agreement with this note he copied into his notebooks from
Symonds's *Essays Speculative and Suggestive:* "the people have as yet found
no representative in poetry & art. The *sacer vates* of Democracy has not
appeared" (*LN,* 2:41).

2. I have provided an account of Hardy's relationship to Keats's writing in my
chapter on *Tess.* Though it is not what I have done, one could read Hardy's
relationship to culture as Marjorie Levinson reads Keats's relationship to
culture in *Keats's Life of Allegory: The Origins of a Style* (London: Basil
Blackwell, 1988), and with equally remarkable results. Hardy's "life of
allegory" strikes me as similar in its conflicts and textual effects to Levinson's characterization of Keats's life of allegory. In *Jude* then we have a text
which reflects those characteristic symptoms and textual mediations of class
conflict which are manifest in Keats's poetry; both canons are the work of
lower-class "tradesmen in letters" who aspire to upper-class culture. In this
regard, *Jude* is a genuine confession of Hardy's struggles and anxieties when
a young man—and Jude dies young—while it is an admission of Hardy's
psychic failure to feel at home in upper-class culture. Late in life, Hardy did
in fact see himself as an artist with a Shelleyan sensibility who had to deal
with "the squalid real life . . . imposed upon him by the [class] restrictions
common to all mankind, by the quirks of his own personal fate, and by the
harsh necessities of that system of commercial publishing through which
alone he could win his way to a fuller self-expression" (Millgate, *Hardy,*
374). Thus Hardy could praise Henry James for being "a real man of
letters," with the implication that he himself was a "false" man of letters, a
copyist who was "clever" but whose novels held only an "antiquarian
interest" and little literary merit (Millgate, 374,533). In my reading of
Wessex, I have agreed with Hardy's self-estimate in every instance by
characterizing him as "a tradesman in letters" who nonetheless provides us
with a portrait of a historically "real man of letters."

In this respect, *Jude* is more autobiographically revealing than Hardy's
Life and Work which is, after the deceptions are cleared away, an *allegory* of
the "man of letters" presented as a biography whose structure and construction is, appropriately, modeled upon Hallam Tennyson's biography of his
father's life and works. In terms of genre, Hardy fathers himself into history
as a man of letters by writing a novelistic account of his ideal self. By the
long way round, *Jude* is a biography because it represents the history of
Hardy's struggle to become a figure of culture, while his autobiography is
an allegory of that struggle from which the class-marked anxieties and
regrets have been deleted. In *Jude,* we see something of the emotional
history of Hardy's plight in culture, while in his *Life and Work* we see mostly
Hardy's attempt to present himself as someone who never severely felt
subject to that plight and who eventually overcame it, which in many ways
he never did.

Notes

3. The conflict of interpretations regarding the narrative framing of *Alastor* is fully set forth in Stuart Curran's "Percy Bysshe Shelley" in *The English Romantic Poets,* ed. Frank Jordan, 640–58. The ambiguity and dialogical nature of *Alastor* enriches Hardy's narrative in *Jude.* Like Shelley's poem, *Jude* is at once a criticism of other forms of romanticism and a self-criticism, the combination of which results in poetic self-aggrandizement and self-flagellation within a text essentially sympathetic to the idealist's form of aspiration.

4. Stuart Sperry's estimate that *Alastor* allowed Shelley "to rework in imagination the central predicament of his career to date, to recognize his pattern of recurrent failure, yet at the same time to forgive himself" and so "to come to terms . . . with some of the most painful disappointments and miscalculations in his life" applies with equal force to Hardy's *Jude* (Sperry, *Shelley's Major Verse,* 27). In *Jude,* Hardy wants to forgive himself for the generous error of his cultural ambition which had its successes and its disappointments. By severing his ties with Wessex, Hardy gained the right to speak for Wessex; in effect, he "trades in" Wessex, in the sense of betrayal and merchandising. He becomes the chronicler of Wessex at the cost of distancing himself from his natural culture, thus gaining admittance to another cultural realm in which he is always naturally alienated. Even though his regret at not having stayed at home and remained a small-town architect might be the sentimental luxury of the successful overachiever and so the obverse of Jude's final resentment, *Jude* nonetheless affords Hardy a way of imaginatively coming to terms with "the central predicament of his career" by "figuring out" his own cultural ambitions and their result, after which he can forgive himself for following their imperatives at the risk of an irreversible alienation from hearth and home.

5. Hardy satirizes the conservative views espoused by George Eliot in "An Address to the Working Man, by Felix Holt." Given the enfranchisement of working-class men in 1867, John Blackwood asked Eliot to write "a first rate address to the working men on their new responsibilities" *(Felix Holt,* 412; henceforth cited as *FH).* Eliot did so, and the address was published in the January 1868 issue of *Blackwood's Edinburgh Magazine.* In her address, Eliot effectively issues a restraining order on the working class's cultural desires. She argues that "to be well off, [society] must be made up chiefly of men who consider the general good as their own" *(FH,* 415). Such men, she continues, would see "Class Interests" as "Class Functions or Duties." Only "Roughs, who have the worst vices of the worst rich . . . sots, libertines, knaves, or else mere sensual simpletons and victims" would not submit themselves "to the great law of inheritance" *(FH,* 417, 421). The great law of inheritance dictates that the "classes who held the treasure of knowledge [or] refined needs" should not be asked to "stop too suddenly any of the sources by which their leisure and ease are furnished" (419). For the working class to forgo their "function" which she redefines as a "duty"

and ask that their "refined needs" be satisfied would break "the law of inheritance" and "do something as shortsighted" as "the acts of France or Spain" during their socially disruptive revolutions (419). As I have argued, Hardy depicts Jude as one of Eliot's sensual simpletons. Jude's desire runs counter to Eliot's "law of inheritance," and he would readily abandon his class function which he does not see as a class duty but as a harsh necessity. As "Hearts Insurgent," in Hardy's initial title to the novel, Jude and Sue revolt against Eliot's law in accordance with their Shelleyan proclivity for liberty over and against duty. Their crime is that they want too much too fast in "these uprising times," as Jude says in his Christminster Sermon (J, 398). He "followed his nature" and not his class, only to learn that "it takes two or three generations to do what [he] tried to do in one" (J, 398). Had he accepted Eliot's guidance, he would have appreciated and accepted his "little center of effort" in the Christminster stone yard and not aspired to acquire "the treasures" of culture which are jealously guarded by the worm of society in the maze of Christminster-Oxford's college precincts. Given Jude's desire and his labor of reading, Eliot's conservative program seems unsympathetic and limited in its regard for the working classes. Like the advice which the master of Biblioll College kindly gives to Jude, Eliot's understanding offers "terribly sensible advice" which "exasperates" him (Jude, 167). In Jude's sermon, Eliot's views are legitimized yet at the expense of a devastating cultural critique. Interestingly enough, Hardy's first novel, The Poor Man and the Lady, also bears evidence of his having borrowed from Eliot's "Address." Thus, Hardy's "assault on upper-class attitudes and privileges . . . pressed home in specifically political terms" (Millgate, Hardy, 111) in The Poor Man and the Lady returns in Jude to close the circle of his prose satires.

6. In Simulations, Baudrillard claims that the moment of semiotic disjunction between sign and reference occurred during the French revolutionary period when the skeptical consciousness of the late eighteenth century surpassed, neutralized, or, what amounts to the same thing, negated traditional perceptions about reference. Significantly, Hardy was obsessed with this historical moment; his interest in the history of the French Revolution and the Napoleonic era rivals his interest in letters. My assumption throughout this study has been that his dual interest in history and in letters combines in novels which chronicle the difficulties involved in semiotic conjunction in postrevolutionary times when the world is conceived of as "a cerebral phenomenon" (Tess). Hardy's double interest finds its most explicit figuration in The Dynasts which presents the discursive effects of semiotic disjunction during the time when those effects were first being felt by culture—1804–1815—according to Baudrillard.

7. The relationship between Wordsworth and Hardy is as complex as that between Shelley and Wordsworth in Alastor and elsewhere. Miller's claim that "Hardy's work . . . might almost be defined as from beginning to end a large-scale interpretation of Shelley" (Linguistic Moment, "Shelley," 115) is

Notes

equally true for Hardy's "work" with regard to Wordsworth. The wisdom
and life-affirming values that Wordsworth finds in his Cumberland rurals,
Hardy does not find in his Wessex rurals after 1886, the year he published
The Mayor of Casterbridge. All Wessex folk play minor roles in his major
fictions from *The Mayor of Casterbridge* onward. Nor is the isolation of the
woodlands ever a source of strength for Hardy as it clearly was for
Wordsworth. Hardy's desire, like Jude's, is to escape the woodlands and
head for the city. One effect, then, of reading Hardy alongside Wordsworth
is that we see that Hardy never holds nature as a source of inspiration, nor
are his Wessex rurals much more than quaint figures endowed with nostalgic value—a nostalgia gained through distance, or, in other words, through
a cultivated loss. Such a reading, of course, tacitly demands that we reassess
the role played by Wessex folk culture in Hardy's novels where it is a device
for distancing the author from his own heritage. In order to begin such a
revaluation, we need only apply the full force of Coleridge's estimate of
Wordsworth's use of woodland culture in chapter 17 of *Biographia Literaria*.

8. The relationship between Hardy's aesthetics, at least in the novels, and
Burke's *Enquiry into the Sublime and the Beautiful* deserves more attention
than it has received to date. In this respect, so do Hardy's politics in relation
to Burke's *Reflections on the French Revolution*. Carlyle relies on Burke when
writing his *French Revolution* and Hardy relies on Carlyle when writing *The
Dynasts*, to cite but one instance of an intertextual relationship rich in
interpretive possibilities. Statuesque or "still" characters in Wessex are
"beautiful," while "moving" or energetic characters are "sublime." Jude
begins his life in letters as an obscure and thus sublime character, a figure of
Burke's gothic imagination; yet he concludes a statuesque cadaver, a figure
of Burke's rational beauty which implies that his romantic revolt has concluded and that the formal, neoclassical world has been restored. The implication of his progress from the sublime to the beautiful inverts the trajectory
of aesthetics for Burke and the eighteenth century. And this inversion is
thematic. That is, Jude bears himself into history as the dead letter of
romantic revolt. What is most intriguing about his "obscurity" then is that
it is so transparent and obvious. Thus the chronicle of his form of obscurity
constitutes a highly formal account of what is "usually the case" for romantics of his type. Ultimately, Jude becomes a Christminster statue, a beautiful
representation of a once-vibrant romantic faith which is now as "dead as a
fern-leaf in a lump of coal." At the end of his history, which is typological
in character, he appears as a beautiful *figure* of the once-energetic sublime.
For a brief gesture pointing toward a remarkably rich field of intertextual
engagements, see S. F. Johnson's "Hardy and Burke's Sublime" which
appears in *Style in Prose Fiction*, 55–86.

Bibliography

Abrams, M. H. *The Mirror and the Lamp*. New York: Oxford University Press, 1953.
———. *Natural Supernaturalism: Tradition and Revolution in Romantic Literature*. New York: W. W. Norton, 1971.
Arnold, Matthew. *Essays in Criticism, Second Series*. 1888. Reprint. New York: AMS Press, 1970.
———. *God and the Bible*. 1875. Reprint. New York: Macmillan, 1903.
———. *Literature and Dogma*. 1873. Reprint. New York: Macmillan, 1906.
———. *The Poetry and Criticism of Matthew Arnold*. Edited by A. Dwight Culler. Boston: Houghton Mifflin, 1961.
Bailey, J. O. *The Poetry of Thomas Hardy: A Handbook and Commentary*. Chapel Hill: University of North Carolina Press, 1970.
Bakhtin, M. M. *The Dialogic Imagination*. Translated by J. Michael Holquist. Austin: University of Texas Press, 1981.
———. *Speech Genres and Other Essays*. Translated by Vern W. McGee and edited by Caryl Emerson and Michael Holquist. Austin: University of Texas Press, 1986.
Barthes, Roland. *Roland Barthes on Roland Barthes*. Translated by Richard Howard. New York: Hill and Wang, 1977.
———. *Writing Degree Zero*. Translated by Annette Lavers and Colin Smith. New York: Hill and Wang, 1968.
Baudrillard, Jean. *Simulations*. Foreign Agent Series of Semiotext(e). New York: Semiotext(e), 1983.
Berle, Lina Wright. *Thomas Hardy and George Eliot: A Contrast*. 2d ed. Folcroft, Pa.: Folcroft Press, 1969.
Bersani, Leo. *A Future for Astyanax: Character and Desire in Literature*. Boston: Little Brown, 1976.
Björk, Lennart, ed. *The Literary Notebooks of Thomas Hardy*. Vols. 1 and 2. New York: New York University Press, 1985.
Blake, William. *The Poetry and Prose of William Blake*. Edited by David V. Erdman. New York: Doubleday, Anchor, 1970.

Bibliography

Bloom, Harold. *The Ringers in the Tower*. Chicago: University of Chicago Press, 1971.

―――. *The Visionary Company*. 1961. Reprint. Ithaca: Cornell University Press, 1971.

Blunden, Edmund. *Thomas Hardy*. 1942. Reprint. London: Macmillan, 1967.

Bostetter, Edward. *The Romantic Ventriloquists: Wordsworth, Coleridge, Shelley, Keats, Byron*. 2d ed. Seattle: University of Washington Press, 1975.

Boumelha, Penny. *Thomas Hardy and Women: Sexual Ideology and Narrative Form*. Totowa, N.J.: Barnes and Noble, 1882.

Brenneke, Ernest. *The Life of Thomas Hardy*. New York: Greenpoint Press, 1925.

―――. *Thomas Hardy's Universe: A Study of the Poet's Mind*. London: T. F. Unwin, 1924.

Brooks, Jean R. *Thomas Hardy: The Poetic Structure*. Ithaca: Cornell University Press, 1971.

Burke, Edmund. *Enquiry into the Nature of the Sublime and the Beautiful and Reflection on the French Revolution*. 1756 and 1791. Reprint. Harvard Classics. New York: P. F. Collier, 1937.

Butler, Marilyn. *Romantics, Rebels, and Reactionaries: English Literature and Its Background 1760–1830*. Oxford: Oxford University Press, 1981.

Cameron, Kenneth Neill. "The Social Philosophy of Shelley." In *Shelley*, edited by Donald Reiman and Sharon Powers. New York: W. W. Norton, 1977.

Carlyle, Thomas. *Critical and Miscellaneous Essays*. 5 vols. Vol. 1 "Goethe's Helena" (1828), 146–98. Vol. 3 "Characteristics" (1831), 1–44. 1899. Reprint. New York: AMS Press, 1969.

―――. *The French Revolution: A History*. 1831. Reprint. 3 vols. New York: Scribner's, 1898.

―――. *The Life of Friedrich Schiller*. 1825. Reprint. New York: AMS Press, 1969.

―――. *On Heroes, Hero Worship, and the Heroic in History*. 1841. Reprint. London: Oxford University Press, 1959.

Casagrande, Peter. "Hardy's Wordsworth: A Record and A Commentary." *English Language in Transition*. 20 (1977):210–37.

Castle, Terry. "Phantasmagoria: Spectral Technology and the Metaphorics of Modern Reverie. *Critical Inquiry* 15, no. 1 (Autumn, 1988): 26–61.

Caudwell, Christopher. *Illusion and Reality: A Study of the Sources of Poetry*. 1937. Reprint. Woodstock, N.Y.: Beekman, 1973.

Chew, Samuel. *Thomas Hardy: Poet and Novelist*. New York: Russell and Russell, 1964.

Coleridge, Samuel Taylor. *Aids to Reflection*. 1925. Reprint. Edited by Thomas Fenby. Edinburgh: John Grant, 1905.

―――. *Biographia Literaria*. 2 vols. 1817. Reprint. Edited by John Shawcross. Oxford: Clarendon Press, 1907.

―――. *The Complete Poetical Works of Samuel Taylor Coleridge*. 2 vols. 1912. Edited by E. H. Coleridge. Oxford: Clarendon Press, 1966.

Bibliography

———. *Lay Sermons*. 1816. Reprint. Edited by R. J. White. London: Routledge and Kegan Paul, 1972.

———. *Shakespearean Criticism*. 2 vols. Edited by Thomas M. Raysor. 1930. Reprint. London: J. M. Dent, 1960.

DeLaura, David. " 'The Ache of Modernism' in Hardy's Later Novels," *Journal of English Literary History* 34 (September, 1967):380–99.

de Man, Paul. *Blindness and Insight: Essays in the Rhetoric of Contemporary Criticism.* New York: Oxford University Press, 1971.

———. "Political Allegory in Rousseau." *Critical Inquiry* 2 (1976): 649–75.

———. *The Rhetoric of Romanticism*. New York: Columbia University Press, 1984.

Dowden, Edward. *The Life of Percy Bysshe Shelley*. 1886. Reprint. New York: Barnes and Noble, 1966.

Eliot, George. *Felix Holt, The Radical*. 1866. Reprint. Edited by Fred C. Thomson. Oxford: Clarendon Press, 1980.

———. *Middlemarch*. 1871. Reprint. Harmondsworth, England: Penguin Books, 1971.

Fairchild, Hoxie. "The Immediate Source of *The Dynasts*," *PMLA* 67 (March 1957):43–64.

Flaubert, Gustave. *Madame Bovary: Patterns of Provincial Life*. 1857. Reprint. Translated by Francis Steegmuller. New York: Random House, 1957.

Frederick, Karl. "*The Mayor of Casterbridge*: A New Fiction Defined." *Modern Fiction Studies* 21, no. 1 (Autumn, 1975), 424–28.

Freud, Sigmund. *The Standard Edition of the Complete Psychological Works of Sigmund Freud*. Edited and translated by James Strachey. Vol. 21 "Fetishism" (1927); vol. 23 "Splitting the Ego in the Process of Defence" (1940). London: Hogarth Press, 1957–74.

Fry, Northrop. *The Secular Scripture: A Study of the Structure of Romance*. Cambridge: Harvard University Press, 1976.

Garrison, Chester A. *The Vast Venture: Hardy's Epic-Drama "The Dynasts."* Salzburg: Universitat Salzburg, 1973.

Gide, André. *The Immoralist*. 1921. Translated by Richard Howard, New York: Knopf, 1970.

Giordano, Frank R. *"I'd Have My Life Unbe."* Tuscaloosa: University of Alabama Press, 1984.

Goethe, Johann Wolfgang von. *Elective Affinities*. 1807. Translated by James Anthony Froude. New York: Frederick Ungar, 1977.

Gossman, Lionel. "History as Decipherment: Romantic Historiography and the Discovery of the Other." *New Literary History* 18, no. 1 (Autumn 1986):23–59.

Hardy, Evelyn, and F. B. Pinion, eds. *One Rare Fair Woman: Thomas Hardy's Letters to Florence Henniker 1893–1922*. Coral Gables, Fla.: University of Miami Press, 1972.

Hardy, Thomas. *The Collected Letters of Thomas Hardy*. Vols. 1–6. Edited by

Bibliography

Richard Little Purdy and Michael Millgate. Oxford: Clarendon Press, 1978–87.

————. *The Complete Poetical Works of Thomas Hardy*. Edited by James Gibson. New York: Macmillan Publishing Co., 1976.

————. *Far From the Maddening Crowd*. 1874. Reprint. Harmondsworth, England: Penguin Books, 1984.

————. *Jude the Obscure*. 1896. Reprint. Harmondsworth: England: Penguin Books, 1984.

————. *The Life and Work of Thomas Hardy*. Edited by Michael Millgate. Athens: University of Georgia Press, 1985.

————. *The Mayor of Casterbridge*. 1886. Reprint. Harmondsworth: England: Penguin Books, 1978.

————. *Thomas Hardy's Personal Writings*. Edited by Harold Orel. Lawrence: University Press of Kansas, 1969.

————. *Tess of the d'Urbervilles*. 1891. Reprint. Harmondsworth: England: Penguin Books, 1978.

————. *The Woodlanders*. 1887. Reprint. Harmondsworth: England: Penguin Books, 1978.

Jacobus, Mary. "Tree and Machine: *The Woodlanders*." In *Critical Approaches to the Fiction of Thomas Hardy,* edited by Dale Kramer. Totowa, N.J.: Barnes and Noble, 1979.

Jameson, Fredrick. *Marxism and Form*. Princeton: Princeton University Press, 1971.

Johnson, S. F. "Hardy and Burke's Sublime." In *Style in Prose Fiction,* edited by Harold Clark Martin. New York: Columbia University Press, 1959.

Jordan, Frank, ed. *The English Romantic Poets: A Review of Research and Criticism*. 4th ed. New York: Modern Language Association, 1985.

Keats, John. *The Poetical Works and Other Writings of John Keats*. Vols. 1–8. Edited by H. Buxton Foreman. New York: Phaeton Press, 1970.

Lacan, Jacques. *Feminine Sexuality*. Edited by Juliet Mitchell and Jacqueline Rose. Translated by Jacqueline Rose. New York: W. W. Norton, 1982.

————. *Four Fundamental Concepts of Psychoanalysis*. Translated by Jacques-Alain Miller. London: Hogarth Press, 1977.

Laplanche, Jean. *Life and Death in Psychoanalysis*. Translated by Jeffrey Mehlman. Baltimore: Johns Hopkins University Press, 1976.

Lemaire, Anika. *Jacques Lacan*. Translated by David Macey. Boston: Routledge and Kegan Paul, 1977.

Lyotard, Jean-François. *The Postmodern Condition: A Report on Knowledge*. Vol. 10, *Theory and History of Literature*. Translated by Geoff Bennington and Brian Massumi. Minneapolis: University of Minnesota Press, 1984.

Mill, John Stuart. *On Liberty*. 1859. Reprint. Harmondsworth: England: Penguin Books, 1985.

————. *Nature and Utility of Religion*. 1874. Reprint edited by George Nikhnikian. New York: Bobbs-Merrill, 1958.

Bibliography

Miller, J. Hillis. *The Linguistic Moment: From Wordsworth to Stevens*. Princeton: Princeton University Press, 1985.

Millgate, Michael. *Thomas Hardy: A Biography*. Oxford: Oxford University Press, 1985.

Monk, Samuel Holt. *The Sublime: A Study of Critical Theories in XVIII-Century England*. Ann Arbor: University of Michigan Press, 1960.

Nietzsche, Friedrich. *The Birth of Tragedy*. 1871. Reprint translated by Francis Golffing. New York: Doubleday, 1956.

Orr, Linda. "The Revenge of Literature: A History of History." *New Literary History* 18, no. 1 (Autumn 1986): 23–59.

Pater, Walter. *Gaston De Latour: An Unfinished Romance*. London: Macmillan, 1910.

———. *The Renaissance: Studies in Art and Poetry*. London: Macmillan, 1910.

Paulson, Ronald. *Representations of Revolution (1789–1820)*. New Haven: Yale University Press, 1983.

Pinion, F. B. *A Hardy Companion: A Guide to the Works of Thomas Hardy and Their Background*. New York: St. Martin's Press, 1968.

Plottel, Jeanine Parisier. "Introduction." In *Intertextuality: New Perspectives in Criticism*, vol. 2. Edited by J. P. Plottel and Hanna Charney. New York: New York Literary Forum, 1978.

Purdy, Richard Little. *Thomas Hardy: A Bibliographic Study*. London: Oxford University Press, 1954.

Ragland-Sullivan, Ellie. *Jacques Lacan and the Philosophy of Psychoanalysis*. Urbana: University of Illinois Press, 1987.

Rajan, Tillottama. *Dark Interpreter: The Discourse of Romanticism*. Ithaca: Cornell University Press, 1980.

Riffaterre, Michael. *Semiotics of Poetry*. Bloomington: Indiana University Press, 1978.

Rutland, William. *Thomas Hardy: A Study of His Writing and Their Background*. Oxford: Basil Blackwell, 1938.

Salomon, Roger B. *Desperate Storytelling: Post-Romantic Elaborations of the Mock-Heroic Mode*. Athens: University of Georgia Press, 1978.

Schapiro, Barbara A. *The Romantic Mother: Narcissistic Patterns in Romantic Poetry*. Baltimore: John Hopkins University Press, 1983.

Schiller, Friedrich. *Naive and Sentimental Poetry, and On the Sublime*. 1796. Reprint translated by Julius A. Elias. New York: Frederick Ungar, 1966.

Shelley, Mary Wollstonecraft. *Frankenstein or The Modern Prometheus (The 1818 Text)*. Edited by James Rieger. New York: Bobbs-Merrill, 1974.

Shelley, Percy Bysshe. *Shelley's Poetry and Prose*. Edited by Donald H. Reiman and Sharon Powers. New York: W. W. Norton, 1977.

Sperry, Stuart M. *Shelley's Major Verse: The Narrative and Dramatic Poetry*. Cambridge: Harvard University Press, 1988.

Springer, Marlene. *Hardy's Use of Allusion*. Lawrence: University Press of Kansas, 1983.

Bibliography

Symonds, John Addington. *Essays Speculative and Suggestive.* 1890. Reprint. New York: AMS Press, 1970.

Trilling, Lionel. *Sincerity and Authenticity* Cambridge: Harvard University Press, 1972.

Weber, Carl J. *Hardy of Wessex: His Life and Literary Career.* 1940. Revised edition. New York: Columbia University Press, 1968.

Weiskel, Thomas. *The Romantic Sublime.* Baltimore: Johns Hopkins University Press, 1976.

Weissman, Judith. *"Tess of the d'Urbervilles:* A Demystification of the Eternal Triangle of Tennyson's *Idyls of the King." Colby Quarterly* 11 (1975):189–97.

Wells, John E. "Wordsworth and the Railroads: 1844–1845." *Modern Language Quarterly* 6 (1945): 38–47.

White, Hayden. *Tropics of Discourse.* Baltimore: Johns Hopkins University Press, 1978.

White, R. J. *Thomas Hardy and History.* New York: Harper and Row, 1974.

Williams, Raymond. *Culture and Society 1780–1950.* New York: Columbia University Press, 1958.

Wolfson, Susan J. *The Questioning Presence: Wordsworth, Keats, and the Interrogative Mode in Romantic Poetry.* Ithaca: Cornell University Press, 1986.

Wooton, George. *Thomas Hardy: Towards a Materialist Criticism.* Totowa, N.J.: Barnes and Noble, 1985.

Wordsworth, Jonathan. *The Music of Humanity: A Critical Study of Wordsworth's "Ruined Cottage."* London: Nelson, 1969.

Wordsworth, William. *The Early Letters of William and Dorothy Wordsworth (1785–1805).* Edited by Ernest De Selincourt. Oxford: Clarendon Press, 1935.

———. *The Letters of William and Dorothy Wordsworth: The Later Years.* (1841–50). Oxford: Clarendon Press, 1939.

———. *The Poems.* Edited by John Hayden. New Haven: Yale University Press, 1977.

———. *The Prose Works of William Wordsworth.* Vols. 2 and 3. Edited by W.J.B. Owen and Jane Worthington Smyser. Oxford: Clarendon Press, 1974.

———. *Selected Poems and Prefaces.* Edited by Jack Stillinger. Boston: Houghton Mifflin, 1965.

Wright, Walter. *The Shaping of "The Dynasts."* Lincoln: University of Nebraska Press, 1967.

Index

315

Index

Index

Index

About the Author

KEVIN Z. MOORE, scholar, critic, and writer, has published articles on classical Greek drama, medieval hagiography, Near Eastern politics, and Hardy's novels. He has taught at the University of Pennsylvania and is now visiting assistant professor at Temple University. He has recently been awarded a Pennsylvania Council of the Arts grant for a novel in progress.